West Cotton, Raunds

A study of medieval settlement dynamics AD 450–1450

Excavation of a deserted medieval hamlet in Northamptonshire, 1985–89

East Coker

In my beginning is my end. In succession
Houses rise and fall, crumble, are extended,
Are removed, destroyed, restored, or in their place
Is an open field, or a factory, or a by-pass.
Old stone to new building, old timbers to new fires,
Old fires to ashes, and ashes to the earth
Which is already flesh, fur and faeces,
Bone of man and beast, cornstalk and leaf.
Houses live and die; there is a time for building
And a time for living and for generation
And a time for the wind to break the loosened pane
And to shake the wainscot where the field-mouse trots
And to shake the tattered arras woven with a silent motto.

T S Eliot, *Four Quartets*, 1940
(from *Collected Poems 1909–1962*, 1974 Faber and Faber, London)

This wooden gatepost, with a length of rusty chain still wrapped around it, and its partner even more effectively concealed by hawthorn and brambles, flank a gateway that was abandoned following the introduction of modern farm machinery after World War II, when a more convenient gate was made at the corner of the field.

*It lies at the access from Cotton Lane to the West Cotton hamlet,
marking 1000 years of continuity of access, now lost.*

West Cotton, Raunds

A study of medieval settlement dynamics
AD 450–1450

Excavation of a deserted medieval hamlet in Northamptonshire, 1985–89

RAUNDS AREA PROJECT

Andy Chapman

with major contributions by

Umberto Albarella, Tony Baker, Paul Blinkhorn, Gill Campbell,
Paul Courtney, Simon Davis, Tora Hylton and Mark Robinson

contributions by

Marion Archibald, Pat Chapman, Simon Mays and Barbara Niemeyer

Illustrated by

Tony Baker, Leslie Collet and Alex Thompson

Oxbow Books
Oxford and Oakville

Published by
Oxbow Books, Oxford, UK

ISBN 978 1 84217 389 3

A CIP record for this book is available from the British Library

This book is available direct from

Oxbow Books, Oxford, UK
(Phone: 01865–241249; Fax: 01865–794449)

and

The David Brown Book Company
PO Box 511, Oakville, CT 06779, USA
(Phone: 860–945–9329; Fax: 860–945–9468)

or from our website

www.oxbowbooks.com

Library of Congress Cataloging-in-Publication Data

Chapman, Andy, 1951-
  West Cotton, Raunds : a study of medieval settlement dynamics, AD 450-1450 : excavation of a deserted medieval hamlet in Northamptonshire, 1985-89 / Andy Chapman ; with major contributions by Umberto Albarella ... [et al.] ; contributions by Marion Archibald ... [et al.] ; illustrated by Tony Baker, Leslie Collet and Alex Thompson.
     p. cm.
  "Raunds Area Project."
  Includes bibliographical references and index.
  ISBN 978-1-84217-389-3
 1. West Cotton (Raunds, England) 2. Excavations (Archaeology)--England--Raunds. 3. Raunds (England)--Antiquities. 4. Archaeology, Medieval. I. Albarella, Umberto. II. Archibald, Marion. III. Raunds Area Project (England) IV. Title.
  DA690.R24C53 2010
  942.5'54--dc22
                    2010018123

Printed and bound by
Short Run Press, Exeter

Contents

PART 1: THE DEVELOPMENT OF SETTLEMENT AT WEST COTTON

1 Introduction

2 The Documentary Evidence by Paul Courtney

3 The Prehistoric to Middle Saxon Occupation

4 The Late Saxon Settlement (AD 950–1100)

PART 2: THE MATERIAL AND ENVIRONMENTAL EVIDENCE
      (On CD inside back cover)

10 The Saxon and medieval pottery by Paul Blinkhorn

11 Other finds by Tora Hylton
with contributions by Andy Chapman, Graeme Lawson, Marion Archibald and Barbara Niemeyer

12 The environmental evidence by Gill Campbell and Mark Robinson

13 The animal bones by Umberto Albarella and Simon Davis

14 The human bone by Simon Mays

Acknowledgements

The excavation of the West Cotton deserted medieval hamlet spanned a period of five years and the process of analysis and preparing the original report occupied a similar time-span. During both stages many people and organisations contributed to the final result and, as principal author, I must acknowledge a great debt to all of them. The first draft of the report was completed in 1994. While the report has undergone reorganisation and editing in 2005/06 and final editing in November and December 2008, it has not been possible to fully revise the text to take account of all changes in thinking and new data accumulated over the past decade or so.

The excavations were conducted by the Northamptonshire County Council Archaeology Unit. They formed part of a much larger programme of excavation, fieldwork and documentary research, the Raunds Area Project (RAP), a joint initiative between English Heritage (HBMCE) and Northamptonshire County Council. The project was co-ordinated by a management group comprising Varian Denham, Brian Dix, Andrew Fleming, Alan Hannan, John Hinchcliffe, and Mark Robinson, with the support of the successive regional Inspectors of Ancient Monuments, Michael Parker-Pearson and Andrew Fleming. A particular mention must be made of the then County Archaeologist, the late Alan Hannan: it is a great pity that he did not live to see the publication of the Raunds reports as the final fruit of his own efforts, which were central to the creation of the project.

I must also acknowledge that the contribution of Dave Windell cannot be overstated. He was site director throughout the five seasons of excavation and guided the early stages of the post-excavation programme. There were so many inherent complexities in answering to several different funding bodies and functioning within the broader programme of the area project, that keeping West Cotton on the road was a major achievement. In addition, the excavation had to work within the constraints of rescue archaeology while operating on the scale of a major research project, but with the core of the digging team comprising local people with no previous archaeological experience or knowledge. Without Dave's skills of organisation and his determination to keep the project on course the results presented here would not have been achieved.

Of the many other people who had a long-term commitment to the project, particular mention must be made of Jo Woodiwiss, who was a site supervisor throughout the excavation and into the initial stages of post-excavation, while Tony Baker was a site supervisor in the later years of excavation as well as post-excavation assistant and principal illustrator throughout the preparation of the report in the early 1990s.

Funding was provided by English Heritage, Northamptonshire County Council (Planning and Transportation Department), the former Manpower Services Commission (MSC) and the Training Commission. Assistance with machinery and other co-operation were provided by ARC (Eastern), largely through the good offices of the quarry manager Mr Ron Binder. Other local organisations provided considerable assistance, particularly Raunds Town Council and Wellington Tannery, Raunds under its director Mr Thompson, and the project is indebted to these and all the other organisations and their individual representatives who have helped to make the project a success. In addition, the people of Raunds and the surrounding area must be thanked for the interest and goodwill they have shown to all the excavation and survey work carried out within the area since the late 1970s.

Over 300 people worked at West Cotton for periods ranging from a week or two up to months or even years. Andy Chapman, Jo Woodiwiss, Phil Voice and Tony Baker served as site supervisors, while the bulk of the workforce came from schemes under the MSC Community Programme and, in the final year, the Training Commission. Without these schemes it would have been impossible to even consider excavating on the scale that was achieved. Some of the people who started on the MSC projects gained sufficient skills to be retained on a longer-term basis to form the core of the excavation team, and some are still with *Northamptonshire Archaeology* or are working elsewhere in archaeology today. The long-term members of the digging team were mentioned individually in the interim report (Windell *et al* 1990).

The post-excavation project has been funded largely by English Heritage, with Varian Denham acting as co-ordinator between the numerous specialists contributing to the work programme in the early 1990s. The initial stages of post-excavation and the preparation of the interim report (Windell *et al* 1990) were conducted by Dave Windell, Jo Woodiwiss and Andy Chapman, with Chris Jones and Tony Baker as illustrators. The bulk of the full analysis of the structural evidence and the report preparation was conducted by Andy Chapman and Tony Baker under the direction of Brian Dix, as principal archaeologist for the contracts section of the Archaeology Unit and latterly as Chief Archaeologist, Northamptonshire Archaeology. Within Northamptonshire Archaeology, Paul Blinkhorn prepared the pottery report and Tora Hylton the finds report. The many external specialists who have made both major and minor contributions to this report are individually acknowledged within the appropriate sections of the report, but particular mention must be made of Mark Robinson and Gill Campbell, both then of the University Museum, Oxford, for their long involvement with the project through both excavation and post-excavation, and to Umberto Albarella and Simon Davis for their work on the faunal remains. Mention must also be made of the documentary studies for the project provided by Paul Courtney, with the support of Christopher Dyer.

The final stage of report editing has been carried out by Andy Chapman, as Senior Archaeologist, Northamptonshire Archaeology, under Steve Parry, Principal Archaeologist, with proofreading by Pat Chapman. Helen Keeley has supervised the process on behalf of English Heritage with much patience and support. The publication of the report has been funded by English Heritage through the Aggregates Levy Sustainability Fund.

The illustrations of the structural evidence have been prepared by Tony Baker and the finds illustrations are by Lesley Collet. The reconstruction drawings are by Alex Thompson.

Tables

Illustrations

PART 1, COLOUR PLATES (between pages 18 and 19)

PART 2: THE MATERIAL AND ENVIRONMENTAL EVIDENCE

Preface

Through the winter of 1984–85 I shared an office with Dave Windell as he put together his plans for a nine-month excavation of a series of medieval tenements at West Cotton in advance of the construction of the Raunds and Stanwick bypass. I was committed to other projects and remained in the office in the spring as Dave and his team began work on the site.

A few weeks later I happened to be in the main office when Glenn Foard arrived clutching the photographic prints from his first fly-over of the site. These showed a long transect across the settlement with the gleaming white limestone of the rubble-covered buildings and boundary walls emerging as the team cleaned away the debris from the machine stripping. Within the rubble, robber trenches and lengths of standing wall were clearly visible; with three tenements sitting there just waiting to be explored. One glance was enough; this was a project that I just had to be involved with. A few weeks later one of the supervisors left and I grabbed the opening, happily taking a demotion to work for Dave and to be part of this unique opportunity.

I was warned when I took the post that, as a supervisor on the Manpower Service Commission scheme, I was only guaranteed nine-months employment, and there was no promise of being involved with the post-excavation. I am not sure what my reaction would have been then if I could have foreseen that, after five seasons of excavation and four and a half years of post-excavation, 23 years later I would be sitting in another office writing this preface as part of the final stage of editing prior to the report finally going to press.

With the benefit of two decades of hindsight, there are still no regrets that I happened to be in the right place at the right time to see a set of photographs that changed the course of my archaeological career, and my life. The five seasons of weekly commuting from Northampton and living on-site during the week in a caravan with my wife, children and dogs complemented the experience provided by the archaeology. The excavation of West Cotton was a great adventure in many ways, and the world of contract archaeology in the 1990s and 2000s has not offered a more substantial or more satisfying challenge. The end result was the product of team work involving numerous people, and the quality of the archaeology was always an inspiration, and both the fieldwork and the site record were of high quality.

There is regret that the report did not appear in the mid-1990s, as it might have done, but at that time the whole of the Raunds Area Project lost momentum following the completion of the fieldwork and the departure of many of the central figures that had helped to create it. At that time we were also busy learning how to make a living in the new world of commercial archaeology. As a result, West Cotton has not yet taken its rightful place as a major contribution to medieval settlement studies. However, despite the passing of so many years this is not just an old excavation that requires the formality of some sort of report so we can finally say, job done. The site was well-preserved, produced far more than was ever anticipated, and in those heady early years of the Raunds Area Project, supported by the Manpower Services Commission who provided us with a constant supply of diggers, we had both the time and the people to do justice to the archaeology. In addition, the site does not sit alone, but takes its place within a broader understanding of the medieval settlement of the area generated by the work of the Raunds Survey and the excavation of contemporary settlement within Raunds itself. It also sits within the broader chronological perspective provided by the work on the Mesolithic, Neolithic, Bronze Age, Iron Age and Roman utilisation of the same landscape. It will be a great disappointment if we do not see the data contained in this body of work on the medieval settlements being utilised by students of medieval settlement studies to help progress our understanding of that crucial theme, the origin of the English village.

Andy Chapman, Senior Archaeologist
Northamptonshire Archaeology
December 2008

Summary

The open area excavation of nearly a half of the small deserted medieval hamlet of West Cotton, Raunds, Northamptonshire has revealed the dynamic processes of constant development in a way that has rarely been achieved on other comparable sites in England. Its origins have been seen to lie in the mid tenth-century plantation of a planned settlement based on regular one-acre plots, which occurred within the political context of the reconquest of eastern England by the Saxon kings and the subsequent reorganisation of settlement and society within the Danelaw. The settlement contained a major holding comprising a timber hall with ancillary buildings and an adjacent watermill, with perhaps a second similar holding and dependent peasants nearby. It was established on the edge of the floodplain at the confluence of a tributary stream with the River Nene, on a major valley-bottom route way.

The processes of redevelopment which led to the rebuilding in stone in the twelfth century, as a small Norman manor house; the probable relocation of the manor buildings in the thirteenth century; and its final form in the fourteenth to mid-fifteenth century as a hamlet of peasant tenements have been well documented by the archaeological evidence. In particular, it has been vividly shown how the final form of the settlement, preserved in earthwork, was merely a fairly brief episode at the end of this extended process of development, while the historic evidence provides no hint of the higher-status elements that had formed an integral part of the settlement until the final century of its occupation. Desertion appears to have been a gradual process, with the tenements abandoned one-by-one through a century of economic and social disasters, of which the Black Death was the most notable, as families presumably moved to better quality land then readily available elsewhere.

The role of the local environment in the processes of change has also been well documented, with the abandonment of the watermill in the twelfth century resulting from a disruption of the water supply caused by a period of intense flooding and alluviation, when the very survival of the settlement was only ensured by the construction of a protective flood bank.

The excavated structural evidence is of high quality, and has provided numerous complete building plans ranging from the timber halls of the tenth and eleventh centuries, through the manor house of the twelfth to thirteenth centuries, to the well-preserved tenements of the fourteenth century. This is complemented by substantial artefact assemblages, and the consideration of the local economy and environment is largely dependent on the analysis of the faunal evidence and the environmental evidence derived from an extensive programme of soil sampling.

Résumé

La fouille systématique de près de la moitié du hameau médiéval déserté de "West Cotton, Raunds, Northamptonshire , a révélé les processus dynamiques d'une évolution continue de façon rarement égalée sur d'autres sites comparables d'Angleterre. Les origines du hameau remontent à l'implantation, vers le milieu du dixième siècle, d'un habitat planifié basé sur des parcelles régulières d'un demi hectare chacune environ (1 acre). Cette première occupation des lieux se produisit dans le contexte politique de la re-conquête de l'est de l'Angleterre par les rois saxons, et de la réorganisation de l'habitat et de la société dans les territoires dits du « Danelaw ». Le hameau comprenait une tenure principale dotée d'un manoir en bois avec dépendances, et d'un moulin à eau adjacent. Il est probable qu'une seconde tenure de même caractère, accompagnée de petits lopins paysans, se trouvait à proximité. La colonie fut établie en bord de la plaine inondable, au point de confluence d'un petit cours d'eau avec le fleuve « Nene », sur une voie de passage importante en fond de vallée

Les résultats des travaux illustrent clairement les processus évolutifs qui conduisirent, au douzième siècle, à la reconstruction en maçonnerie de ce qui devint alors un petit manoir normand, puis au redéploiement des bâtiments manoriaux au treizième siècle et, finalement, au hameau de tènements paysans des quatorzième et quinzième siècles. Il a été démontré de façon particulièrement saisissante comment la phase finale du hameau, préservée par ensevelissement, ne fut qu'un bref épisode clôturant une longue période de développement. Cependant aucunes des sources historiques existantes ne laissaient présager du rang social élevé de certains des éléments qui firent partie intégrante du village jusque dans le dernier siècle de son existence. Le site fut abandonné graduellement semble-t-il, au cours d'un siècle de catastrophes économiques et sociales, dont notamment la Peste, les lopins étant désertés un par un par des familles migrant vraisemblablement vers de meilleures terres devenues disponibles ailleurs.

Le rôle joué par l'écosystème local dans le processus évolutif est également bien illustré par les preuves archéologiques. L'abandon du moulin hydraulique au douzième siècle fut causé par une perturbation de l'alimentation en eau due à une période d'inondation alluvionnaire intense, alors que le village ne devait sa survie qu'à l'existence d'une digue de protection.

Les vestiges structuraux mis à jour sont de très grande qualité. De nombreux plans complets de bâtiments ont été recouvrés, depuis les manoirs en bois des dixième et onzième siècles, en passant par le manoir en maçonnerie des douzième et treizième siècles, jusqu'aux tènements paysans du quatorzième siècle. Ces résultats sont étayés par d'importantes collections d'objets, alors que l'interprétation de l'économie et de l'environnement naturel local s'appuie essentiellement sur l'analyse d'ossements animaux et d'échantillons de sol provenant d'un programme de prélèvement extensif.

Zusammenfassung

Durch die großflächige Ausgrabung von fast der Hälfte der kleinen mittelalterlichen Dorfwüstung von West Cotton, Raunds, Northamptonshire, konnten dynamische Prozesse einer ständigen Entwicklung mit einer Genauigkeit nachvollzogen werden, wie sie auf anderen, vergleichbaren Fundplätzen Englands bisher nur selten erreicht wurde. Die Ursprünge des Dorfes gehen auf die Mitte der 10. Jahrhunderts zurück, als im Zuge der Wiedereroberung Ostenglands durch die sächsischen Könige und der folgenden Neuorganisation der Siedlungsmuster und Gesellschaft des Danelags eine einen Hektar große, geplante Siedlung mit regelmäßigen Parzellen angelegt wurde. Die Ansiedlung umfasste ein größeres Lehensgehöft, das aus einer Holzhalle mit Nebengebäuden und einer daran anschließenden Wassermühle bestand. In der Nähe befanden sich vielleicht ein zweites, ähnliches Gehöft und abhängige Bauern. All dies wurde am Rand der Talaue nahe der Mündung eines Baches in den Fluss Nene errichtet, entlang eines bedeutenden Verbindungsweges auf der Talsohle.

Weitere Entwicklungsprozesse waren gut am archäologischem Material nachweisbar: der Neubau in Stein als kleines, normannisches Herrenhaus im 12. Jahrhundert; die wahrscheinliche Verlegung dieser Gebäude im 13. Jahrhundert; und die endgültige Form des Ortes, vom 14. bis zur zweiten Hälfte des 15. Jahrhunderts, als ein Weiler aus an Bauern verpachteten Grund. Es konnte vor allen Dingen klar aufgezeigt werden, dass die Endform der Siedlung, die oberirdisch als Erdwerk erhalten ist, nur eine relativ kurze Episode am Ende dieses lang andauernden Entwicklungsprozesses darstellt, während die historischen Quellen keinen Hinweis auf die höhergestellten sozialen Elemente enthalten, die bis zum letzten Jahrhundert der Siedlungstätigkeit eine wesentliche Rolle gespielt hatten. Die Aufgabe des Weilers scheint ein allmählicher Prozess gewesen zu sein. Im Laufe eines Jahrhunderts von wirtschaftlichen und sozialen Katastrophen, allen voran die Pest, wurden die Pachten eine nach der anderen aufgelassen, als Familien wohl auf besseres Land auswichen, das zu dieser Zeit andernorts leicht zu bekommen war.

Die Auswirkungen der örtlichen Umweltgegebenheiten auf diese Veränderungsprozesse konnten ebenfalls gut dokumentiert werden. So lässt sich die Aufgabe der Mühle im 12. Jahrhundert mit einer Unterbrechung der Wasserzufuhr erklären, deren Ursache in einer Periode heftiger Überflutungen und Anschwemmungen zu suchen ist, während der das Überleben der Siedlung selbst nur durch den Bau eines schützenden Hochwasserdammes gesichert werden konnte.

Die ergrabenen Gebäudeüberreste sind von hoher Qualität. Zahlreiche komplette Grundrisse konnten nachgewiesen werden, angefangen von den Holzhallen des 10. und 11. Jahrhunderts, über das Herrenhaus des 12. und 13. Jahrhunderts bis hin zu den gut erhaltenen Gehöften des 14. Jahrhunderts. Sie werden von umfangreichem Fundgut ergänzt. Die Betrachtungen zur örtlichen Wirtschaft und Umwelt beruhen hauptsächlich auf der Analyse der Fauna und auf Erkenntnissen aus den zahlreichen, planmäßig entnommenen Bodenproben.

1 Introduction

A Day on Site

In the morning at the Site everybody comes for work. They take the tools out to the Site and get to work. Some are trowling to clean up so daddy can take a photograph. Some are digging and some are planning. You see you plan a wall so wen it is gon you no wot it was like. Wen I help I choose a person to help trowling or digging. We find pot and bone and put it into a tray, but iron we mesher in and level. The soil we put in the wheelbarrow and push it to the spoilheap and empty it.

We are here becaus Daddy works here as a supervisor. The caravan is next to the Site and we live in it during the week. Every morning we walk up the track to get the milk. In the morning we have to chase a cow out. We have picked Elderflower and blackberry in summer, elderberry in ortum. Later we will pick hawthorn and sloes.

Eleanor Chapman, aged 7, 1985

The Raunds Area Project

The Raunds Area Project was a major programme of archaeological research examining the development of a midland England landscape within part of the Nene valley in Northamptonshire (Fig 1.1). The project area encompassed four medieval parishes, Raunds, Stanwick, Ringstead and Hargrave, covering a total of 40sq km.

The project had developed out of the rescue excavation of Furnells manor in Raunds between 1977 and 1982 (Boddington 1996; Audouy and Chapman 2009). Concurrently, a detailed examination of the priorities for rescue archaeology in Northamptonshire (Foard 1979) had shown Raunds to be the most intact area of historic landscape in the upper Nene valley, but with many of the well-preserved grouping of key sites of prehistoric, Roman, Saxon and medieval date likely to be destroyed during the 1980s. The academic basis and a broad framework for future work was defined in 1983 (Foard 1983) and the Raunds Area Project as a joint venture between Northamptonshire County Council and English Heritage was formally established in 1984.

The research was primarily based on a series of extensive open area excavations conducted in advance of new development, particularly road construction, gravel extraction, and new housing and industrial projects, which all posed direct threats to a number of identified key sites (Fig 1.2). Each aspect of the project is the subject of a separate major report.

Beside the River Nene there was a group of known early prehistoric ritual and burial monuments, and through the first year of excavation at West Cotton it became apparent that further monuments, previously unknown, lay beneath the medieval hamlet itself (Harding and Healy 2007). Only 1km south of West Cotton there was a major focus of Iron Age and Roman settlement at Stanwick, with further Roman settlement to the north, at Mallows Cotton (Crosby and Neal forthcoming). Finally, there were the important areas of Saxon and medieval settlement at the northern end of Raunds village (Audouy and Chapman 2009) and beside the river at West Cotton, Raunds. The excavations were complemented by documentary research and an area survey, utilising intensive fieldwalking, cropmark analysis, geophysical survey and small-scale excavation (Parry 2006).

For the Saxon and medieval periods the project was conceived as an investigation at the lowest administrative level of society. Systematic field survey and the excavation of key sites threatened with at least partial destruction were to be supported by a programme of documentary research. The published volumes on Saxon and medieval Raunds (Boddington 1997; Audouy and Chapman 2009) and the area survey (Parry 2006) complement the present volume and include details and an overview of the local settlement pattern and topography, and the broader documentary evidence omitted from this volume.

Location and topography

Raunds lies within east Northamptonshire on the eastern margin of the Jurassic uplands of Central England (Fig 1.1). There is undulating higher ground to the west and the low flat landscape of the fens is not far to the east. The drift (Boulder Clay) covered lowland plateau lies at 70–88m OD and is intersected by the River Nene, rising above Northampton and flowing north-east across the county and past Peterborough on its course to the Wash. It forms the western boundary of the study area.

The village of Raunds lies on the western margin of the plateau. It straddles the Raunds Brook which runs westward

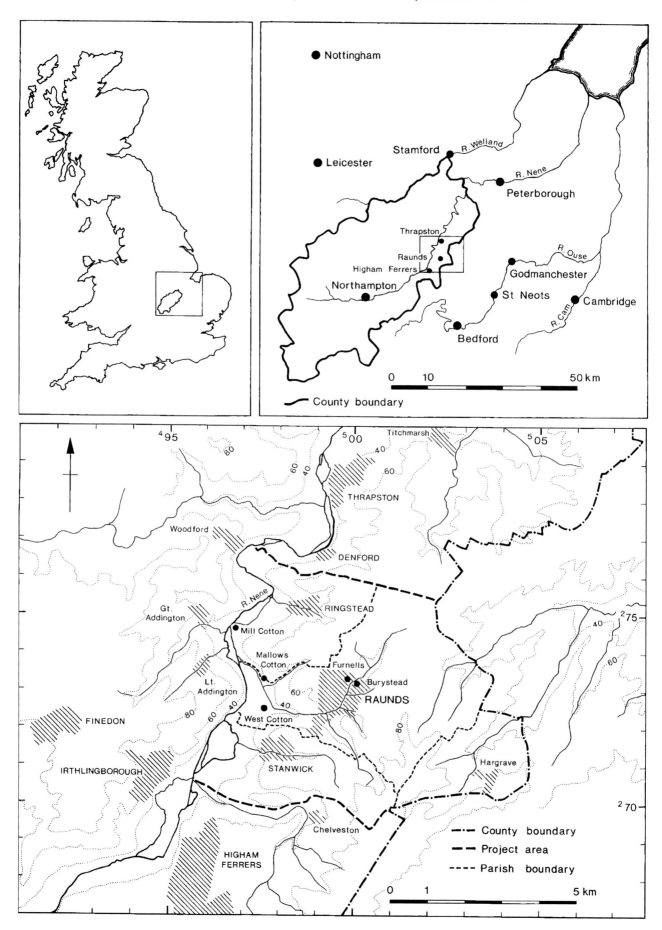

Fig 1.1: Location maps and the Raunds Project area. © Crown copyright. All rights reserved. Northamptonshire County Council: Licence No. 100019331, Published 2009

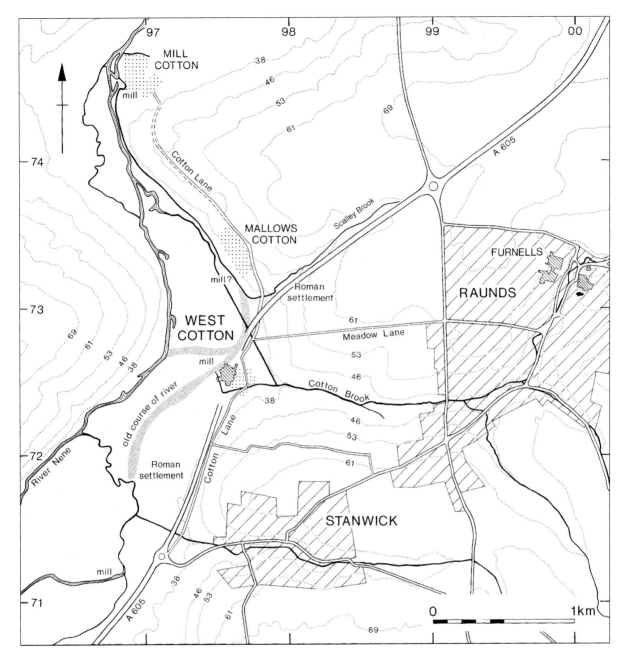

Fig 1.2: The location of West Cotton and other settlements within the Nene valley (contours in m). © Crown copyright. All rights reserved. Northamptonshire County Council: Licence No. 100019331, Published 2009

passing West Cotton, as the Cotton or Tipp Brook, before joining the Nene (Fig 1.2).

The valley slope between Raunds and West Cotton cuts across a complex geological sequence comprising Oxford Clay, Cornbrash, Great Oolite Clay, Great Oolite Limestone, Lower Estuarine Series, Northampton Sand with Ironstone and Upper Lias Clay. These deposits provided a ready source of both limestone and ironstone that has been utilised in the area for building stone from at least the Roman period onward.

West Cotton lay on the eastern margin of the floodplain of the Nene, adjacent to its confluence with the Cotton Brook tributary. It also straddled the Cotton Lane, which

survives here as a farm track, but was once a medieval road running along the edge of the floodplain from Higham Ferrers in the south to Thrapston in the north, and perhaps following a Roman predecessor linking settlements at Higham, Stanwick, Mallows Cotton and Ringstead (Figs 1.1 and 1.2, Plate 1).

The modern floodplain of the River Nene is locally up to 900m wide and relatively flat, with the river running along the western margin. The general level of the floodplain, prior to the gravel extraction, lay at 36–37m OD while the earthworks at West Cotton lay at the lower level of 34.5–35.0m OD. This anomaly was the result of major hydrological changes in the twelfth century when the deposition of up to 1.0m of alluvial silts across the valley floor concealed the earlier topography and formed the raised and level floodplain of subsequent centuries. At this time the settlement was surrounded by a clay flood bank to protect it from inundation, which produced the anomaly of the buildings then lying below the level of the floodplain. Prior to this, the settlement had occupied a gravel platform that stood above the valley floor. It was then flanked by a major channel of the River Nene, which had been open from at least the later Neolithic period, but this became redundant by around the end of the twelfth century and was itself buried beneath the alluvial silts (Fig 1.2). The tributary stream has also seen a succession of diversions related to the creation of the mill leats in the tenth century, the alluviation in the twelfth century and a final diversion at the time of enclosure in the eighteenth century (Fig 1.3, the Hog Dyke).

West Cotton: previous fieldwork

The medieval and post-medieval documentary evidence indicates the presence of three deserted settlements in the valley of the River Nene within the parishes of Rounds and Ringstead (Fig 1.2). The location of two of these, Mill Cotton and Mallows Cotton, had long been known as both were described in the mid-eighteenth century by Bridges (1791, 190), and their main earthworks had been depicted on Ordnance Survey maps from the late nineteenth century. The documentary and archaeological evidence for these two settlements has been summarised within the Raunds Survey volume (Parry 2006, 177–195). Both were much larger than West Cotton and are documented as including substantial medieval manors. Much of Mill Cotton, including a moated manor site, was lost to gravel extraction in the early 1970s with only limited salvage excavation, while Mallows Cotton survives intact as a well preserved earthwork site under pasture, and is a Scheduled Ancient Monument.

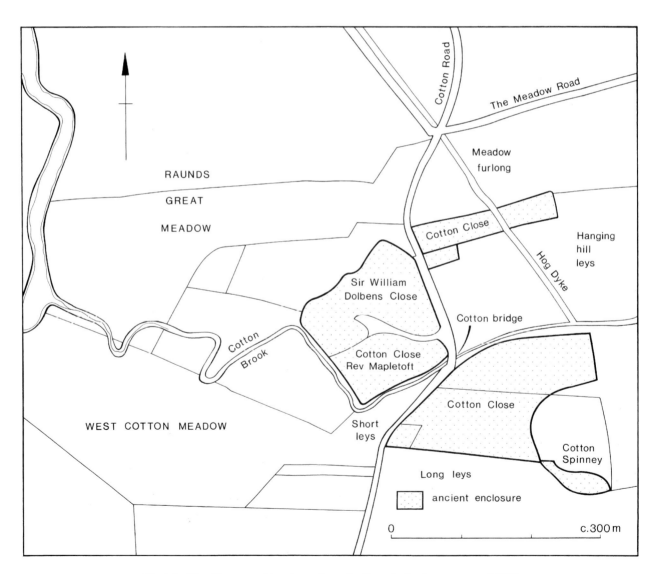

Fig 1.3: West Cotton and its closes from the Raunds Enclosure map of 1798

In contrast, the location of the deserted settlement of West Cotton was not recognised until the 1960s. It was listed as unlocated in *The Deserted Villages of Northamptonshire* (Allison *et al* 1966, 38). However, as David Hall has noted (Hall *et al* 1988, 32), its location could have been easily deduced from the Raunds Enclosure Map of 1798 (NRO and Fig 1.3), and Hall also records that it had been recognised through fieldwork in 1962. The first published reference to its location dates to 1967 (Brown 1967, 28) when the late A E Rowlings recorded the presence of a limestone wall footing, pits and ditches, together with pottery dating to the twelfth to fourteenth centuries, while observing the digging of a new pipe trench to the east of Cotton Lane (Fig 1.4, J).

The survival of the main settlement of West Cotton as low earthworks within a pasture field to the west of Cotton Lane (SP 976 725) was confirmed in 1972 (Hall and Hutchings 1972, 15), and a description and earthwork survey was published in 1975 (RCHME 1975, 81–83). This recorded two building groups (Fig 1.4, F and G,) as

earthwork remains to the immediate west of Cotton Lane, while a third complex in the ploughed field to the east was indicated by an area of building-rubble associated with medieval pottery (H). It was concluded that "the settlement never consisted of more than two or three farmsteads or cottages" (*ibid*, 83). The settlement earthworks and the surviving ridge and furrow of the field system to the immediate south had been surveyed by David Hall in 1973, but the settlement survey was only published in 1988 near the end of the excavations reported here (Hall *et al* 1988, 34, fig 5).

The West Cotton Project

As a largely intact site threatened with partial destruction by road construction, the A605 Stanwick and Raunds bypass, the deserted medieval hamlet of West Cotton was one of the key Saxon and medieval sites of the Raunds Area Project (Foard 1983, appendix 2).

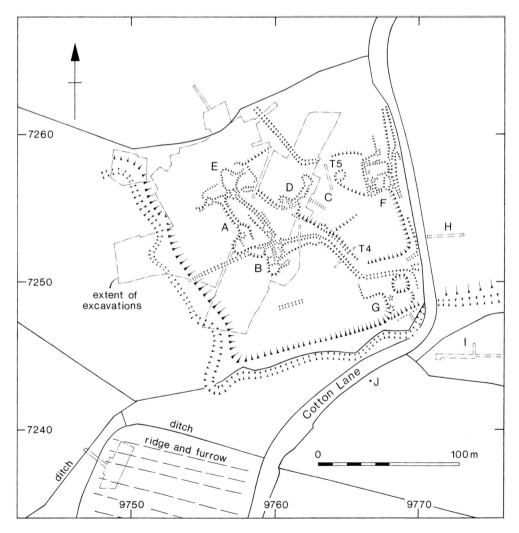

Fig 1.4: West Cotton, the earthworks prior to excavation. © Crown copyright. All rights reserved. Northamptonshire County Council: Licence No. 100019331, Published 2009

Earthworks

Early in 1983 the main earthworks were surveyed by Glenn Foard and Dave Windell (Figs 1.4 and 1.5). This revealed a considerably larger and more complex settlement than had been apparent from the Royal Commission survey. The presence of several discrete tenements was defined by low building platforms set around a central yard (A-E) and flanking the Cotton Lane (F and G). The bank and stream course to the south and west, and the field system to the south were surveyed during the excavations, and some details of the field system are taken from D Hall's unpublished survey.

The earthworks of the medieval tenements were of fairly low amplitude. Both on the ground and from the air (Fig 1.5) the most prominent feature was the bank surrounding the central yard and flanking the access road, which has been shown to post-date the desertion of the central tenements. The flood bank to the west, flanked by the post-medieval stream course, was also visible, although its rounded profile rendered it less prominent from the air than on the ground. The ridge and furrow of the field system in the field to the south was also evident, along with a series of linear and curvilinear ditches of a later date. Ploughing to the east of Cotton Lane had levelled all former earthworks, with the exception of the flood bank and former stream course.

Evaluation

In November 1983 a "short programme of trial-trenching was carried out to ascertain the state of preservation, depth of stratification and probable date-range of the earthworks to assess the value of the site" (Windell 1984, 1). Five trenches, each 20m long by 1.75m wide, were sited to reveal the nature of the remains while avoiding severe damage to the apparent building platforms. Three of these trenches were later absorbed within the main excavation area while the other two lay to the east (Fig 1.4, T4 and T5). This evaluation indicated that the earthworks did "represent well-preserved buildings of medieval date" (*ibid*, 2), with a probable late Saxon origin indicated by the tenth to fourteenth-century date range of the recovered pottery.

Aims and objectives

It was anticipated that the excavation of the settlement would contribute to three of the broad academic objectives of the Raunds project:

a) The investigation of the origins of the medieval nucleated village from the presumed dispersed settlement pattern of the middle Saxon period. To be achieved by establishing the date and form of the original settlement.

b) The relationship of "daughter" settlements, as represented by the three Cottons, to the main parochial centre at Raunds. To be achieved by establishing the status and the form of the occupation in order to provide comparative data to that obtained in north Raunds.

c) The desertion of secondary settlements and the

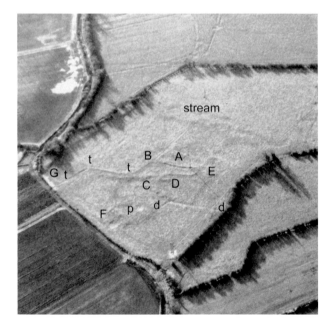

Fig 1.5a: Aerial photograph of the West Cotton earthworks in December 1982, prior to excavation, looking south with Cotton Lane to the east (left) (Glenn Foard, NMR 2221/16, NCC SP9772)

Fig 1.5b: The West Cotton earthworks labelled to show the trackway, t, the late drainage ditch, d, the pond-like feature, p, the medieval tenements surrounding the central yard, A–E, the tenements adjacent to the Cotton Lane, F and G, and the course of the late medieval to post-medieval stream

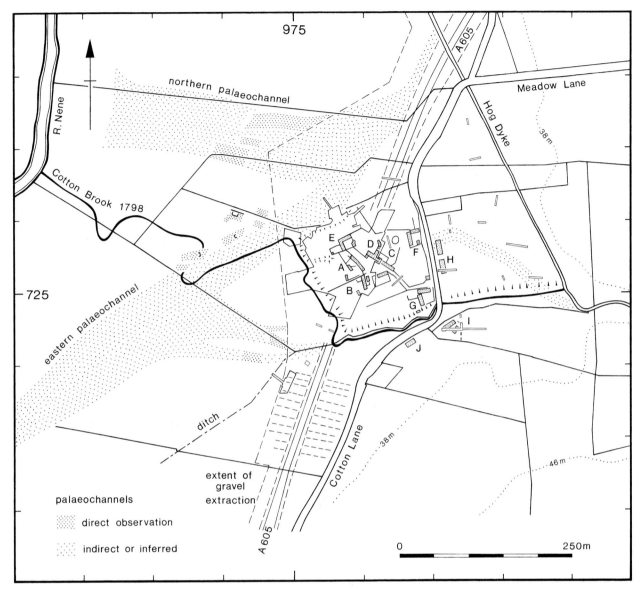

975

northern palaeochannel

R. Nene

Cotton Brook 1798

eastern palaeochannel

725

ditch

palaeochannels

direct observation

indirect or inferred

extent of
gravel
extraction

A605

Meadow Lane

Hog Dyke

38 m

Cotton Lane

38 m

46 m

0   250m

Fig 1.6: West Cotton, showing the medieval tenements, the field system and the palaeochannels. © Crown copyright. All rights reserved. Northamptonshire County Council: Licence No. 100019331, Published 2009

relationship of this to changes at the parochial centre. To be achieved by establishing the date and the processes leading to desertion.

In addition, from the beginning an intensive programme of environmental sampling, determined in consultation with Dr Mark Robinson of the University Museum, Oxford, was undertaken in order to examine both the agricultural economy of the settlement and the wider environmental background.

The excavation

Excavation began in March 1985 with the opening of a single, elongated area along the intended line of the new road. This initial area, 140m long by 30m wide, took in most

of the central medieval tenements (A, B, C and D), as well as parts of the stream courses to the north and south (Figs 1.6 and 1.7, Plates 2, 9–11). It had been anticipated that full excavation could be achieved within a single season of some nine months. However, the medieval buildings were better preserved than expected, while the discovery of partially intact prehistoric mounds beneath added an additional, and completely unexpected, dimension. As a result, the excavation of the initial area of 6000sq m was only completed towards the end of 1986. It was then backfilled prior to the commencement of road construction early in 1987.

In 1987 gravel extraction by ARC (Eastern) began to the north-west, with the extent of the concession including the western margins of the settlement area and the adjacent stream and river palaeochannels. Excavation therefore

Fig 1.7: West Cotton in May 1985, looking south-east, showing the initial area of excavation with tenements C/D (left), tenement A (bottom centre) and tenement B (top centre) covered by spreads of demolition rubble (Aerial photograph by Glenn Foard for NCC)

recommenced in April 1987 with the opening of a second large area immediately adjacent to, and partly linking with the previous work, and taking in the final central medieval tenement, E (Figs 1.8–1.11 and Plates 1, 3 and 12). Beneath and around this tenement work in 1988 and 1989 explored the stone-built manor house of the twelfth century (Plate 5) and the timber ranges of the late Saxon settlement (Plate 4).

To test for the suspected presence of a watermill, in 1987 a detached trench was opened immediately to the north-west, while a trench was cut across the palaeochannel to the north to obtain environmental samples from the sequence of waterlogged river silts. In addition, smaller areas were opened in the field to the south to investigate further prehistoric monuments. Through the duration of the gravel extraction of the adjacent areas in 1987, an informal watching-brief resulted in the location of parts of the local palaeochannel system (Fig 1.6).

In early 1988 the entire Project was comprehensively reappraised and the Research Design was updated (Foard and Parker-Pearson 1989). With the excavation approaching its conclusion, the results achieved had defined the potential for further and more specific areas of study:

a) The potential to examine the regular lay-out of the late Saxon settlement together with its internal organisation.

b) The location of the watermill, at the time suspected but not confirmed, as potentially of national significance given the few excavated examples and the exceptional circumstance of the close relationship with an extensively excavated settlement.

c) The examination of the nature and the social context of the complex transition from the late Saxon settlement, with only a single building complex within the excavated area, to a medieval peasant hamlet, where five tenements lay within the excavated area.

d) The continuation of the programme of environmental sampling along with the recovery of waterlogged environmental samples from the adjacent palaeochannel. This was particularly significant given the close physical relationship to the settlement and the results already achieved within the dry-land excavations.

In 1988 the open area was extended northwards to link the palaeochannel with the dry-land excavation, and this led to the discovery of the watermill complex (Fig 1.12 and Plate 6). The further investigation of both the watermills and the palaeochannel led to a succession of further small extensions in 1989. Following the excavation of the watermills and the timber buildings of the tenth-eleventh centuries, work came to an end in December 1989. By this time a total area of 13000sq m had either been fully or extensively excavated, along with accompanying watching brief, salvage recording and trial trenching to the north, west and south.

A total of 46 months had been spent on site, 920 days, and the labour input is estimated at 14000 person days. At current charging rates for site staff in commercial archaeology this would represent over £2 million of labour costs alone. At the time, the site staff employed through the Manpower Services Commission received £10 a week above the basic rate of unemployment benefits.

Other work of relevance was conducted by the Survey

Fig 1.8: West Cotton in June 1987, looking north, with road construction in progress over the initial area of excavation, while a new area has been opened (left), which included medieval tenement E. (Aerial photograph by Glenn Foard for NCC)

Fig 1.9: West Cotton in June 1987, looking east, with road construction in progress over the initial area of excavation, while in the new area to the west (bottom) the demolition rubble covering tenement E has been exposed. (Aerial photograph by Glenn Foard for NCC, NMR 3423/24)

Fig 1.10: Aerial photograph 1987, showing medieval tenement E, arranged around a courtyard and with a walled yard to the west (left). The kitchen/ bakehouse of the earlier manorial range is also visible (top left) (Aerial photograph by Glenn Foard for NCC)

Fig 1.11: Aerial photograph in 1988, looking west, showing the triangle of the unexcavated eastern half of the hamlet (foreground), with the excavated western half surrounded by the quarry (Aerial photograph by Glenn Foard for NCC)

Fig 1.12: West Cotton in May 1989, looking south-west, showing the partially excavated late Saxon timber ranges (centre) and the watermill system and river palaeochannel (bottom left) (Aerial photograph by Glenn Foard for NCC)

team under the direction of Steve Parry. In 1988 trial-trenching to the east of Cotton Lane located previously unknown medieval buildings (Fig 1.6, I). In 1990 a series of trial-trenches in the field to the immediate east of the main settlement investigated the presence of early–middle Saxon features beneath a pottery scatter located in field walking, and a trench immediately beside the lane confirmed the suspected presence of a further medieval tenement or tenements (Fig 1.6, H).

Excavation methodology

The removal of both topsoil and subsoil was achieved using a mechanical excavator with a 5 or 6-foot toothless ditching bucket: a toothed bucket was only used on the deep deposits of intractable clays over the river palaeochannel. Across the building platforms the walls and demolition rubble were usually covered by little more than the turf, requiring careful control of the machine to minimise damage when exposing the rubble spreads. Within the associated yards the upper part of thick soil horizons that had accumulated within them were also removed, with a consequent loss of a small proportion of the pottery, other finds and animal bone.

In 1985 an area north of tenement C/D had been stripped directly to the natural gravel in order to establish at an early

stage the presence and date of cut features pre-dating the buildings (see Fig 7.3). This provided the first recognition of the presence of an earlier boundary ditch system, as well as the unexpected discovery of the ditches encircling a Bronze Age round barrow.

The alluvial clays around the margins of the settlement were also removed by machine in order to expose the buried prehistoric and late Saxon deposits. This included the removal of the twelfth-century flood embankment, which was therefore only seen in section.

Following machine stripping, all areas were cleaned, photographed and planned prior to excavation. With the later medieval buildings and yards the initial approach was to establish running sections, requiring the temporary provision of narrow baulks at each stratigraphic level. Although of some initial use, while the team became familiar with the stratigraphy, these were soon found to be more inconvenient than useful and this method was rapidly abandoned in favour of full area excavation of both the buildings and yards.

All of the stone medieval buildings, apart from some marginal areas that lay beyond the road take, were totally excavated in order to expose the underlying levels. The late Saxon timber buildings were also fully excavated. These posed considerable technical problems as there was a minimal distinction between the wall-trench fills and the soil horizon into which they were cut. The occasional presence of limestone, largely within the subsidence fills, identified short lengths of wall-trench but, despite careful trowel-cleaning of the surface, it was never possible to define a full building plan in advance of excavation. The approach adopted was to excavate the definable lengths and then to carefully work the sections along into the unknown. This inevitably resulted in some loss of information, particularly the relationships of some intersecting wall-trenches, and it is also likely that at least some evidence for the presence of basal hollows indicative of post positions was also missed.

The tenth to twelfth-century system of boundary ditches was extensively excavated in an attempt to provide broader finds samples to enhance the overall dating and perhaps to define the presence and nature of adjacent activity areas, although this latter objective was not achieved. One of the major problems with the boundary system was the lack of evidence for their individual dates of origin, as recutting had either removed or at least mixed the earlier ditch fills, so that in many cases only their infill dates can be defined. With more careful excavation it might have been possible to define localised pockets of early fills, which were certainly present in places, but in practice ditch excavation was often given to the less experienced site workers who would not have recognised such subtleties. The dating of the origin of the system is therefore primarily based on the pottery assemblages from a few lengths of ditch that were abandoned and filled in at an early date.

In the 1985 and 1986 seasons the importance of the development of the natural watercourses to the overall history of the settlement was not fully appreciated and, as a result, the difficult task of exploring the area of alluvial silts and underlying stream channel deposits at the northern end of the site was not carried through. Similarly, a full section was not obtained of the southern stream when it was exposed in the quarry edge.

Bulk finds of animal bone and pottery were allocated to both context and a 5m grid-square, while other finds were recorded by three-dimensional coordinates. The locations of all bulk soil samples were recorded to context and by coordinate.

Recording systems

The site grid was established on the alignment of the intended new road, with site north to the east of Ordnance Survey grid north. Across the excavated area a grid of metal pegs at 5m intervals was established using the basic theodolite surveying techniques of setting out successive base lines with cross-checking of right-angles and the alignment and lengths of diagonals, using Fibron tapes for the linear measurements. There is an estimated error of ±0.10m between points some 50m or more apart, largely resulting from a systematic error in the original base line. A basic grid of metal rods, driven to ground level and protected by small cairns of limestone, has been left *in-*

situ across the eastern, unexcavated part of the settlement. The site location relative to the Ordnance Survey base was established by tacheometric survey to fixed points within the modern landscape, to an estimated surveying accuracy of ± 0.5m.

The planning system was based on A2-sized sheets of drafting film, enabling two 5m grid squares to appear on each sheet at a scale of 1:20. Composite plans show the entire palimpsest of contexts exposed at successive stages of the excavation of a given area. Intermediate plans, showing only one or more specific contexts, were used as required, while small details were sometimes recorded on A4 sheets. All areas containing buildings and other major feature groups were planned stone-by-stone at 1:20, but in the later excavation seasons lengths of boundary ditch and some minor features were often planned at 1:50. Some marginal areas or detached trenches were recorded at 1:100. Sections or profiles were drawn of most individual features at 1:10 and major sections, generally those provided by the edges of excavation areas, at 1:20. In total there are around 1700 plans and 1500 section drawings.

The context numbering system comprised a single numerical sequence, running from 1 to 7398. During the first season of excavation there was no allocation of blocks of numbers to specific areas of the site, but in subsequent seasons each supervisor was allocated a block of 1000 numbers. This system had the advantage of providing more rapid access to blocks of related information. A total of 5390 context numbers were allocated to Saxon and medieval contexts, and the remainder are accounted for by either unused numbers at the ends of some blocks and the numbers allocated to the prehistoric elements of the site. All context information was recorded on individual pro-forma sheets; soil colour descriptions were purely verbal, colour charts were not used.

The allocation of context numbers was pragmatic. An individual posthole, say, might have been given separate context numbers for its cut and fills when these showed some complexity of form, but in other instances a single fill would be subsumed under the feature context. Such simplifications occurred more frequently as the excavation progressed into its later seasons. Context numbers also had a wider usage in defining archaeological actions. Whilst the major areas of the site were allocated letter codes during the course of excavation (A, B, C etc) individual trenches within or beyond the open area excavation were identified by a general context number. A few individual structures or smaller areas of specific investigation, such as box-sections examining ditch intersections or general areas of cleaning, were also given general as well as specific context numbers.

Stratigraphic sequence diagrams, or matrices, were not compiled during the course of the excavation, although sequences for some complex areas were produced between excavation seasons.

Throughout the excavation the normal process of site photography used 35mm single-lens reflex cameras, and ranged from individual contexts to whole-site photographs, duplicated in black-and-white and colour transparency. From 1987 colour print film was also used for any subjects likely to provide popular shots for use in public displays. Well over 200 films were exposed, producing some 3,500 negatives and 3,500 transparencies offering over a 1000 separate views of the excavations in progress, with two to four images of each view taken in each format. High-level photographs were taken utilising either a high ladder or a scaffolding tower, while on one occasion a mobile hoist was hired. The site photographs are complemented by aerial photographs taken by Glenn Foard during flights sponsored by the Royal Commission on Historic Monuments (England). The colour slides resulting from these flights are deposited with the Northamptonshire Historic Environment Record and the black and white negatives are deposited with the National Monument Record (NMR) at Swindon.

Geophysical Survey

In order to enhance the understanding of the layout of the settlement beyond the excavated areas, a programme of geophysical survey, using both magnetometer and resistivity techniques, was conducted by Andy Payne of the Ancient Monuments Laboratory in 1991 (Figs 1.13–1.15). This was supplemented by further magnetometer (Figs 1.16 and 1.17) and resistivity surveys (not illustrated) in the field to the east of the Cotton Lane, carried out by Peter Masters for Northamptonshire Archaeology. The results of these surveys in defining further medieval buildings and boundary ditch systems have been incorporated within the period and phase plans depicting the overall development of the settlement, while further probable prehistoric monuments were also located (see Harding and Healy 2007, 129, fig 3.65).

Interim publications

Annual summaries or interim statements were published in national, regional and local journals:

Medieval Archaeology: 1987, **31**, 153–4; 1988, **32**, 266–7; 1989, **33**, 204–6; and 1990, **34**, 204 and plate 12A
The Medieval Settlement Research Group Annual Report: 1987, **2**, 23–4; 1988, **3**, 22–3; and 1989, **4**, 41–3
South Midlands Archaeology: 1988, **18**, 51–60; 1989, **19**, 35–9; and 1990, **20**, 45–50
Northamptonshire Archaeology: 1985, **20**, 3–8; 1986–7, **21**, 25–9
Archaeology Review, English Heritage: 1988–89, 18 (plate) and 36
Current Archaeology: 1987, **106**, 337–9.

In addition, a series of short, illustrated leaflets were produced; largely for local distribution to site visitors, organised tours and at the annual public open days.

Following the completion of excavation, a comprehensive interim report was produced to cover both the prehistoric and the Saxon to medieval aspects of the site: Windell, D, Chapman, A, and Woodiwiss, J, 1990, *From Barrows to Bypass: Excavations at West Cotton, Raunds, Northamptonshire, 1985–1989*. This presented an outline interpretation of settlement development based on the empirical understanding that had evolved through the course of the excavations. The major differences between the interim account and the model of site development presented in this report are the more detailed and reliable chronology established by the pottery analysis and the more complex story that has emerged for the conversion from manor to hamlet in the late thirteenth to early fourteenth centuries.

A summary of the site chronology was also published in the Raunds Survey volume (Chapman in Parry 2006, 172–177).

Post-excavation methodology

In the analysis of the context information only a single additional level of post-excavation coding was introduced: the provision of Structure Group codes. For this a mnemonic system was chosen, so that the nature and, in broad terms, the date range of any defined structure group was readily apparent from its code. The buildings were numbered in a single sequence but given a prefix letter defining their building group, which was drawn from the on-site area codes. Thus, the medieval buildings of tenement A are coded A1–A3, while those of tenement B are B4–B7, and so on. The buildings of the post-Conquest manor and the late Saxon timber buildings are prefixed S (stone) and T (timber) respectively. The definition of individual rooms was achieved by a suffix, so building A1 comprises rooms A1/1 to A1/5. The medieval yards have been given an additional Y prefix and are numbered separately within each tenement; thus AY1–AY6 and BY1–BY7. The earlier boundary ditch system and the plots defined by them are coded respectively as LSD's (late Saxon ditches) and LSE's (late Saxon enclosures). Any further definition is by reference to the original context numbers, but the use of these has been kept to the necessary minimum.

A single site context matrix was not compiled, as the site comprised coherent blocks of stratigraphy but with few links between tenements or the detached buildings of a single tenement. A diagrammatic representation of the sites overall development was provided at structure level in combination with the pottery phase dating, and this provided a sufficient tool to explore the complexities of site development.

The full analysis of the archaeological evidence led to the production of a written text, the site narrative, accompanied by post-excavation drawings of all major structures, building groups and general period plans, and most of the final drawings are taken directly from them.

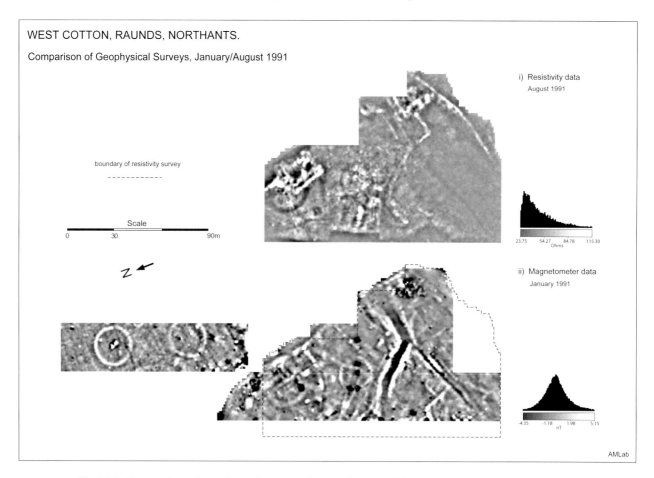

Fig 1.13: Comparison of geophysical surveys, January/August 1991 (Ancient Monument Laboratory)

The site archive

The archive will comprise all the original records generated during the excavation and all the collected finds, which include retained environmental residues although all waterlogged wood has been discarded following analysis. The written notes are largely in the form of individually numbered context sheets, which have been organised in structural groups rather than simple numerical order. The drawn records comprise separately numbered plan and section drawings in numerical order. The photographic archive comprises black-and-white negatives and prints, colour transparencies and some colour-print negatives and prints.

During post-excavation computerised database catalogues were compiled for most aspects of the site archive and hard copies of these are included in the archive. In addition, there are full narrative descriptions and discussions of all excavated features by period and structural group, accompanied by over 100 plan and section drawings in a single numbered sequence (PE drawings).

Copies of all written and drawn archive material will be available on microfiche in the National Monuments Record. It is intended that the full report will be made available online five years after publication, and a full digital archive of all the illustrations and photographs will be retained as a resource available for use by other researchers. At the time of writing Northamptonshire does not have an established county archaeological archive, so it is not possible to state where the physical site archive will eventually be deposited. The archive will be retained in temporary store by Northamptonshire Archaeology until a suitable store becomes available.

Further comments on the future availability of the West Cotton material are included in Chapter 8.

Summary of the chronological sequence

The chronological sequence

As an introduction to the description of the excavated evidence, a simple tabulation of the full chronological sequence is provided (Table 1.1 and Fig 1.18). The earliest features at West Cotton date to the early Neolithic, with the sequence of burial monuments running through to the early Bronze Age. These aspects of the site will be briefly summarised in Chapter 3, and are dealt with in detail within the account of all the prehistoric aspects of the Raunds Area Project (Harding and Healy 2007).

No features or finds of late Bronze Age or Iron Age date were identified, but a late Bronze Age field system and an extensive area of Iron Age settlement lay 1km to the south. There was a considerable scatter of residual Roman finds, and perhaps some specific activity related to the adjacent river palaeochannel, and 1km to the south the earlier settlements were overlain by a major Roman settlement and villa. This and all other aspects of Iron Age and Roman in the Raunds Area will be dealt with in another separate volume (Crosby and Neal forthcoming).

The main excavation located minor episodes of early Saxon occupation, while a further focus in the field to the east of Cotton Lane was defined in the field survey. Middle Saxon activity is apparently limited to use of the adjacent river channel for flax retting, as determined by radiocarbon dating. The early and middle Saxon episodes fall within the broad pattern of dispersed settlement as established by the work of the survey team (Parry 2006).

The archaeological importance of West Cotton lies in it comprising a small settlement of which a large proportion has been excavated. This has provided a sound model for examining many aspects of the processes of village formation and development in Central England from the tenth century onward, and set in the local context of the reorganisation of settlement and society in the wake of the early tenth-century reconquest by the Saxon kings and the subsequent establishment of order within the Danelaw. The evidence from West Cotton also complements the parallel evidence from the village of Raunds itself, where the manorial centre of Furnells manor, with its associated church and churchyard (Boddington 1996), and the parts of the manorial demesne farm of the Burystead manor, adjacent to the present parish church on the opposite side of the Raunds Brook, were also extensively excavated in the 1970s and 80s (Audouy and Chapman 2009).

The 500–year period from the tenth-century settlement formation at West Cotton to the late medieval desertion has been divided into three main periods (Table 1.1 and Fig 1.18a). The late Saxon settlement saw the formation of a new, planned settlement with its timber buildings and watermill. The early twelfth century saw the replacement of the timber buildings with a small Norman manor house in stone, whose prosperity was immediately under threat when a period of flooding and alluvial deposition rendered the watermill redundant and necessitated the building of hundreds of metres of protective floodbank (Fig 1.18b).

The thirteenth century saw a reorientation of the economic base, with an emphasis on crop storage and processing, presumably at least in part to produce marketable cash crops. This was initiated as part of the direct farming of the manorial demesne, but by the middle of the thirteenth century the settlement underwent a major reorganisation in which the manor was relocated away from the redundant river channel and mill, and onto the plots adjacent to Cotton Lane (Fig 1.18c). This episode also

saw the formation of new tenements on the former manor house plots, as the beginning of the end to direct farming of the manorial demesne. By the fourteenth century the buildings of the new manor had been converted to further tenements, and the site was then truly a peasant hamlet, with the production of malt and perhaps the fulling of woollen cloth providing additions to the economic base of arable and pastoral agriculture.

This episode was to be short-lived as the tenements were deserted one-by-one through the fourteenth century and into the fifteenth century as part of the nationwide process of desertions that occurred in the wake of the series of the famines of the early part of the fourteenth century, when a colder and wetter period hit both crop returns and the animal livestock, and the Black Death and subsequent lesser epidemics that so drastically reduced the population and left the marginal settlements unviable when better land was unoccupied and going to waste.

The basis for the site chronology

While a small group of radiocarbon dates provide corroborative evidence, the basis for the site chronology comes from the analysis of the pottery carried out by Paul Blinkhorn. This is fully detailed and discussed in the pottery report, but the broad basis is summarised below for the general reader.

The dating is based on the use of a Relative Seriated Phase Dating System (RSP). This technique was first used during the analysis of the late Saxon and medieval pottery from the sites in north Raunds (Blinkhorn 2009), and was based on the dating of the pottery types that are common to both Raunds and Northampton, where there was an established history of pottery research (Denham 1985). The analysis of the West Cotton pottery has confirmed the original seriation of the major wares, while the assemblage has also provided an opportunity to enhance some areas of the RSP established for the Raunds sites.

The RSP technique establishes a series of ceramic phases defined by the introduction of particular pottery forms, with the commencement of the phase being the *terminus post quem* (TPQ) for the introduction of those particular forms. There are separate ceramic phases for the late Saxon (LS1–LS4) and the medieval pottery (Ph0–Ph5) and these are tabulated below (Tables 1.2 and 1.3):

Throughout the report when dates are quoted they will usually include the ceramic phase date, eg (ph 1, 1150–1225), so that if future research refines the absolute dating of any ceramic phase it would be possible to revise the site chronology derived from the pottery assemblages.

It must also be remembered throughout that, apart from any direct references to documentary evidence, all dates are approximate. However, rather than cluttering the text with a *circa* attached to every date these have often been omitted and the reader is asked to recognise their invisible presence.

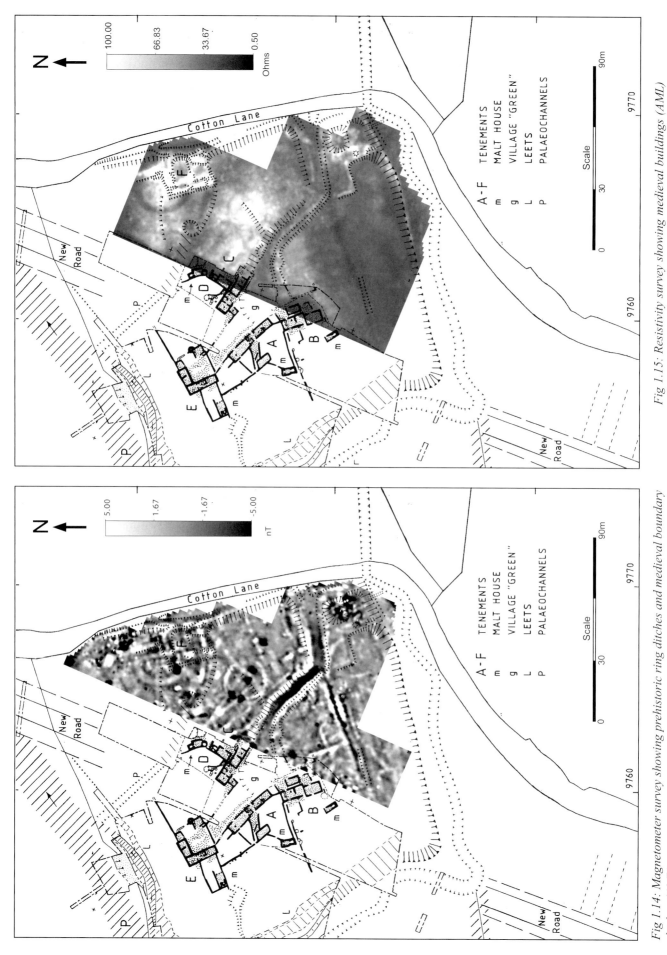

Fig 1.15: Resistivity survey showing medieval buildings (AML)

Fig 1.14: Magnetometer survey showing prehistoric ring ditches and medieval boundary ditches (AML)

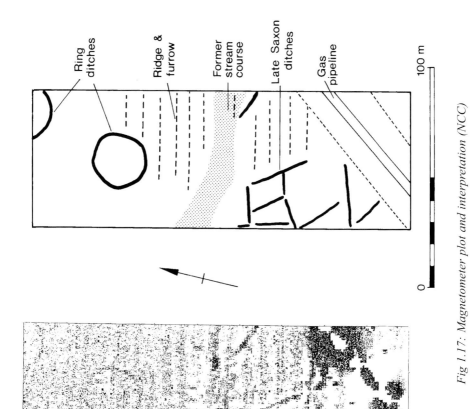

Fig 1.17: *Magnetometer plot and interpretation (NCC)*

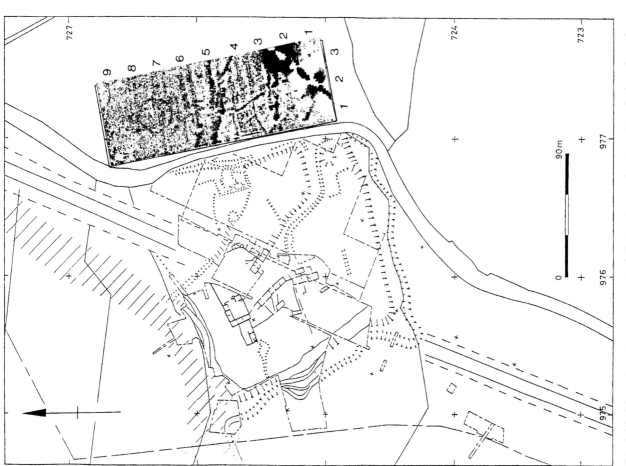

Fig 1.16: *Magnetometer survey east of Cotton Lane, showing ring ditches, boundary ditches, possible former stream and gad pipeline (NCC)*

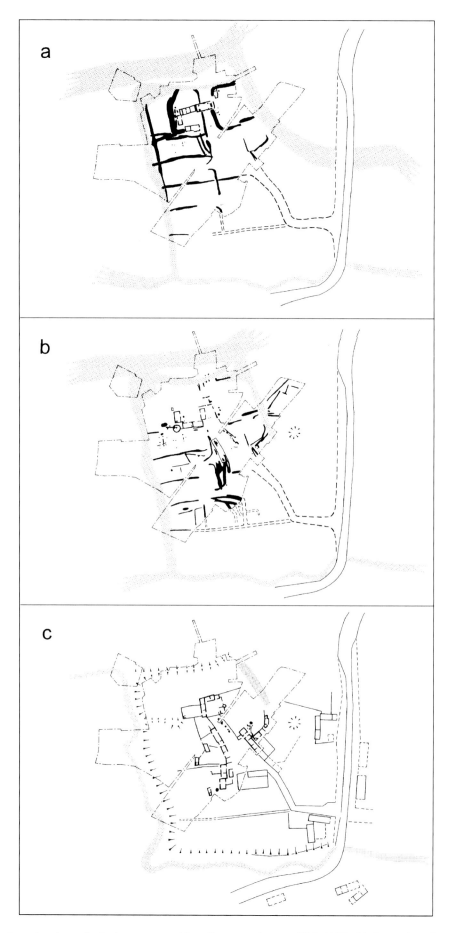

Fig 1.18: West Cotton, the chronological sequence; a) late Saxon settlement (950–1150), b) the medieval manor (1150–1250), c) the medieval manor and hamlet (1250–1450)

Plate 1: Aerial photograph in 1988, showing West Cotton (bottom) with Cotton Lane and the new road running south, with Stanwick Roman villa (centre), the quarry processing plant (top), and the River Nene and the old railway line (top right) (Photograph by Glenn Foard for Northamptonshire County Council (NCC))

Plate 2: Aerial photograph of West Cotton in 1985, looking south-east, showing the initial area of excavation along the proposed road corridor set within pasture fields (Glenn Foard for NCC)

Plate 3: A similar view in 1987, showing the landscape transformed by road construction and quarrying, with West Cotton preserved as a green square in the centre, while the former river and stream channels form raised areas of unexcavated ground within the quarry to the west (right) (Glenn Foard for NCC)

Plate 4: The late Saxon courtyard manor, defined by the wall trenches, looking south, with the leat feeding the watermill complex in the foreground

Plate 5: The medieval manor (AD 1100–1250), looking south, showing the heavily truncated buildings set around a courtyard; hall to left and kitchen range to the right (Glenn Foard for NCC)

Plate 6: The early watermill, M27, with planks simulating the location of the sluice gate and feeder trough, with the metalled and wattle-lined wheel pit in the foreground

Plate 7: Reconstruction of the medieval hamlet as it may have looked in the later thirteenth century, with the manorial barns fronting onto the central yard (left) and the new peasant tenements at the western end (top centre and right) (Alex Thompson)

Plate 8: April 1985, showing the initial cleaning of the demolition rubble over medieval tenement B, with tenement A in the background

Plate 9: Excavation of the domestic range of tenement A, with tenement B in the background and late medieval drainage ditch along the frontage

Plate 10: Excavation of tenements C/D , with tenement A in the background on the opposite side of the central yard, which was filled with alluvial clayey silts

Plate 11: The malt house of tenement C during excavation, showing the circular vat stand with the rectangular oven chamber in the background

Plate 12: Tenement E, following removal of demolition rubble from the buildings and central yard

Plate 13: The carved-stone figure, 'Norman Morris', from a stone-lined bin in tenement D, building D11

Table 1.1: Summary of the chronological sequence

MAJOR PERIODS	DATE RANGE
The prehistoric monument complex	**Neolithic to early Bronze Age**
Romano-British activity	
Early to middle Saxon occupation	**AD 500–800**
The late Saxon settlement	**AD 950–1100**
The formation of the settlement	AD 950– 975
The late Saxon settlement	AD 975–1100
The medieval manor	**AD 1100–1250**
The medieval rebuilding, and abandonment of the watermill system	AD 1100–1200
The initial development of the frontage	AD 1200–1250
The medieval manor and hamlet	**AD 1250–1450**
The relocation of the manor	AD 1250–1300
From manor to hamlet	AD 1300–1350
The medieval hamlet, decline and desertion	AD 1350–1450
Post-medieval activity	**AD 1450 onward**

The organisation of the report

Compiling the results of any major long-running excavation into a single document that can both catalogue the mass of data and provide a meaningful overview and discussion, but without becoming so voluminous that it intimidates both the mind and the pocket of the potential reader, is not an easy task. In the draft of the mid-1990s the approach taken was to compartmentalise the data into a series of thematic chapters – comprising a general overview of the development of the site, a period by period cataloguing of the excavated evidence, and then a general discussion of site development processes and specific discussions of particular aspects of building form and use.

This approach necessitated considerable repetition of some details, and was largely written without the benefit of being able to integrate the results of the various specialist studies, apart from the chronological base provided by the pottery, as the analysis and reporting of the pottery, other finds, the environmental evidence and animal bone were all in progress concurrently. These deficiencies were ruthlessly exposed by the anonymous reader of that draft.

The document presented here has been extensively reordered and revised. The approach taken is to chronicle the development and structure of the settlement period by period, so that each chapter provides a self-contained account of the archaeology of that period.

Following the presentation of the documentary evidence, each period-based chapter begins with a broad overview of the development of the site through the period in question accompanied by an overview of the key points emerging from the specialist studies relating to status and the economic basis of the settlement. There then follows more detailed description of individual elements of the site, with the many well-preserved buildings catalogued in some detail. Broader overviews of building techniques are provided for the timber buildings of tenth and eleventh centuries, and the chapter detailing the conversion from manor to hamlet also provides an overview of all of the stone buildings of the twelfth to fourteenth centuries. At the middle of the thirteenth century the chronological narrative is interrupted by a chapter dealing specifically with the particular evidence for the development and demise of the watermill system, and the associated history of the river palaeochannels.

The story of West Cotton has been left largely in isolation from the rest of the medieval settlement of Raunds, and the reader is referred to both the Raunds survey volume (Parry 2006) and the account of the contemporary settlements in north Raunds to find more extensive descriptions and discussion of the broader pattern of medieval settlement

Table 1.2: The late Saxon Relative Seriated Phase Dating System (RSP)

LS1	LS2	LS3	LS4
St Neots T1(4)	St.Neots T1(3), Stamford Ware	Cotswolds type Oolitic Top Hat Jars	St Neots T1(2)
AD 850–950	900–975	975–1000	1000–1100

Table 1.3: The medieval Relative Seriated Phase Dating System (RSP)

Ph0	Ph1	Ph2/0	Ph2/2	Ph3/2	Ph4	Ph5
T1(2) St Neots SHC, SAC	Lyveden A	Lyveden B Brill	Potterspury	RRW	Lyveden D LMR	LMO
AD 1100–1150	1150–1225	1225–1250	1250–1300	1300–1400	1400–1450	1450–1500

SHC, Medieval Shelly Coarseware; SAC, Medieval Sandy Coarseware
RRW, Raunds-type Reduced Ware; LMR, Late Medieval Reduced Ware
LMO, Late Medieval Oxidized Ware

development (Audouy and Chapman 2009, Chapter 3: A panorama of settlement development, 22–50).

The full specialist reports will form Part 2 of this report, and will appear on a data CD attached to the printed volume, as well as being made available online. This approach will not endear the principal author to the specialists who devoted so much time and effort to the project, to whom I apologise, but the decision was taken on the basis that these studies do have a restricted appeal and it has been considered more important to keep the overall volume to a reasonable length, and cost, to attract the less specialist reader.

Various aspects of the specialist studies have already been made available to fellow workers. The function of the pottery vessels within the medieval hamlet has been considered by Blinkhorn (1998–99), and an overview of the principal results from the analysis of the charred plant remains was published in the mid-1990s (Campbell 1994). The animal bone report, containing all the figures, diagrams and plates has been available to interested specialists since the 1990s as an English Heritage Ancient Monuments Laboratory report (AML 17/94), and only the text is reproduced in full in this volume.

2 The Documentary Evidence

by Paul Courtney

As part of the Raunds Area Project, a one-year programme of documentary research was funded, with Professor Christopher Dyer as project advisor. In this volume, only the evidence directly pertaining to the deserted hamlet of West Cotton is considered in detail. The reader is referred elsewhere for fuller discussions of the evolution of the Anglo-Saxon estate, and of the manorial structure of the Raunds area (Courtney 2006). A further volume contains a discussion of the relationship of the manorial building complex on the northern holding at West Cotton to the superior manor at Furnells in Raunds village (Courtney 2009). These discussions are, however, briefly summarised below.

A wide range of documentary sources have been utilised and they are listed below along with the abbreviations used in the text references:

BF	Book of Fees
CFR	Calendar of Fine Rolls
DB	Domesday Book
CIPM	Calendar of Inquisitions PostMortem, Public Record Office
CIPM-Rec Comm	Calendar of Inquisitions PostMortem, Record Commission
NRO	Northamptonshire Record Office
PRO	Public Record Office
Rot Hund	Rotuli Hundredorum temp. Hen. III and Edw. I, Record Commission
VCH	The Victoria history of the Counties of England: Northamptonshire

Feudal overlords

Raunds is believed to have been a component of a late Saxon estate centred upon Higham Ferrers. By the time of Domesday Book this estate was in a process of fragmentation giving rise to a complex tenurial landscape. Domesday Book indicates that two major holdings dominated the area of the former estate. One fee belonged to the King's thegn Burgred in 1066 and had been granted to the bishop of Coutances by 1086. This estate comprised lands and rents in Raunds, Ringstead and the Cottons and included a manor in Raunds which can be identified with

Furnells (*DB* I, f 220c). It later belonged to the Clares (as part of the honor of Gloucester) and the Staffords. It continued to be known in the post-medieval period as the Gloucester fee. By the twelfth century the Clare/Gloucester fee had its chief court at Denford and the three main post-Conquest manors associated with the Cottons all owed suit to its court leet. The other major fee belonged to the Countess Gytha in 1066 and was in the hands of the Peverel family by Domesday. It was later held by the Ferrers family, the earls of Lancaster and from 1351 as part of the duchy of Lancaster. The manorial centre was at Higham Ferrers, and Raunds, Burystead, which possessed lands and tenants in Raunds, Ringstead, Hargrave and Stanwick, appears to have been a berewick (dependent demesne) in Domesday Book.

Table 2.1: The descent of the two chief Raunds Fees

1066	1086	1200	1300	1400
Burgred	Coutances	Clare	Clare (Gloucester)	Stafford
Gytha	Peverel	Ferrers	earl of Lancaster	Duchy of Lancaster

Documentary sources

Any understanding of the history of West Cotton, and the other Cottons, is severely hindered by the paucity of sources, especially the lack of early manorial documents for the dominant Gloucester fee. The Cottons do not appear in the Domesday Book, where they are subsumed within the larger estates. The first reference is in the twelfth-century Northamptonshire Survey and this only refers generically to "the Cotes" (*VCH*, 1, 377; see also Glover *et al* 1938, 194–5).

The documentation is also highly biased to its feudal overlords with a lack of evidence relating to its medieval peasant inhabitants. The main sources of information include the records of central government, especially *inquisitions post mortem*, taken on the deaths of the feudal tenants, as well as other lists of feudal tenure, but there is a chronological bias to the period after its decline as a settlement. Manorial records are limited to references in the court rolls of the duchy manor of Raunds, from 1349 onwards, and the Clare/Gloucester fee court based in Denford, from 1514 onwards.

The Cottons

Raunds lay within the hundred (or rather hundred and a half) of Higham, which was named after the major estate centre at Higham Ferrers. In the tenth century, the royal manor (*cyninges tun* or *regia villa*) had been replaced as the basis of royal administration by a new system based on the hierarchical units of county, hundred and vill. All the Cottons along with Raunds, Ringstead and the part of Hargrave in Northamptonshire (rather than Huntingdonshire) formed a single vill into the late fourteenth century. It is not therefore normally possible to distinguish the Cottons from the other components of the vill in taxation records. However, in the 1220 carucage Ringstead and Cotes (probably Mill Cotton) were assessed at 9 1/2 ploughs and 'Cotes and the other Cotes' (probably Mallows Cotton and West Cotton) were assessed the same (*BF*, 1, 3210). This was a property tax on plough teams (8 oxen), supposedly as yoked on June 21 1220 (Mitchell 1957, 136). The Ferrers lands (later the duchy) seem to have been excluded from the Higham hundred assessments. This taxation, if reliable, seems to imply considerable agrarian resources attached to the Cottons.

The excavations at West Cotton have clearly revealed a high-status site of late Saxon origin and it has been argued that all three Cottons may have had similar origins, not as secondary settlements but as an integral part of the tenth-century re-planning of the landscape (Courtney 2006). In Domesday Book the Cottons were clearly not regarded as manors. However, many such subordinate units (eg the Peverel holding in Raunds) possessed demesnes, subordinate peasantry and presumably halls at which dues and services were rendered. The tenure and social status of the late Saxon holder of West Cotton is far from clear. Nevertheless, it seems likely that its holder would have been a minor thegn, sokeman or freeman. Domesday Book suggests that there was an overlap in economic status between the lesser thegns and the wealthier freemen; Abels (1988, 144) has argued that some sokemen and freemen attended the king's army alongside thegns, either to discharge their own tenurial obligations or those of their landlord.

One must also distinguish between the hall as an architectural type, as revealed by excavation, and the hall as a legal concept, as revealed by the documents. However, it is possible that West Cotton had its own unfree tenants who rendered rent and labour services at its hall. Indeed, in economic rather than tenurial terms it may have differed little in its operation to Furnells. In regard to the material culture of the two sites, it is not impossible that the residents of the Cottons could have been of a higher status and wealth than the farmer who actually lived at Furnells.

Place names

The place-names *Cotes* and *Cot(t)on* are Middle English plural forms derived from the Old English word for cottage, *cot(e)*. They are normally associated with sites of low status; cottagers and bordars were peasants with only small holdings of land who lived primarily from hiring out their labour. However, Gelling (1976, 924–5) has previously drawn notice to a higher status *Cotes* place name in Buscote, Berkshire. Particularly pertinent is the classic analysis of the surviving 1279 hundred rolls for the south Midlands by the Russian historian, Kosminsky (1956, 256–318). He demonstrated the lesser role of villeins and customary labour in relation to smaller manors, which instead must have been largely dependent on hired labour. This offers an explanation for the co-existence of minor manorial sites and settlements of cottagers. Both Mallows and Mill Cotton appear to have had peasant settlements existing alongside manorial sites in the high Middle Ages. The 'Cotton' place-names seem likely, therefore, to be derived from the low-status elements of this settlement pattern. As they are not documented before the twelfth century it is possible that they replaced earlier names. There is no evidence at West Cotton for peasant settlement before the thirteenth century reorganisation of the manorial complex. It is possible, however, that earlier peasant dwellings existed outside the main area of excavation, either within the eastern enclosures or to the east of Cotton Lane (Fig 1.6).

West Cotton appears in the medieval records as West Cotes, Little Cotes and Wilwencotes with various spellings. It is first specifically identified in a feet of fine of 1247 which records the transfer of land and meadow in Raunds and Westcotes; the meadow was probably the portion in West Cotton (PRO CP25(1)/175/36/551). The name Little Cotes (*Parva Cotes*) is first used in the hundred roll of 1274–5 (*Rot Hund*, 2, 10) and *Wylewynecotes* first appears in an inquisition of 1307 (*CIPM*, 4, no. 435). The duchy court rolls show that the form *Cot(t)on* or *Cot(t)en* alternates with *Cotes* from the early fifteenth century (NRO 705–7). West and Little Cotes (Cotton) predominate in the duchy sources and, as far as can be discerned, appear to be interchangeable terms. Wilwencotes is the usual form in the Gloucester fee documents and incorporates the Old English word *welig*, probably in its dative plural form meaning 'at the willows' (cf Smith 1956, 2, 266–7 and Wrander 1983, 108).

The manorial descent

The Clare/Gloucester fee manor

The Clare/Gloucester fee dominated the three Cottons. The Northamptonshire Survey of the twelfth century records three lords holding lands 'in Cotes' from the fee of Denford (*VCH*, 1, 377). It is not clear who held the 'fee of Dennford' at this date and it may have been farmed from the crown.

The three twelfth-century 'manors' may correspond to the Domesday holdings of either three named men of uncertain status (Robert and Geoffrey each with 1 hide or Algar with 1 1/2 virgates), or else three un-named sokemen who held two hides between them (*DB*, 1, 220c). The Domesday Book hidages do not equate with those in the Northamptonshire Survey but are likely to represent fiscal units, prone to reassessment, rather than measured acreage.

The three lords of 'Cotes' recorded by the Northamptonshire Survey were John Bidun, Gilbert fitz Richard (de Clare) and Frumbold de Denford, and their holdings can be identified (by means of their later descents) with Mill, Mallows and West Cotton, respectively. Frumbold de Denford also held lands in nearby Knuston. It is unclear on what terms, possibly temporary, these lands were initially held but they clearly soon became hereditary holdings. This can be seen as part of the rapidly evolving trend of major lords to sub-infeudate lands to knights in return for homage and military service. The Normanville family had succeeded the de Denford family in Knuston by 1232 (PRO CP25 (1)/172/23/246) and also held land in West Cotton, indicating the identity of Frumbold's half hide (*VCH*, 4, 22). By the early twelfth century it is clear therefore that West Cotton was a minor manor and the excavated high status building complex of twelfth to early thirteenth century date may possibly be equated with the 1/2 hide of Frumbold de Denford.

The hundred roll of 1274–5 refers to the men of Ralf Normanville in (West) Cotton. However, it also refers to the men of Henry de Albotesk, who is not otherwise documented in West Cotton (*Rot Hund*, 2, 10). This may indicate that Frumbold's manor had already been split, as is indicated in later documents. The inquisition *post mortem* of Gilbert de Clare in 1314 records that both Richard Chamberlain and Ralf Normanville held 1/40 of a knight's fee in Wilwencotes (*CIPM*, 5, no 538). In 1373 the fees are described as 1/16 and 1/40 parts, the smaller belonging to Ralph de Normanville, and by 1387 the Chamberlain family was in possession of both (*CIPM*, 13, no 210 and 16, no 454). In 1399, John Wolf, successor to the Normanville family at Knuston, is recorded as possessing the 1/40 part of a fee but is not mentioned again (*CIPM*, 17, no. 1282). In 1397 and 1406 the Chamberlain holding is described as 30 acres of land and meadow and 3s 4d of rent of divers tenants, held by 1/20 of a knight's fee (*CIPM*, 17, no. 779; *CFR* 1405–13, 39). However, in 1413 the possessions of Johanne (Joan), widow of Richard Chamberlain, held of the earl of Stafford, are described in more detail. They were said to comprise: a messuage, one virgate plus 3 acres of land and a watermill held by 1/8 of a knight's fee; two other messuages and 1 1/2 virgates held by military service; and one cottage, a virgate, two tofts, nine acres of land and 3s 5d of rent also held by military service (PRO C138/3). These separate units are presumably a reflection of the peasant holdings.

The watermill is not mentioned in a more cursory description in an inquisition of 1496 (PRO C142/11/4).

The Chamberlains also owned manors locally at Ringstead, Denford and both Mill and Mallows Cotton, as well as several manors in adjacent counties. Their main residence from at least the late fourteenth century was the mansion called Chamberlain's Place (*mansi vocat' Chaumberlainplace*) at Mill Cotton (*CIPM-Rec Comm*, 4, 2).

Wilwencotes manor, along with manors in Mill and Mallows Cotton, Ringstead and Raunds, was sold by Sir Edward Chamberlain to Robert Dormer in 1530. By 1535 they had been purchased by the FitzWilliam family who sold them in 1559 to the Pickerings of nearby Titchmarsh (*VCH*, 4, 33; Bridges, 2, 190). After this date Wilwencotes manor ceases to be mentioned and its lands were probably sold off by the Pickerings. A deed of 1545 records the sale of a close in West Cotton from Thomas Hopkyns to John Taylarde and notes that it was bounded by a close of Richard FitzWilliam to the north and a close of Thomas Infylde to the south (NRO S of O 63), see discussion of mills below, unfortunately these closes cannot be traced in later documents.

In 1598 only two tenants, both freeholders, were recorded as owing suit to the Clare/Gloucester fee court in Denford; Thomas Harrison and Thomas Tawyer, gent. It is possible that Harrison only held meadow, while the Wilwencotes section of the court rolls records that, between 1601 and 1603, Thomas Tawyer 'gent' sold off 36 acres of arable and 3 roods of meadow to 5 individuals. Several of the new owners are subsequently listed as owing suit of court for Wilwencotes (NRO X884 and X887:23–8, p 219). It is uncertain if the arable lay in the close vicinity of West Cotton or was more scattered, being attached to a former messuage there. Unfortunately, none of these holdings can be traced subsequently with any degree of certainty. It seems likely that these lands are the same as those held by the Chamberlains in the fifteenth century, Tawyer having purchased them from the Pickerings, but this is unproven.

The Clare/Gloucester court rolls record Wilwencotes as a separate tithing from the earliest surviving Denford court rolls of 1514 until it disappears sometime between 1622 and 1628. A tithing was a group of men who were bound to stand security for each other's good behaviour. Two tithingmen or officials for the tithing of Wilwencotes were appointed by the court into the seventeenth century (1514–1622), though they repeatedly failed to give suit of court in the reign of James I. An annual 'cert' payment of 6d was also paid by the tenants to the Denford court. Several tenants are named as owing suit but there is no evidence that any of them actually lived in the hamlet; in the 1514–21 rolls William Clark was one of the two tithingmen for West Cotton as well as tithingman for Middle (Mallows) Cotton. Occasional references to the inheritance or sale of portions of meadow or pasture in Wilwencotes also occur (NRO X884–5).

Duchy lands

Although the Clare/Gloucester fee dominated the three Cottons, the duchy certainly had meadow and cottagers at both Mallows and Little Cotton. These were not sub-infeudated, like the Clare/Gloucester fee lands, but were farmed as demesne (land worked by tenants or hired servants for the direct profit of the lord) administered from Burystead. The duchy baliff's accounts regularly record 1 acre and 2 rods of Burystead demesne meadow in West Cotton (eg PRO DL29/324/5292). A duchy court roll of 1349 is the sole survivor from that century and contains a reference to a tenant holding a portion of meadow in West Cotton. Frequent references to holdings of meadow by duchy tenants occur in the court rolls from around 1400 onwards and in the fifteenth century tenants were sometimes ordered to scour ditches in West Cotton or at Cotton Bridge (NRO X705–7); which probably carried Cotton Lane, linking all three Cottons and Stanwick, over the Cotton (Tipping) Brook (Fig 1.6). These include orders in October 1433 for Walter Johnson to repair the ditch at Wilwencotes and in April 1434 to do the same at Litelcotes, demonstrating that the names were interchangeable. The fifteenth-century duchy accounts also include portions of meadow in West Cotton included among the lists of decayed rents for which tenants could no longer be found (eg PRO DL29/326/5344).

A duchy court roll of 1520 (NRO X706) refers to a cottage in 'Little Cotes', formerly belonging to Walter Johnson, with 3 acres of pasture and an acre of willows (later located by the Tipping Brook). The same property is also recorded in the duchy rental of 1552–3, and in court rolls of 1603 and 1723 (NRO X707; FH 565 and QCR 51) where the cottage is described as a messuage now a close of pasture, indicating desertion. This appears to be the only post-medieval evidence for occupation in West Cotton and suggests abandonment of the cottage in the late sixteenth century, if not before given that time-lag in such documents is always a possibility.

Another problem is posed by the existence of a duchy manor of Cotes held by the Chamberlains. A chancery case of 1378–9 records that the manor was taken into the hands of the king's father (Edward II, 1342–77) because Richard Chamberlain had alienated it without licence to William Mercer and Hugh Seneschal (PRO C44/10/3). Richard argues that the manor was held of the honor of Peverel and not in chief (directly from the crown). Neither the outcome of the case or the location of the manor is known, but it is likely to have been either at Mallows or West Cotton. If the latter was true, it would indicate the presence in West Cotton of a manor belonging to the Duchy fee, in addition to the Clare/Gloucester fee manor.

The eighteenth-century records

A Gloucester fee estate document of around 1735 describes both *Wilwencotes* and *Middlecotes* as 'entirely demolished' (NRO X887 23:12, 2–3). At the time of the 1739 terrier the area to the west of the Cotton Lane appears to have been occupied by two closes. The south close held by Elizabeth Morris and the north close by Lady Dolben, inheritor of the duchy estate of Burystead. Lady Dolben had held 'Cotton Close' in 1723, when it is listed alongside the Burystead estate, suggesting that it was a distinct acquisition (NRO QCR 25). Both closes were almost certainly freehold but their descent prior to 1739 remains obscure. A claim relating to the intended enclosure of Raunds in 1797 (in the possession of Mr T C Smith of Raunds to whom we are grateful for access) indicates that the north close was still in the hands of the Dolben family while the south close was then held by the Rev Mapletoft and his wife, Margaret (Fig 1.3). The enclosure map of 1798 (NRO map 3124) clearly shows that the northern close included the former tenements A, E, C, D and F while the southern close included tenements B and G (Figs 1.3 and 1.6). To the west, the depicted boundary between the closes can be equated with a post-medieval boundary ditch that had replaced the former walled boundary between tenements A and B. The 1797 claim also refers to the Pen Pound and this may equate with the walled enclosure occupying the medieval central yard, also clearly shown on the enclosure map.

The 1798 enclosure map also reveals 'ancient' enclosures to the east of the Cotton Lane. The elongated form of the most northerly enclosure clearly reveals its origins as an open field strip. To the south of the Cotton Brook lay two larger and adjacent closes, both of which are referred to in the 1739 Gloucester fee terrier (NRO ML 124).

Fields and meadows

West Cotton lies on the boundary separating the two ecological zones of the arable and meadow of the medieval and early-modern field system. David Hall has argued that the three Cottons once possessed an independent field system (see Parry 2006) though it appears to have become integrated within the Raunds field system by the late fourteenth century.

The meadows were divided between the two fees. In 1086 both the Bishop of Coutances and William Peverel were assessed as holding 20 acres (probably a fiscal measure) of meadow in demesne. The meadow, like the arable, was divided into strips or doles of intermixed ownership, though the detailed division between the two fees is uncertain. Meadow was an especially valuable resource providing hay to feed the livestock over the winter. After the hay was mown, meadows were laid open for common grazing, often between Lammas (August 1) and sometime in November or December, but regulations were quite variable (see Ault 1972). In 1298, an extent of the lands of the earl of Lancaster valued (ie when farmed or rented out) the Burystead meadow at 2s an acre, while the arable was only worth 6d (PRO C133/81: Kerr 1925, 34).

There were two meadows in Raunds, West Cotton Meadow and Raunds Great Meadow (NRO ML 124: 1739 terrier) and these, like the arable, were enclosed in 1798 (Fig 1.3). The 1797 enclosure claim clearly locates West Cotton meadow as abutting the Short Leys, an arable/pasture field immediately south of West Cotton. The two meadows were probably separated by the Cotton Brook, which then partly followed the former river channel that may have provided a previous boundary.

In addition, in the same enclosure claim rights of common in the Pen Pound, identified above, and the Great Green were claimed by the Rev Mapletoft, Sir William Dolben and three others, from Lady Day to Old Midsummer, after which they were laid open as common with the rest of the fields and meadows. A similar right of common was also claimed by a nearly identical list of farmers on the Little Green near Cotton Bridge. Both the Great Green and the Little Green are also recorded in a Terrier of 1768. This clearly indicates that the Great Green lay adjacent to West Cotton Meadow, although its exact location is still uncertain, while the Little Green abutted the southern side of Meadow Furlong, a field to the immediate east of Cotton Lane, identifying it as a part of the former settlement area to the east of Cotton Lane and north of Cotton Brook. These restricted rights of common probably preserve rights held by the medieval inhabitants of West Cotton.

3 The Prehistoric to Middle Saxon Occupation

The prehistoric monument complex

The prehistoric activity at West Cotton has been discussed in a separate volume covering the prehistory of the entire Raunds Area (Harding and Healy 2007), while interim statements were published during and immediately after excavation (Windell 1989 and Windell *et al* 1990). As a result, this evidence is only briefly summarised here.

The group of prehistoric monuments at West Cotton lay at the northern end of a complex that extended south for over 2km and spanned the early Neolithic to early Bronze Age and included a broad diversity of monument types. The group at West Cotton formed the most concentrated cluster, situated on an area of slightly raised gravel immediately adjacent to the easternmost channel of the River Nene (Fig 3.1). At this time the valley floor would have comprised a series of gravel islands between multiple, braided river channels; as explored within the Raunds Area Project and more recently in a watching brief during the final stages of gravel extraction at Stanwick Quarry (Chapman 2004). The monuments were constructed either on the gravel islands or at the margins of the valley floor, as at West Cotton, and there is no evidence to suggest that flooding and alluviation was occurring at this early date.

Wood from one of three pits sealed beneath the western end of the Neolithic Long Mound (Fig 3.1, LM) has been radiocarbon dated to the early fifth millennium BC, and may relate to a short-term or seasonal occupation, perhaps related to tree-clearance.

Monument construction appears to have begun began in the early to mid-4th millennium and at West Cotton this included the Long Mound and the Long Enclosure (LM and LE). There was a second period of monument construction in the late Neolithic and early Bronze Age, which comprised a series of round barrows and associated inhumation and cremation burials. At West Cotton there was a triple-ditched round barrow (B), with a central inhumation accompanied by a long-necked Beaker, a flint dagger and a V-perforated jet button. Several unexcavated ring ditches lie to the immediate north-east (Fig 3.1, RD).

In addition, at the edge of the prehistoric river palaeochannel there was a timber platform largely of alder (T), which is dated to the early to mid 3rd millennium BC.

It has recently been suggested that the creation of this platform may have been related to tree-felling by beavers, perhaps with additional human modification (Coles 2006, 90–95), and a beaver bone, radiocarbon dated to the late Bronze Age, was recovered from medieval silts above this (see Chapter 9).

One subject that is of direct relevance to the later settlement history is the prehistoric river system, which will be discussed in more detail in Chapter 6. The location of the Neolithic timber platform shows that the main eastern river channel was stable, and the late Saxon river edge lay only a few metres to the north of its Neolithic predecessor (Fig 6.5c). The difficulty of interpretation relates to the confluence of the Cotton Brook with this channel, as the early history of the watercourses to the north and the south of West Cotton was not resolved by excavation, leaving the sequence of channel evolution undefined. It is suggested by the author that the prehistoric stream course lay to the north (Fig 3.1, northern stream), while the southern channel was of a later date, cutting across the southern end of the Long Enclosure (LE) and eroding the prehistoric ground levels in this area, and was evidently the major channel at the formation of the late Saxon settlement.

There is no evidence of any activity at West Cotton during the middle to late Bronze Age or in the Iron Age. The three excavated prehistoric mounds, two immediately beneath the medieval settlement and one beneath the medieval field system to the immediate south, were all well preserved, standing up to 0.30–0.50m high, and this might suggest that the area had not been subject to long-term arable exploitation during the later prehistoric and Romano-British periods. Most of the evident disturbance of the mounds resulted from activity post-dating the early Saxon period, although it is possible that this could have removed evidence of lesser earlier disturbance.

Romano-British activity

Romano-British settlement within the Raunds area will be considered within a separate volume (Crosby and Neal in preparation). A sparse scatter of residual Romano-British

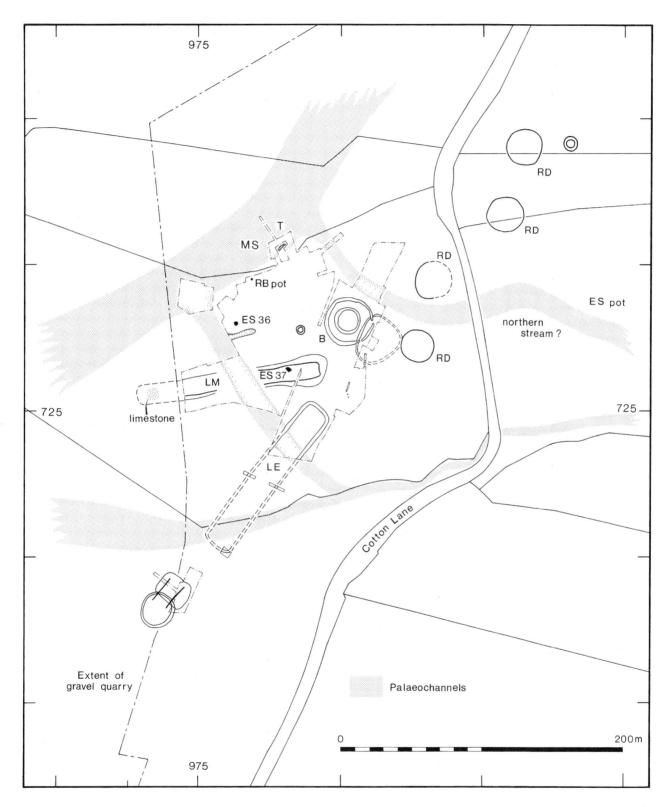

Fig 3.1: West Cotton, prehistoric, Romano-British and early/middle Saxon activity. © *Crown copyright. All rights reserved.*
Northamptonshire County Council: Licence No. 100019331, Published 2009

domestic debris was recovered, including 157 sherds of pottery, 33 coins, other copper alloy finds and some ceramic tiles. This includes some early second-century coins but most of the material is dated to the third to mid-fourth centuries. It can be accounted for as material brought to the site either deliberately or accidentally in the late Saxon and medieval periods from the nearby Roman settlements at Stanwick, 1km to the south, and Mallows Cotton, 0.5km to the north. It is possible that much of the domestic debris came within cart loads of building stone brought to West Cotton along the Cotton Lane from these nearby Roman ruins, which would have provided the nearest sources of building stone.

However, a single near complete pottery vessel of Roman date was recovered from the silts of a watercourse sealed beneath the late Saxon mill leats (Fig 3.1, RB pot). This does suggest the probability of a Romano-British presence in the immediate vicinity of West Cotton. The form this may have taken is unknown, but the presence of small quantities of ceramic tile could suggest that there was a building or buildings not far beyond the excavated area. In addition, even though the lane was not tested by excavation at West Cotton, it seems likely that the Cotton Lane followed, or at least closely respected, the course of a Roman road linking the settlements along the eastern side of the floodplain at Stanwick, Mallows Cotton and between Mill Cotton and Ringstead (Fig 1.2).

Early to middle Saxon occupation (AD 500–800)

There is evidence for two separate episodes of activity within the early to middle Saxon period, occurring in the sixth and eighth centuries respectively.

Early Saxon occupation

The early Saxon occupation comprised a sunken-featured building and another poorly preserved structure some 45m away set on top of the prehistoric Long Mound (Fig 3.1, ES 36 and ES 37). Early/middle Saxon pottery was recovered from both and also from the final fills of a silted watercourse immediately to the south of the sunken-featured building. There was a sparse early/middle Saxon pottery scatter across the remainder of the excavated area. A total of 262 sherds was recovered, mainly small, undecorated body sherds although a few larger rims are present, along with a single stamped sherd and four with incised decoration.

None of the Raunds sites has produced pottery or other finds that can be dated to before the end of the fifth century and this, together with the absence of Maxey and Ipswich-type wares at West Cotton, is consistent with two residual brooches of late fifth to early sixth-century forms and a Kentish-style disk brooch dated to the sixth century. The radiocarbon date from the sunken-featured building provides a broader date range from the early fifth to the end of the sixth century (420–600 cal AD; 95% confidence; 1548± 333 BP; UB-3418).

In addition to the pottery, the excavated structures produced domestic items such as loomweight fragments and spindle whorls, but the only personal items of this date, two brooches and a decorative mount, were recovered as residual finds in later contexts.

The lack of any further structures, particularly post-built halls, or specific pottery concentrations indicates that these were isolated, individual structures and not merely the only identified elements of a more extensive settlement. However, fieldwalking to the east of Cotton Lane also produced a scatter of early/middle Saxon pottery, suggesting that there may have been contemporary activity of at least a similar nature 200–250m to the east. These two areas lay on either side of the course of the northern channel of the Cotton Brook. The early Saxon activity at West Cotton may therefore have formed one of the bifocal settlements, of which several have been identified from fieldwalking within the Raunds Area, with occupation located on either bank of a stream course (see Parry 2006, 92–94).

The upper levels of the sunken-featured building were partially truncated by an homogeneous soil horizon of red-brown sandy loam with sparse pebble inclusions. This occurred across most of the site and the late Saxon occupation was cut through it. It appears to represent a plough-turned soil derived from a period of arable cultivation occurring sometime between the demise of the sixth-century occupation and the appearance of the main settlement in the tenth century, reinforcing the conclusion that there was no continuity of settlement.

Structure 36, sunken-featured building

The steep-sided, flat-bottomed pit was 2.50m wide by 0.35m deep (Fig 3.2, ES 36). A single posthole, 0.50m deep, lay at the centre of the slightly rounded eastern end, but the southern end had been removed by a later ditch system.

The mixed fills of grey silty clay with gravel contained substantial quantities of Hazel (*Corylus*) charcoal, much of it 50–200mm in length (from which a radiocarbon date was obtained), and an assemblage of early Saxon pottery, three sherds of Romano-British pottery, a spindle whorl, loomweight fragments and a perforated stone block with a worn surface, possibly used as an anvil or hammer stone (see Figs 11.1 and 11.2). The larger charcoal fragments lay above the basal fill and they may have come from carbonized timbers of a floor, or the walls and roof, burnt at demolition and collapsed into the pit. The upper fill was closely comparable to the overlying soil horizon.

To the immediate south of Structure 36 there was a linear ditch, 6.0m wide by 0.40m deep, which was largely filled with mottled water deposited silts (Fig 3.1). Some early Saxon pottery came from the upper fills and continued over and immediately beyond the northern edge, and may derive from external activity associated with the nearby building.

Structure 37

This structure was initially defined by a localised scatter of early Saxon pottery on the surface of the prehistoric Long Mound (Fig 3.1, ES 37). In excavation it was only visible as a shallow and poorly defined oval to sub-rectangular depression, 5.50m long by 3.30m wide and at most 0.12m deep (Fig 3.2, ES 37). The fill of grey to brown sandy loams with some gravel was generally slightly lighter than the underlying mound material. There were two internal postholes 1.25m apart and 0.45 and 0.18m deep. A linear concentration of charcoal, perhaps the remnant of a single short plank, 1.0m long by 0.2–0.3m wide, lay between them. The absence of any other structural postholes leaves the building form uncertain, although the presence of the pottery scatter, a decorated bone spindle-whorl, a ceramic spindle-whorl and fragments of clay loomweight suggest that it had been a roofed structure.

Middle Saxon activity

An episode of middle Saxon activity took place on and adjacent to the river channel, and is dated to the eighth century by three radiocarbon dates. A slight shift of the channel edge had truncated earlier silts and partially re-exposed parts of the Neolithic timber platform. Oak (*Quercus*) stakes were driven, apparently deliberately, into the two largest alder trunks, and flax seeds and capsules came from silts above these stakes. Any other stakes that had just been driven into the earlier silts might have been lost in the initial machine stripping of the channel silts.

The two oak stakes and the flax debris have given radiocarbon dates between the mid-seventh to late ninth centuries: (650–860 cal AD; 95% confidence; 1297 ±49 BP; UB-3328); (660–890 cal AD; 95% confidence; 1264±52; UB-3323) and (620–890 cal AD; 95% confidence; 1295±70 BP; OxA-4079). In addition, a displaced hazel stake from the nearby first watermill gave a date in the same range (660–880 cal AD; 95% confidence; 1258 ± 36 BP; UB-3322), and is presumed to be residual within its context.

The consistent date ranges suggest that this was probably a short-lived phase centred on the mid-eighth century, with the flax seeds and capsules in the silts being the debris from flax retting. In this process bundles of flax stems would have been dumped into the water and retained within timber structures supported by stakes driven into the river bank below water level. The flax was left to decay, so that the flax fibres could be easily extracted from the rotted residue. Flax retting is well known to contaminate the water in which it takes place, and for this reason would preferably be carried out at some distance from a settlement, and downstream rather than upstream.

The absence of features and pottery dated to this period from the main excavations supports the interpretation that this activity was limited to the riverside area.

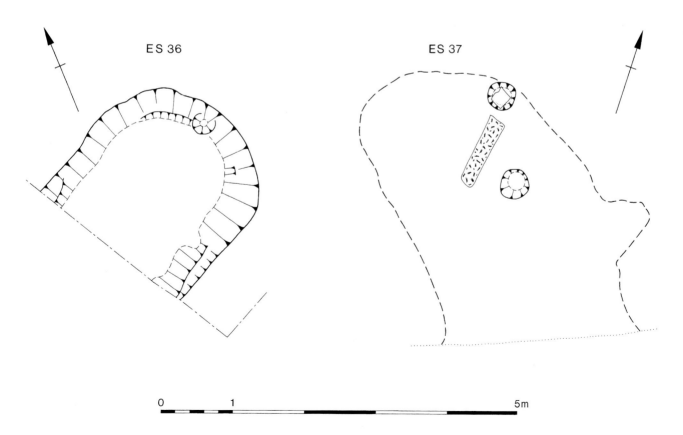

ES 36   ES 37

0   1   5m

Fig 3.2: The early Saxon buildings, ES36 and ES37

4 The Late Saxon Settlement (AD 950–1100)

While there was evidence for limited occupation at West Cotton in the sixth century and for utilisation of the river channel in the eighth century, there was no indication that the foundation of the settlement in the tenth century owed anything to these previous episodes other than coincidence of common usage of a favourable location. It can therefore be regarded as a new foundation, with the tenth-century arrangement destined to provide the underlying structure for the subsequent development of the site up to its final form as a medieval hamlet 400 years later.

The choice of location was primarily based on the local topography. The settlement was situated on a slightly raised peninsular of gravel terrace that lay near the confluence of a tributary stream, the Cotton Brook, with a major channel of the River Nene (Fig 1.2). The other two deserted settlements to the north, Mallows Cotton and Mill Cotton, also lay adjacent to tributary streams, with Mill Cotton similarly positioned on the edge of the floodplain, while Mallows Cotton lay on slightly higher ground, above a steeper fall to the valley floor.

The raised location at West Cotton was even slightly enhanced in places by the presence of upstanding prehistoric mounds. The settlement was therefore ideally placed to exploit both the valley slope and the river valley environments, and a controllable water supply to power a watermill may well have been a major consideration, as it was at Mallows and Mill Cotton, where there were also watermills.

The new settlement, based on regular plot sizes, containing a high-status complex of timber buildings and standing beside a small watermill, may have been the residence of a minor Saxon thegn. At its formation in the mid-tenth century, the provision of a partially enclosing ditch and a timber palisade harked back to earlier times, with probable Scandinavian influences added to the new concepts of plot layout brought in with the reconquest of the Danelaw by the Saxon kings. However, by the beginning of the eleventh century these semi-defensive elements had been swept away and a new courtyard arrangement marked the emergence of what must be considered to be a proto-manor house.

The formation of the settlement (AD 950–975)

The date of the formation of the settlement is crucial to placing the site within its historical context, but the dating is necessarily largely dependent on the pottery evidence, which is not as precise as would be wished. However, it was possible to isolate a few lengths of boundary ditch that had been backfilled early in the life of the settlement. The earliest watermill and the backfilling of the area prior to the digging of a new mill leat was another early event. Within these assemblages an earlier form of St Neots ware bowl was absent but a later bowl type was relatively common. At Northampton, these types have been dated respectively to AD 800–950 and AD 900–1150, indicating that the occupation probably began in the decades around AD 950.

It is therefore likely that the establishment of the settlement post-dated the reconquest of the Danelaw, which occurred between AD 918–24, and West Cotton can be seen to be part of a widespread episode of social and economic reorganisation of the Danelaw in the following decades. Part of this process may be typified by the appearance of new planned settlements with a regular arrangement of ditched plots, which echo in form and dimensions elements of late Saxon town planning.

The planning and metrology

The main settlement area was near square in plan form, occupying 2.4 hectares or about six acres (Fig 4.1). It was bounded to the east by the Cotton Lane, which may have respected a Roman predecessor linking the valley bottom settlements at Stanwick, to the south, and Mallows Cotton and Ringstead, to the north. At West Cotton the road was diverted eastward and then back northward at two dog-legged turns. This may have been a deliberate realignment to help accommodate a square settlement area, and these are the most marked deviations in the course of the lane along this length of the valley. Any evidence for a former linear road would lie beneath the unexcavated eastern half of West Cotton, although a metalled surface was not evident on the geophysical survey of this area.

To the south the settlement was also bounded by the Cotton Brook, while a western limit was created by the

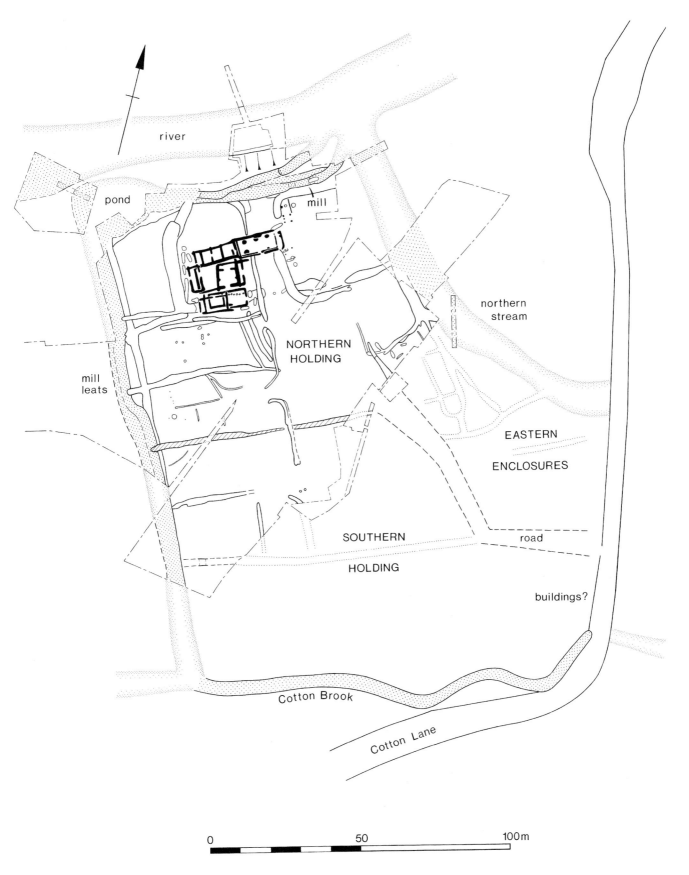

river

pond

mill

mill
leats

NORTHERN
HOLDING

northern
stream

EASTERN

ENCLOSURES

road

SOUTHERN

HOLDING

buildings?

Cotton Brook

Cotton Lane

| 0 | 50 | 100m |

Fig 4.1: The late Saxon settlement, 950–1100

establishment of an artificial leat system to divert water northward to a pond and watermill. The northern boundary was provided by the watermill system and the adjacent river channel. The only deviation from a rectilinear plan lay to the north-east, where a largely redundant stream channel, the northern stream, cut diagonally across the site, and clearly influenced the setting out of the nearby boundary ditches. This channel was probably not carrying any stream flow at this time, but it may have held seasonal water and back flow from the river during times of flood.

Within the settlement rectangular plots were defined by a system of linear boundary ditches. Excavation at the northern end of Raunds village has shown the appearance of similar boundary systems at around the same date across an extensive area either side of the valley, taking in two manorial centres and plot systems beyond (Audouy and Chapman 2009). West Cotton, where the evolution of the boundary system has been most clearly established, provides a good model for the process of creating such regular plot systems in the mid-tenth century.

In particular, the regular rectangular plots along the western side of the site enable a full metrical analysis of the system to be undertaken (Figs 4.1 and 4.2). The western ditches were spaced at close to 20m centre-to-centre. Taking the rod of 16.5 feet (5.03m), as defined in many later medieval documents (Zupko 1968, 144–5), a 4-rod length of 20.13m closely fits the measured ditch spacing. It is more difficult to establish a precise metrology for the length of the western enclosures. While the eastern end is defined by an original linear ditch system, the western end could have lain anywhere within the broad expanse of the westernmost boundary ditch and the adjacent mill leat. If the mill leat system is adopted, it may be suggested that the intended length was 50m or 10 rods. This provides idealised dimensions for the smallest plots of 4 by 10 rods, and this immediately suggests a connection with a standard medieval land measurement, the statutory acre. This is defined in later medieval documents as a field strip 4 rods wide by 40 rods long (Zupko 1968, 3). The 40-rod length is 1/8 of a mile, the furlong or furrow length. The small western enclosures were therefore quarter-acre plots, a quarter the length of a statutory acre.

However, the internal partitioning of the site may actually have been founded on the three principal east-west ditches, which were spaced at 40m or 8 rod intervals with the same spacing to the northern and southern settlement boundaries. These ditches may be modelled on a length of 100m or 20 rods, twice the length of the quarter-acre western enclosures, even though they actually terminated at an irregular line formed by either the northern stream or the access road, showing how the metrical model was necessarily modified by the site topography.

The general argument is therefore that the primary settlement arrangement comprised a line of four one-acre plots to the west, each 8 rods wide by 20 rods long, half the length and twice the width of the statutory acre (Fig 4.2). To the east, the addition of a further two one-acre

plots provides an idealised, near-square plan of six acres. However, given the presence of the northern stream, which lay at an oblique angle, it was necessary to modify the model layout in order to fit a plot beside the stream. To achieve this, the line of the access road departed from the rectilinear to allow some extra space for the provision of a roughly rectangular, nominal one-acre plot set between the access road, the northern stream and Cotton Lane. The end result was that this obliquely aligned eastern plot was actually slightly less than an acre in extent as a result of accommodating the site typography.

While it has not been established whether there was any tenth-century occupation beyond this main settlement area, it is suggested that the coherence of the plan indicates that this probably formed the full extent of the original planned settlement, with the spread of settlement to the east of the Cotton Lane resulting from subsequent expansion.

Having established a simple model for the original plan form, it is of immediate interest to note how this was modified through the subsequent development of the site, so that only a few clues to its presence survived to the final period of occupation, the medieval hamlet, the earthworks of which were available for study and interpretation without excavation. The eastern boundaries of the regular western plots were to show a steady eastward drift, so that the plot length, the most uncertain of the original measurements, was lost, although the medieval tenement boundaries did run on much the same lines as their late Saxon predecessors and therefore retained a recognisable spacing at 40m or 8 rod intervals, although there was a loss of regularity resulting from slight drifting of the boundaries through time.

As a result, given only the medieval evidence, it would be possible to suggest the provision of regular widths for the western tenements, but the extent of the later changes left no clue that the original planning had been based on regular plot sizes based on the statutory acre. Analysis of earthwork plans showing the final settlement arrangement is therefore unlikely to provide a full understanding of the principles underlying the original settlement organisation.

The arrangement of the settlement

From the available evidence the settlement area appears to have comprised three principal zones; the northern holding, the eastern enclosures and the southern holding, which are a combination of the tenurial and functional divisions of the original settlement arrangement (Fig 4.1).

The northern holding

This was the only area to be fully excavated, and the core of the description of the late Saxon settlement is the story of the development of the northern plot system (Figs 4.3 and 4.4). It comprised a high-status building complex set within the northern one-acre plot. To the south-east there was an open yard, with a nominal area of a half-acre, and to the south-west there were two quarter-acre plots, both with

0   50   100 m

0   100   300 ft

20 rods

4 rods	
10 rods	½ acre
¼ acre	

8 rods   1 acre

Fig 4.2: The metrology of the late Saxon settlement boundaries

access onto the yard, at least one of which was probably used for stock control. In addition, a watermill lay on the leat system running along the northern margin of the plots.

On the basis of several pieces of circumstantial evidence, it is suggested that this two-acre plot system constituted the major part of a single holding. In particular, the southern boundary of the holding was formed by a continuous ditch

that was the only boundary to be closely respected not only throughout the lifetime of the medieval hamlet, when it was the only boundary marked by two parallel walls, but through to the end of the eighteenth century, when it was the tenurial boundary between two separately held closes (see Fig 1.4). Another significant factor relating to this boundary was the complex sequence of reordering at its western end, which ran down to metalled fords providing passage across the mill leats, and perhaps located here as a crossing shared by both the northern and southern holdings (Figs 6.2 and 6.6).

The exact status of the individual who farmed this holding eludes us but, as concluded in the study of the documentary evidence (Chapter 2), it is most likely to have been held by a freeman/sokeman or a minor thegn, although we have no documentary evidence to confirm this.

The eastern enclosures

The eastern enclosures comprised the less regular plots, with a nominal area of one acre, set between the access road, the northern stream and Cotton Lane. Very little of this area was excavated, so its form and function is undefined. The excavated boundary ditches at the northern end showed a complex pattern of recutting, and initially there may have been a bridged crossing (Fig 4.1). The ditches also contained quantities of domestic debris of tenth and eleventh-century date, which may have come from nearby occupation. A scatter of postholes and small pits within the small area of the interior that was excavated perhaps provide an indication of the broader pattern of activity (see Fig 4.36). The only evidence for the interior arrangement comes from geophysical survey. This suggests the presence of a central sub-division, and numerous linear features within the northern half may include both ditch lines and the walls of timber buildings.

It is suggested that this occupation may have been associated with peasant settlement related to, and probably dependent on, the domestic focus of the northern holding. A later connection between the northern holding and the eastern enclosures was evident in the way that the twelfth-century manor on the northern holding was relocated in the thirteenth century onto the eastern enclosures, and it is considered most likely that they were always parts of a single holding.

The half-acre or so of land at the northern corner of the settlement, beyond the northern stream, might also be included. Any early features would have been sealed by alluvial silts deposited in the early twelfth century, and these were not excavated. As a result, the nature of any activity here in the tenth and eleventh centuries has not been established, but as it was largely low-lying it seems unlikely that there was any significant domestic activity within an area which must always have been prone to flooding.

The full extent of the northern holding and the eastern enclosures therefore comprised 3.5 acres, over a half of the original settlement area.

The southern holding

Only part of the southern holding was excavated, but it is suggested that it may have been a near mirror image of the northern holding. To the north, it comprised two quarter-acre plots that may have opened into a half-acre yard to the east. The smaller plots contained few features, although there was a transverse sub-division within the southern plot (Figs 4.1 and see 4.28).

On the basis of the mirror imaging of the smaller plots and the yard, it is suggested that the unexcavated southern plots, totalling 1.5 acres, may have contained a building complex of similar size to that within the northern holding. With a total extent of 2.5 acres, the southern holding can be seen to have been only slightly smaller than the northern holding, indicating that it was perhaps of similar status.

The idea that the original settlement held two high-status holdings may be supported by the documented presence of two overlords throughout the medieval period and beyond. It is suggested that the physical expression of this tenurial division lay at the heart of the original settlement, and the analysis of subsequent periods of activity shows that this fundamental division was maintained throughout the lifetime of the settlement.

The early development of the northern holding (AD 950–975)

As the whole of the northern holding was excavated its development can be reconstructed in some detail. In the later tenth century it comprised a yard to the south giving access to two smaller enclosures to the west (Fig 4.3). These areas were separated from the main domestic buildings and the watermill by a substantial ditch system. With this arrangement it seems to fall halfway between being a fully enclosed settlement, as would often have been constructed up to this time, and an open settlement form going with the introduction of regular plots. What may have been an initial suspicion of the new open settlement form evidently faded, as through the eleventh century the major ditches were progressively abandoned and the arrangement of the buildings similarly became more open, taking on a simple courtyard form (see Figs 4.5 and 4.8).

The original arrangement of the buildings comprised a single square building set within a rectangular, timber palisade (Fig 4.4a). For a brief period this building may have stood alone, and it was perhaps only ever intended to be a temporary structure; perhaps the equivalent of living on-site in a caravan while building a house. It was closely followed by the construction of the timber palisade, which to the west and south was flanked by a substantial broad, U-shaped ditch, up to 4.0m wide by 1.0m deep. These dimensions may be contrasted with the 2–3m wide by 0.4–0.7m deep ditches forming the other ditched boundaries. A bank may have been thrown up against the western and southern sides of the palisade, but no traces survived.

The lengths of shallow ditch to the north of the palisade lay nearly 20m from the main boundary, and may have been part of the initial establishment of the plot boundary layout. They would have been rendered obsolete by the new defensive ditch and the construction of the main domestic buildings.

The construction of the main timber hall probably followed fairly closely (Fig 4.4b). This entailed the removal of the north-eastern corner of the timber palisade, which was then closed by new transverse walls extending from the north-east corner of the original building, which was also rebuilt. The provision of principal posts perhaps suggests that an upper storey was added as part of the rebuilding.

The domestic range abutting the western end of the hall was probably the last to be constructed, as the culmination of the initial phase of development (Fig 4.3). The northern side of the palisade would have been demolished, but the remainder appears to have been retained, abutting the end walls of both the hall and the domestic range. The building within the palisade was demolished, its provision of temporary on-site accommodation being no longer required. There was little direct evidence for the constructional details of the timber buildings, but what there is indicates that they were stave-built, with timbers

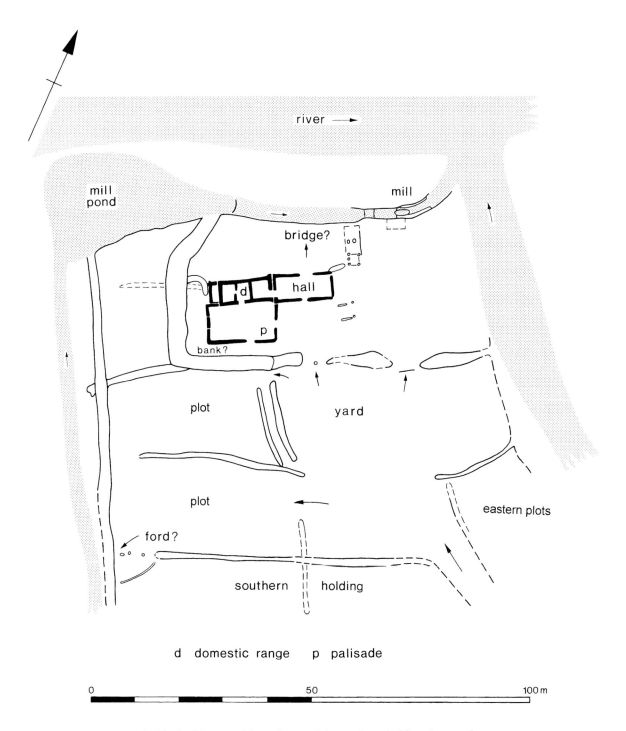

d domestic range   p palisade

Fig 4.3: The buildings and boundaries of the northern holding, late tenth century

of near equal dimensions but including more deeply-set posts for at least some of the doorways.

While the palisade, the ditch and the possible bank would have formed an imposing facade that could have provided some degree of defensive protection, this would have been largely negated by the more open aspect to the east. Here, the boundary ditch system was less substantial and was broken in two places, including a direct access to the hall. The defensive ditch originally ended in line with the palisade, to leave a broad opening, 11.5m wide (Fig 4.4a). This was later narrowed to 5.0m by the addition of a large pit at the end of the defensive ditch. A central post-pit in this opening may suggest the provision of a gated entrance (Fig 4.4b). The earliest surviving metalled surface along the access to the hall was of compacted gravel. It contained pottery dated to the earlier twelfth-century, although the road may have had an earlier origin.

The separate opening to the east may have provided direct access to the watermill. The watermill flanked the northern side of the holding, with the mill pond to the west. It was a vertical-wheeled, undershot mill. Millstone Grit, lava and at least one finer sandstone millstone were recovered from the leat fills, confirming its use as a corn mill. Given the complex sequence of activity relating to the form and development of the watermill system spanning the mid-tenth to mid-twelfth centuries, a chapter has been devoted to this topic, Chapter 6. A small timber building, more lightly built than the other contemporary ranges, lay between the hall and the mill and seems most likely to have related to the use of the mill (Fig 4.3). Its exact function is unknown, but large internal post-pits might have held a timber frame for lifting heavy weights, such as millstones, suggesting that it may have been a workshop used for preparing and recutting millstones.

The southern half of the northern holding was probably divided from the beginning between an open yard to the east and two smaller plots to the west, but the earliest pottery assemblages from these boundary ditches are

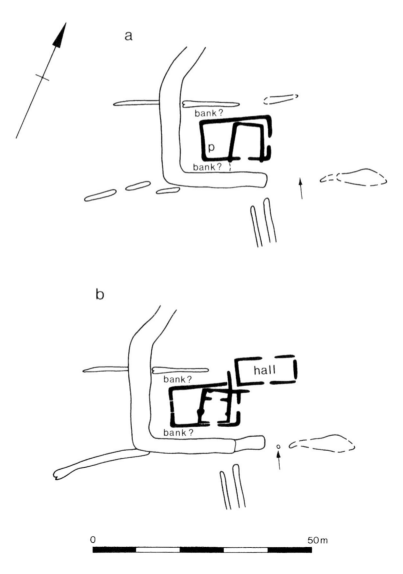

Fig 4.4: The initial development of the late Saxon buildings; a) the palisade enclosure, b) the addition of the hall

only eleventh-century in date. Initially, the northern plot seems to have been closed off from the yard by a double ditch system, while the southern plot opened directly onto the yard. To the west the plots were separated from the western mill leats by a ditch system that became filled with water deposited, homogeneous clayey silts, presumably as a resulting of flooding from the mill leats, and this back boundary was redundant by the early eleventh century.

At the western end of the ditched boundary between the northern and southern holdings there was a line of post-pits, and a later date there is evidence that there was a ford across the mill leat here, probably shared by both holdings.

The redevelopment of the northern holding (AD 975–1000)

The defining feature of the second phase of the pre-conquest settlement was the reorganisation of the buildings of the northern holding at the end of the tenth century. In this reorganisation most of the former defensive features were removed and new buildings were introduced to create a complex set around a central courtyard (Fig 4.5 and Plate 4). There were also associated modifications to the boundary system.

With the reorganisation of the domestic buildings into a

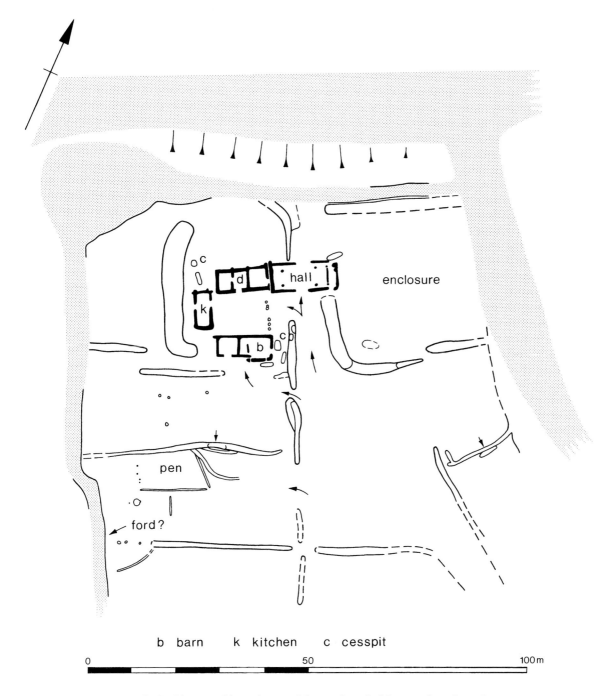

Fig 4.5: *The buildings and boundaries of the northern holding, earlier eleventh century*

courtyard arrangement, comprising a hall, domestic ranges, a detached kitchen and a barn, and a new watermill (Fig 4.6), we can see the northern holding in its fully developed form; clearly possessing the attributes of what in post-conquest terms would be regarded a small manor house (Fig 4.7). The evolution of this plan form through the second half of the tenth century may be a physical expression of how the concepts of social organisation and the origins of the feudal system were developing within England in the century prior to the Norman Conquest.

The southern arm of the semi-defensive ditch system was backfilled with clean sand and gravel, probably derived from the levelling of an associated bank, and the timber palisade was also removed. This created space for the provision of the central courtyard and the addition of new building ranges (Fig 4.5). To the west a smaller range with opposed central doors was probably a detached kitchen range, as its stone successor certainly was. To accommodate this building the small westernmost room of the domestic range was removed, but otherwise this range was largely unaltered.

The eastern end the new courtyard was separated from the access road by both a fence, defined by several post-pits, and by a ditch blocking the southern half of the opening. Two possible post-pits in the base of the ditch terminal may suggest that a fence with deep terminal posts may have preceded the ditch. The courtyard area therefore served only the domestic ranges, and was kept physically separate from the access to the hall.

On the southern side of the courtyard a range was constructed over the backfilled ditch. The main doors of this building faced south into the adjacent plot, rather than into the courtyard. The eastern room, with its broad southern doorway and projecting porch, may have served as a barn or byre, but there was probably also a small door in the northern wall to give access from the courtyard. The ditched boundaries to the south were modified to provide and control access to the new building.

The hall was also rebuilt during the eleventh century. It was widened slightly, with the new southern wall lying south of its predecessor, and internal principal posts were also introduced. These were not fully paired-posts, suggesting that they supported upper end chambers, rather than forming an aisled hall. The narrow bay at the eastern end of the hall was possibly the foundation for an external stairway serving these upper chambers.

The introduction of new ditch systems flanking the access to the hall made the approach narrower and more restricted, and a ditched plot, possibly with a gated entrance onto the yard to the south, was formed to the east of the hall. A ditch system along the northern side kept this plot separate from the watermill system to the north.

The development of the watermill system cannot be precisely paralleled with the redevelopment of the domestic buildings, and there is no reason why they should have been developed directly in parallel. However, at around the end of the tenth century the original mill was demolished and the leat was backfilled with sand and gravel. It is possible that following this there was a period without a functioning

Fig 4.6: The late Saxon timber buildings, looking east, with the mill leat (left) and the defensive ditch (foreground)

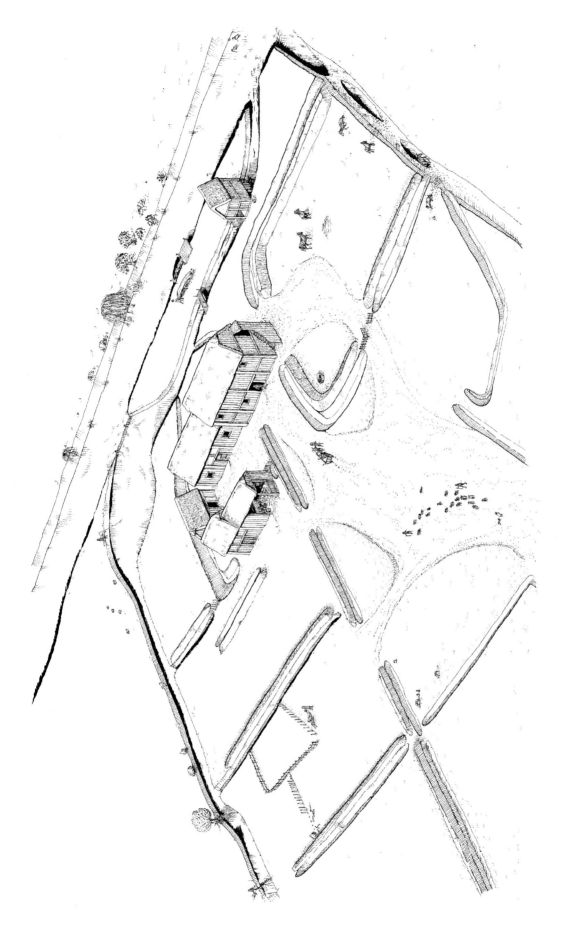

Fig 4.7: West Cotton as it may have looked in the eleventh century (Alex Thompson)

mill. A boundary ditch and a broad flat-bottomed leat to its immediate north both partly overlay the early mill (Fig 4.5). This new leat may have functioned as a water channel carrying the surplus outflow from the pond, and a temporary absence of a mill might provide a context for the subsequent change in the mill technology, from a vertical to a horizontal wheel.

Later alterations to the northern holding (AD 1000–1100)

Through the eleventh century there were further modifications to the buildings, the boundaries and the watermill system (Fig 4.8). After the probable period of disuse, a new mill was probably constructed quite early in the eleventh century. This was poorly preserved but was probably a horizontal-wheeled mill, as was its successor, which had been constructed by the mid-eleventh century (Fig 4.8). It is possible that it was this mill that appears as the lesser of the two Raunds mills in the Domesday Book, valued at 12d. With the continued use of the ditched plot to the south of the mill, access to the mills was restricted, with direct access only through the hall itself. There was also a bridged crossing of the mill leat to provide access to the river beyond.

The ditch at the western end of the courtyard, the final remnant of the earlier more defensive arrangement, was

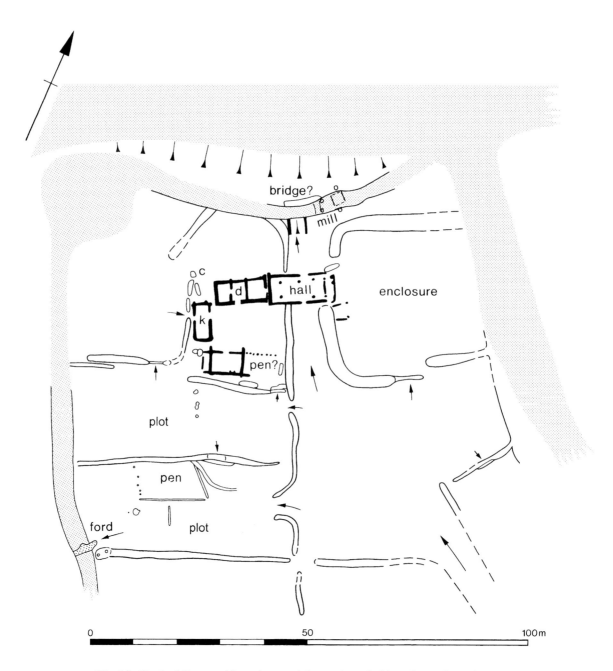

Fig 4.8: The buildings and boundaries of the northern holding, later eleventh century

probably backfilled quite soon after the construction of the adjacent kitchen range. It was replaced by a much smaller ditch, with an opening providing access to the western door of the kitchen range.

The southern range was also replaced, and the new single-roomed building had a northern doorway giving access into the central courtyard (Fig 4.8). A line of post-pits suggest that a fence extended eastward, perhaps to form a pen, and there was a new boundary ditch to the south of the building and the pen. Within the plot to the south of the buildings, a line of post-pits indicate that a fence formed a partial transverse sub-division.

The southern plot contained many more internal features (Fig 4.8). A sub-rectangular pen abutted the northern boundary, and to its south there was a partial transverse sub-division. To the east of the pen the open boundary ditch may have been spanned by a timber bridge founded in the base of the ditch. The entrance from the open yard to the east was refashioned, with the ditches curving inwards to form a funnelled entrance. The control of the access and the provision of sub-divisions suggest that the plot was used for stock penning.

At the western end of the southern boundary ditch a raised metalled surface of compacted limestone within the mill leat provided a fording point giving access to the west (Fig 4.8 and see Fig 6.2).

The material and environmental evidence

The full reports on the pottery by Paul Blinkhorn, the other finds by Tora Hylton, the environmental evidence by Gill Campbell and Mark Robinson, and the faunal evidence by Umberto Alberella and Simon Davis, are available in Part 2 of the report, but some significant general points will be summarised within each period overview to characterise the domestic activity and the economic base of the settlement.

The pottery in use through the tenth and eleventh centuries was dominated by St Neots-type wares, with over 8000 sherds recovered of this shelly coarseware for daily functional use. It formed the primary pottery style for the region at this date and, while kiln sites are rare, pottery of this type is believed to have come from multiple production sites in the eastern counties, and was evidently traded over a wide area. The vessel types included jars and bowls, with the occasional spouted or socketed bowl. The distinctive Top Hat jars, with their near vertical sides, were common in St Neots ware fabrics, but also continued until the mid-twelfth century in medieval Shelly Coarseware, when some primary groups of discarded vessels were found dumped in the boundary ditches. These particular vessels have been recovered in quantity within the Raunds sites, and had seemed to be confined to this area, but examples are now being found more widely, including sites to the south and east at Milton Keynes and Bedford. The smoking

and burning on the exterior of these jars and organic lipid residues suggest that they were specialist cooking vessels, set in the hot ashes as slow cookers, and with the inturned rim bowls potentially acting as lids. Similar ranges of utilitarian vessels, but in much smaller quantities, were also being obtained from production centres to the west, the Cotswold-type Oolitic wares.

The finer glazed Stamford ware, for the table, made up the rest of the late Saxon assemblage, although most of the Stamford ware came from twelfth-century deposits. There is a limited number of vessel forms, mainly jugs and pitchers, together with jars and flange-rim bowls. A single pedestal-based cresset lamp was also found.

A further pottery type produced in the eastern counties, Thetford ware, was present but in small quantities, and only from twelfth-century deposits. It had come from no more than half-a-dozen of the distinctive handled, large storage jars, products of the kilns in Thetford itself, which had perhaps been used for transporting goods to the site.

While late Saxon pottery was plentiful, the majority of it had been recovered from deposits of later date due to the lack of surviving floor levels and other undisturbed late Saxon deposits. This effect made it even more difficult to securely attribute many other finds to this period. The only individual items of note are a small barrel padlock key from the cess pit at the eastern end of the timber southern range (T34), parts of two barrel padlocks from the floors of the overlying building (T33), and a whittle-tang knife with copper alloy hilt fittings from the fills of the second mill leat (M26). In addition, there is a single pre-Conquest coin, a penny of Cnut from the Stamford moneyer, Oswere, dated to around AD 1024–30. The only other finds group of late Saxon date is the assemblage of millstone fragments from the watermills, which are summarised in Chapter 6.

The agricultural economy of the settlement involved a mixed farming regime. Wheat was plentiful in the charred plant remains and of particular importance was the recovery of tetraploid free-threshing wheat, probably rivet wheat (*Triticum turgidum*), from ditches filled in by the end of the tenth century, making it the first pre-Conquest record for this type of wheat in Britain. Its appearance at this time may be associated with the laying out of the open fields and the adoption of a new agricultural system.

None of the sampled assemblages produced only hexaploid or tetraploid free-threshing chaff, which may suggest that the two were grown as a mixture, and cultivation experiments have shown that both will ripen together.

Charred seeds and chaff indicate that barley, oats and rye were also grown. The barley and oats could have been grown together as a mixture, and sown in the ratio 1:1 it was known as dredge or drage in the medieval period, and was typically spring sown. From the twelfth century onward there were specific malt ovens attached to the major building groups, in which sprouted barley and oats was dried to produce the malt for brewing, with this a major product of the settlement for some centuries. No malt ovens can be dated to the tenth and eleventh century settlement, but a dump of burnt debris on the raised river bank adjacent to the watermills, and broadly contemporary with them, contained charred germinated barley and oat grain. This may suggest that malting was being carried out as early as the eleventh century, but as the feature can only be broadly dated to the eleventh to mid-twelfth century this is still uncertain.

The faunal assemblage that can be securely assigned to the tenth and eleventh centuries is too small to draw any general conclusions, although it is dominated by cattle, sheep and pig, with horse present in smaller numbers.

The late Saxon timber buildings

This section provides a catalogue and discussion for the seven timber buildings within the northern holding that were constructed and in use during the period AD 950 to AD 1100 (Figs 4.9 and 4.10). They were demolished within the first half of the twelfth century as they were progressively replaced by the buildings of the new medieval manor, which were largely stone-built.

These buildings were characterised by continuous, linear wall-trenches, indicating that they were post-in-trench structures, and most probably stave-built, comprising similar-sized timbers along the entire wall line. More deeply-set timbers, probably of greater diameter, were sometimes provided as door-jamb posts and in some instances at corners and wall junctions, where they may indicate the provision of principal posts in buildings with upper storeys. The eleventh-century rebuilding of the hall (Fig 4.11, T29), with the introduction of internal principal posts may provide further evidence for the presence of upper storeys.

The hall (T29) and the domestic apartments (T30)

The hall, T29

The hall was up to 15.5m long by 6.5m wide (Fig 4.11). To the west it adjoined the narrower domestic range, T30, to form a building complex 30m long. The junction of the two buildings was not fully understood, but the differing building widths and the double wall-trenches indicate that they were separate and abutting structures. There were two distinct constructional phases.

Phase 1 (Fig 4.12, a)

The original hall was 14.0m long by 6.2m wide, with a floor area of 61.5sq.m measuring 12.3m by 5.0m. The long walls were founded in deep wall-trenches, 0.60–0.70m wide by 0.30m–0.45m deep. Closely-spaced oval hollows in the base of the trenches indicate that they were stave-built (Figs 4.11 and 4.13, and see Fig 4.26). There was a central doorway defined by a 1.0m-wide break in the southern wall trench, with shallow post-pits at the inner

edge. A central doorway in the northern wall was defined by a construction pit, 3.30m long by 0.45m deep, both broader and deeper than the wall trench. Terminal post-pits to hold timber door jambs, cutting down a further 0.05–0.10m, indicate that the doorway was 1.80m wide. This doorway may have belonged to the second phase, with its construction removing all traces of an earlier, less substantial door surround.

The end walls of the building were founded in shallower wall-trenches, 0.40–0.60m wide and 0.15–0.30m deep, indicating that the end walls were of a lighter construction. There may have been a doorway at the southern end of the western wall, where there was a break in the wall trench of the domestic range. A pair of post-pits in the eastern wall trench may have held the jambs of a narrow central doorway.

A floor surface of compact gravel pebbles in a matrix of orange-brown sand survived at the north-eastern end of the building, sealing a small internal posthole, 0.25m deep, to the east of the northern doorway. Across the western half of the building later disturbance had removed any floor surfaces, but there was a remnant of a hearth, up to 0.90m in diameter, comprising cobbles and pieces of limestone with worn edges set within a shallow hollow in a matrix of pale yellow clay. The surface was only lightly scorched, suggesting that hearth surface had been lost. The floor and hearth could belong with either building phase.

Phase 2 (Fig 4.12, b)

The new southern wall lay 0.50m south of its predecessor and, at 0.30–0.40m deep, the wall-trench was 0.10m shallower. A central doorway was defined by a break in the wall-trench, but this was disturbed by later activity. A possible western door-jamb post-pit, 0.60m deep, may suggest that the doorway was originally 2.5m wide. The continuation of the wall-trench to the east of this indicates that the doorway was either always 1.50m wide or was later narrowed by relocating the western door jamb.

The northern wall was either retained or rebuilt within the original wall trench. The broad northern doorway, with timbers set in a construction pit, may have been part of this rebuilding. However, the second post-impression in the base the construction pit at the western end, might suggest that the doorway was narrowed at some stage, most probably at the introduction of the internal principal posts, as one of these would have partially blocked access to the full width doorway.

There were two sets of opposed pairs of principal posts at either end of the hall. They were set 3.90m apart and defined end chambers 2.50m long. Along the northern wall there was also a central post-pit, the one partly blocking access to the northern doorway, but this was not paired with a southern post. The arrangement therefore falls short of forming an aisled hall, and it is suggested that the introduction of the principal posts was to support upper storeys over the two end bays of the hall.

Fig 4.10: The timber buildings of the northern holding looking west

The post-pits were typically circular or sub-rectangular, 1.50–1.70m in diameter and up to 0.45–0.55m deep (Fig. 4.27). In most, the post location was indicated by a 0.10–0.20m deep circular hollow within the base of the cut, suggesting that the posts were probably around 0.40m in diameter. The fills of the post-pits contained varying quantities of tumbled limestone, including larger slabs probably from displaced packing. In one instance, the central post-pipe had been filled with a stack of flat-laid limestone slabs. In the central post-pit on the northern side the post position was particularly well defined by vertically pitched slabs of limestone, indicating that it had held a squared post measuring 400mm by 350mm.

The new eastern wall was set in a shallow wall-trench, 0.15m deep, running between two principal posts. The northern end cut the fill of the post-pit, indicating that it post-dated the erection of the principal post. A second shallow wall-trench lay a further 2.50m to the east, flanked on its inner edge by shallow postholes. These eastern wall-trenches formed a sub-chamber or outshot, 2.00m wide, giving the building a total length of 15.5m.

The western wall-trench was more substantial and contained both principal posts and posts of similar dimensions at the corners of the building. In addition, there was a central doorway opening defined by hollows that had held the door jamb posts.

In the new arrangement, the central bay was 7.50m long, presumably still open to the roof, with two narrower, 2.5m long, end chambers with first-floor rooms above. It

is suggested that the narrow bay at the eastern end of the building held an external timber stairway giving access to the eastern upper chamber. The solitary principal post near the northern doorway is difficult to explain, unless it supported a narrow gallery running along the northern wall of the building to provide access to the upper chamber at the western end of the building.

Immediately beyond the north-eastern corner of the building there was an elongated pit, 4.00m long by 0.40m deep, which closely abutted the wall-trench. This may have been merely a short length of ditch, blocking access between the hall and the boundary ditch to the north-east. Alternatively, it may have served as a cess-pit for the hall, although the fills provided no evidence of such a function.

The later cut of the southern wall-trench produced 24 sherds of St Neots-type pottery, mainly the later type, and the post-pits produced a smaller, but similar assemblage. This suggests that the refurbishment of the building occurred within the eleventh century (ph LS3/2, 1000–1100). It was demolished in the earlier twelfth century (ph 0, 1100–1150), when the overlying timber building (T28) was constructed.

The domestic range, T30

The domestic range adjoined the western end of the hall, T29, and had a total length of 14.5m and a width of 5.5m, with rooms 3.9m wide. The three main rooms, 1–3,

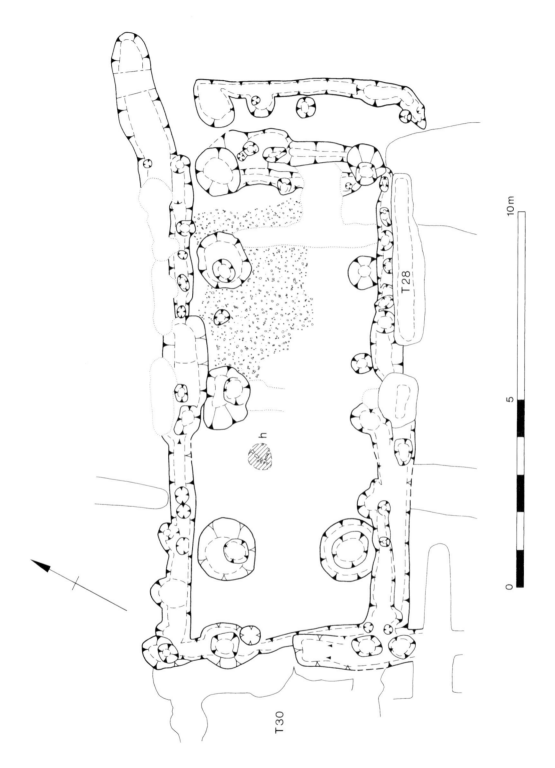

Fig 4.11: The late Saxon timber hall, T29

a

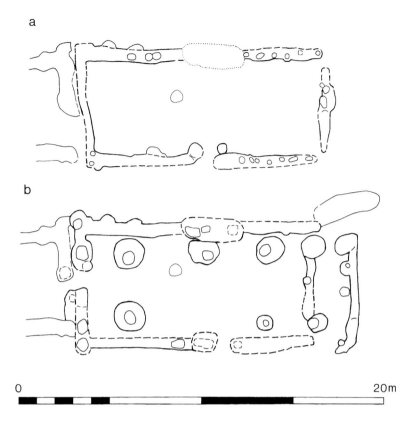

b

0   20m

Fig 4.12: The development of the hall, T29; a) stave built, tenth century, b) principal post construction, eleventh century

Fig 4.13: The timber hall, T29, looking west

were of a single build, at a length of 12.3m, with a small chamber, 4, attached to the western end of the range (Figs 4.14 and 4.15).

The northern wall-trench was 0.70m wide by 0.20–0.30m deep. The southern wall-trench was slightly wider but this was a result of the southern wall running along the line of the earlier timber palisade, T38, and the recutting of the earlier trench was evident in section. The lower fills of the wall-trenches were clean sands and gravel containing little evidence for any timbers.

The northern wall-trench contained no deeper post settings to suggest the location of a doorway. At the centre of the southern wall trench, a pair of post-pits, 0.65m deep, may have held the jambs of a 1.00m wide doorway opening into Room 2.

The northern end of the eastern wall-trench was of comparable depth to the long walls. To the south, a pair of post-pits indicates the position of a doorway giving access to the hall. The wall-trench between Room 3 and Room 4 was of the same depth as the main wall-trenches, suggesting that this was the original end wall of the building, with Room 4 abutted against it, and founded in wall-trenches of similar depth. The westernmost trench contained hollows for the provision of at least three principal posts, presumably related to successive door jambs. This wall-trench was partially backfilled with flat-laid limestone, particularly to the south. The stone had

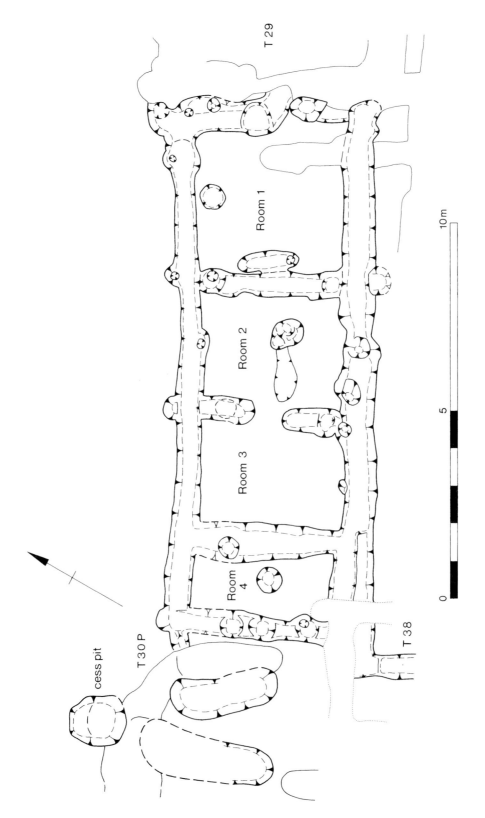

Fig 4.14: The late Saxon domestic range, T30

Fig 4.15: The late Saxon domestic range, T30, looking south, with building T32 (right) and T34 (top)

probably been introduced to consolidate the backfill when the end chamber was levelled to permit the building of an adjacent kitchen range, T32.

The two internal wall-trenches, separating Rooms 1, 2 and 3, were 0.10m shallower than the main walls. Basal hollows at three of the four junctions with the main walls indicate that the internal walls terminated at principal posts abutting the long walls.

Room 1, to the east, was near square in plan, at 3.80m long. To the west, a shallow, stone-lined, construction slot, with a 0.20m-deep posthole at the southern end, lay adjacent to the partition wall and was presumably related to the framing of a central doorway. A 0.25m deep pit on the northern side of the room might be a later feature.

Room 2, the central room, was 2.80m long. To the west, a 0.75m-wide break in the partition wall indicates the provision of a central doorway. Immediately south of the central doors, a shallow linear hollow, 0.15m deep, which terminated to the east at a complex post-pit up to 0.25m deep, may have held a partition wall. The fills of both features contained burnt loams, ash and charcoal, perhaps derived from a hearth either within this or an adjacent room. This internal partition may have screened access to the doorway opening into the central courtyard to the south.

Room 3, to the west, was 2.60m long, and contained no internal features. A possible post-pit in the western wall-trench may indicate that there was a central doorway opening into the western chamber. Room 4 was only 1.50m long, and the internal pit might be a later feature.

No floor levels survived in any of the rooms, making it difficult to define the construction and occupation dates. Pottery from the upper fills of the wall-trenches is dated to the first half of the twelfth century (ph 0, 1100–1150), and defines the demolition date.

To the west of the building there was a complex of pits and ditches. An L-shaped length of ditch (Fig 4.14, T30P) flanked the west wall of Room 4 and turned westward towards the main enclosure ditch, perhaps serving to close the gap between the building and the ditch. It comprised two elongated pits, each 0.45m deep, linked at the corner by a shallower arc of ditch.

Three pits partially cut into the ditch fills. A sub-square pit to the north, near vertical-sided and flat-bottomed, 1.55m diameter by 0.65m deep, had a distinctive primary fill of yellow-green silts indicative of its use as a cess pit. The two elongated pits to the south, were up to 0.50m deep, and may also have served as cess pits, but there was no clear indication of this within their fills.

Building T31

This building lay at the centre of the complex and was closely related to the timber palisade, T38, as part of the first phase of building development (Figs 4.16 and 4.17). It was up to 8.7m long and from 7.2m to 7.9m wide, with a trapezoidal plan, widest to the south. No contemporary floor surfaces survived. The recutting of the eastern wall-trench indicates that there were two phases of building.

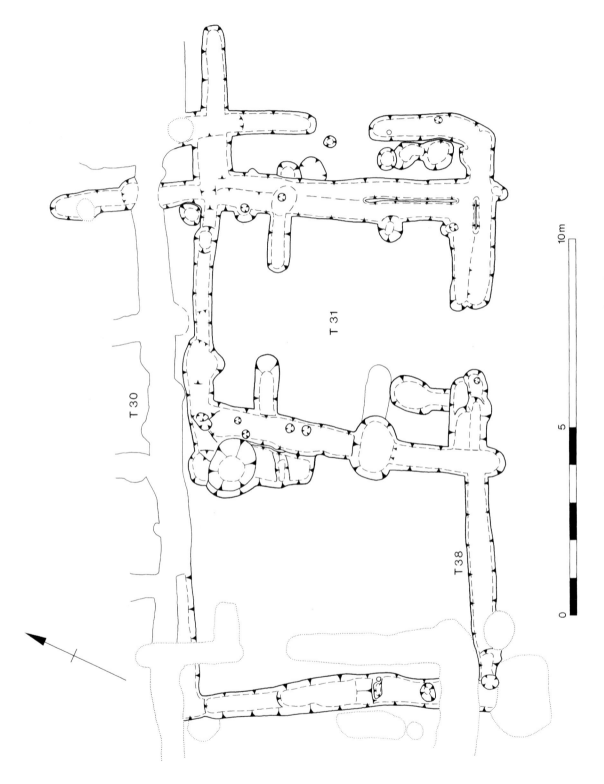

Fig 4.16: The late Saxon timber palisade, T38, and building T31

Fig 4.17: The palisade and building T31, looking west

The original building probably possessed a single open room with internal dimensions of 6.40m north-south and 5.50–6.60m east-west, a floor space of 38sq.m. The main entrance was a 1.70m wide opening within the southern wall-trench. Hollows towards either end of the northern wall-trench may have held principal posts forming a 2.5m wide doorway belonging to either or both phases of use. The wall-trenches were 0.55–0.75m wide and 0.35–0.45m deep.

In the second phase, a new eastern wall lay inside its predecessor, reducing the width of the building to 5.10–5.90m, a floor space of 34.5sq.m. In addition, there were paired internal slots towards the north, and to the south there were post-pits against the internal wall faces. These features define a central bay, 3.00m wide, and they may have held principal posts, independent of the main walls and perhaps supporting an upper storey raised over the central bay. An external construction pit abutted the northern end of the western wall, and contained two post-pits. The southern setting was elongated east-west suggesting that it had held a transverse post or plank, while the large circular pit to the north may have been a result of the digging out of the post. It is suggested that this feature held a ladder-like stairway providing access to an upper storey.

From the north-east corner of the building construction trenches extended 4.0m to both the north and east. They ran less than 1.00m from the walls of the hall, T29. They were probably introduced when this corner of the original timber palisade was removed to permit the construction of the hall, T29. They may have held a new L-shaped length of timber palisade to reinstate the removed corner.

The palisade, T38

The palisade comprised surviving linear construction trenches to the east, south and west. The northern trench had largely been removed at the building of the domestic range, T30 (Figs 4.16 and 4.17). The palisade enclosed an area 14.0–14.5m long, 7.6m wide to the west and 8.3m wide to the east; an area of 114sq.m. More than half of this was occupied by the central building, T31, leaving a narrow space, 1.00m wide, to the east and an open space to the west 5.50m long.

The construction trench was typically 0.60–0.70m wide and 0.30–0.45m deep, and the only evidence for any timber settings was a couple of post or plank impressions in the base of the western arm. There were simple openings through the palisade to the east, 1.40m wide, and south, the latter coinciding with the doorway to the central building, T31. In addition, a central deepening on the western trench and a differential fill above this, may indicate that there was a western entrance, perhaps inserted at a later stage.

To the south the palisade lay 2.50–2.80m from the inner edge of the enclosing ditch, and to the west it was 4.50–5.00m from the ditch (Fig 4.9). Given the width of this berm, it is possible that a bank had been thrown-up against the palisade to the south and west, although no evidence for this was obtained. The combination of ditch, bank and timber palisade would have created an imposing facade.

The courtyard fence

Following the demolition of the central building, T31, and the palisade, T38, the enclosed compound became an open courtyard. A rough line of small post-pits to the east of Building T31 may have formed a post-built fence, with a central opening, that would have closed the eastern end of the new courtyard (Fig 4.16). Some of these post-pits must have cut the fills of the wall-trenches forming Building T31 but, given the similarity of the clean fills, these relationships were not seen in excavation. To the

south, there was a group of four pits, from 0.10–0.40m deep, while a similar group to the north were largely lost in the fills of the earlier wall-trench. There was a central entrance, 1.5m wide.

The kitchen, T32

This building lay at the western end of the central courtyard (Fig 4.18). It is interpreted as a kitchen on the basis that its stone-built successor was a kitchen range. It was 9.0m long by 4.2m wide, with a floor space of 22.5sq.m measuring 7.5 by 3.0m. The wall-trenches were 0.60–0.80m wide and 0.35–0.40m deep. Towards the southern end of the eastern wall, a slightly darker fill defined a central slot tapering from 0.50m wide at the surface to 0.15m wide at the base. This may indicate that the wall timbers were at least 150mm thick. The southern wall-trench was slightly curved and both wider and deeper, at 1.10m wide by 0.50m deep, probably terminating at principal posts. This may indicate that this wall had been rebuilt. To the north the wall trenches extended beyond the corners by up to 0.40m, and a deepening in the base of one of these extensions may indicate that it held a rectangular post or plank.

Opposed doorways were set to the north of centre. The

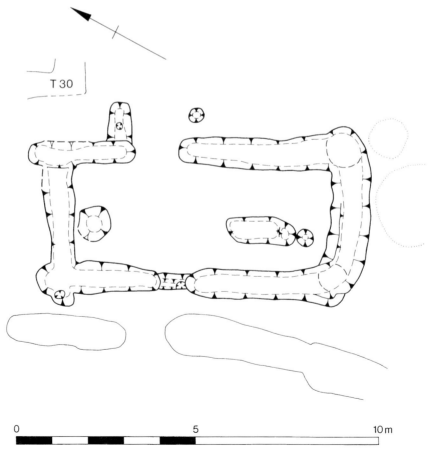

Fig 4.18: The possible late Saxon kitchen, T32,

eastern doorway was 1.15m wide and was screened on at least its northern side by a short external stub-wall, set in a slot 0.28m deep. The western doorway was narrower, at 0.85m wide, and a 0.18m-deep slot across the threshold would have held a sill beam.

No floor surfaces survived. There was a shallow pit, 0.35m deep, at the northern end of the room, and an elongated pit and an adjacent posthole, 0.25m deep, lay to the south. These features lay beneath the eastern wall of a later building (S21) and it is possible that they were related to the construction of that building.

Very small groups of pottery from the wall trenches date its demolition to the earlier twelfth century (ph 0, 1100–1150).

The southern range, T34

This two-roomed building, 12.8m long (Figs 4.19 and 4.20), was constructed over a backfilled ditch. The probable broad doorway in the eastern room indicates that it was an agricultural building, probably a barn or byre.

Room 1, to the west, was near square at 5.3m long by 4.9m wide, with a floor space of 14.8sq.m, measuring 4.1 by 3.6m. The wall-trenches were 0.55–0.70m wide by 0.3–0.4m deep, although the southern wall-trench was 0.10m shallower. The corner post-pits were 1.00m in diameter by up to 0.60m deep, generally 250mm deeper than the wall-trenches. Their fills differed from the wall-trench fills in containing pieces of limestone, with particular concentrations in the southern two.

A central doorway within the southern wall-trench was 1.30m wide, defined by a linear slot with terminal postholes. A floor of gravel in a matrix of orange-brown sandy loam partially survived, and a hearth was defined by a circular area of burning, 0.85m in diameter. Surface patches of brown loam with charcoal inclusions and a scatter of pottery and animal bone appear to represent trampled occupation debris. The internal postholes to the west could belong with either this or the later building.

Room 2, to the east, was 7.5m long and from 5.0–6.0m wide, with a floor space of 26.2sq.m, measuring 6.9 by 3.8–4.7m. The northern and eastern wall-trenches were 0.70–0.80m wide by 0.35–0.45m deep. The offset wall-trench forming most of the southern wall was slightly deeper, at 0.55m. This plan form is assumed to indicate the presence of a projecting doorway, 4.00m wide and founded on a sill beam, presumably to add support to a heavy timber door surround and a set of heavy wooden barn doors. Two internal post-pits, 0.30–0.40m deep, with an irregular feature between them, might have held posts supporting the main roof at its junction with the projecting doorway structure. At a later date, the width of the doorway was probably reduced, with a post-pit just east of centre in the wall-trench holding the new eastern jamb of a doorway 2.00 or 2.50m wide.

There may also have been successive doorways in the northern wall. A doorway, 1.30m wide, was defined by an

external slot with terminal postholes, while two post-pits set on the inner edge of the wall-trench may have framed a broader doorway, 1.70m wide. The break in the eastern wall-trench indicates the provision of an end door at least 1.00m wide. No floors survived. A slot to the west of the southern doorway may have held a partial subdivision, forming a western chamber, only 1.70m wide.

There were three external pits at the eastern end of the building (Fig 4.19, cess pit). A pit adjacent to the eastern wall, 2.80m long by 1.50m wide and 0.65m deep, had a distinctive lower fill of fine, dark green to grey-green silty sand, characteristic of a cess deposit, and it also contained a substantial pottery assemblage. A group of shallow postholes around the northern end suggest the provision of a light wooden screen. A pit adjacent to the southern wall, 3.00m long by 1.15m wide and 0.40m deep, was introduced after the narrowing of the doorway, but the fill gave no indication that it had been used as a cess pit. Further to the east there may have been another broadly contemporary pit, but it lay beneath a later building (S20) and was not clearly defined in excavation; it was 2.50m long by 0.80m wide and 0.30m deep, and filled with orange-brown sandy loam with some blackened (burnt) loam.

The internal features of Room 2 and the cess pit adjacent to the eastern wall were sealed by a distinctive layer of grey-brown loam heavily mottled with fine grey ashy material including much charcoal. A similar deposit was also present beyond the western end of Room 1. These deposits appear to derive from the destruction of the building.

The pottery from the floor of Room 1 and from the fills of the cess pit to the east comprised over 200 hundred sherds of St Neots-type ware, including the later style bowl rims, suggesting that it was constructed in the later tenth century (AD 975). It continued in use into the earlier eleventh century.

The new southern range, T33

The original range, T34, was demolished and replaced by a new building (Fig 4.21). This was 9.7m long by 5.3m wide, comprising a rectangular room of 6.7m by 4.0m, an internal floor space of 26.8sq.m, with a narrow, 1.20m wide, bay attached to the western end.

The wall-trenches were 0.60–0.75m wide by 0.45–0.60m deep. A post-pit at the north-eastern corner, identified by differential filling, may suggest the provision of principal posts at the corners. There were extended slots, from 1.30–2.00m long, at the corners. To the west, the extended wall slots and a shallower slot, 0.16m deep, beyond the western wall, suggest the provision of a narrow lean-to.

A narrow break in the wall trench, 0.45m long, and an external threshold slot ending at small postholes, defines a 1.0m wide doorway in the northern wall.

A floor of mixed grey-brown loam with some burning, clean orange sand and gravel with some pieces of limestone, partially survived. Postholes against the southern and northern walls may indicate that there were internal fittings.

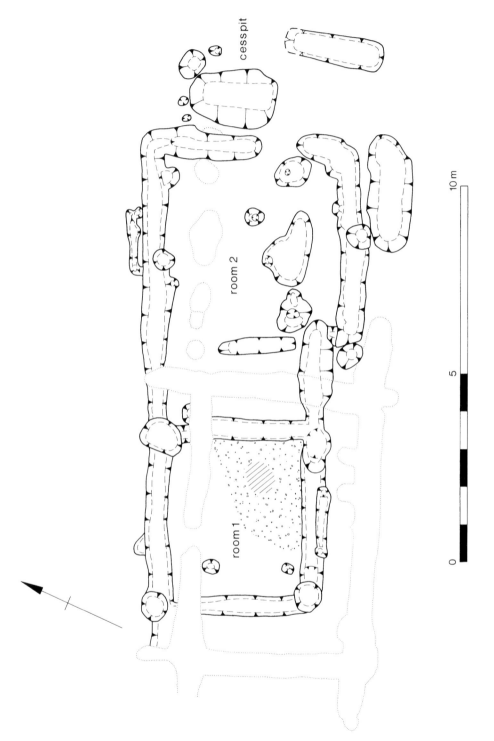

Fig 4.19 : The late Saxon southern range, T34

Fig 4.20: The southern ranges, T34 and T33, looking west

To the north-west two external pits, 0.20 and 0.40m deep, may have been contemporary with the building. They were filled with orange-brown sandy loam with some gravel and the larger of the two contained quantities of limestone.

A line of seven or eight post-pits, 0.20–0.40m deep and spaced 0.70–1.70m apart, ran eastward for at least 7.0m, and probably held posts supporting a substantial timber fence. Three smaller, but truncated postholes may represent a southward return to form a small pen, bounded to the south by a ditch system, 5.

A later stone-built range, S20, lay largely to the east of this building, but with its western wall directly overlying the eastern wall-trench. It is therefore possible that the timber range could have been retained to abut the new stone-built range (see Fig 5.17).

The assemblage of 84 sherds from the floor indicates that the building was in use in the eleventh century (ph LS3/2, 1000–1100). Later pottery from the wall-trench fills might support the postulated retention of the building into the twelfth century (ph 0, 1100–1150).

The ancillary mill building, T35

This building was of a much lighter construction than the other contemporary structures (Fig 4.22 and 4.23). It lay beside the watermills and is assumed to have been part of the mill complex, with its distinctive constructional form perhaps suggesting that it had some specialised function.

The large post-pits within the building might indicate the provision of a timber frame capable of carrying a substantial weight, so one possibility is that it may have been used for the preparation and maintenance of the millstones.

The northern end and western wall had been destroyed by ditch system 19, and truncation had lowered the ground level by up to 200mm, down to the surface of the natural gravel. The building was in excess of 7.8m long and Room 1 was 4.0m wide. A linear setting of flat-laid limestone slabs within the upper fill of the adjacent boundary ditch, 19a, lay on the line of the western wall at the same level as the base of the eastern wall-trench. They might indicate that the building had extended over the early phase ditch, to a total length of 10m, which would make it contemporary with the second watermill, M26, and dated to the eleventh century. Following abandonment, a good group of earlier twelfth-century pottery (ph 0, 1100–1150) was deposited in the filling of both the sunken-floor and within ditch system 19.

The wall-trench of Room 1 was 0.30–0.40m wide and 0.20m deep. To the south it terminated at a short transverse slot, 0.13m deep, which probably held a plank, and part of a similar transverse plank-slot was all that survived of the western wall. Within the room there were two large post-pits, 0.35m deep, and the western pit contained a possible post-pipe of 250–300mm diameter.

Room 2, to the south, was a narrower, sunken-floored chamber, 2.80m square, with a floor area of only 4.8sq.m.

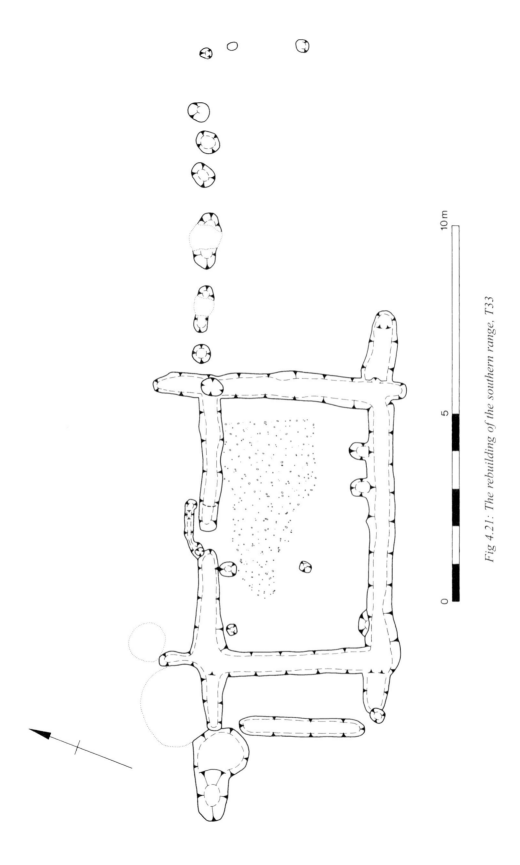

Fig 4.21: The rebuilding of the southern range, T33

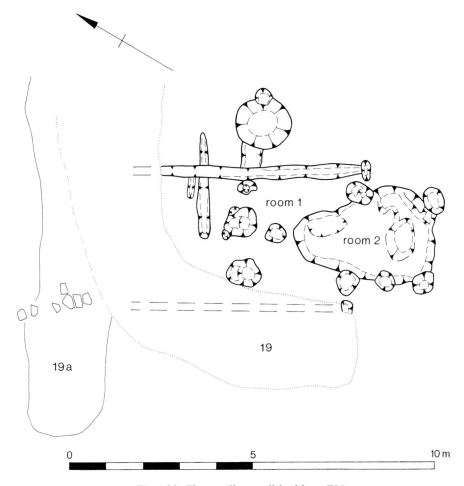

Fig 4.22: The ancillary mill building, T35

Fig 4.23: Building T35, looking west, with ditch system 19 in the background

It was of separate build, founded on four principal posts, with the post-pits 0.35–0.40m deep. A central post-pit in the western wall, 0.25m deep, may have held a door jamb. The sunken floor was 0.30m deep, with an uneven and undulating surface. The hollow was steep-sided, except to the north where a shallower slope extended into Room 1, indicating that they were interconnected.

A steep-sided pit, 0.45m deep, to the east of the building was linked to the wall-trench by a broad but shallow slot. The shallow slots further north post-dated the filling of the wall-trench and derive from later activity.

The timber buildings: general discussion

The hall

The timber halls at a number of broadly contemporary settlements show a similar pattern of development to the West Cotton hall (Fig 4.24). At Goltho (Beresford 1987) successive stave-walled, open halls (Period 3) were replaced by successive aisled halls (Period 4) and finally by a hall of principal-post construction (Period 5). At Faccombe Netherton (Fairbrother 1990, fig 4.55, 185) there was a transition from a pre-Conquest stave-built hall (building 9) to an aisled hall with walls comprising infilling between intermittent principal posts (building 11). At Furnells manor, Raunds the original open hall was also replaced by an aisled hall of significantly greater width (Audouy and Chapman 2009). In all of these instances the halls were adjoined by a further range, typically narrower and often sub-divided into several small chambers that are believed to provide domestic apartments; they are referred to as the camera at Faccombe Netherton and the bower at Goltho (see Audouy and Chapman 2009, 55, fig 4.2, for comparative plans of these halls).

The close comparability of general form between the halls and domestic apartments at West Cotton and Furnells manor (the long range) has previously been noted (Audouy and Chapman 2009, fig 4.2), but it is possible that the comparison may be valid at the more fundamental level of the actual building dimensions. At Furnells manor the complex sequence of later rebuilding left the constructional form of the original hall uncertain. The stated length of 19.0m exceeds the 15.5m length of the hall at West Cotton. However, at Furnells the total length includes a broader northern chamber and the length of the West Cotton Hall includes the possible external stairway that belongs with the second phase of building. If these elements are ignored, the basic structures of both halls are closely comparable at about 13.0m long. The internal widths of both halls are closely comparable at 5.00–5.50m, although the loss, or reuse, of most of the southern wall at Furnells has left the original width uncertain. The internal width of the associated domestic apartments is precisely comparable, at 3.90m. The main chamber of the domestic apartments

at Furnells, Room 2, was 11.5m long, closely comparable to the 12.0m length of Rooms 1–3 in the West Cotton apartments. The differing overall lengths of 14.5m at West Cotton to 19m at Furnells, may be accounted for by the provision of only a short end bay at West Cotton as opposed to two extra, near square rooms at Furnells.

It may be that the ranges at West Cotton and Furnells were constructed independently to similar specifications, but the close comparability of dimensions does raise the possibility that they were based on common specifications, perhaps even constructed by the same builder and they may even have utilised pre-cut timbers prepared off-site to standard dimensions. This suggestion, that the respective halls and apartments were effectively off-the-peg constructions utilising prefabricated timbers but with additional individual tailoring in the form of extra chambers added to the ends of the core buildings, may be seen in the context of the construction of both halls as part of the same episode of reorganisation of settlement at around the middle of the tenth century.

The speculative suggestion is that the provision of these buildings at West Cotton and Furnells may have occurred within such a short time-span that it was achieved through intensive, off-site prefabrication of semi-standardised buildings. Thereafter, the respective halls and apartments at West Cotton and Furnells were redeveloped in distinctly different ways, presumably reflecting their subsequent differences in status and prosperity. If this hypothesis has any validity, it would suggest that other contemporary settlements within the Raunds area would also possess hall and apartment complexes not only of similar form but also of closely similar core dimensions.

Building dimensions

Many studies of Saxon timber buildings have examined their size ranges and proportions, often whilst seeking to determine the possible use of certain standard length measurements (eg Fernie 1991; Huggins 1991; Marshall and Marshall 1991). The West Cotton buildings (Fig 4.24) can be compared to the results from these studies and, given the use of the 16.5-foot rod (5.03m) in the setting out of the plot system there is also a need to examine the possible utilisation of this particular measurement. In addition, we may test for the possible presence of the Germanic rod of 4.65m, as apparently utilised in the early Saxon buildings at Mucking, Essex (Huggins 1991). However, a major difficulty in attempting to define the use of any specific length measurement is that with the wall trenches having basal widths of 0.35–0.50m, the buildings have a range of 0.75–1.0m in the measurable dimensions (Table 4.1).

The widths of the buildings had an extreme range of 2.9–6.7m, but three buildings, T34, T33 and T30, lay within a narrower range of 4.9–5.2m. These values agree with the major grouping identified by Marshall and Marshall (1991, 35–6 and fig 4) of widths between 4.5 and 5.5m, while the width of the later hall, at 5.7–6.7m, falls within their

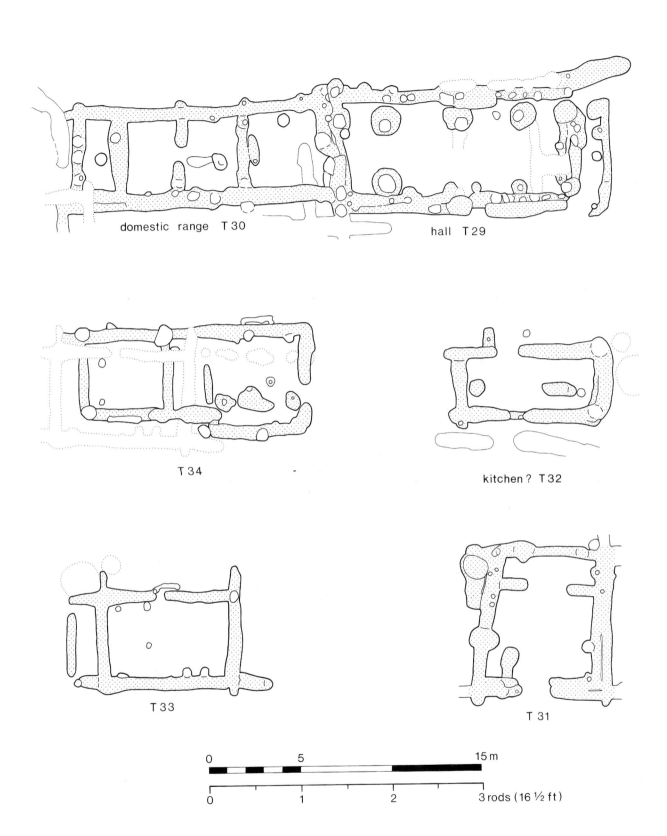

domestic range T 30

hall T 29

T 34

kitchen? T 32

T 33

T 31

0   5   15 m

0   1   2   3 rods (16 ½ ft)

Fig 4.24: The late Saxon timber buildings, comparative plans

Table 4.1: The late Saxon timber buildings; dimensions and length/width ratios

Building	Width (m)	Length (m)	Length/width ratio
Western range (T32)	2.9–3.7	7.6– 8.5	2.3–2.6
Early southern range (T34)			
room 1	3.8–4.9	4.4– 5.1	1.0–1.2
room 2	3.8–4.9	7.1– 7.8	1.6–1.9
Later southern range (T33)	4.3–5.0	7.0– 7.8	1.6
Domestic range (T30) rooms 1–3	4.2–5.2	10.6–11.8	2.3–2.5
Early hall (T29 phase 1)	5.3–6.2	12.6–12.9	2.1–2.4
Later hall (T29 phase 2)	5.7–6.7	12.1–12.8	1.9–2.1
The palisade (T38)	7.8–9.5	14.5–15.7	1.7–1.9
Building T28	6.1–7.0	6.4– 6.5	0.9–1.0

secondary grouping of 6.0 to 6.5m. The western range lies within their lowest width grouping, of 3.0 to 3.5m.

The building lengths range from 7.0–12.8m, although if the narrower end chambers of both the domestic range and the later hall are included these buildings would measure 14.5 and 15.5m respectively. This is in good agreement with the typical range of 6m to 15m identified by Marshall and Marshall (1991, 37–39 and fig 6), and there is some support for their suggested clusters at 7–8m, buildings T32 and T33, and 14–15m, the hall, T29 and domestic range, T30.

While the building widths provide no convincing conformity to any set unit of measurement, the clustering of lengths at 7–8m, 10–11m, and 14–15m identified by Marshall and Marshall suggests a possible relationship to the 16.5ft rod (5.03m); at lengths of 1.5, 2.0 and 3 rods. This appears to be confirmed by individual buildings at West Cotton. The early southern range, T34, had room lengths of 1 and 1.5 rods, while the later southern range, T33, was 1.5 rods long. The hall, T29, was also 2.5 rods long, while the inclusion of the end bay would extend this to 3 rods. The spacing between the principal posts of the enlarged hall, at 2.5m (0.5 rod), with the central span measuring 7.5m (1.5 rods), may also confirm this. The particularly short and narrow western range, T32, does not appear to fit this scheme, and neither does the domestic range, T30.

This analysis of the building dimensions does suggest that at least the lengths of some major buildings at West Cotton may have been set out as simple multiples of the 16.5ft rod (5.03m) (Fig 4.24).

Stave-walled buildings

The linear wall-trenches had been cut down through a pre-building soil horizon of sandy loam so that they bottomed on or up to 100mm into the underlying natural gravel (Fig 4.25). The consistency of the bottom levels in relation to the gravel, despite variations in the depth at which it was encountered, suggests that the trenches were quite deliberately cut to the gravel, most probably to provide both a solid base and the best possible drainage at the base of the wall timbers. The trenches were typically steep-sided and flat-bottomed, from 0.60–0.80m wide at

ground level and 0.35–0.50m wide at the bottom; they ranged from 0.20–0.60m deep, although the shallower examples had probably all been truncated by later lowering of the ground surface.

The wall-trenches and their fills provided little direct evidence for the nature of the timbers that had been set within them. As excavated, the base of the wall-trenches were roughly level, although it is probable that basal hollows derived from post impressions were missed in at least some instances through overcutting. This was largely a result of the excavation technique of working along the trenches, rather than excavating longer lengths in plan, a method necessitated by the difficulty encountered in defining the wall-trenches in plan at ground level.

The only clear evidence for a sequence of individual post positions came from the long walls of the original timber hall, T29. The bottoms of both the northern and southern wall-trenches contained well-preserved oval depressions, 0.40–0.60m in diameter, 50–200mm deep and spaced on average at intervals of 0.75m centre-to-centre (Fig 4.26). The consistency of size and spacing suggests that this was a stave-built wall, comprising closely-spaced timbers of similar size, rather than comprising lighter infilling between more widely spaced principal posts.

The spacing of the individual staves suggests that more shallowly founded timbers would have been required as infilling between them, and if the staves had measured 350–450mm, then there would have been a further 300–400mm of infilling between them, so that the walls may have comprised alternating posts of two sizes. A similar, but better preserved, pattern of rectangular post impressions was recorded along a length of wall-trench in the 'weaving shed' at Goltho (Beresford 1987, 56–57, figs 55 and 56) and the reconstructed wall elevation (*ibid*, fig 56B) is probably indicative of the form of the hall walls at West Cotton.

The wall-trench fills were of homogeneous, clean sandy loams with some gravel but rarely containing other inclusions or artefacts. This suggests that they comprised the material originally excavated from them used as a backfill around the inserted timbers. The absence of distinct post-impressions within the fills indicates that the timbers had not been left to decay *in situ*, implying that the buildings had all been systematically dismantled. In a number of buildings it was noted that the fills against the trench sides were both cleaner and more compact than the central fills, and a central core of darker fill was quite clearly defined along part of the eastern wall of the kitchen range, T32, tapering from 0.50m wide at the surface to 0.15m wide at the base of the slot. This suggests that the timbers had generally been set centrally and not against one side of the trench. The relatively undisturbed nature of the fills also indicates that base plates had not been set along the bottoms of the wall-trenches, as either their decay in-situ would have left clear evidence or their removal would have involved the digging out of the original backfill resulting in more mixed fills than were encountered.

In some buildings the wall-trenches extended beyond the wall line by between 0.50m and 1.75m (Fig 4.23; T30, T32 and T33). Similar features have been noted in buildings at Faccombe Netherton, where it was suggested that 'this results from the preliminary setting out, where the end walls were not positioned until the long walls were determined and the post positions established' (Fairbrother 1990, 193). Similar features also appear on a few buildings at Furnells, Raunds (Audouy and Chapman 2009, figs 5.22 and 5.24).

At West Cotton, extensions to both long and end walls were recorded, suggesting that the explanation proposed for Faccombe Netherton is inadequate. It seems more likely that these features had a definite structural function, and in one instance, building T32, the extension contained a transverse, elongated slot suggesting that it may have

Fig 4.25: A typical length of steep-sided wall trench, bottoming just into the natural gravel

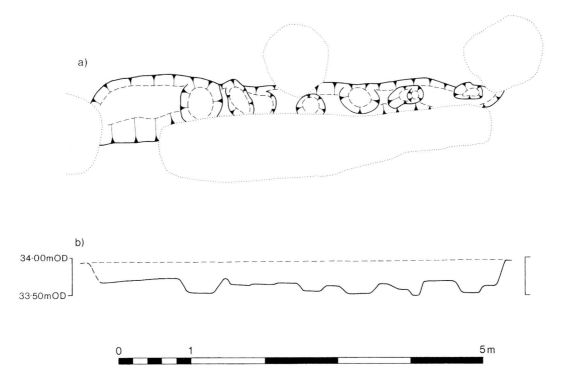

Fig 4.26: The wall trench of the hall, T29, showing stave construction; a) plan, b) reconstructed longitudinal profile

held a rectangular post or plank. Such external posts may have provided additional support to either wall corners or, as in the domestic range T30, at major wall junctions. No structural details were recovered from the longer extensions on building T33, but perhaps here we can suggest the provision of major corner buttresses. Whether these would have been original features or later additions to support points of developing structural weakness has not been established.

The provision of upper storeys

Sub-circular hollows in the bottoms of the wall-trenches indicate the occasional provision of principal posts, probably squared posts of 300–400mm diameter, set up to 200mm deeper than the main wall timbers. Some were clearly door jambs, see below, but others occurred either at corners (Fig 4.24, T34) or immediately inside the external wall lines at apparent internal divisions, T30 and T31. In most instances these post-pits were also defined by differential fills, typically darker and looser and usually including some limestone, probably from displaced packing. The use of principal posts within otherwise stave-built walls may indicate that some buildings required additional structural support, and this may suggest the presence of partial or even full upper storeys in a few buildings.

The corner posts of the square western room of the southern range provided a simple provision of larger corner posts (Fig 4.24, T34). However, building T31, within the palisade enclosure, had a more complex arrangement of short internal wall trenches and post-pits, defining a central bay, with posts set inside the line of the main wall. There was a

similar arrangement around the central room of the domestic range, T30, with post-pits set in the internal partition wall trenches immediately inside the main wall line.

Most elaborately, when the hall, T29, was rebuilt, there were free-standing principal posts within the hall (Fig 4.27), and principal posts on the same lines were also set within the end walls. This rebuilding only increased the width of the hall by 0.50m, to 6.7m wide, so the introduction of arcade posts to carry the roof load, as in an aisled hall, was not necessary. It may also be noted that the central principal post to the north had no partner on the opposite side of the building. It is therefore suggested that the principal posts were related to the provision of first-floor chambers over the end bays. The narrow bay at the eastern end of the building may have contained an external stairway giving access to the upper chamber at this end of the building, with perhaps a gallery running along the north wall to the opposite chamber.

The halls of similar structural form at both Faccombe Netherton (Fairbrother 1990, building 11, fig 4.20) and Goltho (Beresford 1987, fig 65) have been reconstructed as single-storey buildings but Beresford noted that there was no apparent reason for the adoption of such a narrow-aisled hall at Goltho as 'very little extra width was gained by the change of construction' (*ibid*, 67).

Doorways

The simplest doorway form was a plain opening in an otherwise continuous wall-trench (Fig 4.24, T31 and T32). In these instances it would appear that the door jambs were provided by terminal stave-posts that were not

Fig 4.27: Section of post-pit holding arcade post in the timber hall, T29

significantly larger or more deeply set than the rest. The opposed doorway of building T32 was of the same basic form, but a shallow, steep-sided slot running across the opening indicates the additional provision of a sill beam between the jambs.

In three instances doorways comprised shallow sill-beam slots with terminal postholes, containing timbers 100–150mm in diameter, set at or just beyond the external wall face, indicating the provision of shallow porches. In building T34, two such porches flanked continuous wall-trenches, and provided the only indication of the presence of doorways, while in building T33 a sill-beam slot flanked a simple opening in the wall-trench.

The southern doorway of the central room of the domestic range, and a doorway at the western end of the same building (Fig 4.24, T30) were defined by post-pits deeper than the continuous wall-trenches, and their fills contained limestone probably from displaced packing. These probably held substantial door jamb posts, possibly with sill beams set between them, and in these instances it is suggested that the lintels may have been raised above eaves height.

The original southern doorway of the hall (Fig 4.24, T29) appeared to have had a plain opening, with small internal postholes suggesting either that the door was recessed or that there were short internal screens. Following the rebuilding, the new doorway was probably flanked by deeply-set door jamb posts, while the opposed northern doorway possessed substantial door jamb posts set at either end of a construction pit. Both of these doorways were later narrowed by resetting the western posts. As in the domestic apartments, we may suggest the provision of elaborate doorways with raised lintels.

The broad doorway of building T34, which was 4.0m wide, possessed the most complex structural form, The continuous wall-trench with terminal posts appears to denote the presence of a broad, barn-like doorway set forward of the main wall line by 1.0m, perhaps to form a porch raised above eaves height. Subsequently, this doorway was apparently narrowed to some 2.5m wide by the insertion of a new eastern door jamb post.

Floors

The floor surfaces had been lost in all of the early buildings with the exception of the southern ranges, T34 and T33, where floor and occupation levels had survived as a result of subsidence of the underlying ditch fills. These floors comprised gravel in sandy loam, and with the ready availability of gravel from the boundary ditches this may also have been used for the floors in other buildings.

Repairs

The kitchen (Fig 4.24, T32) had terminal post-pits at the ends of a wide and curving wall-trench, which bore little resemblance to the other end of the building. These differing forms may suggest that this end wall had been rebuilt, with the digging out of the old timbers and the insertion of the new wall explaining the width of the trench, while the corner posts would have provided the structural link to the existing walls. No other buildings show a similar rebuilding of a single wall, as the other instances all appear to have involved a total rebuild of the entire structure.

Roof form

There may be an indirect indicator of the possible form of the roofs. The wall-trenches for the end walls were generally slightly shallower than those for the long walls, but there was no substantial distinction between them, except in the shallow and irregular wall-trenches forming the end walls of the hall (Fig 4.24, T29). This suggests that in most buildings the long and end walls probably contained timbers of closely comparable size and load-bearing capacity. In a gabled roof the weight would be fully carried by the long walls, so that the end walls need be no more than a light weight, non-structural infilling, as is apparent in the hall. In the other buildings, as the end walls could have provided structural support equal to that of the long walls, it is suggested that they may have had hipped roofs.

The boundary and plot systems

This section provides a discussion and catalogue of the evidence for the development of the boundary and plot system, which has been central to modelling the general development of the site between the tenth and twelfth centuries (Fig 4.28). It should be noted that the later phases of both the boundary system and the features within the plots were contemporary with the medieval manor and, whilst illustrated here, they will only be seen in context within the following chapter discussing the medieval manor and its form and development.

The ditched boundary system

In post-excavation each individual boundary ditch system was numbered in sequence running from south to north for both the western and eastern halves of the ditch system: Late Saxon Ditches (LSD) 1–21. Similarly, the enclosed plots were also numbered in sequence from south to north: Late Saxon Enclosures (LSE 1–13) (Fig 4.28).

In formulating the strategy for post-excavation analysis it initially appeared that the detailed development of each individual ditch system could be given a fairly cursory examination, but this conclusion was shown to be false. Ditch recutting was found to be not just a product of re-establishing ditches that were silting, but was often a result of realignments and slight modifications of the ditch systems that reflected aspects of settlement structure and reorganisation, including redevelopment of the buildings.

It was therefore the combination of all aspects of the archaeological record that allowed the development of the settlement to be described in such detail. A distinct contrast may be drawn between West Cotton and Furnells manor, Raunds (Audouy and Chapman 2009), where the analysis of the site within discrete structural groups, with insufficient consideration of the relationship of buildings and boundaries, limited the scope for a detailed interpretation and modelling of the overall site development, leaving the buildings stranded within a palimpsest of multi-phase ditches, sometimes with no apparent access to adjacent plots. In addition, given the limited dating evidence from

the timber buildings, the larger quantities of pottery from the ditches, and the presence of a few sealed assemblages from lengths of ditch abandoned early in the development of the settlement was crucial in defining the overall chronology.

These conclusions have important implications for the excavation of boundary ditches on comparable sites. The resolution achieved was only possible because the boundary systems had been extensively excavated, revealing details of realignments, the presence of earlier openings, relocated ditch terminals defining entrances, as well as possible bridging points spanning the open ditches. It is therefore suggested that at any major late Saxon settlement site it is essential to understand the detailed form and development

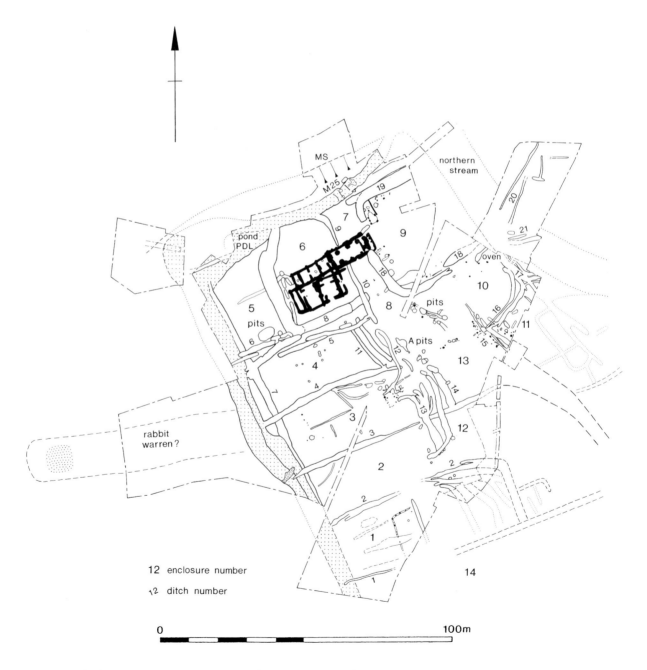

Fig 4.28: The late Saxon settlement, showing ditch system (small font, angled) and plot numbers (large font, upright)

of the individual boundary systems in order to build a comprehensive understanding of the whole site.

Probable bridging points

In three instances distinctive features within and alongside boundary ditches are interpreted as indicating the provision of small timber bridges spanning the open ditches. All three shared common features including distinct basal slots, narrow lengths of ditch with multiple recuts converging from either side, as if respecting a fixed point, and flanking lengths of ditches or slots beside the main ditch, sometimes associated with postholes (Fig 4.29, a–c).

At the eastern end of ditch system 5 (Fig 4.29, a), the ditch terminal contained a steep-sided slot, 3.50m long and 0.10m deep, total depth 0.55m, with probable postholes set towards either end, 1.50m apart centre-to-centre. The upper fill contained a concentration of limestone, which was only sparsely present within the ditch fills further west. Within ditch system 4 (Fig 4.29, b) there was a similar basal slot, 4.20m long by 0.20m deep, total depth of 0.75m, although no evidence for postholes was recovered. There was an adjacent length of shallower ditch or slot, up to 0.40m deep, with steep sides and a flat base, which at either end deepened and turned abruptly towards the ditch. Multiple recuts converged at either end of this length. The third example lay on the northern boundary of the eastern enclosures (16) (Fig 4.29, c). Within the ditch there was

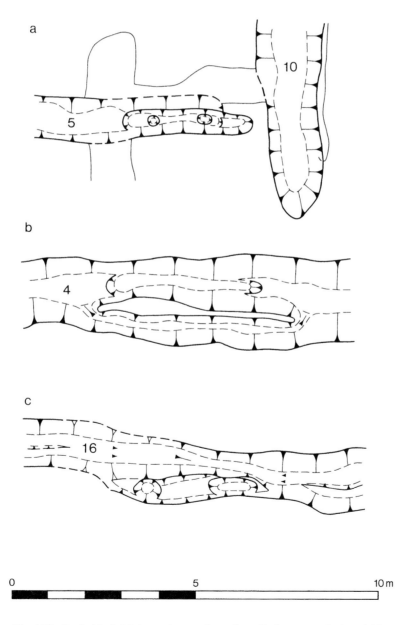

Fig 4.29: Probable bridging points on boundary ditch systems 5, 4 and 16

no clear definition of a basal slot, but for a length of 4.5m the ditch was particularly narrow, suggesting that the recuts converged here. This was flanked by a shallower, flat-bottomed ditch or slot, 3.80m long by 0.20m deep, with postholes set towards either end, 0.35–0.45m deep and 2.00–2.50m apart. A possible fourth example, not illustrated, may have lain at the eastern end of the northern ditch of ditch system 6, defined by a narrow, slot-like length of ditch probably with a post-pit at its eastern end, but this area had been disturbed by later activity.

The basal slots and postholes are interpreted as having held pairs of timber uprights and sill beams supporting simple plank bridges, at least 1.50m and possibly as much as 2.00 to 2.50m wide. It is more difficult to explain the additional provision of shallow ditches or slots adjacent to the ditch systems, unless these held gateways set at the end of a bridge to provide more formal control of the use of such bridging points.

Possible fences

In the latest phases of recutting on ditch systems 2, 3, 4, 13, 15 and 16, there were a number of examples of steep-sided slots, typically more regularly linear than the ditches they replaced. It is suggested that these may have held timber fences, although no direct evidence for this was recovered. The clearest example was provided by the final northern boundary to the eastern enclosures (Fig 4.36, 16). The western end comprised a linear, steep-sided and flat-bottomed slot (1244) and to the east this ran directly into a deeper, broader and curving ditch (1268), suggesting the provision of a boundary with both fenced and ditched lengths. These fenced boundaries appear to have been introduced in the mid to later twelfth century (ph 1, 1150–1225), with the provision of fences marking a growing redundancy of the use of ditched boundaries, and presaging the medieval use of walls for any boundary that did not also act as a drainage system.

The usage and filling of the ditches

The fills of the boundary ditches showed distinct general patterns. To the west they were typically of homogeneous clayey silts, water deposited and presumably derived from flooding both while the mill leats were in use and through the earlier twelfth-century flooding at the around the time of the abandonment of the watermills. These deposits contained few finds, probably resulting from a combination of the silting process and the distance from the main buildings.

Around the buildings of the northern holding and along the frontages onto the central yards the fills were of sandier loams and these did produce considerable quantities of finds. Few came from the rapidly accumulated primary fills, and articulated portions of animal carcases from the lower fills of ditches, 16, of the eastern enclosure and the northern holding, 4, appear to be isolated occurrences.

Similarly, the surviving secondary fills of the earlier ditches also contained few finds. In contrast, the secondary and final fills of the latest recuts often produced large quantities of pottery, fragmented animal bone, limestone and burnt debris. This suggests that there was little long-term use of the ditches for rubbish disposal, as much of the material had come in only when the ditches were being backfilled at major changes of settlement organisation, presumably in association with the demolition of buildings.

As a result, the pottery assemblages are typically well-mixed and fragmented, with a high proportion of late Saxon types occurring within otherwise twelfth-century groups. The only good primary group came from the final terminal of the ditch system 4, within the northern holding, where there was an exceptionally clearly defined horizon related to a single act of infilling. The light silty fills of the large ditch, 8, flanking the southern side of the late Saxon timber buildings (Fig 4.31, 7290), were sealed by a thin, 50–100mm thick, layer of distinctive grey loam with charcoal producing a sparse pottery scatter but invariably of large sherds.

The ditch system, 18, flanking the eastern side of the road approaching the buildings of the northern holding produced one of the largest pottery assemblages. The fill containing this material may have been dumped in the twelfth century when the first stone buildings were appearing on the northern holding. Further south, the final filling of the same ditch comprised dumped limestone rubble and mortar, perhaps the disposal of debris from building construction.

Evidence for deliberate filling was also provided by the pottery, finds and burnt debris within the ditches along the western frontage onto the central yards (Fig 4.31, 14). Some burnt debris, burnt soil and charcoal, was present within the fills of the earlier cuts and suggests sporadic earlier dumping, presumably derived from use of the contemporary activity area to the north, which probably contained at least one oven. The final fills contained consistently more such debris, along with pottery and animal bone, and this may relate to a clearance of the activity area to the north immediately prior to the appearance of a new building range, S17. This activity was all contemporary with the twelfth-century manor, and is more fully described in chapter five.

The enclosed plots

There is a strong chronological bias in the dating of the features within the enclosed plots. The only major feature that produced a pottery assemblage with a pre twelfth-century date was a transverse internal ditch within plot 1, and even in this instance the adjacent fenced pen was in use in the twelfth century. Similarly, the successive gated entrances to plot 3 and the palimpsest of postholes and pits within the eastern plots, 11, are also dated to the earlier twelfth century.

There is, therefore, virtually no evidence that the

features related to stock control were present through the tenth and eleventh centuries. However, it is suggested that many of these features probably were in use much earlier, and that the dating evidence is probably indicative of the date of disuse. This suggestion is also supported by the known twelfth-century expansion of the domestic enclosure of the medieval manor and the appearance of numerous pits and ovens, all generally containing much burnt debris, showing that these processing activities were supplanting the use of the adjacent enclosures for stock control.

The ditches and plots of the southern holding

Ditch system 1 (LSD1)

This was a primary east-west boundary that formed the central division within the southern holding (Figs 4.28 and 4.30, 140). Only the south-western end lay within the excavated area, but its continuation was confirmed both by partial survival as an earthwork and by geophysical survey. The short excavated length to the west was V-shaped, 0.60m deep, with a narrow basal slot. It was filled with water-deposited silts and clays, and the five sherds of pottery are dated to the earlier twelfth century (ph 0, 1100–1150). After the accumulation of 0.20–0.30m of silts across this western area through the later twelfth century, the ditch was re-established at a higher level (104), but only the very base of this feature suvived.

Ditch system 2 (LSD2)

This was an intermediate boundary separating two quarter-acre plots. To the west there were two parallel ditches (Fig 4.30, 81 and 160), and the northern ditch was probably the later cut. They were only 0.10–0.35m deep, but this was a result of the clays into which they were cut being truncated in machine stripping. It is uncertain whether the break in the ditch further to the east was a result of machine removal or indicative of the presence of a real break providing access between the two enclosures. The small quantity of pottery recovered is dated to the first half of the twelfth century (ph 0, 1100–1150).

To the east, a sequence of four ditches formed the southern side of an entrance to the plot to the north. Geophysical survey showed that they turned southward to form a frontage onto the central yard. Although there were insufficient relationships to establish a full sequence, there was probably a steady eastward encroachment onto the central yard, as was demonstrated for ditch systems to the north. The southernmost ditch (1682) turned southward within the excavated area probably as part of the eastern boundary to the original quarter-acre western plots. Some small pottery groups from these ditches comprised only St Neots ware and some Stamford wares and suggest the presence of fills dating to the tenth century (ph LS2, 950–975).

The ditches were 0.30–0.50m deep, but both the southern and northern ditches (1682 and 1667/1701) deepened to the east, to 0.40–0.80m deep, indicating that the frontage had been recut and deepened on more than one occasion. To the north, a steep-sided slot (1672), up to 0.65m deep, may suggest the addition of a timber fence as a final definition of the frontage.

The fills of the northernmost ditch (1667/1701) contained quantities of burnt soil and charcoal, similar to deposits in ditch systems 13 and 14 to the north. This ditch was largely filled by the middle of the twelfth century (ph 0, 1100–1150), but smaller quantities of later twelfth-century pottery (ph 1, 1150–1225) suggest that the boundary may even have overlapped with the appearance of the first stone building in medieval tenement B.

Two small pits (1746 and 1751), 0.80–1.00m in diameter by 0.35m deep, may indicate the provision of posts flanking the enclosure entrance at some stage.

Plot 1 (LSE1)

This was a quarter-acre plot divided into western and eastern ends by a linear ditch (72), 1.30m wide and 0.35m deep (Fig 4.30). A shallow, L-shaped slot (22/30) containing regularly placed postholes formed a small enclosure or pen adjacent to the ditch, measuring 13.5m by 7.5m, an area of 100sq.m. The slot was 0.40–0.50m wide and 0.15m deep, with postholes in the base spaced between 0.80m and 2.90m apart. While the fills of the ditch contained a good pottery assemblage of later tenth-century date (ph LS2, 950–975), the slot produced a small amount of pottery dated to the earlier twelfth century (ph 0, 1100–1150). Within the enclosure there was a shallow, sub-rectangular pit (73), 0.75 by 0.60m and 0.10m deep, with a post or stakehole at either end, 0.10m deep. The lower fill was of dark grey-brown silty clay heavily flecked with charcoal, and above this a layer of scorched (red-brown) clay and two pieces of burnt limestone appeared to be the *in situ* remnants of a drying oven, and concentrations of charred cereal grain within nearby features and the boundary ditch to the north may have come from here.

A shallow linear hollow (24) up to 3.0m wide but no more than 0.06m deep, ran across the western slot and may have been an eroded pathway leading into the pen. A shallow linear slot to the north (31), 0.6m wide but only 0.03m deep, was aligned with the pen and may have held a further length of fence. To the north there was a shallow oval hollow (165), 5.00m long by 1.50m wide and up to 0.10m deep.

Plot 2 (LSE2)

Access to this quarter-acre plot was from the central yard through a broad, 5.50m wide, opening in the boundary ditch systems, 2 and 13, to the east (Fig 4.28). Initially this had been a simple opening between plain ditch terminals, but with the eastward migration of the eastern boundaries it was furnished with flanking ditches forming a funnelled

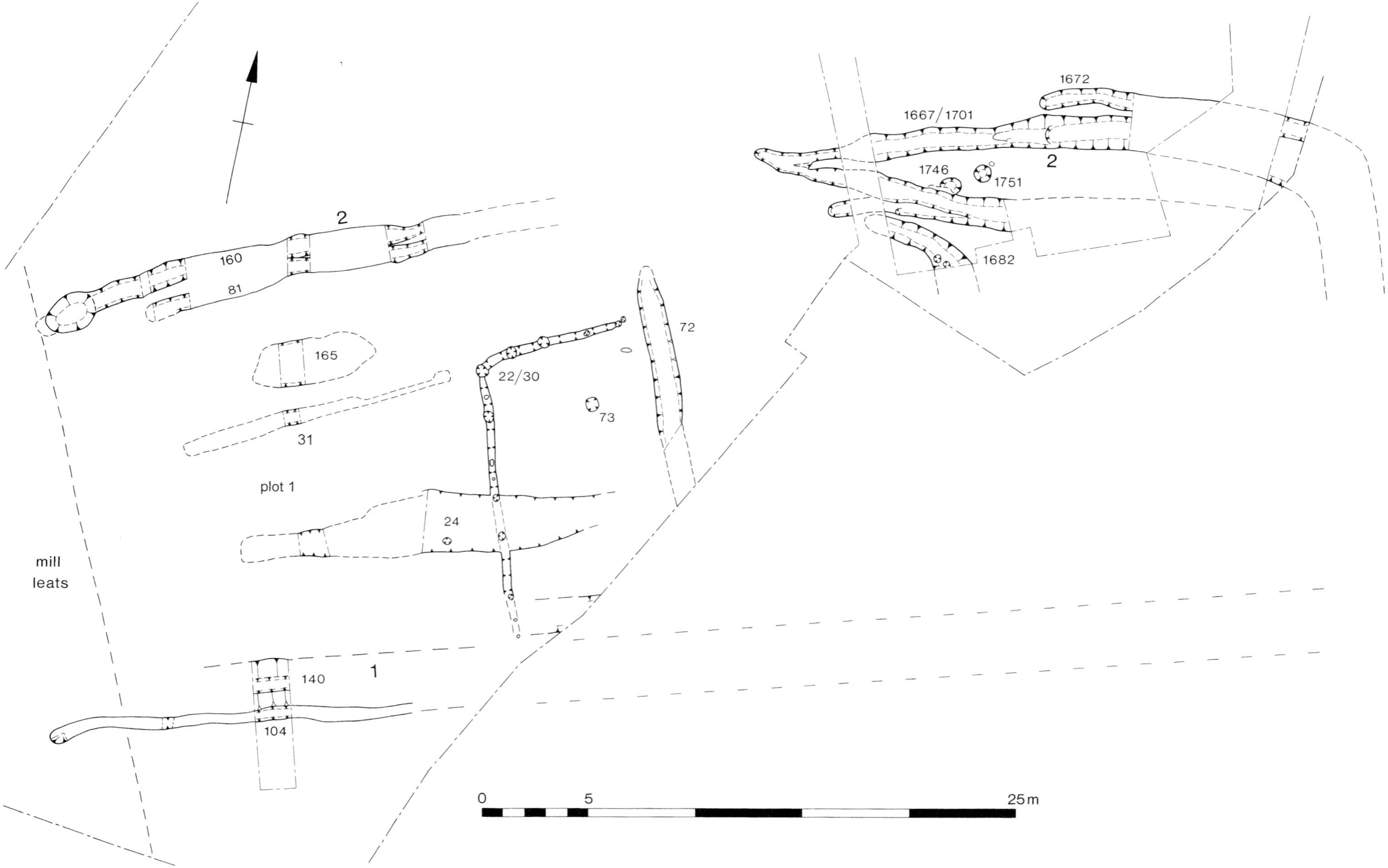

Fig 4.30: The southern holding, plot 1 and ditch systems 1 and 2

entrance passage. The interior of the plot was almost devoid of features, but the heavy machining of this area would have removed any shallow features. To the west an arc of gully (5203), 0.40m wide by 0.05m deep, may have held a fence connected with the control of access to the fording point across the adjacent mill leats (see Fig 6.2).

Plot 12 (LSE12), the southern central yard

The part of the central yard related to the southern holding lay largely beyond the excavated area, but the strip outside the entrance to plot 2 was devoid of any early surfaces or features (Fig 4.28). Geophysical survey indicated that in the south-western corner there was an L-shaped ditch forming a small sub-square enclosure, measuring 12m by 10m, perhaps a small pen or even a timber building. A twelfth-century date would be suggested by the way it appears to abut the most easterly boundary ditch.

The tenurial boundary: ditch system 3 (LSD3)

This was a primary boundary system that is interpreted as the tenurial boundary between the northern and southern holdings (Figs 4.31 and 4.32). In the later medieval period it was replaced by a double-walled boundary and following desertion a new ditched boundary lay between separately owned closes.

The original ditch was perhaps broken only where the original eastern frontage, ditch system 13, bisected it (Fig 4.32). A short length of the original flat-bottomed ditch, up to 0.60m deep, survived to the immediate east of this intersection, between ditch systems 13 and 14. It had been backfilled at an early date with clean gravel and sand, with the small pottery group dated to the later tenth century (ph LS2, 950–975). The second phase to the east had a terminal several metres east of ditch system 13. It was up to 1.00m deep with a V-shaped profile and a distinct basal slot (Fig 4.33). As the frontage moved eastward, to ditch system 14, the ditch terminal also migrated eastward. The ditch was only partially recut, so it then formed a U-shaped ditch half its original depth. The final fills contained quantities of burnt debris similar to the final fills of ditch system 14.

To the west of the frontage the ditch terminated 1.0m short of the transverse boundary. The distinct basal slot suggests that it was probably frequently scoured, and there was a complex history of recutting. The central section showed three surviving cuts shifting progressively northward. The earliest, 0.60m deep with a well defined basal slot, ran to within 10m of the mill leats, where it terminated adjacent to a curving length of gully within the enclosure to the south, which may have controlled access through this opening (see Fig 6.2). Three pits in the base of the later ditch, each 0.60–0.80m in diameter and 0.10–0.15m deep, may have been the truncated bases of post-pits beyond the original terminal, or perhaps a bridged crossing.

A further use of posts followed the abandonment of both the western boundary ditch, 7, and the second mill leat. A large pit (Fig 6.2, 6977), at least 3.60m long by 2.40m wide and 0.60m deep, contained two sub-square pits, 0.25–0.45m deep, suggesting the provision of a pair of posts set 2.40m apart. The distinctive form of this western end of the boundary system may have been determined by the presence of an adjacent fording point across the mill leats, the posts perhaps marking its location, and reflecting the more intensive usage of the area as the only point of access onto the area west of the mill leats.

By the earlier twelfth century (ph 0, 1100–1150), probably at the abandonment of the mills, the posts had been replaced by a continuous ditch, (5066/1281) typically 0.50m deep, running to the edge of the stream and terminating beside a surfaced ford. A final ditch recut at the western end was 0.30–0.40m deep. In part its profile was steep-sided and slot-like, and to the east the final recut along the northern edge of the system (Fig 4.32, 1155) was consistently a narrow, steep-sided slot, 0.65m wide by 0.50m deep, with a well defined terminal 19m west of ditch system 13. The profile suggests that it may have held a timber fence. The fills of this final recut contained some later twelfth century pottery (ph 1, 1150–1225).

Along part of the western length of this boundary there was an eroded remnant of bank, up to 0.35m high, comprising red-brown sandy clay with a little gravel. Although it had spread across much of the ditch system, it had clearly originally lain on the southern side.

The northern holding: the western ditches and plots

Ditch system 13 (LSD13), the early western frontage

This complex system of ditches formed part of the eastern frontage to plots 2 and 3, and thus formed a frontage to parts of both the northern and southern holdings (Fig 4.32, 13). The plan form shows that while the ditch recutting on the two holdings ran in parallel, the northern and southern halves were quite distinct. On the southern holding, the ditch sequence showed a minimal drift to the east, while to the north there was a substantial movement eastward, with the successive ditches fanning out from a near common origin with the neighbouring system. The central convergence of the ditches made it difficult to correlate the northern and southern sequences, but the presence of several butt-ends in this area, indicated by distinct basal steps, suggests that in many instances there were separate, but contemporary, northern and southern ditches which either closely abutted or even interlinked.

The earliest ditch to the north appeared to have a plain terminal, but it was soon replaced by an inturned ditch (937) forming part of a gated entrance to plot 3, and paralleling the development of ditch system 12 on the opposite side of the entrance. Thereafter, there was a succession of four plain terminals with a steady eastward drift. Two later cuts

Fig 4.31: The northern holding, showing the plots and boundary systems (including the twelfth-century oven and pit groups)

were narrow and steep-sided, up to 0.75m deep, and were either timber-slots or had filled very rapidly. The final recut (935) was also a narrow, steep-sided, slot, up to 0.80m deep, which may have held a fence. It was broadly contemporary with the latest recuts of the southern sequence, where at least the final two of a sequence of six or seven cuts were also narrow and steep-sided, up to 0.80m deep.

The ditch fills were consistently of red-brown sandy loams with pebble inclusions, although the fills of two of slot-like cuts to the south did contain some charcoal and burnt soil.

The ditches produced a large quantity of pottery, but much of this cannot be assigned to specific recuts as these were only defined in the drawn sections and not during excavation. Most of the system produced earlier twelfth century pottery (ph 0, 1100–1150).

Ditch system 14 (LSD14), the later western frontage

The eastward drift of the frontage culminated in the abandonment of the original ditch system and the provision of a completely new eastern frontage formed by two parallel ditches, each of which was recut a number of times (Fig 4.32).

On the western ditch (1662), the inturned entrance to plot 2, to the south, was an original feature, and contained a substantial assemblage of earlier twelfth-century pottery (ph 0, 1100–1150). The later cuts all had plain terminals, and the upper secondary fill of the latest cut contained multiple, interleaved lenses of burnt (reddened) sands with much charcoal and some pieces of burnt limestone. A pit (1674), 1.50m diameter by 0.80m deep, of similar depth to the ditches, lay adjacent to these terminals, and also contained some charcoal and burnt soil.

The easternmost ditch terminated adjacent to ditch system 3, which probably then had a western terminal at about the same point. There was a sequence of at least three cuts and, as with the western ditch, the upper secondary fill of the final cut contained much grey, charcoal flecked loam with burnt (reddened) soil.

At the northern end of both ditches there were pits which also contained burnt debris, these appeared to be related to the oven and pit group (1162/1355) further to the north.

The pottery from the western ditch was largely of earlier twelfth-century date, but one or two groups contained small quantities of later twelfth century date (ph 1, 1150–1225). The eastern ditch produced large quantities of later twelfth-century pottery, suggesting that it was retained after the western ditch was out of use, and may even have replaced the western ditch at around the middle of the twelfth-century.

Ditch system 4 (LSD4)

This was an intermediate boundary, separating two quarter-acre plots, with multiple recutting (Fig 4.32). The earliest

ditch to the west may have been the most northerly (5031). This terminated 7.0m from western ditch system (see Fig 6.2), suggesting that, like boundary system 3 to its south, there was an original opening to the west. The later recuts to the west cut across the abandoned western ditch and appeared to terminate within the fills of the second mill leat.

Any physical link between the earlier ditches to the west and the east was lost where they converged to a single narrow ditch, where a slot-like deepening within the base of the ditch and an adjacent length of slot have been interpreted as the foundations for timber beams supporting a bridge (see Fig 4.29b).

The earliest cut at the eastern end (1352/1432) lay to the south and had the most easterly terminal, which pre-dated the extension of the frontage ditch, 12, to form the inturned plot entrance.

In subsequent recutting the terminal retreated westward. The final recut at the eastern end (1430) was a steep-sided, slot-like cut, 0.55m deep, which contained much limestone, some of which was steeply pitched and may have been displaced packing for a timber fence. It also contained one of the few primary pottery dumps recovered, including several near complete vessels both of earlier twelfth-century date (ph 0, 1100–1150) and also a good group of Lyveden A-ware dated to the later twelfth century (ph 1, 1150–1225).

Plot 3 (LSE 3)

Access to this quarter-acre plot was probably originally through a simple, 9.0m-wide opening in the eastern boundary, but this was soon replaced by a funnelled entrance provided with a post-built double gateway, which presumably formed a pen with gates at either end for stock control, particularly the separating or shedding of animals (Fig 4.32, g1; Fig 4.34).

The gateway, g1, was defined by a regular line of eight postholes to the west, typically 0.30–0.50m diameter by 0.10–0.15m deep, and three to the south, in line with the ditch terminal. On the eastern side there was a more irregular scatter of postholes, and some may have been removed by the later entrance. Along the northern side there was a length of ditch (1115), which had probably removed further postholes. It contained flat-lying slabs of limestone, with a 0.25m deep posthole at the western end. Within the gateway there was a compact layer of orange-red clay with sparse pebble inclusions and occasional burnt patches, measuring 3.60m by 3.40m, probably created by trampling. Above this there was a 30mm thick layer of compact orange-brown sandy loam mottled with patches of either reddened or blackened burning.

With the eastward migration of the boundary, a new gateway was formed further to the east, g2. The western side comprised a slot, 0.60m wide by 0.15m deep, which broadened and deepened at either end. Along the southern side a further length of slot, up to 0.90m wide by 0.20m

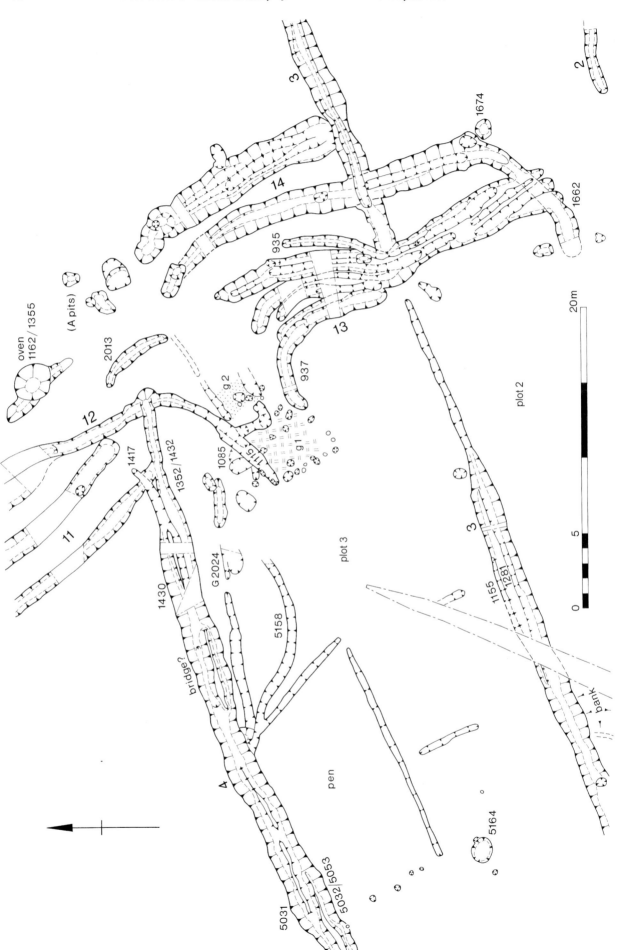

Fig 4.32 : The northern holding, plot 3 with gated entrance (g1 and g2), and boundary ditch systems 3, 4, 11, 12, 13 and 14

deep, ran eastward but was largely removed by later activity. To the north there was a parallel length of slot, 0.50m wide by 0.15m deep. This was also partly removed by later activity, but a faint soil-mark suggested that it was 6.6m long, running to the terminal of a shallow ditch (2013). The new gateway therefore comprised an elongated entrance passage, 3.50m wide, with remnants of a laid surface of gravel and limestone at its western end.

There were several features within the plot (Fig 4.32). A pen, 8.0m wide and 12–15m long, enclosing an area of 108sq.m, was defined by two linear slots, 0.50m wide and 0.10–0.16m deep, and a line of five postholes to the west, 0.27–0.48m diameter and 0.06–0.12m deep. To the south there were two further short lengths of slot. A sub-circular pit (5164), 1.70m diameter by 0.54m deep, had near vertical sides and a flat-bottom. It had a posthole on its eastern edge with a further posthole 0.70m to the west, perhaps suggesting that they supported some structure or device suspended over the pit, but there was no further indication of its function.

To the east of the pen a curving ditch or slot (5158), 0.64m wide by 0.45m deep, had probably held a timber fence, and to its north there was a shallower interrupted linear slot or ditch (G2024). These were probably both concerned with controlling access to a possible bridge crossing the adjacent boundary ditch.

Immediately north of the enclosure entrance there was a cluster of small pits, no more than 0.30m deep. The southernmost pit (1085), 2.30m by 0.90m and 0.25m deep, contained flat-lying pieces of limestone.

Fig 4.33: The primary boundary ditch, 3, separating the northern and southern holdings, looking west

Fig 4.34: The postholes of the double gateway entrance to plot 3, looking east

Ditch system 11 (LSD 11)

Two parallel and slightly curving ditches, 2.0m apart, ran between the domestic enclosure and ditch system 4 (Figs 4.31 and 4.32). They were both shallow, only 0.30–0.35m deep, with no evidence of recutting. They probably belonged with the late tenth-century arrangement and were abandoned before the end of that century.

Ditch system 12 (LSD12)

This ditch formed the frontage to the northern quarter-acre plot (LSE 4), probably replacing ditch system 11 (Figs 4.31 and 4.32). In its original form it comprised a single elongated pit, 7.0–8.0m long by 3.00m wide and 0.20m deep. This was replaced by a ditch, which was later extended southward and curved to the west to meet the northern side of the gateway to plot 3. The small quantity of pottery recovered was of earlier twelfth-century date (ph 0, 1100–1150).

Plot 4 (LSE 4)

While the main access to this plot was generally from the east, for a period in the eleventh century the barn, T34, to the north had its main doors opening into this enclosure. The changes in access involved a number of realignments of the adjacent ditch systems (Fig 4.9).

There were few internal features (Fig 4.31). A line of four irregularly spaced post-pits, 0.40–0.50m deep, formed a partial transverse subdivision, and two postholes to the west, 2.0m apart, may have formed a small two-post structure.

By the middle of the twelfth century, and the introduction of the stone-built manor house, this area had been absorbed into the domestic enclosure of the northern holding, with a new building, S24, occupying the western end.

Ditch system 7 (LSD7), the western boundary

This ditch system ran parallel to the earliest western mill leat, and was cut by the second mill leat, indicating it had been at least partially abandoned by the end of the tenth century (see Fig 6.2). The northern end was retained slightly longer, and cut into pond silts which had probably accumulated during the use of the first watermill, but there was no indication that it was in use into the twelfth century, when the transverse boundaries, 3, 4 and 6, were extended across it.

The original ditch (Fig 6.2, 5082) was a broad, flat-bottomed cut, up to 0.50m deep, which had largely silted before it was recut along its eastern side (5081). The homogeneous fills of clayey silts suggest that it silted rapidly, probably largely as a result of the deposition of clayey silts through overflow from the mill leats.

The northern holding: the northern ditches and plots

Ditch system 8 (LSD8), the defensive ditch

This substantial, L-shaped ditch partially enclosed the original timber buildings of the northern holding (Figs 4.9 and 4.31). It was both broader and deeper than any of the other boundary ditches.

The southern arm (Fig 4.31, 7290; Fig 4.35) was 3.50m wide with a broad, flat-bottom, 0.60m deep, and a steep-sided slot to the north, 1.10m deep. The same profile was evident along much of the western arm, which was 4.00–5.00m wide. This profile was probably a product of successive cuts, but later recutting had removed the relationship. Originally, the western arm continued northward and opened into the mill leats. The deep slot was filled with loose clean yellow sand and gravel with a few pieces of limestone, while red-brown sands with some gravel had accumulated against the edges of the broader ditch.

The ditch was recut within its former limits as a broad and flat-bottomed ditch, 2.00–2.50m wide by 0.60m deep. The primary fill of mottled silty clays, containing some water snails, suggests that at this stage there was frequently standing water within the ditch, perhaps because the western arm now terminated short of the mill leats. Above the primary silts on the southern arm a distinctive layer, 50–80mm thick, of brown loam mixed with grey charcoal flecked sand and fine, grey ashy material, had been deposited from the inner side of the ditch. It contained scattered clusters of large un-abraded pottery sherds, often from single vessels, dated to the later tenth century (ph LS2, 950–975). The remaining fill comprised up to 0.40m of homogeneous and clean red-brown sand with very frequent pebble inclusions, a dumped deposit probably derived from the levelling of an internal bank.

At the eastern end of the southern arm there was a detached ditch segment (Fig 4.31, 7328), 6.70m long, 2.75m wide by 0.55m deep, with a broad flat-bottom, separated from the main ditch by a low ridge. This had a similar sequence of filling, with the final dumped fill of sand and gravel appearing to be contiguous with the final filling of the main ditch.

The western arm was retained through the eleventh century (Fig 4.9). It was filled with sandy loams with pebble inclusions and some limestone, generally more clayey towards the northern end. The upper secondary fills contained more limestone and towards the northern end there were also deposits of burnt debris, reddened soil, grey loams and much charcoal.

At the northern end, a final recut (Fig 4.9, 4803) extended further northward to open into the latest mill leat, M25. Its fills contained frequent large pieces of limestone. The general fill of the subsidence hollow above the western ditches contained both disordered limestone and mortar broadly contemporary with the construction of the stone-built kitchen/bakehouse, S20, which partially overlay the ditch.

Fig 4.35: The excavated southern arm of the early defensive ditch system (8, 7290) enclosing the timber buildings, looking west, showing the broad, flat-bottomed cut with a steep-sided slot to the north (right)

Once the western arm was largely filled, it was replaced by a shallower ditch system lying to the immediate east, with an opening providing access to building T32. The steep-sided cuts suggest either the provision of a timber fence or rapid filling. The southern end cut the secondary fills of the main ditch, and may have continued across to meet ditch system 6 to the west.

The bulk of the large pottery assemblage from the upper fills of the western arm was of earlier twelfth century date (ph 0, 1100–1150), while the limestone and mortar fills of the subsidence hollow above this produced a large group of later twelfth century pottery (ph 1, 1150–1225).

Ditch system 5 (LSD5)

This boundary replaced the southern arm of the domestic enclosure ditch 8 following its backfilling and the introduction of a new timber building range, T34.

The original linear ditch, 0.45m deep, was broken to the east to provide access to the southward facing doors of the new range (Fig 4.9). The ditch was recut (4617) following the demise of this building. The eastern end, abutting the frontage boundary, 10, contained a narrow basal slot and a pair of shallow postholes, perhaps suggesting the provision of a narrow timber bridge (Fig 4.29a).

The small pottery assemblage is dated to the earlier twelfth century (ph 0, 1100–1150). By the later twelfth century this area had been sealed beneath gravel and limestone surfaces, SY2.

Ditch system 6 (LSD6)

This system comprised two short lengths of recut ditch filling the gap between the western boundary, 7 and domestic enclosure ditch, 8 (Figs 4.9 and 6.2). The southern ditch, 6a was the earliest and comprised two or three lengths of ditch separated by openings. It abutted the corner of the main enclosure ditch, 8.

The later ditch, 6, lay to the north on a slightly different alignment (see Fig 6.2, 4578). The eastern end had been heavily disturbed by a later oven and pit complex, but a narrower, slot-like cut with a post-pit (4900), up to 0.75m deep, at the eastern end may indicate the provision of a bridged crossing.

The earlier ditch produced 12 sherds of St Neots-type ware suggesting that is was filled before the end of the eleventh century (ph LS3/2, 1000–1100). The northern ditch was probably filled well before the middle of the twelfth century (ph 0, 1100–1150), as the overlying oven and pit group were in use at that time.

Plot 5 (LSE5)

This north-western corner of the northern holding lay adjacent to the mill pond (Fig 4.31). The only early feature was a shallow linear ditch filled with clean orange-brown sandy loam, almost identical to the soil through which it is cut, and predating ditch 8. To the east further ditches with similarly clean fills pre-dated the construction of the domestic range and the hall, and it is suggested that they formed an intermediate boundary that was set out but was then abandoned and backfilled to permit the construction of the original buildings and the semi-defensive enclosing ditch, 8.

Plot 6 (LSE6), the domestic plot

This plot contained the timber buildings of the northern holding (Figs 4.31 and 4.9). The open area to the north of the buildings and adjacent to the mill leats was devoid of features.

As noted above with respect to plot 5, lengths of ditch which pre-dated the hall, T29, and domestic ranges, T30 (Fig 4.9, D), had been filled with orange-brown sandy loam containing some clean gravel. They appear to have been part of an intermediate boundary ditch that was set out, but not fully excavated, before it was backfilled to permit the construction of the buildings.

Ditch system 9 (LSD9)

The northern end of this ditch cut the fills of the earliest mill leat, M27, making it broadly contemporary with the second and final mills, M26 and M25. It formed the northernmost part of the intermittent linear boundary flanking the eastern side of the western plots (Figs 4.31 and 4.9)

To the north the ditch cut the western side of a large, shallow pit (Fig 4.9, 6734), up to 0.35m deep. The pit fill comprised grey clayey loam and gritty sand containing charcoal, mottles of burnt (reddened) sand and grey to red fine ashy material, suggesting that it had been at least partially filled with dumped debris from hearths or ovens. The boundary ditch terminated immediately adjacent to the wall of the timber hall, T29, where it was only 0.15m deep.

The pottery from the ditch is dated to the earlier twelfth-century (ph 0, 1100–1150), and at the northern end the final fill of tenacious clays was contemporary with the final filling of the adjacent mill leat. The boundary was subsequently redefined by a stone wall.

Plot 7 (LSE7)

This area lay to the north of the timber hall, T29, and south of the mill leats (Fig 4.31), where at least the final leat had a bridged crossing providing access to the river. No metalled surfacing or features lay within this area.

Ditch system 10 (LSD10), the western frontage

This boundary lay between the central courtyard of the northern holding and the access road to the east (Figs 4.31 and 4.9). It was introduced following the creation of the courtyard in the later tenth century (ph LS2, 950–975).

The ditch fully blocked access into the courtyard, but the complex sequence of recutting suggests that there had been access points that had been relocated at each refurbishment of the ditch. The earliest ditch only survived to the north, immediately south of the hall, T29. This length was later abandoned, leaving a 6.0m-wide opening between the ditch and the hall, T29. At the new ditch terminal, there was a pair of pits in the base of the later ditch. These may have held deeply-founded posts, perhaps at one stage forming a gated entrance at the south-eastern corner of the courtyard. An intact dog skull, without mandible, lay within the fill of the northern pit, possibly deliberately placed here as a protective deposit. A later shallower recut ran up to the wall of the timber hall, T29. To the south, a shallow slot, up to 0.30m wide by 0.10m deep, partially surviving along the eastern edge of the later ditch may have held a timber fence. At the southernmost end of the ditch the upper fill of the final cut was a mixed deposit of grey loam with charcoal flecks and small pieces of burnt (reddened) clay, similar to the final fills in the ditches to the south.

The pottery assemblage of St Neots-type ware and some Stamford ware suggests that the ditch was largely filled by the end of the eleventh century (ph LS3/2, 1000–1100). However, small pottery groups from both the northernmost end and from the burnt debris at the southern end are dated to the earlier twelfth century (ph 0, 1100–1150), shortly before the construction of the overlying hall, S18.

The access road (LSE 8)

The approach to the hall, T29, between ditch systems 10 and 18, had a metalled surfaced, 80mm thick, of compact gravel and small pieces of heavily worn limestone, typically between 30–60mm in diameter (Figs 4.31 and 4.9). The underlying soil horizon was generally clean and undisturbed and survived here to its greatest thickness, suggesting that this major point of access must have been surfaced from the earliest phase of occupation. The surface survived for a length of 19.0m and was up to 5.5m wide. To the north a narrow 2.0m wide tongue led directly to the southern door of the timber hall, T29.

To the south, an isolated post-pit, 0.80m in diameter by 0.43m deep, set centrally between the ends of the transverse boundary ditches 18 and 8, marked the formal entrance to the domestic enclosure and was perhaps part of a timber gateway.

Over the road surface there was a layer, up to 50mm thick, of red-brown sand with some pebbles and small pieces of limestone. The clean red-brown sand matrix, similar to the pre-late Saxon soil horizon, suggests that this was a dumped deposit perhaps forming a levelling layer beneath a later road surface.

Plot 13 (LSE13), the northern central yard

The trackway from the east entered the northern part of the central yard at the south-east corner, while the access to the timber building complex was diametrically opposite at the north-west corner (Fig 4.31). While a road surface did survive to the north, the area of plot 13 had been disturbed by later medieval activity.

Ditch system 19 (LSD19)

This boundary separated the plot to the east of the early buildings from the watermill complex (Figs 4.31 and 4.9).

The earliest ditch (Fig 4.9, 6788), 2.00m wide by 0.70m deep, cut the fills of the early mill leat, M27, indicating that the boundary was only introduced following the demise of the original watermill. A pit rich in environmental remains was cut into the fills of the original ditch, indicating the deliberate burying of domestic rubbish in the soft ditch fills. The ditch system was recut, with the introduction of a southward return arm (6590). The new ditch was up to 3.50m wide and up to 0.80m deep, and was recut at least once. A good pottery group indicates that it was filled during the earlier twelfth century (ph 0, 1100–1150).

Plot 9 (LSE9)

Much of the enclosed area to the east of the late Saxon buildings had been disturbed by later medieval activity, and only narrow strips alongside the three boundary ditches were stripped to late Saxon levels (Fig 4.31).

A pair of parallel linear slots (Fig 4.9, 7192 and 7193), set 3.00m apart, lay immediately south-east of the hall. They were up to 2.80m long, 0.40–0.60m wide and 0.25m deep, and there were some nearby postholes. They may

have been the wall-trenches and postholes of a small timber structure. To the north, east of the ancillary mill building, T35, there were several small pits or postholes (G7019).

Ditch system 18 (LSD18), the eastern frontage

This ditch system flanked the approach to the hall and also bounded the southern and western side of the plot to the east of the buildings (Figs 4.31, 4.36 and 4.9).

Initially, a linear ditch system formed part of the southern boundary to the domestic plot, and if there was a contemporary ditch flanking the approach to the hall it had been removed by the later ditches. The original boundary comprised two broad but relatively shallow ditches flanking a central entrance. The western ditch (Fig 4.9, 6486) was 2.90m wide by 0.55m deep, becoming narrower and shallower at either end. The homogeneous ditch fill contained much animal bone and a large pottery assemblage, 218 sherds, of St Neots-type ware of later tenth century date (Ph LS2, 950–975), indicating that the ditch system was redeveloped when the courtyard arrangement of the domestic buildings was introduced.

The eastern ditch (Fig 4.36, 79), was of similar dimensions, and had a shallow recut along the northern side. The fill of the subsidence hollow, dated to earlier twelfth century (ph 0, 1100–1150), contained much burnt debris, charcoal, burnt clay and heat reddened limestone, and similar material occurred beyond the ditch as a surface layer. It was all dumped debris from an adjacent malt oven (393).

Within the 6.40m wide entrance there was a narrow linear slot, 3.80m long, 0.20m wide by 0.08m deep, containing three postholes, 0.10–0.15m deep, which probably held the uprights of a timber gateway. A scatter of other postholes to the west might have held a fence between the gateway and the ditch terminal.

At the end of the tenth century the original system was replaced by an L-shaped ditch, up to 0.75m deep, which also flanked the approach to the hall (Figs 4.31; 4.9, 6544 and 4.36, 149). It was recut at least twice and the final recut ran down the centre of the system. The easternmost end was only partially excavated, but for the final 7.0m the ditch comprised successive, slot-like cuts 0.60–0.85m wide and 0.30m deep, perhaps suggesting that there was a new entrance in the same location as its predecessor. The fill of the later southern cut contained burnt debris similar to that over the earlier ditch to the north-east and this presumably also came from the nearby oven.

The secondary and final fills, particularly near the hall, contained much animal bone and a large pottery assemblage dated to the earlier twelfth century (ph 0, 1100–1150). The subsidence hollow above this, of the same general date, contained much large limestone rubble and mortar, probably discarded construction debris from the building of the new stone hall on the opposite side of the approach road.

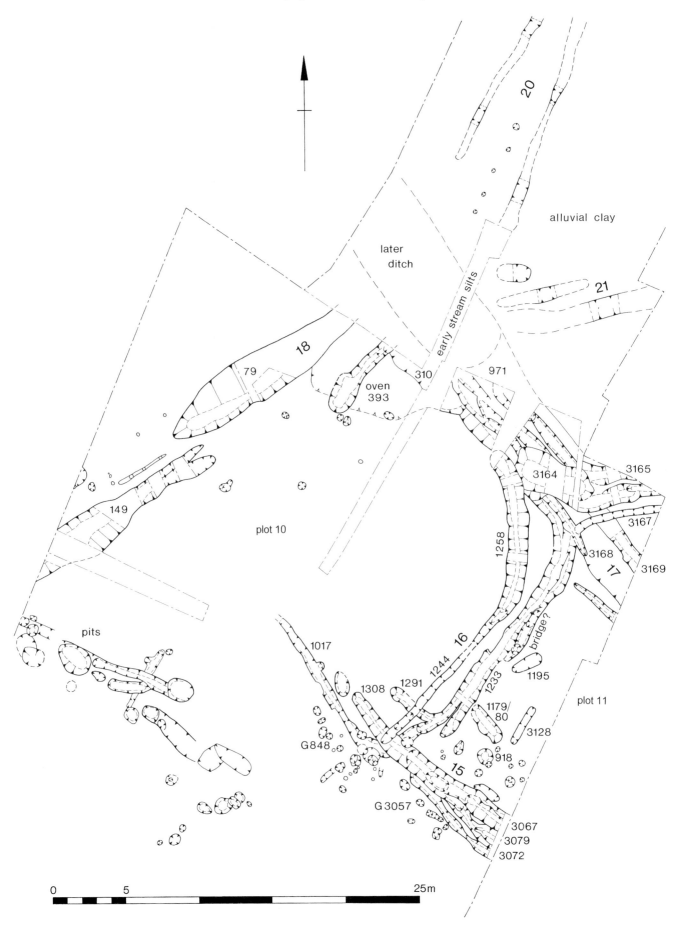

Fig 4.36: The northern holding and the eastern enclosures, plots 10 and 11, and ditch systems 15–18 and 20–21

Plot 10: the central yard (LSE 10)

Initially this area was part of the half-acre open central yard, with the eastern enclosures impinging onto the idealised rectangular plan form (Fig 4.36). There was a sparse scatter of undated small pits or postholes, but there were no major features in this area until it was partly cut off from the yard in the earlier twelfth century, when a linear slot, probably holding a timber fence (1017), was extended northward from the boundary ditches to the south. At this time the malt oven was functioning in the northern corner of the plot.

A linear pit group to the south-west, forming a further encroachment onto the central yard, appeared in the later twelfth century (ph 1), when the area was taken into the extended domestic enclosure of the medieval manor house.

The ditches and plots of the eastern enclosures

The eastern frontage: ditch system 15 (LSD15)

The earliest ditches (Fig 4.36, 3079 and 3072) were partly removed by a recut (1308) that extended further northward. This length had a distinctive secondary fill containing mottles or blocks of distinct soil types, suggesting that it was deliberately infilled in the earlier twelfth century. Later recuts, terminated further to the south-east.

Alongside the ditch system there was a group of shallow pits or postholes (G3057), which may have formed a short length of fence either flanking the ditch or blocking an opening following the final retreat of the ditch terminal. They may have been contemporary with a further group of postholes to the north (G848). The secondary fills of the latest recut produced a large assemblage of earlier twelfth-century date, but including some later material (ph 1, 1150–1225).

Ditch system 16 (LSD16)

The south-easternmost of the two ditch systems was the earlier (Fig 4.36, 1233). At the mid-point the narrowest length was flanked by a flat-bottomed slot with terminal postholes, possibly indicating the provision of a timber bridge (Fig 4.29c). To the north successive ditches turned westward and ran alongside the northern boundary, 17, cutting the earlier phases of that system. At the southern end of the boundary there was a complex series of ditch terminals, which progressively retreated to the north. The earliest ditch had met the south-eastern end of a linear slot (1017), 0.80m wide by 0.40m deep, with a narrow basal width of 0.30m, forming a partial, probably fenced, boundary to enclosure 10 to the north.

The entire boundary was relocated to the west, and the new system had two distinct components. The northern half was a broader and deeper ditch (1258), 1.40m wide by up to 0.50m deep. The southern half was a narrow, steep-sided and flat-bottomed slot (1244), 0.50–0.70m wide by

0.20–0.35m deep, with the fill containing scattered pieces of limestone. It had probably held a timber fence. At the southern end there was a group of postholes and post-pits (G848), some of which contained limestone packing set vertically against the cut sides, while flat-laid or partially disordered limestone also indicates that some had been carefully backfilled.

The fills of the earlier ditches produced good groups of earlier twelfth-century pottery (ph 0, 1100–1150), with a small amount of later pottery (ph 1, 1150–1225) from the final fills. The small quantity of pottery from the post-pits, G848, is dated to the earlier to later twelfth century (ph 0 or 1).

Ditch system 17 (LSD17)

There was a complex boundary system to the north-east alongside the northern stream channel.

The earliest features were two parallel ditches (Fig 4.36. 3168 and 3169), filled with gritty, sandy silts with a high pebble content. The next phase of ditches were on a different alignment (3165 and 3167) and included a large sub-rectangular pit (3164), 5.50m long by 2.70m wide and 0.60m deep. These features had streaked and mottled fills of clayey and sandy silts with moderate pebble inclusions, and contained a small assemblage of St Neots type ware, suggesting a tenth to eleventh century date (ph LS2–LS3/2).

The early ditches were sealed by a layer, up to 0.50m thick, of mixed silty and sandy clays with some pebbles, deposited during the early twelfth-century episode of flooding that led to the demise of the watermills. A boundary and drainage system was quickly re-established by the digging of a broad shallow ditch (971), up to 3.50m wide by 0.90m deep. The primary fill comprised grey clayey loam mottled with brown to greenish-brown sandy clay, indicating that the area was still flooding at intervals. The secondary fill was a similar grey clayey loam but it contained substantial quantities of burnt (reddened) sand, charcoal flecks and pieces and scattered limestone with some burnt pieces and much animal bone and pottery dated to the early twelfth century (ph 0, 1100–1150. A particular concentration of burnt debris at the northern end, including pieces of limestone with reddened edges and small pieces of fired clay may have come from the malt oven to the north (393). The final fills of the ditch and a broader hollow beyond produced a large assemblage dated to the later twelfth century (ph 1, 1150–1225).

Plot 11 (LSE 11)

Only a 5.0–6.0m wide strip at the north-western end was excavated (Fig 4.36). To the south-west there was a scatter of ten postholes and post-pits. The deeper examples, at 1.00m diameter by 0.60m deep, frequently contained limestone, often steeply pitched, derived from displaced packing stones. They may have formed the southern side of an enclosure surrounding a small group of pits. A bowl-shaped pit (918), 1.10m diameter by 0.20m deep, had blackened charcoal-flecked sand against the sides and a fill of tenacious yellow-green clay had its surface fire-hardened and blackened, forming the base of a small hearth or oven. An adjacent similar pit (1179) had been largely removed by an elongated pit (1180), 2.60m long, 0.95m wide and 0.30m deep. A second elongated pit (1195) lay 4.0m to the north-east, and to the south-east there was a linear slot (3128). The postholes produced at total of 38 sherds of pottery dated to the earlier twelfth century date (ph 0, 1100–1150), while the pits produced some earlier and later twelfth century groups (ph 0–1).

Ditch systems east of the northern stream

The area to the north-east of the northern stream channel was the lowest lying area within the settlement, and is largely an unknown quantity as only a small area was partially investigated (Fig 4.36). There was no evidence for any tenth and eleventh century use, although this could have been concealed by twelfth-century alluvial clays which covered the entire area and were not excavated. Ditch systems 20 and 21 were cut into the accumulated alluvial clays in the later twelfth century (ph 1).

Ditch system 20 (LSD20)

A pair of roughly parallel ditches, up to 0.80m wide by 0.25m deep and filled with grey clay, produced a small pottery assemblage dated to the later twelfth century (ph 1, 1150–1225). A line of five postholes lay between them. To the north-east (Fig 4.28) three short lengths of ditch or slot may have formed a small, rectangular enclosure or pen, 7.0m wide by at least 9.0m long.

Ditch system 21 (LSD21)

This boundary comprised two parallel ditches, 1.25m wide by 0.30m, and a pit, 0.65m deep (Fig 4.36). They all had clayey fills with some gravel inclusions and produced small pottery groups dating to the later twelfth century (ph 1, 1150–1225). A later continuation of this boundary line to the east was indicated by geophysical survey, which shows a boundary wall.

The western ditch terminals lay at the southern end of a broad boundary/drainage ditch formed along the northern part of the earlier ditch system and stream channel, which survived as a well defined earthwork (Fig 1.6).

Miscellaneous features to the west of the settlement

A number of isolated features were recovered within the quarry area to the west and south-west of the main settlement area, none of which have been well dated.

To the south of the Cotton Brook two postholes and a larger pit or post-pit were seen in the quarry edge section, cut into the soil horizon sealing a mound of Neolithic date and truncated by the ridge and furrow of the medieval field system (Fig 3.1). They may represent some minor structure or activity possibly of early to late Saxon date.

Towards the western end of the prehistoric Long Mound, an area of limestone and ironstone, 9.0m in diameter and up to 0.50m thick, was observed during the removal of the mound by box scrapers (Fig 3.1). There appeared to be a concentration of the larger limestone blocks, up to 0.60m long, around the circumference, perhaps forming a kerb, with adjacent areas exclusively in ironstone, suggesting some care in its formation. A nearby pit, 1.00m in diameter by at least 0.40m deep and containing some limestone within its fills, was probably associated. A few pottery sherds recovered from this area suggest a possible twelfth-century date.

Immediately beyond the stream course along the western side of the settlement the surface of the prehistoric Long Mound had been disturbed, over an area measuring 26m east-west by 20m north-south, by a convoluted complex of sinuous and intersecting features believed to have been animal burrows. They were observed on the surviving surface of the prehistoric mound and continued right through the body of the mound, a depth of 0.50m, into the underlying soil horizon, but rarely penetrated the natural gravel to any depth. The individual 'runs' were typically 0.20–0.30m wide and they occasionally terminated at broader lobes, 1.00–1.25m long by 0.50–0.75m wide, suggesting the presence of chambers. They were filled with sandy loams similar to the pre-late Saxon soil horizon and, although it was not demonstrated in excavation, they were probably in use prior to the accumulation of the alluvial clays which fully sealed this area.

No animal bones were recovered from these features, but bone preservation was generally poor in this area of the site. These runs may indicate the presence of a small rabbit warren located on the slightly higher, drier and softer ground provided by the prehistoric mound, but there was no indication that this was an artificially created warren and rabbit bones are only sparsely represented in the bone assemblage. While it is undated, the warren could not have appeared until the introduction of the rabbit in the later eleventh century and by the mid to later twelfth century the flooding and the consequent accumulation of alluvial clays across this area would have led to its demise.

5   The Medieval Manor (AD 1100–1250)

The transition from the timber halls forming the residence of a minor late Saxon thegn to the stone ranges of a minor medieval manor house, was a period of physical change that took place in the wake of the political changes resulting from the Norman Conquest. However, the rebuilding took place many decades after the conquest and comprised an almost exact replacement of the timber ranges in stone. Whatever the political changes, the economic function of the manor as the centre of a farm estate, including the running of the watermill, appear to have continued unchanged, at least initially.

Change was not far away, however, as over exploitation of the land for arable cultivation may have been responsible for a period of catastrophic flooding and the deposition of alluvial silts that effectively created the medieval floodplain, threatened the very existence of the settlement and brought the use of the watermill to an end. These new circumstances initiated a response in which the processing of arable products, such as producing malt for brewing and perhaps the fulling of cloth became central, cash producing activities and began a physical reorganisation of the settlement as the need for new buildings brought about the creation of a frontage onto the central yard.

The medieval rebuilding (AD 1100–1200)

The early twelfth century saw the appearance of stone buildings on the northern holding, largely as direct replacements for their timber predecessors. The new arrangement, with its two-storey hall, detached kitchen range, dovecote and other ancillary buildings formed a small manor house, and this is consistent with the documentary evidence that in the twelfth century West Cotton was a sub-infeudated manor, the 1/2 hide held by Frumbold de Denford from the Clare/Gloucester fee (Fig 5.1 and Plate 4). The usage of the plots attached to the manor remained much as before although the domestic plot expanded, taking in the formerly separate plot to its south, while through the second half of the century the boundary systems and clusters of pits, often containing dumped debris from hearths and ovens, encroached onto the margins of the central open yards, reducing the extent of this space (Fig 5.2).

The retention of the boundary between the northern and southern holdings suggests that the southern holding also survived as a separate entity. Little can be said about its development, although the usage of the plots continued with the provision of a pen for stock control and a possible drying oven, and it is suggested that the southern holding may have continued to parallel the development of the northern holding as an independent property, and perhaps a second small manor, but held of the Duchy of Lancaster fee.

Through the first half of the twelfth century there was a dramatic change in the topographical setting of the settlement, which is fully described in Chapter 6. A period of catastrophic flooding carried down quantities of silts and deposited these across the valley floor. It has been argued by Mark Robinson that this was most probably a direct consequence of over-exploitation of arable cultivation on the valley sides and, if so, the process had led to disastrous soil erosion within 150 years of the commencement of the open field system.

With the rising ground levels around the settlement, as the alluvial silts accumulated year by year, the watermill system became inoperable and had been abandoned before 1150. An initial attempt to contain any flooding of the settlement by the provision of drainage ditches along the former mill leats failed, and by the middle of the century a flood embankment had been thrown up around the settlement (Fig 5.3). The stream carrying the water that had formerly supplied the mills ran beyond the bank at a significantly higher level than the former mill leats. A further consequence was that the adjacent river channel also silted, and had probably become largely redundant by the end of the twelfth century, although this event cannot be directly dated.

The redevelopment of the northern holding

The introduction of stone buildings on the northern holding was a progressive, rather than a wholesale, replacement of the late Saxon timber buildings, so that occupation would have continued uninterrupted, if inconvenienced, while building works were in progress. The pottery dating is too imprecise to allow the exact sequence of rebuilding to be defined, and the description follows a logical but not necessarily the original sequence.

The construction of a new hall, set across the formerly

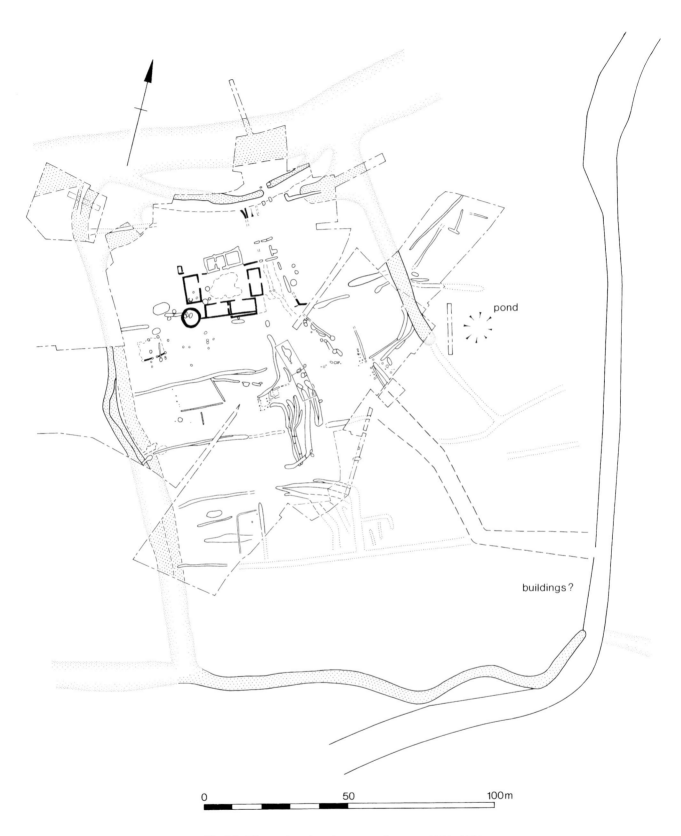

pond

buildings?

0   50   100m

Fig 5.1: The medieval settlement and manor, 1100–1250

open eastern end of the courtyard, may have been the first stage of rebuilding, as it formed the focus of the manor and did not directly replace a preceding timber building (Fig 5.2). The unique presence of scaffolding posts and deeply set, pitched-stone foundations indicate that it stood higher then the other contemporary buildings, so it probably had an upper storey. A remnant of wall to the north may have supported an external stairway. In the hall, the hearth was set against the wall, but the lack of any stone surround indicates that it was probably provided with a smoke hood,

rather than being a full fireplace with a chimney. The road in front of the hall was metalled with gravel and later limestone (Fig 5.4). A pair of postholes cutting the upper metalled surface indicates the provision of a timber gateway in line with the southern end of the hall (Fig 5.3).

A new southern range may have been a closely contemporary construction. The western wall of this building directly overlay the eastern wall of an earlier timber building, suggesting that the timber range may have been retained as an abutting extension. Limestone metalling

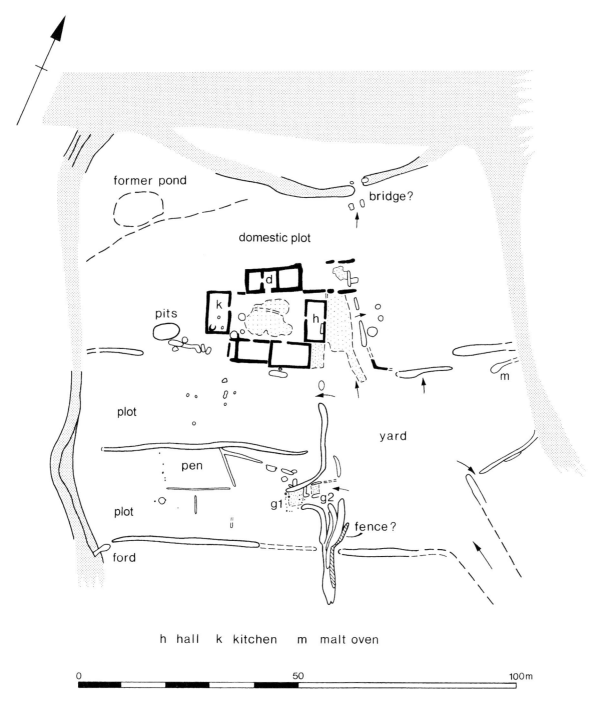

h hall   k kitchen   m malt oven

0   50   100m

Fig 5.2: The manor house, early twelfth century

between the ends of the southern range and the hall suggests the provision of a small lean-to structure. The plot boundary ditch to the south of the new range was also backfilled, and the removal of this boundary suggests that the formerly separate plot to the south was taken into an enlarged domestic plot.

The detached timber range at the western end of the courtyard was directly replaced by a stone-built kitchen/bakehouse, with the southern bay containing a circular corner oven and successive open hearths.

The Saxon timber hall was probably demolished as soon as the new stone hall was completed, but it was immediately replaced by a new, shorter but substantial timber building of principal-post construction. The provision of a drain and soak away pit suggest that it may have served as a byre or stable, although if it did there must have been a broader doorway, perhaps in the western wall.

The old timber domestic range appears to have been retained, so that the courtyard would have been fully enclosed by a combination of stone and timber buildings.

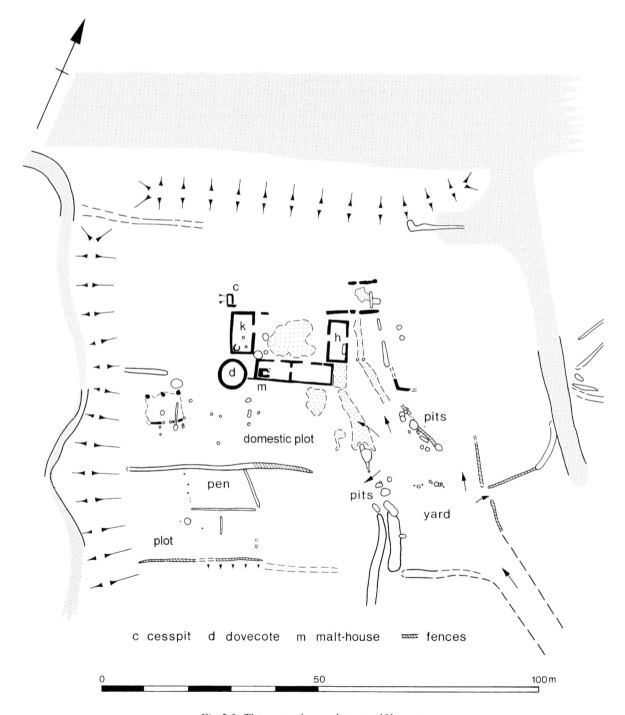

Fig 5.3: The manor house, later twelfth century

To the west of the main buildings a cluster of several pits contained quantities of burnt debris, including fired clay, and at least two pits held *in situ* deposits, indicating their use as external ovens or kilns (Fig 5.2). The carbonised seeds in the fills suggest that they were probably used both as malt ovens and as general drying ovens. At the north-eastern corner of the central yard, well away from the domestic buildings, there was another malt oven, and debris from this was deposited in and over the nearby boundary ditches.

Further redevelopment from the middle of the twelfth century included the demolition of the old timber domestic range. The combined timber and stone southern range was also demolished and replaced by a two-roomed stone range with a malt oven at the western end, the first to be set within a building (Fig 5.3). At least part of the area south of this range was surfaced with gravel and limestone. To the west, between the kitchen and the new malt house, there was a circular dovecote, and a stone-lined cess pit to the north of the kitchen probably appeared at the about the same time. So it is in the later decades of the twelfth century that we see the fully developed stone-built manor house with its buildings set around a courtyard, with the hall dominating the eastern end, and accessible to visitors, while the less savoury aspects of life, the malt house, the dovecote, the kitchen and the cess pit were grouped around the western end of the courtyard, away from the direct sight of visitors (Fig 5.5).

To the south of the buildings there was a new timber range, of principal-post construction but with the sill beam for the southern wall set on stone footings. The provision of an internal drain indicates that it was used as a byre or stable, either complementing or replacing the similar timber structure built over the site of the late Saxon hall.

At the same time, recut boundary ditches and new pit groups encroached onto the central open yard from both the west and east, making the approach to the hall narrower and appearing more elongated. The group of pits on the western side of the yard contained burnt debris and included one possible oven. They may have replaced the general drying oven function of the earlier pits to the west, but much of the debris might have come from the hall and the new malt house. On the eastern side of the yard there was a group of similar pits, and in one instance joining pottery sherds were recovered from pits on either side of the road. A formal southern end to this enlarged domestic plot may have been provided by a line of pits or post-pits running across the open space (Fig 5.3).

The southern quarter-acre plot to the west was retained through the twelfth century, and was slightly enlarged as the eastern boundary was repeatedly recut to encroach further onto the yard to the east. The initial provision of

Fig 5.4: The manor buildings and the metalled road, looking west

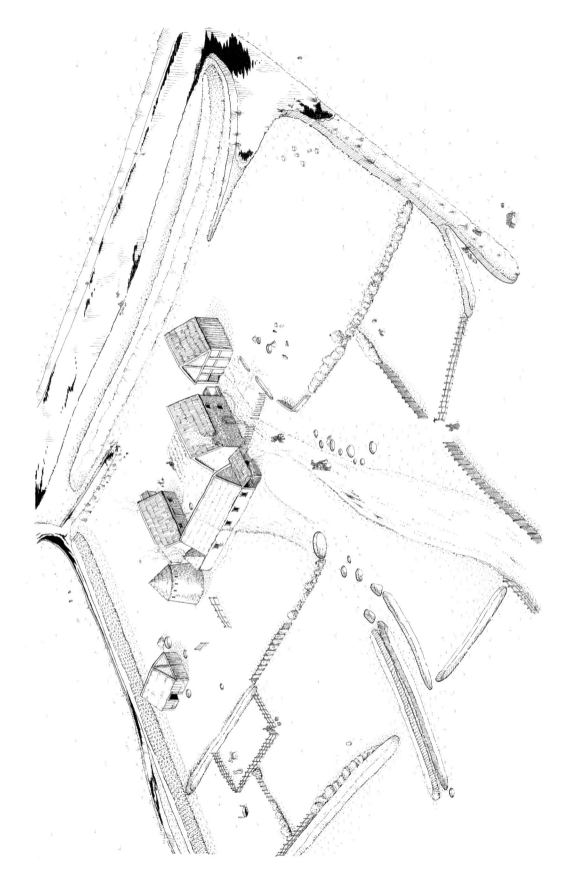

Fig 5.5: The manor house as it may have looked in the later twelfth century (Alex Thompson)

a complex double timber gateway and a second similar arrangement, as well as the internal pens and sub-divisions, indicate that the plot was used to house and manage stock. The later entrances were less complex, perhaps suggesting that such activities were no longer practiced in such close proximity to the manor house.

Although there were changes in organisation, the definition of the plots had still largely been provided by a system of the boundary ditches through the earlier twelfth century. To the north, east of the hall, the substantial late Saxon ditch system was abandoned when the hall was built, with the final ditch fill containing mortar and stone that was probably dumped surplus building material. This ditch was replaced by much shallower ditches and an L-shaped length of wall that marked the approach to the hall.

On the other boundaries many of the latest recuts, and particularly the lengths adjacent to the central yards and the approach to the hall, were steep-sided and slot-like, and may have contained timber fences, although no direct evidence of this was obtained. The boundary between the northern and southern holdings may eventually have been provided with a fence along much of its length. This decline in ditch recutting and the provision of fenced boundaries can be seen as a precursor to the introduction of walled boundaries in the thirteenth century.

The eastern enclosures

As previously, this area may have been either peasant holdings or part of the plot system of the northern manor. There were repeated modifications of the boundary ditches at the northern end, but without any significant encroachment to the west, and many of the later cuts may have held fences. The sequence of ditch recutting has been described in Chapter 4.

The southern holding

Like the northern holding, the recutting of the boundaries at the northern end of the southern holding, showed a progressive encroachment onto the yard to the east. Of the two plots available for excavation, the southern plot contained a substantial pen, formed by an L-shaped post-in-trench structure, and a similarly built sub-division, suggesting that the area was used for stock control. However, a pit within the pen may have been a small drying oven, suggesting an alternative use for at least part of the twelfth century. While there were no stone buildings in this area until the end of the twelfth century, it is suggested that a domestic building complex most probably lay within the unexcavated southern plot, and would be expected to have paralleled the northern plot with timber buildings progressively replaced in stone.

The abandonment of the watermill and the creation of the flood embankment

The abandonment of the watermill was, archaeologically, the most obvious act within a much larger drama that affected the entire settlement during the twelfth century. Given its complex and specialised nature, the evidence relating to the full sequence of the late Saxon and medieval mill system and the subsequent drainage ditches, the flood embankment and the deposition of alluvial silts around the site will be fully described in Chapter 6, and only needs the briefest of summaries here.

It is considered most likely that the latest watermill was still in use when the rebuilding in stone began in the early twelfth century, as there would appear to have been little point in the provision of a new two-storey stone manor house if the threat from flooding and the abandonment of the watermill, and the resultant loss of income from milling, were events that were already in progress.

Immediately following the abandonment of the watermill, the provision of drainage ditches indicates a determination to maintain the manor house once the effort and expenditure of rebuilding in stone was underway. These drainage ditches were inadequate as flooding continued, and the level of the accumulated alluvium would have risen eventually to the ground level within the settlement. The determination to maintain the settlement is vividly illustrated by the provision of over 500 metres of protective floodbank up to six metres wide and approaching one metre high. The bank was formed of the alluvial clays themselves, and so involved no long-distance importation of material, but it obviously required the considerable physical efforts of those dependent on the manor. To the north-east, where there was no bank, a probable former stream channel was partially dug out to form a drainage ditch (Figs 5.3 and 5.5).

Ultimately, the accumulation of alluvial silts beyond the bank raised the ground surface to around 1.0m higher than the ground level within the settlement. Before the end of the century the process was over. The adjacent river channel was redundant or near redundant, and eventually its former course was to be entirely concealed by the general alluvial cover, although exactly when this occurred has not been determined. The digging of new boundaries into the accumulated alluvial silts to the north-east in the later twelfth century suggests that alluvial deposition had ceased or was at least infrequent, with the flood bank apparently providing an adequate protection to the occupied settlement.

The development of the frontage (AD 1200–1250)

During the first half of the thirteenth century the principal buildings of the manor continued in use, but to their south the appearance of new buildings on both the northern and southern holdings formed a western frontage onto the central yard that significantly changed the appearance of the settlement (Fig 5.6). The economic force behind these developments seems clear. The new buildings included a barn and two specialised processing rooms but no certain domestic rooms. There was therefore an expansion of space and facilities for the storing and processing of the products of arable agriculture. This included barley for malting, although the malt house was also used for drying other crops, while the processing rooms were perhaps for the fulling of woollen cloth, to close the weave and remove the grease to make it suitable for use or for sale at market. These developments were just the first stage of expansion of these activities, as will be seen when the slightly later development of the plots to the east, further development of the southern holding and the redevelopment of northern manor house are considered. As might be expected, wheat was the predominant cereal in the environmental record.

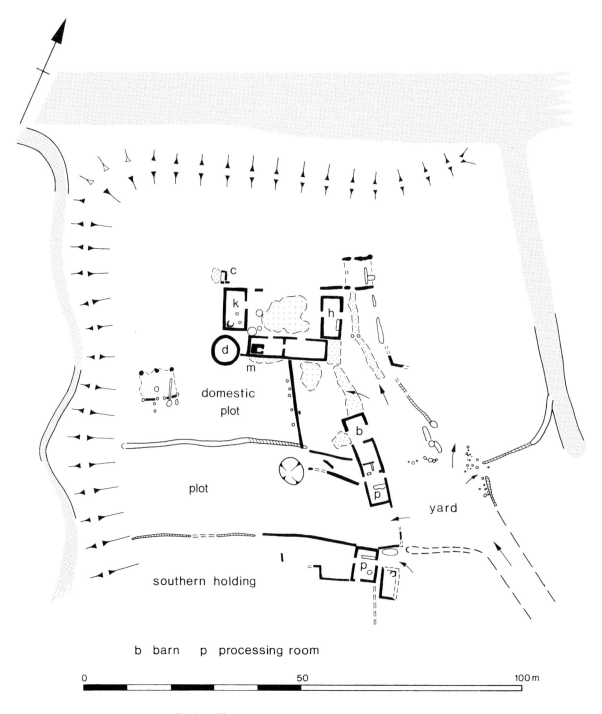

b barn   p processing room

0   50   100 m

Fig 5.6: The manor house, earlier thirteenth century

A manorial barn

The new range was constructed over an earlier pit group and the backfilled boundary ditches that had previously defined the frontage (Fig 5.6, b). The building was poorly preserved, but comprised two large rooms. There was a barn to the north, 11m long with opposed 3.0m wide doorways. The internal features in the southern room, p, included a stone-lined trough, a hearth and a possible stone-packed, soak-away pit, which indicate that it was used for a specialised processing activity, possibly the fulling of woollen cloth.

Contemporary developments in the plot to the rear of the new frontage are difficult to determine, but the first walled yards and boundaries were probably created at this time.

The boundary ditch separating the southern plot from the domestic area appears to have been filled by the end of the twelfth century, but the new north-south and east-west boundary walls converged on its final eastern terminal, demonstrating continuity of the boundary system, and to the west it was probably still marked by some above ground feature, perhaps a remnant of bank, a hedge or even a fence. A north-south wall defined a yard, at least partially surfaced, between the northern buildings and the new range, while a pair of parallel east-west boundary walls flanked a narrow, metalled approach to the rear of the processing room of the new range (Fig 5.6). As in the later periods, the southern plot was a single open area without any surfacing.

The boundary with the southern holding was also retained. To the east the ditch may have been replaced by a wall, while to the west the final, steep-sided recut may have held a fence flanking a remnant of bank, the only instance where a bank and boundary survived into the thirteenth century. The former eastern continuation of this ditch, partitioning the central yard, may have been infilled at this time, to create a single central yard.

The eastern enclosures

Only the northernmost end was available for excavation, but there was more evidence for the provision of fences supplementing or complementing boundary ditches here than was obtained from any other boundary system. This may have resulted from their provision towards the end of the twelfth century, when the boundaries to the west were being largely removed prior to the development of the buildings forming the new frontage.

The southern holding, tenement B

The appearance of a purpose built processing room with a stone-lined trough, large hearth and a rubble filled soak-away pit, may have occurred at around 1200 AD (Fig 5.6), in parallel with the introduction of the barn and processing room on the northern holding. None of the other buildings were certainly introduced at this time, although a small building to the east may have been a

contemporary bakehouse. Remnants of external walls suggest the provision of a small walled yard to the west of the building.

The material and environmental evidence

Pottery use in the twelfth century was very much a continuation from the previous century. Most of the glazed Stamford ware vessels, including spouted pitchers, came from twelfth-century deposits, as well as all of the large Thetford ware storage jars. This may reflect a growing wealth and a more common use of better quality vessels on the table and the importation of goods in the large storage jars. This is also seen in the recovery of a near complete Oxford ware jug from one of the pits and ovens to the west of the manor house, at a time when glazed jugs are far from common household items.

The St Neots-type ware was effectively directly replaced by the medieval Shelly Coarseware tradition, which comprised a similar range of utilitarian jars for daily domestic use, including the distinctive Top Hat jars used for cooking, but now other vessels forms such as larger bowls, some of which were used for dairying, and plain handled-jugs were becoming more common. Cotswold-type oolitic wares offered more in the way of simple decoration including wavy lines and finger-impressed rims, and appear to have come in from somewhere further away, perhaps Lincolnshire.

By the later twelfth century the products of the local pottery industry based on the villages of Lyveden and Stanion, only some 14km (9 miles) to the north-west of Raunds, were taking over the domestic coarsewares, with a range of jars and bowls, sometimes with simple wavy line decoration and finger-impressed rims, and also including some unglazed jugs and a few larger storage jars strengthened with thumb-impressed, applied strips running down the outside.

The finds assemblage associated with the manor includes a number of items common through the twelfth century and continuing into the thirteenth century, but rare or absent within the later tenements. For instance, all three gilded buckle plates (Fig 11.3), the four finger rings and three of the four earrings are associated with the twelfth century manor, and presumably reflect its greater status and wealth in comparison to the later tenements, both in the range and the quality of these quite basic items of dress and jewellery. In addition, the large quantity of finds from the yards of tenement E, which overlay the site of the manor house, must include residual material from the manor and the full assemblage did contain six of the nine brooches from the site, including the two most ornate examples, and four of the six tweezers.

In fact, while the finds do appear to denote that the twelfth-century manor was more affluent and did have higher social pretensions than the medieval tenements, such items as gilded buckle plates are only one short step above the basic level and support the idea that West Cotton lay at the bottom of the manorial ladder.

As a further signifier of status, there are two bone gaming pieces (see Fig 11.9), one of which came from the floor of the hall and another from a later but nearby deposit. These have been interpreted as simple stylised chess pieces worked from lengths of sheep bone, and the playing of chess would denote the presence of educated residents. However, these pieces are very simple and appear to be homemade, and do not approach the elaborate and highly-decorated pieces, often in antler and made by craftsmen, found on other manorial sites, such as a highly decorated rook from the moated manor house at Tempsford, Bedfordshire (Maull and Chapman 2005, 78–80, fig 6.3 and plate 15; Chapman 2005). A bone tableman, decorated with ring-and-dot motifs, was recovered from medieval deposits in tenement E, but may be more likely to have been in use in the manor house.

The residents of the manor house also appear to have had riding horses, as a single prick spur and two snaffle bits come from contemporary contexts (Fig 11.29).

The presence of combined spatulae and pointed-end pinbeaters indicates that the two-beam loom was in use in the twelfth century manor house, but the absence of these weaving implements from later deposits might suggest that weaving was not carried out in the medieval tenements. A further item in bone was a near complete musical pipe fashioned on a long slender bone, possibly a deer metatarsal, which may have been a rare example of a reed pipe, the ancestor of the chanter for the Northumbrian pipes and the Scottish bagpipes (see Fig 11.8)

The weeds present in the charred plant assemblages are the most typical of autumn sown crops on lighter calcareous soils, indicating the cultivation of the valley slopes for cereals. However, other weed species indicate that crops from the heavy calcareous claylands were also being processed. A smaller proportion of the weed assemblage is characteristic of soils likely to be found on the gravels of the floodplain. This latter group are typically present in material from the plots of the manor house, which produced some sprouted grain, relatively high numbers of oat and barley, and relatively little rye. In contrast, the ditches flanking the eastern plots produced much rye, hardly any oat, some barley and no sprouted grain. This would suggest that the manor house was receiving some of its crops from the floodplain, and that these crops were probably oats, barley or dredge intended for brewing, whereas the eastern plots, which may have been occupied by peasant houses dependant on the manor, were probably receiving more crops from the valley slopes where rye, rye and bread wheat maslin, and feed or pot barley were grown.

It is of interest, that a similar pattern was seen later in the life of the settlement, when tenement A was also apparently receiving some of its crops from the floodplain, perhaps suggesting that a specific piece of land originally under the control of the manor later ended up under the control of tenement A. This may have lain on gravels at the margin of the floodplain, and therefore at least largely beyond the area that was subject to alluviation, such as the area of remnant ridge and furrow to the immediate south of West Cotton.

While the arable base of the settlement would have remained largely unchanged, a particular feature of this period was the presence of a number of ovens and associated pits containing dumped debris from the ovens. An earth-cut oven to the east of the manor was evidently a malt oven from the large quantities of charred sprouted barley found in associated features.

However, a demolished oven set in a large pit to the west of the kitchen, and debris from other nearby pits, appear to indicate a broader use for general crop drying. Weed seeds and cereal grain were recovered in roughly equal proportions, but chaff was also common along with large numbers of legume pod fragments, a few seeds of flax and a variety of other material including leaf fragments, thorns and buds, a hazelnut shell, frond fragments of bracken, some possible moss capsules and a large amount of unidentified herbaceous material. The cereal grain component was dominated by free-threshing wheat, but hulled wheat, rye, oat and barley grain were also present, along with hulled wheat, rye and barley chaff.

It can be envisaged that this particular oven was perhaps largely devoted to the general drying of any materials coming in wet from the fields or meadows and requiring drying before going into storage, with this evidently including cereal products, animal fodder and perhaps general herbage and bracken for either strewing across the floors of the manor house or as animal bedding.

The remains showed evidence for the use of a bread wheat and rye mixed together, as a maslin, while rivet wheat and rye maslin was less common. A large quantity of rye chaff from a ditch on the eastern enclosures provided the only evidence for rye being grown as a pure crop, perhaps suggesting that it was associated with dependent peasants rather than the manor house. There was also evidence for oats and barley grown as crops in their own right, and both were perhaps also malted separately. Both two-row and six-row barley were grown although the two-row forms are better suited for brewing, and may have been grown specifically for this purpose.

Oats may also have been grown other than for brewing, perhaps most often as a mixture or dredge, for pottage grain or oatmeal for human consumption, while a sample of charred horse dung indicates that it was also used for animal fodder. Rye straw was also highly valued for thatching and it has been suggested that rivet wheat straw, which has many of the properties of rye straw, might also have been used.

Much of the chaff produced from the winnowing and flailing of the cereals was used as fuel for the drying and malting ovens, rather than going to the animals as fodder, which may suggest that there was enough other winter fodder, probably from nearby hay meadows, together with some permanent pasture. Another reason for the chaff being included in the fuel for the malt ovens may be that malt takes on the flavour of the fuel used, and wheat straw followed by rye, oats and lastly barley were the preferred fuels.

The animal bone assemblage indicates that sheep were the most common animal, followed by cattle, pigs and horses. Contemporary with the twelfth-century manor house, the kill-off pattern for sheep shows that there was a wide range of ages indicating a mixed economy in which meat, milk and wool were important. However, in comparison to the later medieval period, more animals were killed at a younger age, six months to two years, showing a greater interest in meat production, and many bones bore chopping and cut marks indicative of butchery, showing that they had come from food waste.

The kill-off pattern for the cattle is typical of medieval sites, with most animals kept to maturity and exploited for traction power and milk, with a few animals killed when younger for meat.

The pig bones are dominated by immature and sub-adult animals, with only enough kept to maturity for breeding, as is commonly seen. The aim of pig husbandry was the production of meat and lard, while some young males were probably grown on for sale at market.

A number of horses are also present in the bone assemblage, although when measurable they evidently come from pony-sized animals, no more 14 hands and 2 inches high. Dogs were present in all periods, and were generally of average size, but the only two near complete skulls came from near the late Saxon ranges and the medieval manor, and were both from larger animals of Alsatian size, perhaps suggesting the deliberate burial of the skulls of favourite work or hunting animals.

There was a small number of red deer and roe deer, and the bones are from butchered food refuse, indicating that the restricted privileges of the aristocracy were not always respected. A few pieces of antler, at least some of which were shed, had been utilised for craft manufacturing.

There was a small number of domestic fowl, which were slightly more common in the twelfth century, and while they were presumably exploited for meat, eggs and feathers, they were evidently not among the chief food resources. Goose, probably domestic, and duck were present in similar numbers, and were more common in the twelfth century, when the settlement still stood beside an active river channel as well as having its own small mill pond.

Pigeon/dove was the most common bird, although most of those from the vicinity of the dovecote come from deposits of late thirteenth-century date, probably related to demolition and levelling of the building.

A few bones from birds of prey were also present, with three from red kite and one from a buzzard associated with the manor, while sparrowhawk and kestrel bones came from later medieval deposits. Whether the red kite and the buzzard may have come from birds used for hunting, or were merely local scavengers killed for sport is unknown.

Considering the location of the settlement, fish bones were perhaps surprising scarce, although this may partly reflect a low survival rate. Associated with the twelfth-century manor there were bones from eel, perhaps coming from an eel trap on the leat of the final watermill, and from a large perch, while the only sea fish were herring, perhaps arriving smoked or salted.

The timber buildings of the medieval manor

The only two timber buildings constructed in the earlier twelfth century possessed individual post-pits, and so were of principal-post construction (Fig 5.7). This transition from pre-Conquest stave-walled construction to post-Conquest principal-post construction has previously been most clearly seen in the sequence of halls and associated buildings at Goltho, Lincolnshire (Beresford 1987).

Building T28

This building overlay the eastern end of the late Saxon timber hall, T29, and appears to have directly replaced it, perhaps utilising timbers from the hall. It was near square in plan, 6.8m long by 7.3m wide, with a floor space nearly 5.75m square giving a floor area of 33sq m (Figs 5.7–5.10).

The northern wall comprised three elongated post-pits, 2.00–2.20m long and 0.65–0.75m deep, cutting at least 0.20m into the natural gravel. Each had a sub-square deepening at the eastern end to hold a principal post, and the western and eastern pits each had a similar deepening at the western end, presumably for a second but slightly smaller post. A narrow slot at the southern edge of the western end of the western pit suggests the provision of both a post and a plank, and differential fills in the western end of the eastern pit also defined two post-pipes, a circular or sub-square post, 350mm in diameter, and an adjacent, rectangular post or plank on the inner edge, 550mm long by up to 30mm thick.

Most of the southern wall comprised a single wall trench. It lay partially over the wall trench of the late Saxon hall, with this perhaps explaining the difference between the two constructions. The wall trench was 4.6m long, and three squared, post-settings were identified within the fills and a fourth, at the disturbed eastern end, may be inferred (Fig 5.9). They were 400–500mm in diameter and each was partially lined with vertically-pitched limestone. The two to the west also had pieces of flat-laid limestone at the base as post-pads. Between the western posts a looser fill appeared to define a shallow central slot, up to 300mm wide by 200mm deep, which may have held a timber sill beam, set at ground level between the principal posts.

The post-pit at the western end of the southern wall was 1.40m long by 1.00m wide and 0.85m deep. The fill of red-brown sand and gravel to the east contrasted with a looser fill containing steeply-pitched slabs of limestone to the west, suggesting that a single post had been set at the western end of the pit. However, the form of the elongated

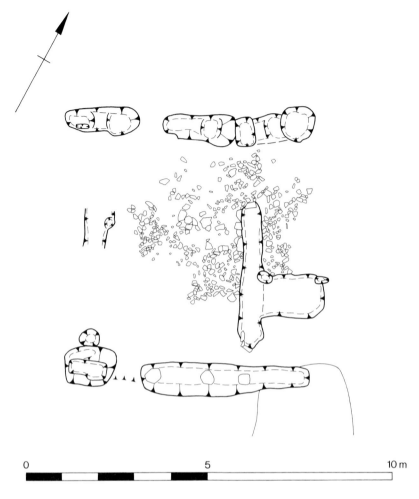

Fig 5.8: The medieval manor, timber building T28

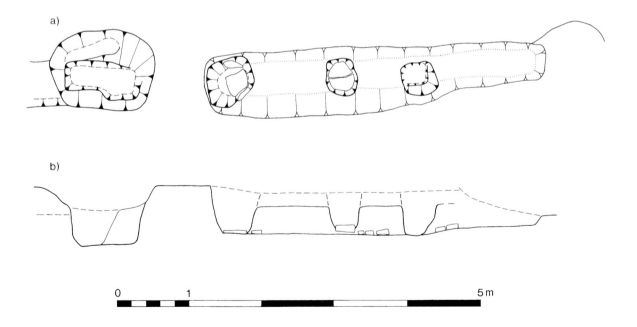

Fig 5.9: Principal post construction, building T28; a) southern wall-trench, b) longitudinal profile of wall-trench

Fig 5.10: Timber building T28, looking north

slot at the base of the cut suggests that originally it may have held two posts.

The form of the northern wall, with its three construction slots, indicates that the basic structure probably comprised three major paired posts, which presumably supported tie beams running north-south, forming a two-bay structure. Within the broader western bay the other posts formed the jambs for doorways in the northern and southern walls, 1.00m and 1.20m wide respectively, which were not quite directly opposed.

The lack of evidence for end walls indicates that these were of a lighter build, probably set in shallow wall-trenches that had been removed by later activity. A short length of shallow trench to the west appears to lie within the probable line of the end wall.

A floor of irregular pieces of flat-laid limestone, often heavily worn, partially survived. In the eastern bay there was a linear slot, 3.95m long, 0.80m wide and 0.10m deep, with a short length of a former stone lining surviving at the northern end of the western side. It was probably a drain that opened into a rectangular pit to the east, 1.70m long by 1.10m wide and 0.20m deep, which was filled with tightly packed pieces of limestone, suggesting that it served as a sump or soak-away. Elongated postholes at either end of the northern side of the pit suggest the presence of either a timber lining or an upstanding timber structure along this side.

The small quantities of pottery from the wall-trenches

and post-pits, none contained more than nine sherds, suggest an earlier twelfth-century construction date (ph 0, 1100–1150). The 58 sherds from the disturbed limestone floor are dated to the later twelfth century (ph 1, 1150–1225).

Building S24

This building was not fully understood during excavation; hence its provisional designation as a stone building (S) on the basis of the stone footings for the southern wall. It lay to the south-west of the main building complex, within an area taken into the enlarged domestic plot (Fig 5.7). The full plan was not recovered, but the building must have been 8.0m long by 7.0m wide; an internal area of 42sq m (Fig 5.11). The post-pit at the east end of the southern wall and the pair of post-pits on the northern wall indicate that it was of principal-post construction. The post-pits were 0.35–0.40m deep, and the two on the northern wall were set 3.70m apart, centre-to-centre. A further two post-pits forming the western wall were not located, probably because they would have been cut into the fills of an earlier boundary ditch.

The southern wall was 0.55–0.60m wide, comprising a single course of large slabs and blocks of flat-laid limestone. It was probably a dwarf wall providing a footing for a timber sill beam. It contained a central doorway

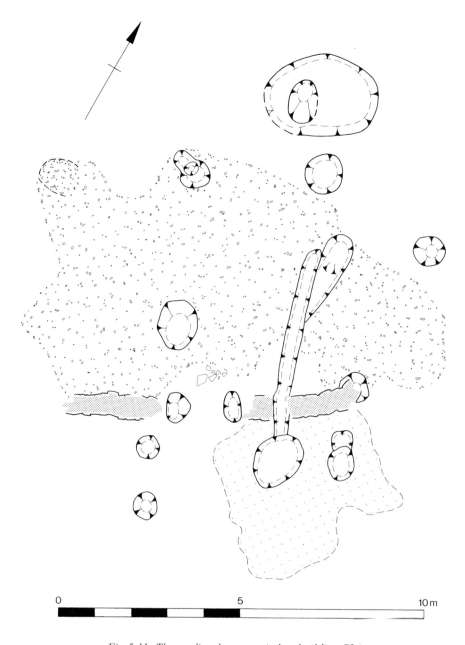

Fig 5.11: The medieval manor, timber building S24

1.30m wide, defined by substantial door jamb post-pits 0.40–0.45m deep (Fig 5.12).

The floor was of gravel with some small pieces of limestone, in a sandy clay matrix. Inside the southern doorway this had been eroded and then patched with larger limestone. Similar gravel surfacing extended beyond the eastern wall, perhaps indicating the presence of a second broader entrance. To the west there was an internal pit, with vertical sides and a flat bottom, 0.65m deep, filled with grey-brown clayey loam with a number of large limestone blocks within the upper 0.4m of the fill. To the east a 0.10m deep, linear drain ran through a gap in the southern wall to

a shallow, 0.22m deep, flat-bottomed pit. As with building T28, the drain suggests that it was used as a byre.

To the south of the building there were a further four small pits, 0.10–0.30m deep. Those to the east were sealed by a roughly square area of metalling comprising disordered pieces of limestone. A further small pit lay to the east of the building while a larger pit, 0.45m deep, to the north was cut into earlier ditch fills. None of the pits contained any distinctive fills or finds to indicate their function or the local presence of any distinctive activity.

The pottery recovered from the various structural features was of later twelfth-century date (ph 1, 1150–1225).

Fig 5.12: Building S24, looking west, showing the western wall and the post-pits holding the timber door surround

The stone buildings of the medieval manor

The twelfth-century stone buildings were not well preserved (Fig 5.7), as they had all been systematically levelled to make way for the thirteenth-century tenements. Only the lowest few courses of walling or the rubble filled, construction/robber trenches survived, along with some floor levels and internal fixtures. The individual buildings are described below, while the general discussion of construction, plan form and usage for the stone buildings appears in Chapter 7, as part of a single discussion of all medieval stone buildings.

The Hall, S18

The hall was 9.55m long by 4.80m wide, with internal dimensions of 8.30 by 3.70m, a ground floor area of 30.7sq m (Fig 5.13). It was the most complex of all the twelfth-century buildings. Uniquely, the mortar-bonded standing walls rested on pitched-stone foundations set in a distinct construction trench, while all of the other medieval stone buildings had no distinct foundation courses. In addition, internal and external lines of stakeholes parallel to the long walls, and sealed beneath floor levels and external surfaces, indicate that scaffolding had been used during its construction. The presence of both the foundations

and the stakeholes are taken as indications that the hall had two storeys.

Scaffold posts

A regular line of five stakeholes, spaced 1.50–1.75m apart, lay 0.85m inside the inner face of the eastern wall, with a line of four stakeholes 0.90–0.95m beyond this wall (Fig 5.13). A much less regular line of stakeholes lay 0.60–1.00m from the western wall. The external areas to the north, west and south had been heavily disturbed by contemporary and later activity, perhaps removing further stakeholes. The stakeholes were typically 0.20–0.40m in diameter and 0.10–0.25m deep, with conical profiles tapering to blunt points, indicating that they were formed by driven stakes. The fills contained mortar and most were tightly packed with small pieces of limestone, suggesting that they were deliberately and carefully backfilled after the stakes had been removed. In two examples, *in situ* pieces of limestone packing defined square stake settings 100mm in diameter. A few examples were more flat-bottomed, suggesting that they may have held posts.

Wall construction

The construction trench for the walls was 0.55–0.65m wide and up to 0.15m deep, with steep sides and a flat

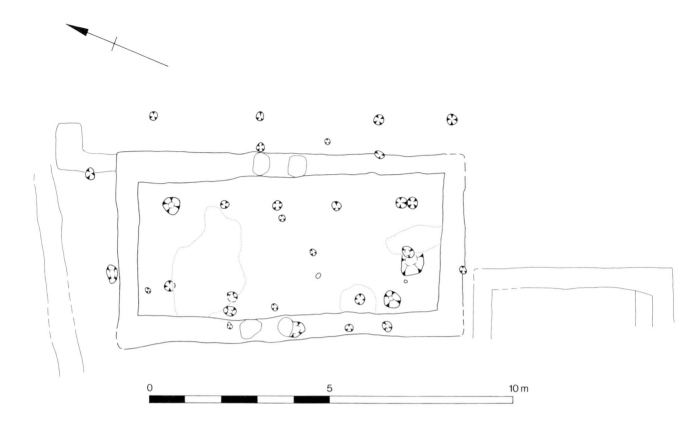

Fig 5.13: The medieval manor; the hall, S18, showing scaffolding postholes

base (Fig 5.14). The foundations comprised inner and outer facings of pitched limestone, set transversely and unmortared, with a central core of smaller limestone rubble either disordered or pitched. A covering layer of mortar formed a flat bed for the standing wall, which had been extensively robbed although at least short lengths survived on all four walls. The best preserved was the southern half of the eastern wall, where both wall faces stood three to five courses high (Fig 5.15). The walls were 0.56–0.60m thick, built in roughly-coursed, flat-laid limestone facings with a core of smaller rubble, all bonded with a yellow sandy mortar. The facing stones were typically only roughly squared, leaving a very uneven wall face, and there were wide joints between the courses.

Opposed doorways lay just north of centre. Originally, they had substantial timber door jamb posts set in deep post-pits (Fig 5.14). Later these were removed and the door surrounds were rebuilt in stone, possibly with less substantial timber jambs (Figs 4.16 and 5.17). The door openings were 0.80–0.85m wide, with square to sub-circular door jamb post-pits 0.25–0.35m deep. The northern post-pits were the deepest and they also contained larger pieces of pitched limestone, probably from displaced packing, perhaps suggesting that both doors had been hung on the northern jambs. Within the doorways the

construction trench was filled with loam mixed with mortar and small pieces of limestone. In the eastern doorway this deposit contained a lead spindle whorl, the only example recovered from the site, and an iron nail. While these may have been random discards, they could be seen as a deliberate protective deposit within the threshold of the main public access to the building, as known from later medieval and post-medieval buildings.

Beyond the eastern doorway a 0.10m deep posthole filled with pitched and flat-lying limestone (a crushed egg shell was found between two of the stones), and set within a shallow linear hollow filled with mortar, may have held a timber screen, but there was no similar feature to the south to indicate that there was a full porch. On the southern side of the doorway a two-course setting of flat-laid pieces of limestone may have formed a low kerb, probably indicating that the approach to the doorway was slightly sunken with respect to the external metalled surface, perhaps as a result of wear and prolonged use.

Floor surfaces

While there were differences in the floor surfaces between the northern and southern ends of the building, as well as a distinct cross-passage, as detailed below, there were

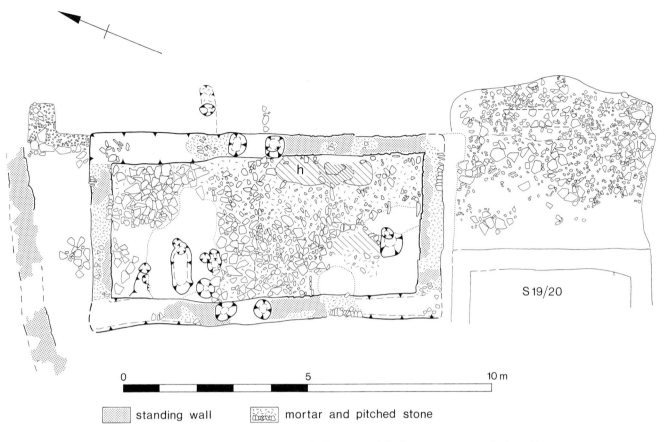

0   5   10 m

standing wall   mortar and pitched stone

Fig 5.14: The medieval manor; the hall, S18, and the lean-to structure (h=hearth)

certainly no stone partition walls (Fig 5.14). There were also no cut features to indicate the provision on any timber partitions, but these could have been founded on ground laid sills that have left no trace. It is suggested that the differential flooring does imply the probably use of some internal partitions.

Southern chamber

Across the southern chamber a sub-floor comprising large slabs of pitched limestone, 200–400mm long, bedded into a thin spread of loam, mortar and some small pieces of limestone, was probably provided to consolidate the soft fills of an underlying length of ditch. The sub-floor continued further north as a contiguous layer of clean yellow sandy mortar with small pieces of limestone, and ended in line with the northern side of the doorways.

The sub-floor was covered with yellow sandy mortar, from which a bone gaming piece, probably a simple chessman, was recovered. Towards the western doorway, where there was no underlying pitched stone, scattered flat-laid limestone was set into the mortar. A hearth was set against the eastern wall. It comprised a central hearthstone, 620mm long by 40mm thick, set in a rectangular layer of clay, 2.60m long by 0.80m wide. For up to 0.30m around

the hearthstone, the clay had a reddened surface mottled with grey ash and was covered with a spread of fine grey ash. There was no surviving evidence for a kerb or for the presence of a chimney, so it is assumed that no more than a smoke hood had been provided.

A layer of mixed grey sandy loam and yellow sandy mortar overlying the hearth included a linear strip which was hardened and heat reddened on the underside. This material was probably a collapsed length of wall rendering which had been scorched and hardened by the adjacent hearth. It indicates the provision of a mortar or plaster wall rendering adjacent to the hearth, and perhaps within the room as a whole. Along much of the frontage south of the doorway there was an external layer of yellow-brown sandy mortar abutting the lower courses of the wall and extending 0.70–1.00m from the wall, which may have derived from erosion and weathering of external wall rendering.

Other features within the southern half of the room included a deposit of grey silty loam mottled with burnt sand and charcoal flecks, which did not appear to derive from *in situ* buring, and against the western wall there was a short setting of vertically-pitched pieces of limestone set in a shallow slot filled with loam and mortar.

The original hearth and floor was covered by a charcoal-flecked loam and a layer of clean yellow-brown sand.

Fig 5.15: The hall, S18, floors removed, looking east

Fig 5.16 : The hall, S18, showing floors, looking east

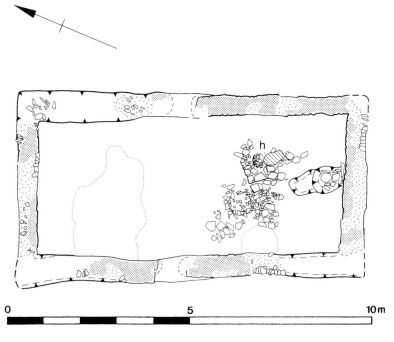

Fig 5.17: The medieval manor; the hall, S18; late floors

A remnant of a new floor above this, comprising mixed flat-laid and pitched limestone bedded in sand, probably belonged with the final use of this building (Fig 5.17). There was then an elaborate open hearth, 1.50m long. A kerb, 0.35m deep, of flat-laid limestone blocks with roughly squared facings surrounded a 0.80m long hearth-base. To the south a square setting of small flat-laid limestone was overlain by a layer of heavily burnt clay, and to the north there was a semicircular setting of flat-laid and pitched fragments of a single sandstone hand-quern. The hearth was covered by a layer of grey loam with some reddened soil. A pit, up to 0.25m deep and partially floored and lined with limestone, that abutted the southern wall may have been contemporary with the hearth. The pit fill was a grey sandy loam containing pitched and tumbled limestone, suggesting that it may have served as a small soak-away pit.

Cross-passage

Between the doorways a cross-passage was defined by a 1.00m-wide floor of flat-laid slabs of limestone with some yellow sandy mortar between. Immediately inside the doorways they had worn surfaces, and a roughly semi-circular area inside the eastern doorway had been relaid with smaller pieces of flat-laid limestone set in yellow sandy mortar.

Northern chamber

Within the northern chamber there was a further area of floor comprising flat-laid slabs of limestone in a matrix of yellow sandy mortar, but these were typically larger and more closely set than those between the doorways. To the west a group of postholes surrounding a linear pit may indicate the presence of some form of internal fitting, but this area had been badly disturbed by later activity.

External stairway

To the north of the building a remnant of a roughly built wall, at least 5.40m long and set at an angle to the northern wall of the hall, may have supported a timber stairway giving access to the postulated upper storey (Fig 5.14). No more than two courses of flat-laid limestone survived with a core of smaller rubble in a matrix of stiff clay, with no mortar. This may have been a dwarf wall providing a low footing for a timber stairway. To the east, an L-shaped setting of small pieces of limestone, faced to the west by flat-laid limestone slabs, ran between the two walls. The larger slabs had worn surfaces and were cracked and flaking from exposure to the elements, and may have formed a threshold at the foot of the stairway.

Dating

As the best preserved building, the dating of the hall was crucial to the understanding of the whole manor house complex. A total of 164 sherds from the wall construction and the sub-floor levels indicate a construction date in the first half of the twelfth century (ph 0, 1100–1150), while the 52 sherds from the earlier floor levels included six sherds of Lyveden A ware, suggesting that these floors continued into the later twelfth century (ph 1, 1150–1225). The later floor level contained 40 Lyveden A sherds, indicating a later twelfth century date. Patchy spreads of burnt debris sealing the levelled eastern wall contained largely twelfth-century pottery but included a few sherds of glazed wares dating to the earlier thirteenth century (ph 2/0, 1225–1250). It is therefore likely that the building was demolished within the second quarter of the thirteenth century (ph 2/0, 1225–1250).

The lean-to

A rectangular area of compact limestone immediately south of the hall, S18, and abutting the eastern end of the southern range, S19, was a hard-standing probably under a lean-to structure set against the end walls of the adjacent buildings (Fig 5.14).

A basal layer of compact stone, comprising flat-lying or gently pitched limestone slabs and small chips of crushed limestone, was set in a matrix of light brown sand. Above this a layer of chips and small pieces of crushed and eroded limestone, 20–150mm diameter, with some larger pieces, formed a compact surface. This extended further to the east, and a number of flat-laid pieces of limestone may have been the badly disturbed remnants of the lowest course of a wall, 0.48m wide, perhaps a dwarf wall for a timber superstructure.

A layer of loam and mortar above this, probably related to demolition and containing the only silver ring recovered from the site, is dated to the earlier thirteenth century (ph 2/0, 1225–1250).

The southern range, S20

The eastern wall of the earlier timber range, T33, directly underlay the western wall of S20, and it is suggested that the timber range was probably retained as a second room (Fig 5.18).

The new stone range was 9.60 long by 5.50m wide, with internal dimensions of 8.20 by 4.50m giving it a floor area of 36.9sq m. The southern and western walls were later levelled, but the eastern and northern walls were at least partially retained when the range was rebuilt, S19.

The eastern wall was 0.50–0.55m wide and survived from one to three courses high (see Fig 5.20). It was built within a shallow construction trench, 0.05–0.10m deep, with the wall founded on a 40–50mm thick bed of mortar. The wall was rubble cored, faced with flat-laid limestone and bonded with a yellow sandy mortar. The surviving remnant of the western wall comprised two more deeply founded courses of flat-laid limestone that appeared to form a partial lining to an adjacent pit, 0.10m deep, which was therefore part of the original construction, although its function is unknown.

There were remnants of a northern wall only to the east and west beyond three post-pits. both containing limestone and mortar, which suggest that there was probably a broad

eastern doorway, 2.0m wide, and a narrower western doorway, 1.5m wide. A shallow construction trench across the eastern doorway contained a remnant of a wall, suggesting that this was probably the original doorway, which was blocked when the building was rebuilt.

To the west a well-defined rectangular setting, 1.40 by 0.90m, of pieces of limestone in a matrix of grey-green loamy clay, edged to the south with vertically pitched pieces of limestone, may have been a threshold abutting the western wall at a further doorway. The surviving limestone floor to the south is dated to the second half of the twelfth century and may be most likely to belong with the rebuilding.

There was little direct dating evidence, but an external layer of mortar abutting the south-eastern corner was dated to the earlier twelfth century (ph 0, 1100–1150), as was further similar material overlying the levelled remnant of the southern wall. However, the pit abutting the western wall contained numerous sherds from a single later twelfth-century vessel (ph 1, 1150–1225), suggesting that the rebuilding occurred during the second half of the twelfth century.

An elongated pit to the south of the building, perhaps used as a sump or soakaway, was probably contemporary with the preceding timber range, T33, but may have been retained as it was only filled in the earlier twelfth century (ph 0, 1100–1150) (Fig 5.7).

The rebuilding of the southern range, S19

The timber building, T33, was levelled and the southern and western walls of the original stone building, S20, were also demolished to allow for the provision of a full range in stone, 18.2m long (Figs 5.19 and 5.20). The details are uncertain, but the construction may have been achieved in two stages as there was a straight joint at the centre of the new southern wall.

The first stage would have comprised the direct replacement of the western timber range, with the new stone walls directly overlying the infilled wall-trenches. The walls had been heavily robbed but a length of the southern wall survived to four courses high, 0.35m. It was founded in a shallow, 0.10m deep, construction trench on a 20–40mm thick bed of mortar with a 0.50m wide, single course foundation of flat-laid limestone. The standing wall, faced with flat-laid limestone and bonded with a sandy mortar, was slightly narrower at 0.45m wide. The western wall had an exceptionally wide foundation course, at 0.60–0.80m, of large limestone slabs, probably due to the presence of a backfilled ditch beneath. The surviving length of standing wall above this was largely in flat-laid limestone, but one course was partly in pitched limestone. In the northern wall, two post-pits, 0.30–0.45m deep, containing displaced limestone packing, held the jambs of a 1.30m wide doorway. The western wall of the original range was probably also demolished at this time, being replaced by a new wall immediately to the west,

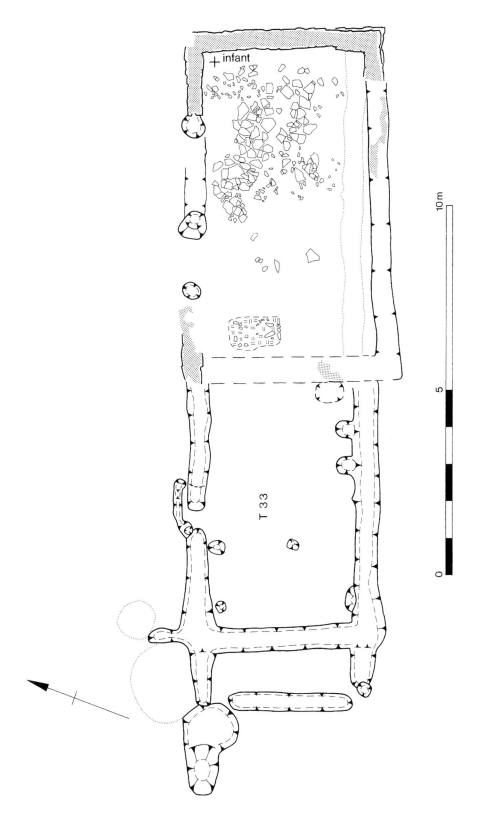

Fig 5.18: The medieval manor: southern range, S20, with retained timber range T33

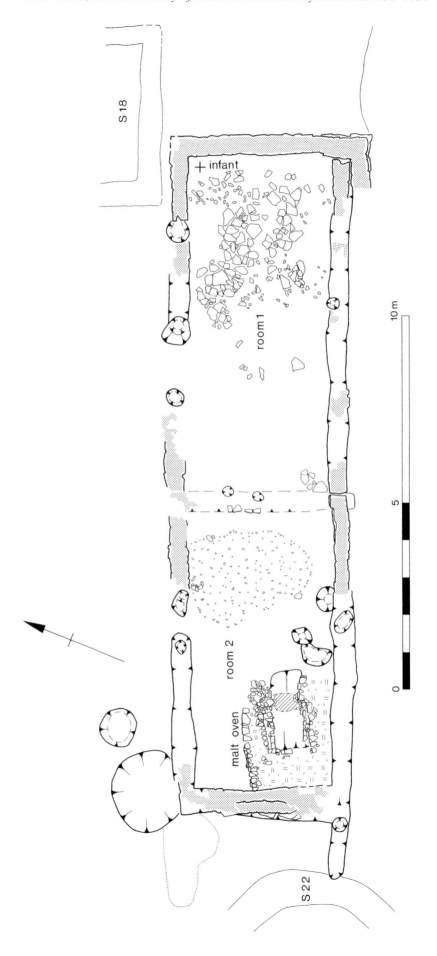

Fig 5.19: The medieval manor: barn and malt house, S19

Fig 5.20: The southern range, S19, room 1, looking west

Fig 5.21: The southern range, S19, room 2, looking north, showing the truncated remains of the malt oven

and contiguous with the new walls of the western room. A pair of post-pits held the jambs of a central doorway. 0.80m wide, and a line of flat-laid limestone formed part of a stone threshold. This wall was probably later removed to provide a single open space.

Subsequently, the southern wall of the original stone building was demolished and replaced by a new wall slightly to the north and in-line with the southern wall of room 2. The northern and eastern walls of building S20 were retained, although the eastern doorway was probably blocked and replaced by a narrower doorway further to the west.

The eastern room, 1, was 9.00m long by 4.00m wide, with a floor area of 36sq m. Across the eastern half there was a floor of large, flat-laid limestone flags, with an infilling of pebbles and smaller pieces of limestone. Within a shallow pit in the north-eastern corner of the room there was an inhumation burial of a neonatal infant (see Chapter 14, burial 4329). There is a direct parallel for the burial of an infant in the corner of a building from the medieval village of Upton, Gloucestershire, which in the 1960s was claimed to be probably "the first human burial recorded from a medieval peasant house" (Hilton and Rahtz 1967; Rahtz 1969, 87–88, fig 6 and Plate III).

The western room, 2, was 7.40m long with a floor area of 29.6sq m. A malt oven occupied just over a quarter of the floor space. The square oven chamber, 1.20m long by 1.10m wide, was set within a shallow pit, 0.20m deep (Fig 5.21). The lining was of small, flat-laid pieces of limestone and between this and the southern and western walls of the room there was a remnant of a mixed mortar and clay infill. To the north, the same filling was retained by a facing of flat-laid limestone. The flue opening was 0.55m wide at its base and widened to 0.63m at five courses high. A rectangular area of scorching indicated the former location of a hearthstone and the immediately adjacent flue lining was also scorched. The base of the chamber was covered with a layer of blackened silt. The side walls of the oven had then been re-lined, narrowing the chamber to 0.80m wide. The oven was later levelled and filled in with mixed mortar, clay, limestone and burnt debris, prior to the building of a completely new malt oven over the top (see Chapter 7, building E16).

Immediately east of the oven there were two shallow pits, 0.15 deep, filled with mixed debris comprising burnt mortar, loam, pieces of limestone and quantities of charcoal. A floor of gravel and small pieces of limestone in a matrix of sandy loam survived across the eastern part of the room, and was covered by mixed deposits of grey-black to orange-brown sandy loam with much charcoal, burnt mortar and pieces of limestone, some of which was burnt.

The small group of pottery from the new walls, as well as the pottery from the floors of both rooms, contained some Lyveden A ware, suggesting that the rebuilding and use occurred within the later twelfth century (ph 1, 1150–1225). The infilling and levelling of the oven chamber, pre-dating the building of a new oven (E16), contained some later pottery, suggesting a demolition date into the thirteenth century (ph 2/0, 1225–1250).

At the south-west corner of room 2 a short length of robber trench indicates that there was a wall linking this range and the adjacent dovecote (S22). At the north-west corner a large pit abutting the wall and a further smaller pit, both 0.40m deep, were filled with mixed loams, and the larger pit also contained a scatter of limestone fragments.

The kitchen/bakehouse, S21

The hearths and corner oven identify this building as a detached kitchen/bakehouse, which partly overlay a timber building, T32, which may have been an earlier kitchen. The new building was 9.50m long by 5.75m wide, with the internal space measuring 8.25 by 4.35m; a floor area of 35.9sq.m (Fig 5.22).

The western wall stood over a backfilled ditch and, as a consequence, had been provided with a broad, 0.63m wide, foundation course of large flat-laid limestone slabs set in a shallow construction trench. Subsequent subsidence into the ditch accounts for the better preservation of this wall. Up to two courses of surviving standing wall, 0.54m wide with an external offset, were constructed in flat-laid and roughly coursed limestone with a core of small limestone rubble, all bonded with a yellow clayey mortar.

A single doorway, 1.1m wide, immediately north of centre in the eastern wall, was defined by door-jamb post-pits, up to 0.35m deep.

In the south-west corner of the room a shallow, circular pit, 1.80m in diameter by 0.20m deep, filled with burnt clay and limestone was the levelled remnant of a corner oven that was contemporary with the construction of the building, as the inner wall face of the adjacent wall was founded within the oven construction pit. It was later replaced by a new, smaller oven set in the upper fill of the pit. Only a single course of the heavily-burnt oven lining survived, but the chamber was 1.20m in diameter. The 0.70m wide flue opening had been damaged and originally it would have been narrower, perhaps 0.40–0.50m wide. The chamber contained a layer of grey-brown loam with charcoal and pieces of burnt clay, mortar and limestone, but a specific floor level was not located.

In the south-eastern corner of the room a square hearth, 1.10m in diameter, was set into a floor surface of pebbles in yellow sand. A single flat-laid limestone slab, with a heavily burnt and cracked surface, remained *in situ* and some smaller pieces embedded in the larger area of scorched floor suggest the former presence of further stones. Occupation deposits of grey-brown loam with charcoal lay against the eastern wall, in front of the corner oven and more patchily across the entire southern half of the room. They overlay the early floor surface and were partially sealed by a later floor of pebbles in orange-brown sandy loam. A hearth near the centre of the room, comprising a single heavily-burnt and cracked limestone slab at the centre of an oval area of burning, was probably contemporary with this later floor.

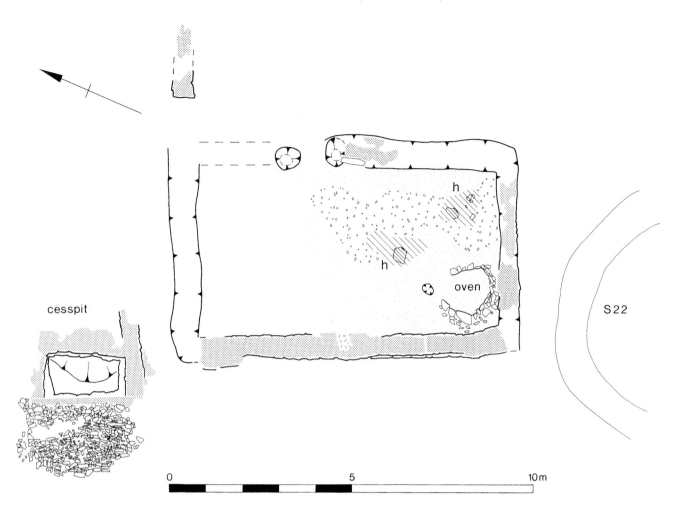

Fig 5.22: The medieval manor; kitchen/bakehouse, S21, and cess pit, S23

The pottery from the disturbed wall footings and the remnant gravel floors suggest a construction date in the first half of the twelfth century (ph 0, 1100–1150). The largest assemblage, 241 sherds, came from the mixed dark loams above the floors. This group was largely of shelly coarsewares, but six sherds of Lyveden A ware, indicate that use of the building continued into the later twelfth century (ph 1, 1150–1125).

The cess pit or garderobe, S23

A well-built, stone-lined cess pit lay immediately north of the kitchen/bakehouse (Figs 5.22 and 5.23). Its construction pit was excavated through the fills of the western boundary ditch, 8, and bottomed on natural gravel. The pit was lined with up to nine courses of flat-laid limestone forming a rectangular chamber with battered faces, 2.20m long by 1.00m wide. To the west it was 0.75m deep while to the east the bottom stepped down to 1.00m deep. On the southern side of the pit an outer wall face at ground level suggests that this side, at least, was flanked by a standing

wall, 0.50m wide, which also continued eastward for at least 1.00m, perhaps to provide a partial screen, although the pit may have been more fully enclosed to provide a roofed structure.

At the base of the pit there was an olive-green discolouration of the natural gravel, which been concreted into a solid mass to a depth of 20mm. Above this there was up to 0.25m of mottled olive green to grey silty clays, indicating the presence of cess deposits. The lower half was mixed and contained some small pieces of limestone, suggesting periodic partial removal of the contents, while the upper half was unmixed, indicating that the final accumulation of deposits had been left *in situ*.

Part of the fill was lifted as a block and excavated in the laboratory. The concentration of mineralised waste decreased towards the bottom of the block. It consisted largely of fragments of coprolite, solid waste which had become mineralised, in which fragments of cereal bran and corn cockle were clearly visible, while detailed analysis showed that wheat and barley were present along with some possible oat and rye fragments.

Fig 5.23: The stone-lined cess pit, S23, looking east (pitched stone ramp removed)

There were also large amounts of herbage, which included some cereal chaff and indeterminate leaf fragments. Fragments of possible *Prunus* sp. (plum etc) skin and pips from an apple or pear (*Pyrus/Malus* sp.) were recorded as well as a large legume, probably a pea (*Pisum sativum*). Arable weeds, familiar from the charred plant assemblages were also present. In addition, large numbers of seeds of elder (*Sambucus nigra*) had not been mineralised, suggesting that they did not enter the deposit with the faecal material. Most of the bone fragments were from fish and Avian egg shell was also common.

Subsequently, much of the lining on the western side of the pit was removed, leaving no more than two courses *in situ*, when a shallow sloping ramp was excavated and surfaced with steeply-pitched pieces of limestone. At this stage the functional depth of the pit may only have been the bottom 0.30m. The ramp presumably provided access into the pit for periodic removal of its contents. A further cess deposit had accumulated and spread across the lower part of the pitched stones before the pit was abandoned. It was backfilled with disordered limestone rubble and mortar, perhaps from a demolished superstructure.

The backfill of the construction pit behind the stone lining produced a large pottery group of 599 sherds dated to the earlier twelfth century (ph 0, 1100–1150), much of which was derived from fills of the subsidence hollow along the underlying ditch. The *in situ* cess deposits contained 31 sherds and the final fill 90 sherds, with the presence of

Lyveden A ware indicating that the pit was in use in the later twelfth century (ph 1, 1150–1225).

The dovecote, S22

This building lay at the south-western corner of the courtyard, with the malt house, S19/2, to its east and the kitchen/bakehouse, S21, to its north (Fig 5.7). It is interpreted as a dovecote on the basis of both its characteristic circular plan and the large assemblage of pigeon bones recovered in the immediate vicinity, largely from overlying demolition levels (Figs 5.24 and 5.25).

It was 6.85m in diameter, with an internal space 5.00m in diameter; a floor area of 19.6sq.m. The wall-trench was 0.16m deep with steep sides and a flat base. It was 1.00m wide suggesting that at foundation level the wall would have been around 0.80m thick, considerably wider than those of the contemporary buildings. On the north-western side a length of wall foundation of flat-laid limestone survived where they had been set to the exceptional depth of 0.50m, replacing the soft fills of an underlying pit. A single course of flat-laid limestone to the north may have formed the threshold of a doorway, 0.85m wide. There was no mortar in the surviving foundations but there was mortar in the fill of the robber trench. No floors had survived across the slightly hollowed interior, which was filled with limestone rubble and mortar, probably a demolition or levelling layer.

There was little direct dating evidence, although a single

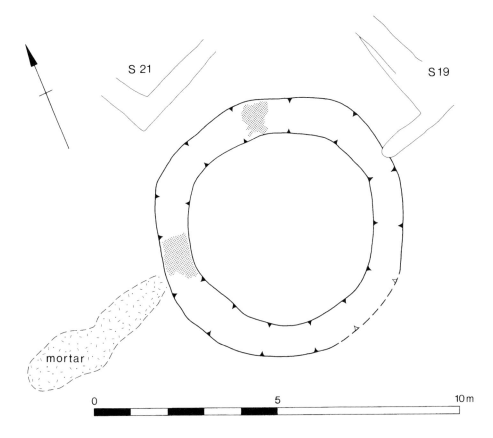

S 21

S 19

mortar

0   5   10 m

Fig 5.24: The medieval manor; the dovecote, S22

sherd from the *in situ* wall footings suggests a later twelfth-century date (ph 1, 1150–1225) for construction, perhaps contemporary with the rebuilding of the adjacent southern range, S19. The building may have been demolished in the earlier thirteenth century, but the overlying demolition levels contained some later thirteenth century pottery (phase 2/2, 1250–1300), perhaps suggesting that the dovecote was retained into the early use of tenement E.

To the west of the building, a 4.50m length of disordered limestone rubble in a matrix of mortar was broadly contemporary with the dovecote. It served no obvious functional purpose and may merely have been a backfilling to consolidate the ground over underlying soft feature fills.

The barn and processing range, S17

This building, the final addition to the twelfth-century manor house (Fig 5.7), served as a barn with an attached processing room (Fig 5.26). It was 21.00m long by 5.20m wide, probably of a single build, and contained two principal rooms of near equal length, with further partial partitions. It was subsequently largely levelled, leaving many of the constructional details unclear.

The later frontage of tenement A almost directly overlay the eastern wall suggesting that this wall may have been partially retained, perhaps with new wall lengths keyed into the existing wall to avoid straight joints. To the south the eastern wall of room 2 was slightly offset from the later wall, perhaps indicating that it was levelled and then rebuilt on almost, but not exactly, the same line. The southern wall did appear to have been retained in the later building, with a ragged joint where it met the new western wall. The western and northern walls were in different locations from their successors, as the later building was slightly narrower.

The eastern wall was 0.50–0.56m wide and was founded within a shallow construction trench, 0.6m wide by 0.10m deep. At its southern end the construction/robber trench extended beyond the southern wall for 1.00m, perhaps indicating the presence of a corner buttress. The western wall was best preserved to the south, where one or two courses of flat-laid limestone facing with a rubble core survived. The southern wall was 0.50m wide but in part the foundation courses were broader, at up to 0.57m wide, and were set within a construction trench up to 0.20m deep where it lay over earlier ditch fills.

The central partition wall between rooms 1 and 2 was largely robbed, but it was 0.40m wide. A slight rectangular hollow to the east of the surviving length might indicate its original extent, suggesting that there was a 1.20m doorway to the east to give access between the two main rooms.

Fig 5.25: The dovecote and the kitchen/ bakehouse with circular corner oven, looking north

Room 1

The northern room measured 10.65m by 4.20m, an internal area of 37.8sq m. The broad opposed doorways to the north of centre, each around 3.00m wide, indicate its use as a barn. The large quoins at the southern side of the eastern doorway survived, and a short length of wall slightly offset to the east appeared to be a remnant of a later blocking wall to reduce the width of the doorway. The location and broad width of the western doorway is only indicated by the 2.50m-wide external metalled surface of flat-laid and disordered limestone pieces. However, a 1.0m-wide ridge within the wall trench suggests that this too was later blocked and reduced to a normal width doorway, standing at the northern end of the barn door opening. Another remnant of external surfacing further to the south comprised a cluster of flat-laid limestone slabs overlain by a spread of yellow clay and mortar. This may suggest the

presence of a further, but narrower, doorway giving access to the southern half of the barn end.

Immediately south of the eastern doorway, a shallow hollow, 0.04m deep, filled with mixed sandy loam, yellow clay and mortar, was presumably the footing for a partial partition wall. There were patchy remnants of a sub-floor or levelling layer of mortar-flecked clayey loam which contained much burnt debris derived from an underlying pit group, and above this the floor was of yellow-brown clayey loam flecked with yellow mortar and some small pieces of limestone.

Room 2

The southern room measured 9.00m by 4.20m; an internal area of 37.8sq m. It had opposed doorways to the north of centre and a narrower doorway or opening at the southern end of the eastern wall (Figs 5.26 and 5.27). The eastern doorway was 1.00m wide, with the quoins partly surviving to the south and an *in situ* pivot stone to the north. The western doorway was 0.95m wide, and was defined by a pair of door-jamb postholes, 0.30m in diameter by 0.10m deep. These were filled with tightly packed pieces of pitched limestone, and a slot for a threshold sill, also filled with pitched pieces of limestone, ran between them.

The opening at the southern end of the eastern wall was only 0.60m wide, with a threshold setting of four flat-laid slabs of limestone. This was either an unusually narrow doorway or was perhaps a low-level opening serving some other purpose, perhaps to allow sacks or other materials to be passed through.

An area of floor survived where it had been overlain by a partition wall within the later building. A scatter of flat-laid limestone slabs was partially overlain by a compact surface of pebbles in a sandy matrix, and above this there was a patchy layer of red to orange burnt loam mixed with fine, pale grey ash and some grey-brown clayey loam.

A small hearth lay immediately inside the eastern door, with an adjacent square base for a respond abutting the wall perhaps to protect the hearth from exposure to draughts. The hearth was 0.70m square with a base of closely packed, gently-pitched pieces of limestone flanked by flat-lying pieces embedded in and partially covered by a clayey loam. The central area of the clay and the tops of the stones were both reddened and blackened, while towards the western side the stones were heavily blackened.

The principal features in the room were the two stone-lined pits occupying the north-west corner (Fig 5.28). The long pit, 1.80m long by 0.50m wide and 0.35m deep, was lined with a mixture of flat-laid limestone slabs and larger, irregular limestone blocks, in up to six rough courses. At the northern end there was a single, steeply-pitched slab of limestone, while at the southern end pitched slabs of limestone had been partially removed when this end was disturbed by the construction of the adjacent rectangular pit. The base was surfaced with flat-laid limestone and much of the base, and the slab at the northern end was discoloured blue-grey by organic chemical staining, and the soil between the stones was stained grey-green. A single flat-laid slab with a blue-grey surface lay at floor level adjacent to the southern end of the pit, and slabs of limestone within the fill and used in the construction of the adjacent pit, may have come from either the upper courses of the lining or an area of adjacent surface. In form and character this pit is identical with a similar feature in contemporary use in the southern holding, tenement B (B5/1) and some of the later tenements. These processing rooms will be discussed in detail in the following chapter, where it is suggested that they were probably used for the fulling of woollen cloth, with the chemicals used producing the grey staining of the limestone.

The smaller, rectangular stone-lined pit, 0.95m long by 0.50m wide and 0.45m deep, was well faced on three sides in up to eight courses of flat-laid limestone, but on the southern side only a partial lining survived. The flat base was not surfaced. To the west the upper two courses of the lining were contiguous with a square base comprising two courses of flat-laid limestone set in a shallow hollow.

To the south of the doorway there was a large, steep-sided pit, 3.10m long, up to 1.30m wide, and 0.45m deep at either end with a shallower, 0.35m deep, central section. The eastern end of the pit was partially lined with large, overlapping slabs of limestone pitched against the cut sides, while the western end was largely filled with closely-set and steep to near vertically-pitched slabs of limestone in a matrix of grey-green silty clay. It is suggested that the pit was probably originally fully-filled with pitched slabs of limestone, and that it served as an internal soak-away pit. A strip 0.50m wide along the southern side was stained grey-green to yellow or orange, suggesting the use of strong organic solutions and a probable direct connection with the use of the long, stone-lined pit to the north. A small pit in the corner of the room, 0.66m in diameter by 0.60m deep, contained some pitched slabs of limestone, perhaps remnants of an original lining, and its fill included a lens of reddened and blackened loam with charcoal and grey-green silty clay particularly concentrated towards the base of the pit. The fill of this pit produced the largest collection of fish bones, all herring, recovered from the site.

The pits pre-dating the building contained later twelfth century pottery (ph 1), and the presence of Developed Stamford ware suggests that the building was constructed in the early thirteenth century, towards the end of ceramic phase 1 (1200–1225). The remnant floors in room 1 produced later twelfth and early thirteenth century pottery (ph 1 and 2/0). The latest burnt layer within room 2 contained a later thirteenth century pottery group (ph 2/2, 1250–1300), as did the earliest floors of the subsequent building, A1, suggesting that the rebuilding occurred within the second half of the thirteenth century.

The access road, courtyards and pit groups

Three areas of external metalled surfaces contemporary with the twelfth-century manor partially survived (Fig 5.7). To the east of the hall, S18, there was a well-preserved length of the main access road; within the central courtyard, SY1, remnants of metalled surfaces survived; and on the yard, SY2, to the south of the buildings there were remnants of metalled surfaces pre-dating the construction of the barn and processing room, S17, while the walled yards were probably contemporary with this building. There were three major pit groups within the extended domestic plot. These lay to the west and south of the buildings, the latter group pre-dating the barn, S17, and to the east on the opposite side of the access road, with an isolated malt oven further to the east. The fills of these pits typically contained considerable quantities of burnt debris, often including pieces of fired

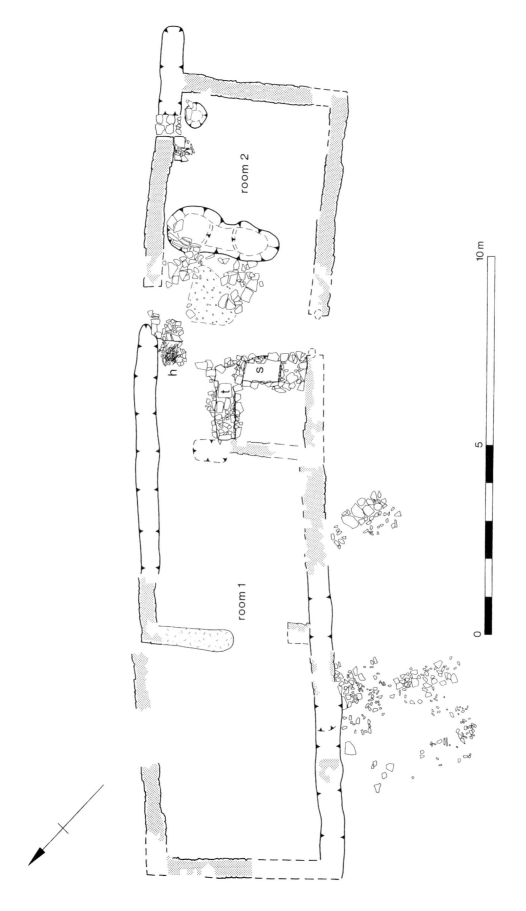

Fig 5.26: The medieval manor; barn and processing range, S17 (h=hearth, s= stone-lined bin, t= trough)

Fig 5.27: The processing room, S17/2, looking west

Fig 5.28: The processing room, S17/2, stone-lined trough and pit.

clay, and it is likely that each group contained the debris from an associated clay-domed drying oven.

The access road

A 20m length of metalled road was well preserved, overlying an earlier gravel surface contemporary with the later use of the timber buildings. Further south any surface had been removed by later medieval activity. The first phase comprised flat laid limestone, typically 150mm long with heavily worn and smoothed surfaces, and some gravel, including small cobbles up to 100mm long (Fig 5.7).

To the east, the late Saxon boundary ditch, 18, may have been retained for a time but it was later backfilled and replaced by a shallow ditch, no more than 0.30m deep. A 2.20m wide opening provided access to the east, and a localised final fill of crushed limestone in the underlying ditch provided a consolidated surface.

Beyond the southern end of the shallow ditch an L-shaped boundary wall was constructed on a dumped layer of yellow sandy mortar overlain by loam and limestone rubble, which formed the final fill of the underlying ditch. The external corner of the wall was sharply angled while internally it was curved. The arms of the wall were 0.60m and 0.50m wide, standing on a broader foundation course. The corner was abutted by a narrow wall, 0.35–0.45m wide, running westward for 1.80m; a single course survived, in both flat-laid and shallowly pitched limestone, and the surviving western end was probably the original terminal. It would appear to mark the southern end of the approach to the new hall.

At a later date, a timber gateway, only 1.15m wide, may have been added to control access to the hall by forming an enclosed court 10.0m long. The post-pits holding the gate posts were up to 0.80m in diameter by 0.55m deep, and lay at the northern side of an oval construction pit, up to 0.15m deep, which was filled with mixed burnt debris and worn limestone from the earlier metalled surfaces. A double posthole to the north-east and the truncated base of a possible further post-pit further to the east may suggest that the gateway stood in front of a timber fence spanning the width of the approach to the hall.

With the introduction of the gateway a new narrow path was provided. It was 1.50m wide and comprised flat-laid limestone, heavily worn, with small, isolated areas of pitched limestone from subsequent repairs. It ran directly to the doorway of the timber building, T28, which had replaced the old timber hall, T29. The eastern edge of the path was closely linear, and at its northern end there was a 2.40m length of a kerb in vertically-set limestone, with the tops of the stones worn smooth and frost shattered. To the east of the kerb there was a shallow, sub-square hollow filled with charcoal-flecked sandy loam and scattered pieces of limestone, and a pair of shallow pits, no more than 0.08m deep, filled with silty loam, pale grey ash and some reddened sand. These deposits were sealed by a worn limestone surface.

The area between the hall, S18, and the path was surfaced with mixed pale yellow mortar, clean sand and small limestone chips, which appeared to be contiguous with the internal floor surface of the hall, and there was an upper surface of mixed sand and gravel.

Over the upper road surface there was a patchy layer of red-brown sandy loam with a scatter of small limestone pieces. This was sealed by a red-brown loam heavily mottled with grey ashy loam and burnt sand with charcoal flecking. This material may have been demolition debris, and similar deposits overlay the levelled eastern wall of the hall, S18.

To the east of the path the earlier road surface had been heavily disturbed, leaving a layer of disordered limestone, much of it worn, in a light brown sandy loam.

The filling of the shallow ditch along the eastern side of the access road is dated to the first half of the twelfth century, while the layer of ashy loam sealing the road included an assemblage of fairly large and unabraded pottery sherds dated to the later twelfth or early thirteenth centuries (ph 1, 1150–1225). Small amounts of later pottery in an overlying surface immediately pre-dating the construction of the northern wing of tenement E, suggest that the road fell out of use around the first quarter of the thirteenth century (ph 1 into ph 2/0, 1225) at the creation of tenement E.

The central courtyard, SY1

The central courtyard was 16.50m long by 9.50–11.25m wide; an area of 171sq m (Fig 5.7). This area had been heavily disturbed by later use, but early metalled surfacing still patchily survived across the central area. The earliest surface comprised three discrete areas of flat-laid limestone slabs, and the westernmost had vertically pitched limestone along its northern side, possibly forming a kerb. These may have been remnants of a path, perhaps 1.00m wide, running between the hall, S18, and the kitchen/bakehouse, S21. To the north there was a small area of worn limestone.

The early limestone surface was overlain by a layer of gravel pebbles, typically 10–40mm diameter, and some small pieces of limestone in a matrix of orange-brown sandy loam. It survived relatively undisturbed in the centre of the yard and beyond this there was much gravel within later layers, suggesting that it had originally covered the entire courtyard. The gravel abutted and lapped over the margins of the original path. Towards the western end of the courtyard there was a single pit, probably recut, 1.60m diameter and 0.25m deep.

To the north, the timber domestic range, T30, was probably retained into the earlier use of the new building complex, and a short length of stone wall, 0.65m wide, may have closed the gap between the stone-built kitchen range to the west and the retained timber range. At its western end a single large slab of limestone spanned the full width of the wall suggesting that this may have been the wall end, which would have left a narrow gateway, 1.00m wide, adjacent to the kitchen range.

Part of the limestone pathway is dated to the earlier twelfth century (ph 0, 1100–1150), while the pottery groups attributed to the gravel surface range in date from the early twelfth to the fourteenth centuries (ph 0 to ph 3/2), but the material is certainly a result of the extensive later disturbance and contamination of these levels.

The western pit group (LSE5)

This pit group comprised two major features: a large oval pit which contained the remnants of a probable square, clay-walled oven (Fig 5.7, 4039) and a linear gully with terminal pits that was probably another oven (4437). These features were rich in charred plant remains, including cereals, field beans, fodder vetch and flax, indicating their probable use as general crop-drying ovens. Bracken recovered from the larger oven may have been used as fuel.

The large oval pit (4039), 6.10m long by 3.70m wide and 0.45m deep, contained a central, 3.00m square, layer of burnt (orange-red) clay pieces, with unburnt limestone embedded in its upper surface, which was probably the levelled remains of a clay-domed oven chamber. Access to the oven was probably from the more shallowly-sloping western end of the pit, where the primary ashy fills were mixed. At the eastern end multiple stratified layers of alternating blue-black and reddish-black ashy silts were probably the debris from successive firings.

The linear oven (4437) comprised a central gully with a elongated pit to the west on the same alignment, and a pit at the eastern end set at an angle, and lying beneath the wall of the later dovecote (Figs 5.7 and 6.2). The central gully was 3.00m long, up to 1.00m wide and 0.35m deep. At its western end on the cut floor there was a spread of grey-black loam with some small pieces of burnt clay. The western pit was 3.50m long and both wider and deeper than the gully, at 1.50m wide and 0.50m deep. It had a primary fill, 0.10m thick, of grey-brown clay-loam containing moderate charcoal flecking. Above this, a 30mm thick layer of burnt (orange) sandy clay was overlain by a fine, light grey ash with much comminuted charcoal, with scorching of the pit sides. The upper fill was a mixed deposit of burnt debris including pieces of burnt or fired clay, and there was a similar upper fill within the gully to its east. The eastern pit lay at an angle, and was sub-rectangular, 2.0m long by 1.2m wide and 0.45–0.55m deep. Against the sides and base there were remnants of a lining of grey-green sandy clay. The fill comprised several thin lenses of burnt (orange-red) sandy clay between thicker deposits of fine, light grey-brown ash with comminuted charcoal. These were either the *in situ* debris from a succession of firings or a sequence of well-stratified dumps of burnt debris from elsewhere. Immediately adjacent there was a slightly shallower pit, 0.40m deep, with similar fills, but without well defined stratification. A third pit further to the east also had similar fills, perhaps suggesting that all three contained dumped burnt debris from multiple oven firings.

The large oven produced a substantial pottery group,

139 sherds, dated to the earlier twelfth century (ph 0, 1100–1150). The linear oven was sealed by a layer of limestone and mortar with an *in situ* vessel at the western end that is dated to the earlier thirteenth century (ph 2/0, 1225–1250).

The southern yard and pit group, SY2 and APITS

Remnant metalled surfaces of gravel in orange-brown clayey loam with much small limestone abutted the walls of the southern range, S19/20, and sparser gravel inclusions in the loams further to the west and south suggest that this surface had once been more extensive (Fig 5.7). To the south-east an area of early metalled surface was better preserved where it had been sealed by later buildings, S17 and A1. It comprised gravel pebbles in orange-brown clayey loam overlain by scattered flat-laid limestone including some stones with worn surfaces.

At the southern end of the surface there was a pit that had possibly held a clay-domed oven (see Fig 4.29, 1162/1355). The pit was sub-circular, 2.40m in diameter by 0.50m deep, with linear gullies forming flues or stokeholes extending to both the north and south for 2.00m. The gully fills contained some charcoal and burnt soils and a similar primary fill in the pit was overlain by a 70mm thick layer of heavily burnt debris, possibly indicative of *in situ* burning (1355). The upper fill also contained much charcoal and burnt sandy clay including small pieces of burnt or fired clay.

There was a cluster of four pits to the south of the oven which also contained burnt debris (see Fig 4.29, A pits), and a further two large pits, which cut the partially filled northern terminals of the double boundary ditch, 14, contained two or three distinct lenses of burnt soils and blackened loams with charcoal. In addition, the upper fills of both boundary ditches also contained considerable quantities of burnt debris. These concentrations of dumped debris were most probably derived from both the nearby drying oven and from general kitchen waste.

The yard surfaces were disturbed and contaminated, resulting in the presence of small amounts of later pottery, but the bulk of the material indicates that the main period of use was during the later twelfth century (ph 1, 1150–1225). The use of the pit group was contemporary with the similar group on the opposite side of the access road, and both are dated to the later twelfth century (ph 1, 1150–1225).

The eastern pit groups

Some distance to the east of the access road, a drying oven lay adjacent to a boundary ditch (see Figs 5.2 and 4.33, 393). A large deposit of carbonized, sprouted barley grain, which must have been accidentally burnt during a firing, indicates that it was a malt oven. The oven comprised a sub-rectangular chamber, 3.00m long by 2.00m wide and 0.50m deep, with a linear gully, 0.90m wide, probably serving as a stokehole, running eastward for 3.00m. A mass of fired clay from within the chamber had come from a clay-domed superstructure. The larger pieces were up to 200mm across and 80mm thick, with one face roughly smooth and sometimes blackened while the opposing face was more irregular and often contained one or two semi-circular impressions, typically around either 15mm or 35mm in diameter, of a wattle framework. The fired clay was hardened, and typically an orange-buff to orange-red in colour. The oven was in use in the earlier twelfth century (ph 0, 1100–1150), and is the earliest appearance of malting within the settlement.

For up to 7.0m to the west and east of the oven there was a surface layer of dark grey silty clay with much charcoal and frequent pieces of burnt clay, with further debris in the upper fills of the nearby boundary ditches, 17 and 18. These were probably dumps of burnt debris derived from both the use and the levelling of the oven.

Immediately along the eastern side of the access road there was a group of pits and gullies, with several pits containing burnt debris, typically burnt sands and fine ash (Fig 5.7, eastern pits). The largest pit, 2.50m long by 1.75m wide and 0.58m deep, was filled with interleaved layers of grey sandy loam, flecked with charcoal and burnt (yellow or red) sand, and red-brown sand free of any burnt debris. A remnant of a burnt clay surface at the northern end may suggest the presence of a hearth or oven built at ground level. These pits are broadly dated to the twelfth century (ph 0 and 1, 1100–1225), and are contemporary with the pit group on the opposite side of the access road (Fig 5.3).

To the east, two elongated pits and some smaller pits, did not contain burnt debris and were slightly later in date, the later twelfth century (phase 1). They were also contemporary with a linear gully, 0.90m wide by 0.25m deep, which cut some of the pits containing burnt debris.

This gully may have held a timber boundary fence, perhaps a precursor of the later boundary wall along this side of the central yard. At the eastern end of this complex a number of pits or post-pits extended southward onto the central yard, where they defined the southern end of the extended domestic plot of the twelfth-century building complex.

The southern walled yards

Walled yards had probably been formed at the introduction of the new barn and processing building, S17 (Fig 5.7). They showed respect for the earlier boundary ditches, showing that the introduction of the walls was just another stage in the development of the plot divisions.

A boundary wall ran south from the southern range, S19, to the old terminal of ditch system 4, blocking off the rear end of the extended domestic plot. It was removed when the manor buildings were levelled for the introduction of the new tenements, and was defined by a robber trench with a little rubble to either side of the trench. The southern boundary to the domestic plot was retained in the introduction of a boundary wall running between the old ditch terminal and the new barn, S17. A second roughly parallel wall, between 3.30m and 5.00m to the south, formed a short access route or a narrow yard, metalled with limestone in mortar, outside the processing room end of the new barn, S17.

To the immediate west of this walled area there was a large pit, 4.50–5.00m in diameter and 0.40m deep. The shallowly-sloping sides led to a central, steep-sided, sub-rectangular pit, 1.80m long by 1.45m wide and 0.30m deep. This may have been a well pit, perhaps supplying water to the trough in the processing room. It was later filled with building debris including pieces of limestone and much crushed limestone, the latter perhaps left over from mortar mixing. The lower fill contained pottery of earlier thirteenth-century date (ph 2/0, 1225–1250) while the upper fills, which included limestone rubble, contained mixed assemblages including pottery of fourteenth-century date (ph 3/2, 1300–1400).

6 The Watermill System (AD 950–1150) and the River Palaeochannels

Given the specialised nature of the evidence, the detailed description of the watermill system, its abandonment and the creation of the flood bank have their own chapter. In addition, the river palaeochannels that were observed and recorded to the west of the hamlet during gravel extraction are also described here (Fig 6.1).

The watermill system appears to have come into use as part of the original establishment of the settlement in the mid-tenth century (see Fig 4.1). The structural elements of the successive mills at West Cotton were only poorly preserved as it went through several refurbishments. One aspect of interest is that the original mill, in the tenth century, was vertical-wheeled while the later phases, in use through the eleventh and into the twelfth centuries, apparently comprised the simpler technology of the horizontal-wheeled mill, with both the wheel and millstone assembly set on a single vertical axle. In addition, much of the associated water supply system was located and partially excavated, providing a broad understanding of the entire system and the work involved in its creation. These elements comprised the 150m of the western leats, which linked the natural water supply with a millpond situated adjacent to the river channel, and the 50m of head race and tail race that served the successive watermills. For each major change in mill construction the entire leat system was renewed, with the preceding leat backfilled while a new leat was cut nearby.

At around the mid-twelfth century a period of catastrophic flooding, which resulted in the deposition of a considerable depth of alluvium across the surrounding landscape, led not only to the disruption of the water supply and the abandonment of the mill system, but also to the creation of a system of flood protection banks, which partly overlay the former mill leats. These flood banks ensured the survival of the settlement despite it then lying up to 1.0m below the level of the newly formed floodplain (see Figs 5.1–5.3). There is a possibility that by the thirteenth century a new watermill had been established on the eastern side of the hamlet, at the edge of the floodplain, but this remains unproven.

Prior to the excavation at West Cotton, only three other watermills of the twelfth century or earlier had been extensively or partially excavated in England. The well preserved timber structure of a mid-ninth century horizontal-wheeled mill at Tamworth, Staffordshire (Rahtz and Meeson 1992) was excavated in 1971 and still stands as the classic English example of this mill type, and the reconstructed plans and elevations of the mill structure have made many appearances in the archaeological literature (eg Longworth and Cherry 1986, 148–9, fig 77). The successive vertical and horizontal mills at Old Windsor, Berkshire, spanning the eighth to tenth centuries, were excavated in 1953–8 by Brian Hope-Taylor and would have formed a major contribution to the understanding of early mills if more than a short note had been published (Wilson and Hurst 1958, 183–5). The twelfth-century watermill at Castle Donington, Leicestershire (Clay and Salisbury 1990, 276–307), was recognised in a watching brief during gravel extraction. Salvage excavations located a mill dam and the timber breasting within which a vertical wheel would have turned, but no other evidence for the mill itself was obtained. At a slightly later date, late twelfth to early fifteenth centuries, the sequence of four well-preserved watermills at Bordesley Abbey (Astill 1993), providing power for metalworking rather than milling, are now our major source of information on the form and working of medieval vertical-wheeled mills.

Fortunately, other useful evidence is available from both Ireland, where a number of early watermills have been excavated (Lucas 1953, 1–35 and Rynne 1989, 13–15), and Scotland, where a late nineteenth-century study of then recently abandoned horizontal-wheeled watermills in the Shetlands (Goudie 1886) provides a full description of their form and function.

A number of more recent discoveries are adding much to the understanding of early watermills, but it has not been possible to take this into account in relation to the mills at West Cotton.

The documentary evidence

by Paul Courtney

Domesday Book (1, 220c) records two mills held by the Bishop of Coutances (later Clare) in Raunds. One rendered 34s 8d and 100 eels, the second richest mill in the county, while the other produced only 12d. Holt (1988, 118–9) has suggested that some at least of such low value mills are likely to have been horizontal-wheeled mills, being cheap to maintain and build but limited in output. They probably belonged to substantial free tenants, such as

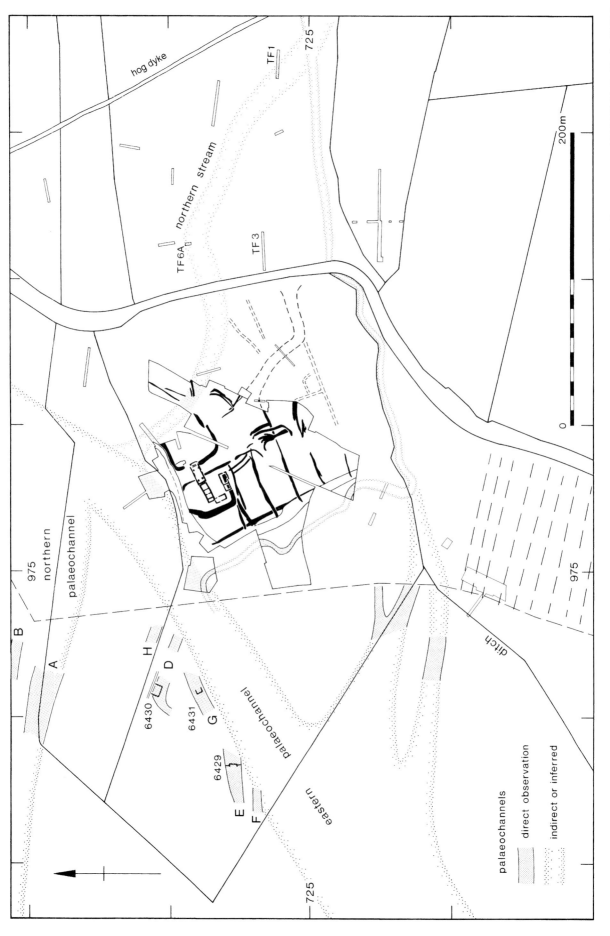

Fig 6.1: West Cotton: the observed river and stream palaeochannels. © Crown copyright. All rights reserved. Northamptonshire County Council: Licence No. 100019331. Published 2009

sokemen, or groups of peasants. It is possible that the 12d mill in Domesday was the horizontal mill excavated at West Cotton.

While there is no archaeological evidence for a later medieval mill at West Cotton, the documentary evidence indicates that Joan Chamberlain had a mill attached to her manor of Wilwencotes in 1413, but both its earlier and subsequent history is unclear (PRO C138/3). It is possible that this was the Chamberlain mill at Mallows Cotton, documented in the 1530s when it was farmed by Thomas Hopkyns (NRO X706: 23–4 Hen VIII), which could have been temporarily attached to Wilwencotes as part of Joan's dowry. However, the possibility of Chamberlain mills in both West and Mallows Cotton cannot be discounted. It is possible that the close in West Cotton sold by Thomas Hopkyns 'miller' of Ringstead in 1545 was attached to a former Wilwencotes mill. The only feasible location for such mill would have been beside the Cotton Brook to the east of the lane, and at the edge of the floodplain, where the buildings of medieval tenement I were investigated by limited trial trenching (see Fig 7.1).

The water supply

The motive power for the West Cotton watermills was provided by the Cotton or Tipp Brook, a minor tributary of the River Nene. It rises 3.5–4.5km to the east of West Cotton as several streams coming off the margins of the boulder clay at around the 75m OD contour (see Fig 1.2). The main tributary stream rises to the north-east of Raunds and flows through Raunds, where it is joined from the east and south-east by further tributary streams. For the final 1.0km of its course to the valley bottom, between the 46m and 38m contours, it flows almost due west down a deeply incised valley. Since the late eighteenth century, the stream has been carried well to the north of West Cotton within a linear channel, the Hogg Dyke (see Fig 1.3). Its previous course took it to the south and west of West Cotton, where it supplied the leats feeding the mill system, with the abandoned course of this stream surviving in earthwork.

Unfortunately, the complex history of the stream system in the immediate vicinity of West Cotton was not fully resolved. In addition to the southern stream channel, there is evidence that there had also been a northern channel. As these channel systems were not fully sectioned, their detailed histories and their inter-relationships remain uncertain, but a possible broad sequence of development has been postulated from the available evidence.

The northern stream

To the east of Cotton Lane geophysical survey and the location of water deposited silts in two trial trenches (Fig 6.1; TF1 and TF6A), suggest that a northern stream channel separated from the southern stream channel at the edge of the floodplain, near the current southern end of the Hogg Dyke (Figs 1.6 and 6.1). The presence of a northern stream channel pre-dating the late Saxon settlement was defined at two locations within the excavated area. North of an earth-cut malting oven in plot 10, the southern edge of a stream channel, at least 0.80m deep, was located in plan and partially sectioned (Fig 4.31, 310). It was sealed by the pre-late Saxon soil horizon. A machine cut trench, 1.0m deep, to the immediate north of this revealed the presence of water-deposited tenacious grey clays and gravel largely sealed by a general layer of alluvial clayey silts. They were not recorded in detail and the bottom of the deposits was not reached, and the location of the northern edge was not established. However, the demise of an active stream channel and the deposition of the alluvial layer by the middle of the twelfth century (ceramic phase 0, 1100–1150) was demonstrated by the excavated sequence within the adjacent ditch system (Fig 4.31, 17), where alluvial clay sealed early ditch fills of sandy silts with gravel.

To the north-west, the outflow channel of the earliest mill (M27) cut through the clay fills of a possible stream that was at least 5.00m wide by 0.85m deep (see Fig 6.9, 7392). By the late Saxon period the northern stream was therefore either narrower or had shifted slightly to the north of its former location.

There is therefore good, if fragmentary, evidence for a northern stream channel that became redundant within the early life of the settlement and which perhaps was already largely redundant when the settlement was created.

The southern stream

The southern stream channel was observed within the quarry edge to the south-west of the settlement, but it was not examined or recorded in any detail here, although palaeochannels on the same alignment were recorded within the quarry further to the west (Fig 6.1). In addition, the northern and southern margins of a broad eroded area to either side of the stream were observed within the southern part of the main excavation area and within detached trenches to the south, where the stream cut across the probable course of a prehistoric monument, the Long Enclosure (Fig 3.1, LE). The recorded truncation of the prehistoric ditches in these areas shows that the prehistoric ground surface had been eroded over an area up to 100m wide, and the area was subsequently buried beneath up to 4.0m of alluvial clay. These factors alone suggest that the southern stream was probably post-Bronze Age in origin, and therefore not the original stream channel, although the actual date of origin has not been established.

It is suggested that the northern stream channel was probably the active channel contemporary with the Neolithic and Bronze Age monuments, and that at some later date a southern channel developed which eventually became the principal stream channel. Whether the process of change was purely natural channel evolution or involved direct human interference is unknown. A further possibility, given the recovery of a beaver bone of late Bronze Age date (1310–

920 cal BC; 95% confidence; 2900 +/-60; OxA-4740), is that the channel evolution may even have been a result of hydrological changes caused by beaver activity, which may have blocked or at least drastically reduced water flow along the northern channel (Coles 2006, 90–95).

The western mill leats

An artificial leat system, 150m long, carried water from the southern stream channel at the south-western corner of the settlement to a millpond at the north-western corner (see Figs 4.1 and 5.1). The junction of the stream and leat system was not excavated but either there must have been a sluice gate to control water flow into the leat system or with the construction of the western leat the natural stream channel further west became redundant, with the entire water flow feeding into the millpond, and then either overflowing into the river or being fed to the watermills.

The creation of this water supply system would have entailed a major input of labour. The leats were from 2.5–4.0m wide and perhaps approaching 1.0m deep with respect to the contemporary ground surface. However, this particular aspect of the labour input was perhaps only broadly equivalent to the creation of the contemporary boundary ditch system, which entailed the digging of a far greater length of ditch, at least some 500m, although these were admittedly typically much narrower and shallower. Of course, in addition to the western leats there was also the labour input involved in the digging of the pond and the 50m of leat for the head and tail races.

A 49m length of the western leats was examined in 1987, with the sequence determined in plan, in two machine-cut sections and in a small area excavation over limestone-surfaced fords at the end of ditch system 3, the primary boundary between the northern and southern holdings (Fig 6.2).

There was a succession of three broad, flat-bottomed leats (Fig 6.3 a–c), and a final narrower and shallower leat probably post-dated the abandonment of the watermills (Fig 6.4 d). Only the small area excavation produced any dating evidence. The silts between two limestone surfaces of the ford within the third leat produced a small group of pottery dated to the earlier twelfth century (ph 0, 1100–1150) and further groups of this date came from the upper silts of the same leat and from the limestone surfacing of the ford within the fourth leat.

It is not possible to make any firm correlation between the western leats and the mill sequence to the north, and it may be noted that three western leats have been identified as opposed to a sequence of four leats relating to the mill system. However, a simple equation would suggest that the first western leat was contemporary with the original mill (M27) and perhaps the following period of disuse as well, while the second and third western leats may have been contemporary with the two horizontal-wheeled mills (M26 and M25).

The first leat (Phase 1)

The earliest leat was steep-sided with a broad flat bottom, 2.40m wide, and was 0.80m deep with respect to the ground level to its east (Figs 6.3a and 6.5, section a–a', 6941 phase 1). The basal levels of 33.25 and 33.15m OD show a gradual fall towards the millpond. The primary silts, up to 0.25m deep, comprised water-deposited silty sands and fine gravel, and was overlain by mixed and convoluted deposits of light grey silty clay and orange-brown sand or sandy clay with coarse gravel inclusions. The upper fills only partially survived, and comprised alternating bands of red-brown sand with some gravel and gravel in red-brown sand, all inclined downwards to the east. They appear to derive from deliberate backfilling of the leat.

The second leat (Phase 2)

The second leat had a steep-sided, flat-bottomed cut, 4.00m wide with a basal width of 3.40m (Figs 6.2, 6.3b and 6.5, section a–a', 6955 phase 2). It was 0.40–0.60m deep, shallower than the first leat, with bottom levels of 33.64 and 33.35m OD at the two sections, again indicating a fall towards the pond. There was a marked dog-leg in its otherwise linear course. At the junction with the pond a partial longitudinal section was obtained, and here the bottom level was at 33.30m OD and it sloped steadily down into the pond.

The leat contained a primary fill, 0.10m deep, of water deposited sandy or clayey silts with moderate gravel inclusions. This was overlain by up to 0.50m of sandy clays and red-brown sands with variable densities of gravel inclusions and some poorly defined tip-lines, which was probably a result of deliberate backfilling. At the junction with the pond a primary fill of orange-brown sandy clay merged into the blue-grey sandy clay of the permanently waterlogged pond silts.

The third leat (Phase 3)

The third leat was from 4.60m to 5.50m wide, broadening towards the north (Figs 6.2, 6.3c and 6.5, section a–a', 6951 phase 3). Along the eastern side there was a double edge formed by a deposit of red-brown sand or grey sandy clay with some pebbles and small pieces of limestone, from 0.30 to 0.80m deep with a steep to near-vertical inner face. In the sections to the north this was seen to sit on a slightly shallower shelf, and it did not have the characteristics of natural silting. It is most likely that it formed a deliberate backfill, perhaps behind a vertical timber revetment of the leat edge, although no stake or postholes were located. One possibility is that the leat was found to be too wide for the water flow and was made narrower. The western side of the leat was also steep-sided. The basal levels varied between 33.25m and 33.35m OD, but with no consistent fall towards the north.

At the end of ditch system 3, the western side of the leat

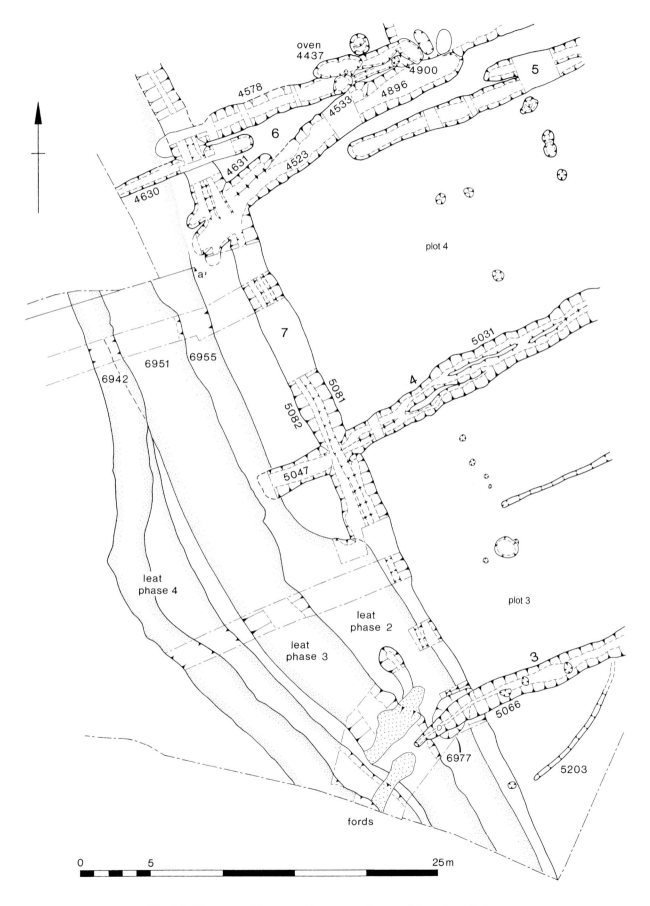

oven
4437

4900

4896

4578

4533

4523

4631

4630

6

5

plot 4

5031

7

6951

6955

6942

4

5081

5082

5047

leat
phase 4

leat
phase 2

leat
phase 3

plot 3

3

5066

6977

5203

fords

0   5   25 m

Fig 6.2: The watermill system; the western leats and boundary ditches

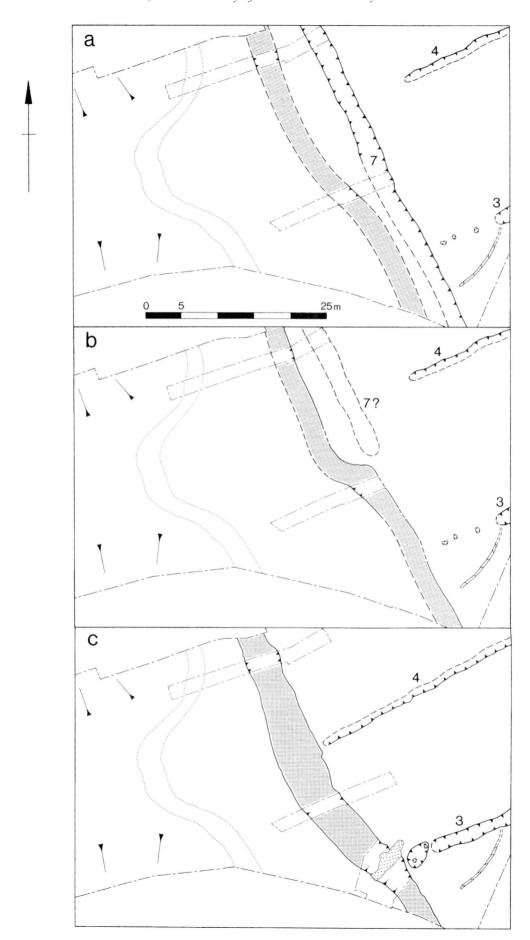

Fig 6.3: The watermill system; the early development of the western leats; a) earliest mill leat and boundary ditch (7), b) second mill leat c) third mill leat, with metalled ford

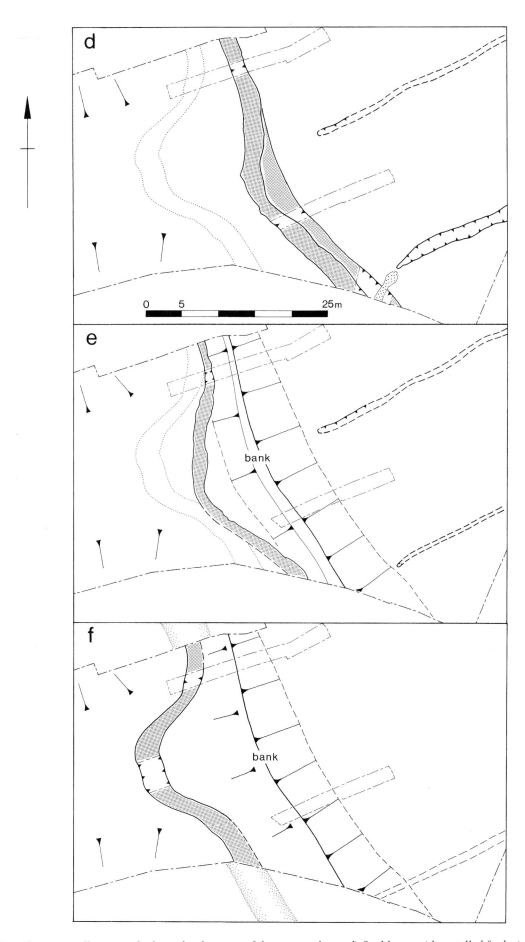

Fig 6.4: The watermill system: the later development of the western leats; d) final leats, with metalled ford, e) flood bank and watercourse, f) flood bank and later watercourse

had a shallow slope. Above a primary fill of up to 0.10m of mixed sandy silts with some ironpanned sand and gravel, there was a 2.00m wide metalled surface of limestone set across the width of the leat, apparently forming a surfaced ford (Fig 6.2). The basal layer comprised a scatter of large, flat-lying limestone slabs, up to 500mm long, while the upper surface comprised closely-set, flat-lying slabs of limestone, up to 400mm long, heavily water worn and ironstained (Fig 6.6). Within the leat the surface was near horizontal, and to the east it climbed up the side of the leat within a shallow ramp cut into the leat side. A comparable western end may have been removed by a later leat. Up to 0.10m of sandy silts with fine gravel inclusions overlay the margins of the original surface and were sealed by an upper limestone surface. This was also up to 2.00m wide, and to the east it too climbed up the side of the leat onto the adjacent ground surface (Fig 6.6). Within the leat it had a slightly domed surface of closely set pieces of limestone, up to 300mm long, with an infilling of limestone chips. The surface was water worn and ironstained.

The fourth leat (Phase 4)

The fourth leat was both shallower and narrower than its predecessors, at 2.20m wide with a broad flat bottom, by 0.30m deep, bottom level 33.65–33.80m OD (Figs 6.2, 6.4d and 6.5, section a–a', 6942 phase 4). To the north only a single cut was recognised, but at the fording point there were successive cuts. The earlier phase had a double eastern edge formed by a band of clayey loam set against the leat side. To either side of the limestone surfaced ford this deposit was retained by large slabs of limestone, up to 450mm long, pitched near vertically to form a revetment. The limestone surface of the ford was up to 1.60m wide and comprised closely-set flat-lying slabs of limestone, up to 300m long, all heavily water worn. The surface was partially covered by ironpanned sand and gravel, no more than 30mm thick (Fig 6.6). To the east the surfacing continued up the side of the leat and across the fills of the preceding leat for 2.00m, although here it consisted of disordered slabs and blocks of limestone up to 0.60m long.

It is suggested that the more sinuous course of this leat, and the fact that it was much narrower and shallower than its predecessors, may indicate that it appeared once the problems of flooding and alluviation were already underway, and it might post-date the abandonment of the mill system but pre-date the construction of the flood banks.

The millpond

The southern margin of the millpond lay within the main excavation area and was partially investigated by a combination of machine and hand-excavation (Fig 6.7). The western end lay within a detached, machine-cut trench to the north-west. This area had been investigated before the mill system was located, and the trench had been opened

in the hope of finding a watermill complex. As a result, the complex palimpsest of successive pond, river and stream silts that were revealed in plan were not fully understood at the time, and can now be only partially interpreted retrospectively (Fig 6.8)

The available evidence suggests that the pond was 40–45m long and 20m wide at its western end. It was probably narrower to the east, with a pear-shaped plan. At the western end the flat bottom of the pond was at 32.30m OD. The bottom level lay 1.50m below the ground level to its south, 0.85m below the lowest point of the first western leat and 0.80m below the highest point on the head race of the earliest mill (M27). This indicates that a depth of water in excess of 0.80m would have been required to provide a water flow to the mill, while a depth of at least 1.00m can be suggested as the minimum for the practical functioning of the early mill. With an original surface area of 500 square metres the water capacity of the pond would have been 500 cubic metres, or around 110,000 gallons.

The western end of the pond contained up to 0.50m of blue-grey tenacious clays, and this accumulation would have raised the base of the pond to above the bottom of the head-race for the second mill (M26) and only slightly below the bottom of the final head race (M25). Most of this accumulation must therefore have occurred no earlier than the use of the final mill and much of it probably after the abandonment of the mills, as otherwise the pond would have had no storage capacity to feed the mills.

The northern side of the millpond lay closely adjacent to the contemporary river channel. The machine-cut trench at the north-western end of the pond indicated the presence of a 3.00–3.80m wide ridge of earlier river silts, capped with up to 0.20m of dumped mixed sandy and clayey silts with gravel, separating the pond from the contemporary river channel (Fig 6.7). The ridge was narrower to the north-east, and it is suggested that the excavated part lay at the western end of some form of overflow from the pond into the river, perhaps either a simple weir or a more elaborate timbered sluice, but no evidence was recovered to determine which.

While the western end of the pond was apparently kept open to near its full depth and width throughout the lifetime of the mills, the sequence of silting and recutting at the eastern end indicates that the pond was not kept fully scoured here, so that there was a progressive retreat of both the eastern end and the southern side. Contemporary with the final mill (M25), the effective length of the pond had been reduced to around 20m, half its original length.

The eastern end of the pond was cut into earlier water-deposited silts of Roman date which may have lain along the southern margin of the river channel. The presence of these underlying silts and the disturbance of the early pond silts by the later leats made it difficult to identify the respective phases of activity in plan excavation. In particular, it is not possible to state with certainty the means used for controlling the outflow from the pond into the head races, as no certain sluice gate foundations had survived at the junction of the

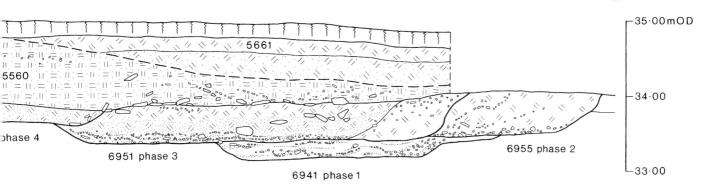

a'

35·00mOD

5661

5560

34·00

phase 4

6951 phase 3

6941 phase 1

6955 phase 2

33·00

mill leats

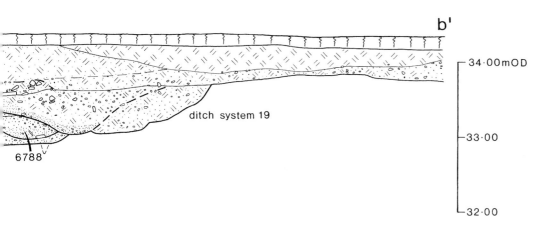

b'

34·00mOD

ditch system 19

33·00

6788

32·00

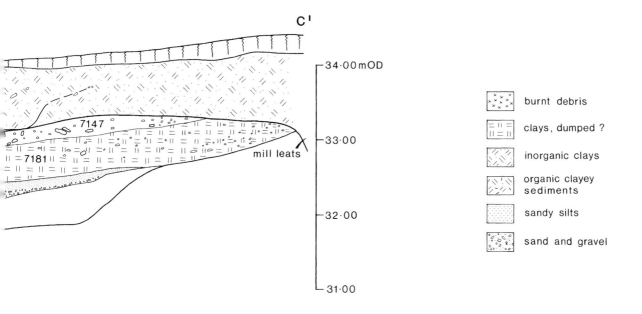

c'

34·00mOD

7147

7181

mill leats

33·00

32·00

31·00

burnt debris	
clays, dumped ?	
inorganic clays	
organic clayey sediments	
sandy silts	
sand and gravel	

10 m

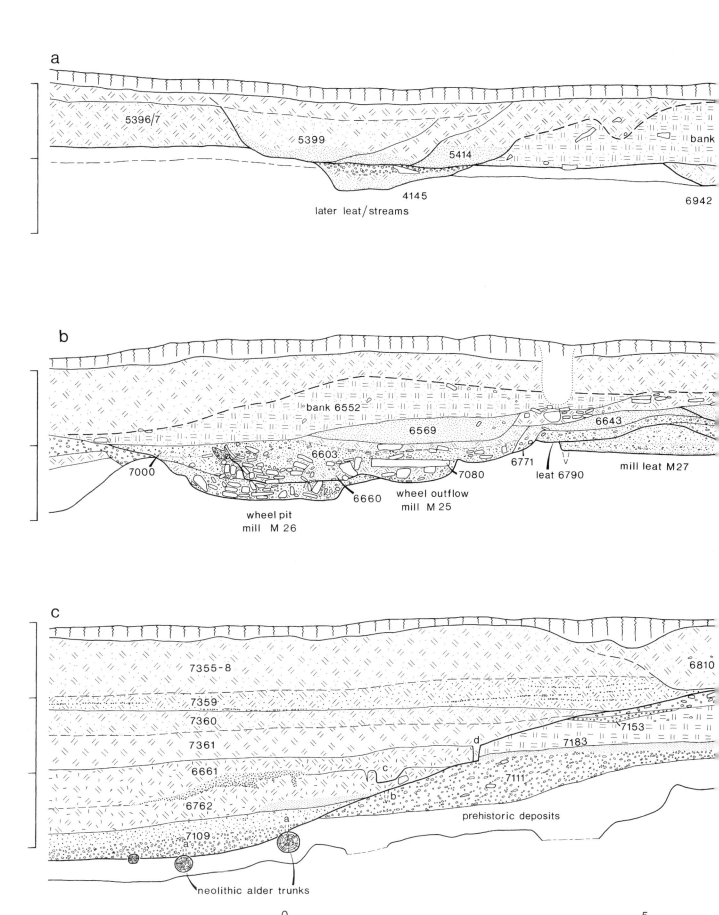

a

5396/7
5399
5414
bank

4145
6942

later leat/streams

b

bank 6552
6569
6643

7000
6603
6771
mill leat M27
6660
7080
leat 6790

wheel pit
mill M 26
wheel outflow
mill M 25

c

7355-8
6810

7359
7360
7153
7361
7183
6661
d
7111
6762
c
b
prehistoric deposits
7109
a
a

neolithic alder trunks

0   5

Fig 6.5: The watermill system, sections; a) the western mill leats, the flood bank and late watercourses, b) the watermills and the flood bank, c) the river channel, riverbank and overlying alluvium

Fig 6.6: The limestone metalled fords on the western mill leats, looking south

pond and the successive leats, and there was no surviving evidence for the provision of bypass channels. It seems most likely that there had been controlling sluice gates at the eastern end of the pond, but that the evidence had either been lost or lay beneath one of the several unexcavated baulks (Figs 6.7 and 6.9). Alternatively, water was free to flow from the pond into the head races, with control of the flow only exercised at the eastern end of the head races.

The only dating evidence from the millpond came from pottery within a dumped layer of mixed occupation debris (Fig 6.7, 6905) filling the subsidence hollow over the accumulated pond silts. This group of 23 sherds is dated to the earlier twelfth century (ph 0, 1100–1150).

The watermills (AD 950–1150)

The series of head races, watermills and tails races formed a complex stratigraphic sequence, containing water-deposited silts, dumped backfills and numerous cut features that had held elements of the timber mill structures that had later been removed. In addition, the area had later been buried beneath the dumped clays of a flood protection bank and accumulated alluvial silts, so that the deepest parts of the mill system lay over 2.00m below ground level.

The mill sequence is therefore only interpretable as a result of excavating it within what became, after a series of extensions, a single open area 35m long (Figs 6.8–6.10). The later mills (M25 and M26) were excavated in 1988. The head race feeding the first mill (M27) was recognised and excavated at the end of the 1988 season. In 1989 the area was extended eastward in two stages to uncover the wheel-pit and tail race of the earliest watermill.

The first watermill (M27)

Although the pottery evidence is scanty, the presence of a St Neots ware, T1(3)-type bowl rim within the wheel-pit revetment suggests a construction date in the second half of the tenth century (ph LS2, 950–975), while a Cotswold Oolitic sherd from the earlier silts of the head race suggest that it was in use until the end of the century (ph LS3/1, 975–1000). The absence of any later pottery suggests that the mill was abandoned and the leats backfilled at the end of the tenth century and this is supported by the eleventh-century dates (ph LS3/2, 1000–1100) for the earliest phase of ditch system 19, which was cut into the mill backfills (Fig 6.9). A displaced hazel stake, presumed to have come from the wheel-pit revetment was submitted for radiocarbon dating but the 8th–9th century date obtained suggests that it was residual from the middle Saxon usage of the adjacent river channel (see Chapter 9, UB-3322).

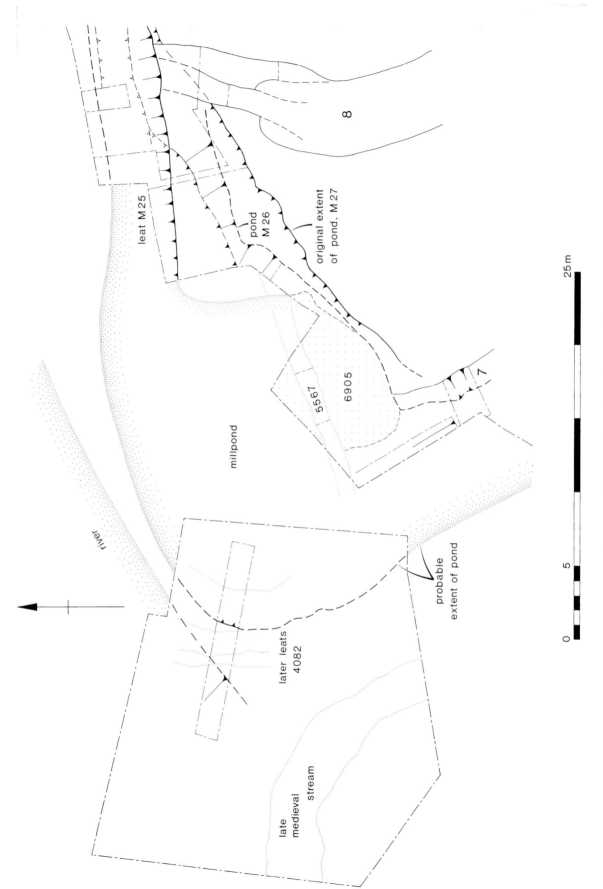

Fig 6.7: The watermill system: the mill pond, general plan

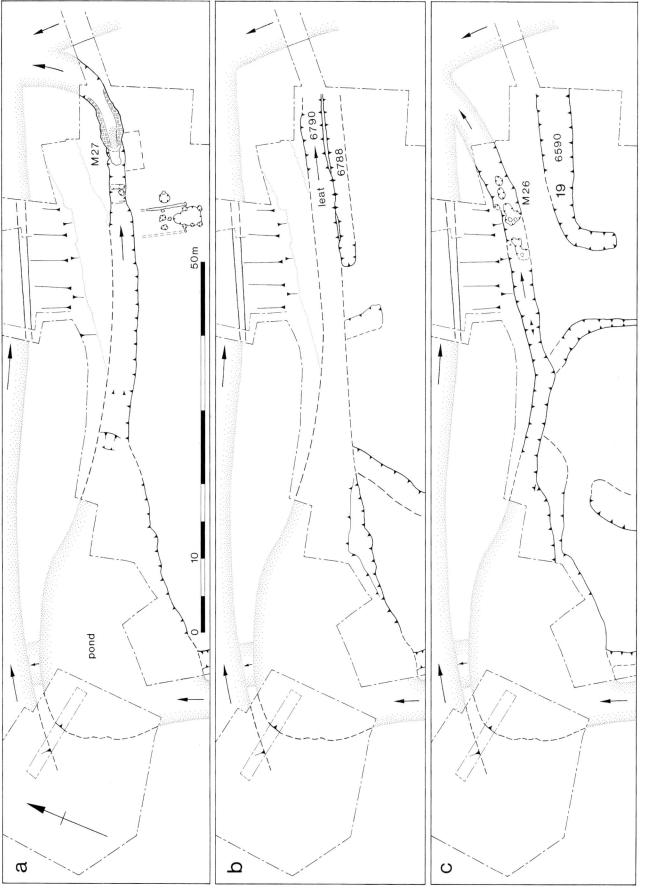

Fig 6.8: The watermill system: the early development of the pond and mills: a) the vertical-wheeled mill, M27, b) the leat system, 6790; probably no functioning mill, c) the second, horizontal-wheeled, mill, M26

The head race

The eastern end of the pond was some 0.20–0.30m deeper than the western end, bottoming at 32.00–32.10m OD, and was 1.90m deep. A shallow hollow, 0.08m deep, filled with limestone fragments, at the base of a 0.30–0.40m high step in the pond floor provided the only evidence for the expected provision of a sluice to control the water flow into the head race, but the feature was too poorly preserved to provide any details of its form (Fig 6.8a).

The head race was a broad flat-bottomed leat, 26.5m long, but for most of its length the northern side had been lost (Figs 6.5, section b–b', mill leat M27; 6.8a and 6.9). At the eastern end it was 2.90m wide at the base, but it was then already tapering towards the dam and sluice (Figs 6.10 and 6.11), so it must have generally been at least 3.10m wide.

The surviving depth of the truncated leat and its fills was typically 0.20–0.40m and never more than 0.60m, although its original depth would have been around 0.85m. The base of the leat was uneven but slightly concave, being up to 0.10m deeper at the centre, presumably as a result of water scouring. The natural gravel on the leat bottom was reddened by ironstaining and hardened by ironpanning, and there was a general fall of 0.30m between the pond and the sluice.

The presence of closely-spaced stakeholes in the base of the leat along the entire southern side and the surviving part of the northern side, indicate the provision of continuous timber revetments between the pond and the sluice (Figs 6.9 and 6.11). The stakes were quite regularly spaced, with an average of 0.44m centre-to-centre, a range of 0.35–0.55m. For the final 8.0m approaching the sluice gate, where the leat was tapering and the speed of the water-flow would have increased, they were slightly more closely-set, averaging 0.37m centre-to-centre, a range of 0.30–0.45m (Fig 6.12).

The stakeholes were typically 150–200mm deep, and 70–80mm in diameter, and tapered to blunt points, indicating that they were the impressions of driven stakes, although no remains of any stakes were recovered. The stakeholes were all filled with light grey silty sand. In many instances the stakeholes were visible as loose silty fills containing small voids within the compact and often partially ironpanned leat fills for up to 0.30m above the base of the leat. Along much of the leat there was also a 100mm thick band of fine silty sand against the near vertical leat side. This silting had probably filled a void left by the decay of the revetment retained by the stakes. No evidence for the nature of the revetment was recovered, but it must have consisted either of planking or wattles and, given the survival of wattles within the wheel-pit, the latter suggestion may be preferred.

The primary fill of the leat comprised up to 0.10m of sandy to clayey silt mixed with some coarse sand and fine gravel. It was sealed by a comparable depth of coarse, gritty sand with pebble inclusions partially consolidated by ironpanning. Above this, there was a repetition of the same sequence of fine and coarser silting, with the coarser upper fill again partially consolidated by ironpanning. These deposits derive from successive phases of use, which may equate with the two phases of wheel-pit.

The final leat fills comprised a water-deposited silty clay with some pebble inclusions and a few small to medium fragments of limestone, indicating a third period of water deposition. This was sealed by a layer of gravel in a sandy matrix, completely consolidated by ironpanning, which appeared to be a deliberately dumped backfill.

The mill

The mill comprised three structural elements and, by analogy with the well preserved mill, dated to the eighth century, at Morett in Ireland (Lucas 1954, 15–23), where the timber superstructure survived, these have been identified as the dam/sluice, the feeder chute, and the wheel-pit (Figs 6.12–6.14 and Plate 6).

The dam/sluice

At the constricted, 1.90m wide, eastern end of the head race the provision of a timber dam/sluice was indicated by a pair of shallow transverse slots (Figs 6.12, 7226 and 7227; Fig 6.15). The western slot (7226) was 0.26m wide by 0.10m deep, with near vertical sides and a flat bottom. It had sub-square terminal postholes, 0.17m diameter and 0.37–0.40m deep, tapering to blunt points. Within the southern posthole there was a partial void and the decaying base of an oak post, up to 250mm long by 60mm thick, but clearly shrunken and distorted as a result of drying. Above this the hole was sealed by consolidated gravel pierced by a rectangular opening measuring 100mm by 60mm, providing minimum dimensions for the original post. It is assumed that horizontal timbers would have been retained between the two posts to form the western end of the dam/sluice arrangement.

The second slot lay 1.70m the east, and was 2.00m long by 0.74m wide, with the ends slightly recessed into the leat sides (7227). It was 0.10m deep, with an irregular central deepening to 0.18m. Several medium to large fragments of limestone lay on the base of the cut along with part of a millstone. This was thicker than the other stones but rested partially within the central deepening, so that the upper surfaces of the stones were near level. The millstone showed little, if any, signs of use, and may therefore have been broken or faulty, explaining its reuse in the mill structure. A smaller, joining fragment was recovered from the fill of the revetment slot along the northern edge of the tail-race. The stone filling of this second slot is assumed to have been a base for a horizontal timber or sill forming the eastern end of the dam/sluice.

The sunken area between the two slots was 1.60m wide and near level, at 32.89m OD. The natural sand and gravel was not reddened and hardened by ironstaining and panning, indicating that the water was carried above this

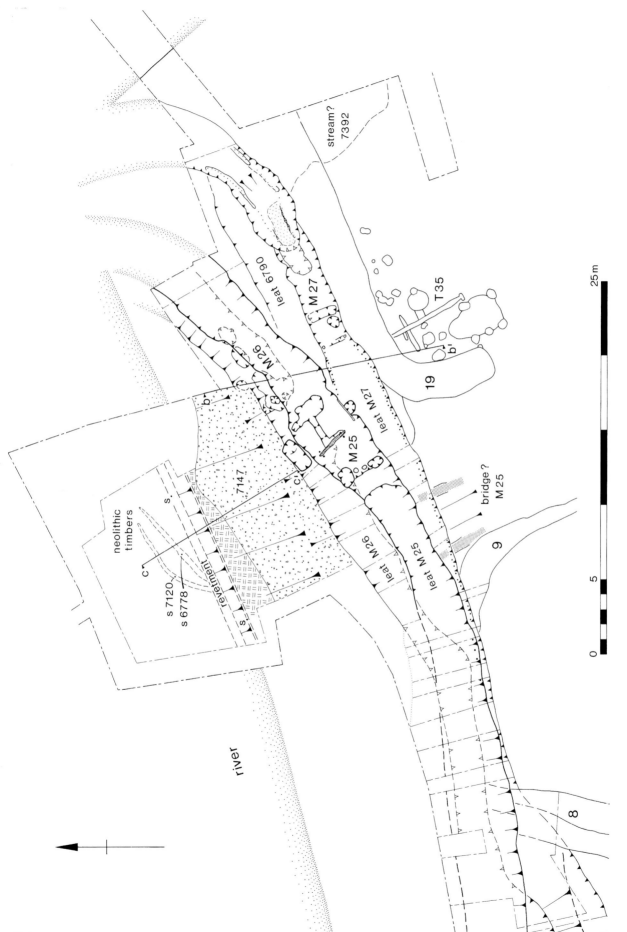

Fig 6.9: The watermill system; general plan of the mills and the riverbank

Fig 6.10 : General view of the mill complex, looking east, after excavation of the third mill, M25 (centre, no baulks), with the second leat and mill, M26 (left) and the first leat, M27 (right) with the first mill still to be uncovered (top right)

Fig 6.11: The first watermill, M27, looking west, showing the stakeholes along the edges of the leat, partly marked with modern posts (top left)

within a timber superstructure running between the two slots. A post-pit towards the southern side was oval in plan, 0.80–0.90m in diameter by 0.26m deep (7228). A sharply defined rectangular deepening in the base, 0.46m long by 0.24m wide and 0.04m deep, may have held a rectangular post, measuring 0.40 by 0.20m, perhaps relating to the control of a sluice gate.

The feeder chute

A timber chute would have occupied the space, 4.70m long, between the dam/sluice and the wheel-pit. This area was 1.80–2.20m wide and 0.10–0.15m deep. Beneath it there was a steep-sided cut (Fig 6.13b, 7308), 1.00–1.40m wide and up to 0.35m deep, which terminated beneath the eastern transverse slot. The homogeneous fill of clean gravel and sand, very similar to the underlying natural, indicates that it was deliberately backfilled soon after it was cut and no purpose related the functioning of the mill can be ascribed to it. It is suggested that it may have provided an access ramp into the wheel-pit during construction, which was

backfilled before the sluice gate was constructed. The gravel in this area showed no signs of reddening and hardening from ironpanning, indicating that the water had been carried above this level in a timber superstructure, the feeder chute. Immediately adjacent to the dam/sluice there were the rounded terminals of two shallow slots (Fig 6.12, 7313 and 7314), 0.25m wide by 0.08m deep, and set 0.50m apart. They ran eastward for at least 0.40m, but further east they had been removed by later activity. They may have held sill beams supporting a timber chute, which would have been at least 0.70m wide.

The wheel-pit

As a result of later activity, the ground level around the feeder chute and the wheel-pit had been lowered by some 0.70–0.90m. As a result, any evidence for the extent and nature of the mill house or of any supports for the wheel itself had been lost. However, there were two successive wheel-pits.

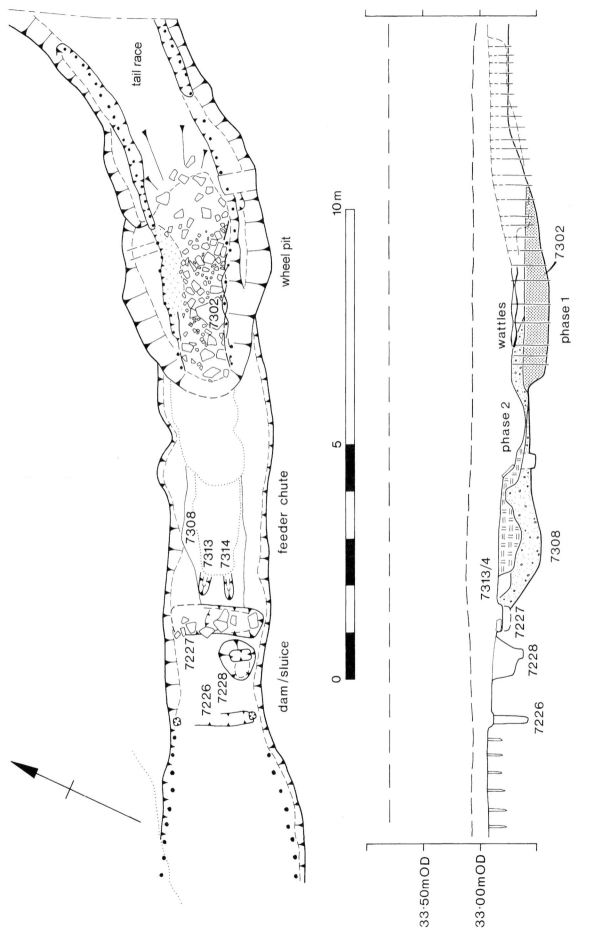

Fig 6.12: The first watermill, M27, with reconstructed longitudinal profile (exaggerated vertical scale)

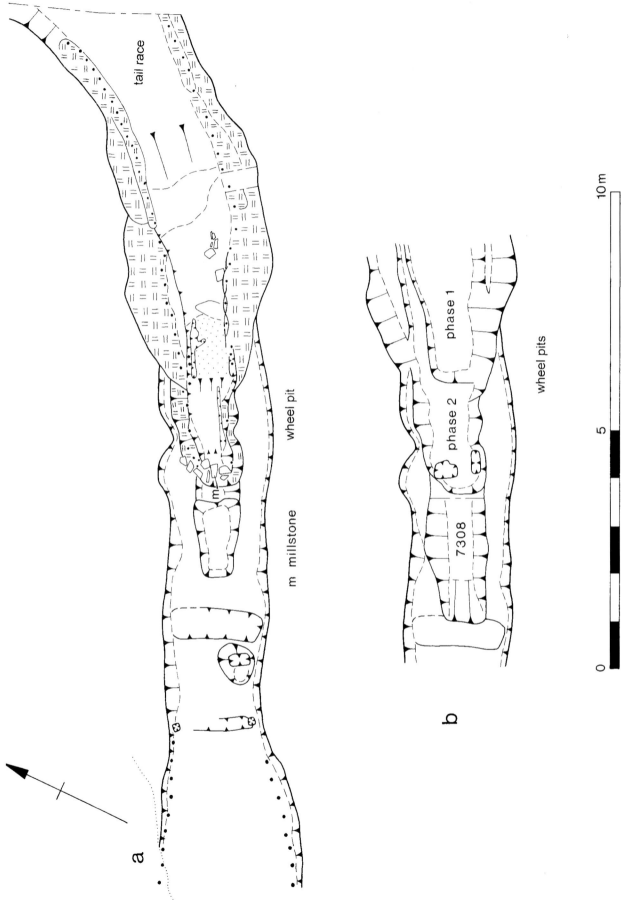

Fig 6.13: The first watermill, M27, a) second phase and b) construction pits

Phase 1

The original pit was up to 3.20m wide, but with shallowly sloping and stepped sides, and survived to a depth of 0.55m, bottom level 32.41m OD, the deepest part of the mill complex (Fig 6.12, section and 6.13b, phase 1). Both sides of the wheel-pit were provided with revetments of closely-spaced stakes and wattles. To the west the revetments were 1.00m apart, but they diverged slightly and then more rapidly to lie 1.80m apart at the junction with the tail race revetments. The former stakes were largely defined by voids within the clay backfill, although in two instances decayed stakes, in oak and Pomoideae type (Hawthorn/apple *etc*), survived *in situ* (Fig 6.16). Along the southern side the stakes had been driven 50–100mm into the base of the construction pit, while to the north they were driven to a comparable depth into a lower ledge on the side, which stood 0.15m above the base of the pit. The westernmost stakes were closely set at 0.20–0.25m intervals, but to the east the spacing increased to 0.30–0.45m. The best preserved stake voids were 30–35mm in diameter. Few of the voids were anywhere near vertical, indicating that there had been later displacement and collapse of the revetments.

Decaying remnants of wattles interwoven between the stakes survived along a 2.50m length of the southern revetment (Fig 6.17). They stood to a maximum height of 150mm and comprised withes 15–25mm thick, identified as Corylus type (Hazel/alder), perhaps indicating the use of a mixture of available woods rather than the use of a single species obtained from systematic coppicing. The longest continuous withy was 1.25m long, and a few others around 1.00m long were also observed.

The gap between the stake and wattle revetments and the sides of the construction pit was partially backfilled with mixed deposits of grey sandy loam and clay, with frequent inclusions of pebbles and limestone chips. This was sealed by a more compact upper layer of grey sticky clay. In places there appeared to be two phases of backfilling along the northern side, suggesting that this revetment had been refurbished. The upper level contained some fragments of broken millstones.

Limestone metalling (Fig 6.12, 7302) ran along the base of the wheel-pit for 4.70m. It was heavily water-worn, ironstained and concreted by ironpanning. To the west it comprised closely-set, flat-laid slabs and fragments of limestone, typically 150–300mm long and from 10–20mm thick; but including a single large block that measured 650 by 600mm. To the east the surface was patchy. The limestone surface was 1.00–1.20m wide, with an additional strip, 0.40m wide, along the northern side surfaced only with gravel pebbles and small fragments of limestone. It is suggested that this latter area may not have formed part of the base of the pit exposed to water action, and that it may have been sealed by some lost structural element, perhaps a horizontal timber set between the revetment and the surfacing.

The metalling was uneven but roughly level, at 32.60–32.65m OD. The floor of the pit was therefore 0.30m below the base of the chute area. An upper surface of pebbles, cobbles and some smaller fragments of limestone, probably resulting from resurfacing, also contained several water worn fragments of Millstone Grit and lava millstones. All but the very eastern end of the surfacing was sealed by a thin layer, 0.05m thick, of light grey sticky clay mixed with some grey silty loam.

Phase 2

In the second phase the wheel-pit lay 2.00m west of its predecessor, but was less well preserved. It was formed by backfilling the sunken base of the western end of the original wheel-pit with clean gravel and orange sand, and cutting into the eastern end of the feeder chute area (Figs 6.12 and 6.13a). The surviving evidence suggests that the sides were retained by stake-supported revetments, but along the southern side only two stake voids were identified, while to the north there were three well preserved stake voids, 50–60mm in diameter, and a further four less well-preserved examples. At the western end pairs of stakes appeared to have been set within two shallow rectangular pits (Fig 6.13b), 0.05–0.08m deep, rather than being driven into the base of the construction pit. Behind the revetments and against the sides of the construction pit there was a backfill of sand and gravel sealed by firm grey clayey loam.

The spacing of the stakes indicates that the wheel-pit had a maximum width of 0.80m, some 0.20m narrower than its predecessor. At the western end there was a curving setting of stones with the central three inclined at 30–45 degrees. They were largely limestone slabs but the central stone was a fragment of Millstone Grit. The floor of the wheel-pit was not surfaced, and it had a concave longitudinal profile with a shallow linear hollow, 1.40m long, 80mm wide and 60mm deep, along its southern margin. Short lengths of shallow slot also lay along either side of the tail race immediately to the east.

The closely spaced stake voids within the southern slot were in-line with the original southern revetment and suggest that this had been retained and perhaps refurbished at this time. The slot to the north, typically 100mm wide by 60mm deep, which contained two stake voids, was set inside the line of the original wheel-pit revetment.

The grey black loam that filled the hollow of the second phase wheel-pit and also extended eastward into the tail race, contained frequent pieces of semi-decayed wood largely in the form of long thin withies, these were presumably derived from collapsed and decaying wattles. In addition, a small piece of spindle wood showing signs of working was recovered from these fills, and was perhaps a remnant of the mill mechanism, possibly a cog-tooth, indicating the selection and use of a particularly hard wood for elements of the mechanism subject to extreme wear.

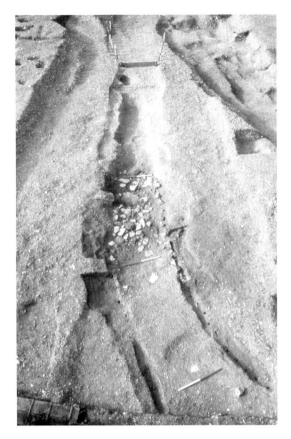

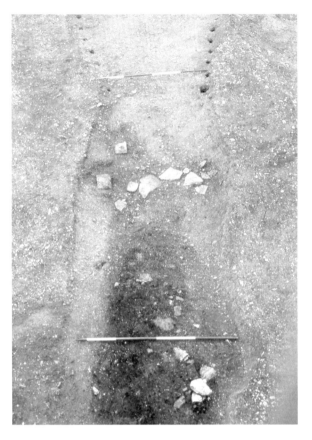

Fig 6.14: The first watermill, M27, looking west (upstream), with the leat and dam (top, marked with modern posts and plank), and the wheel-pit fully excavated to show slots containing stakeholes (foreground)

Fig 6.15: The first watermill, M27, showing the tapering head race and the dam/sluice, looking west (upstream)

The tail race

Roughly in line with the eastern end of the surfaced length of the original wheel-pit, there was a change in the revetment construction (Fig 6.12). The base of the tail race sloped up by nearly 0.20m, to 32.77mOD, and remained near level further to the east, although there was considerable difficulty in accurately defining the base of the tail race due to the merging boundary between undisturbed gravel and the primary fill of clean sands and gravel mixed with grey silty clay. This gave the impression that the natural gravel floor had been churned-up and mixed with water deposited silts, probably a result of the swirling and turbulent water emerging from the wheel-pit. For the first 2.60m the tail race revetments were closely parallel, at 1.8m apart, but beyond this they diverged, and were 2.20m apart at the north-eastern end of the excavated area.

Although the original wheel-pit and tail race revetments appeared to be continuous, with no appreciable change in alignment or the spacing of the stakeholes, the tail race revetments were set within shallow slots, 0.15–0.30m wide by 0.07m deep. The northern slot was 4.60m long, with clearly defined terminals. The slots were filled with mixed grey clay and sandy silt with pebble inclusions, and were capped with homogeneous sticky grey clay free

Fig 6.16: The first watermill, M27, the metalled wheel-pit with modern pegs in stakes voids, looking west (upstream)

Fig 6.17: The first watermill, M27, the preserved stake and wattle revetment

of inclusions. The narrowest length along the northern side also contained a packing of cobbles and limestone, while a single fragment of millstone beside the western terminal joined with a larger portion used in the dam/sluice construction. The stakeholes were typically seen as voids, 30–35mm in diameter, within the slot fill, and they had also been driven 50–100mm into the underlying natural gravel. Along the southern side the stakes were spaced at 0.35–0.40m intervals, while to the north they were typically more closely set, at 0.25–0.30m intervals.

Further to the east the side of the tail race were not supported by revetments. Here the tail race was 3.20m wide and it curved towards the north, presumably to debouch into the contemporary river channel at its junction with the old and redundant northern stream channel.

The vertical-wheeled watermill

The use of an undershot vertical wheel within the earliest mill was indicated by the narrow and shallow channel of the wheel-pit. A simple reconstruction of the basic arrangement of the head race, the dam/sluice, the feeder chute, the wheel-pit and the tail race is based on the evidence provided by one of the few excavated examples of an early vertical-wheeled watermill at Morett, County Laois, Ireland (Lucas 1953), dated by dendrochronology to 770 AD. Here the timber structures of the three main elements were recovered largely intact and the close comparability of general form and dimensions suggests that this mill can be taken as a

model for the West Cotton mill (Fig 6.18). The succession of four mills at Bordesley Abbey also repeats the same basic design (Astill 1993).

At Morett, the dam/sluice comprised converging side beams that held a boarded floor and uprights with vertical boarding set in rebates, although these latter elements had not survived. The side beams were dovetailed into a major transverse timber baulk, and a second timber had originally lain above. These probably held a movable board forming a simple controlling sluice at the end of the dam. The dam/sluice arrangement at West Cotton was shorter but probably of the same general form.

The 4.20m long feeder chute at Morett was hewn from a single timber, with a channel 0.50m wide, which is indicative of the width of the water wheel itself. The chute was only supported by transverse beams at either end, so its presence had left no earth-fast features, and a similar situation pertained in the mill at West Cotton, where the original feeder chute may have been 5.0m long.

At both Morett and West Cotton direct evidence for the precise location of the wheel is lacking. However, at Bordesley Abbey the associated features have been interpreted as indicating that the wheel was centred at the end of the feeder chute, so that the full diameter of the wheel would have spanned the ends of both the feeder chute and the wheel-pit. The diameter of the wheel at West Cotton is unknown, although the minimum width of 1.00m between the wattle revetments indicates that the wheel must have been less than 0.75m wide. At Morett

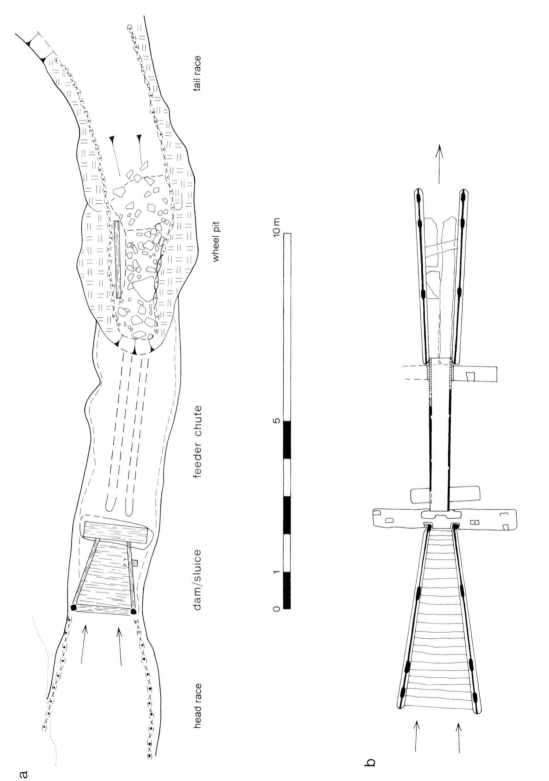

tail race

wheel pit

feeder chute

10 m

5

1

0

dam/sluice

head race

a

b

Fig 6.18: The vertical-wheeled watermill: a) West Cotton, reconstructed, b) the late eighth-century mill at Morett, Co.Laois, Ireland

the wheel-pit comprised a pair of slightly divergent side beams with rebates to hold a boarded floor while the side walls, partially surviving, were of boards slotted into rebated uprights.

The West Cotton wheel-pit was apparently of much simpler design, with the sides of wattles woven between closely spaced stakes, while the base of the pit was metalled with limestone and gravel, unless some more elaborate timber structure set within this had been lost. To the east, the progressive widening of the tail race would have reduced the rate and the turbulence of the water flow, so that first the metalling and then the wattle and stake revetment could be dispensed with.

The comparison between the mills at West Cotton, Morett and Bordesley Abbey is striking in the evident close comparability of both general form and scale (Fig 6.18). We therefore have almost the same mill structure reproduced at three sites, two in England and one in Ireland, over a time span of some seven centuries, from the later eighth to the late fifteenth centuries, and used for both corn milling and metalworking. It would seem that this mill form represented the basic design pattern for a small vertical-wheeled, undershot mill; a design that appears to have been widely repeated for several centuries through much of the British Isles and Ireland with only minor variations.

A period of disuse

The high organic content of the dark loam, containing much partially decayed wood, that formed the primary fill of the wheel-pit of the first mill, suggests that it probably formed in waterlogged conditions. This, as well as the semi-collapsed state of the wheel-pit revetments, indicates that the wheel-pit was left open for sometime following the abandonment of the mill and the probable dismantling of the mill building. The subsequent fill within the watermill area and the head race was of redeposited natural gravel and sand, mixed with some grey loam, heavily ironstained and frequently hardened by ironpanning. This was probably a deliberate backfill, perhaps coming directly from the digging of the next phase of leat and boundary ditches.

The second leat lay immediately north of its predecessor, and was broad and flat-bottomed, up to 3.00m wide and 0.20–0.40m deep, although with respect to ground level it would have been up to 0.80m deep (Figs 6.8b and 6.9, leat 6790). Along part of the northern edge of the leat there was a shallow slot, no more than 0.05m deep, which may have held a timber revetment. The mixed fill of sand, gravel and silt was concreted by ironpanning into a solid mass. The new leat was probably contemporary with the formation of a new boundary ditch system, which lay to the immediate south (Figs 6.8b 6788), with both the leat and the ditch system partly overlying and cutting into, the backfilled first watermill (Fig 6.5, section b–b', leat 6790 and ditch system 19).

Along the surviving length of this leat there was no evidence to indicate the former presence of a watermill.

There appears to be insufficient space for such a structure to have lain to the east, and if a mill had lain to the west it would have to have been totally removed by the construction of the final mill (M25). In addition, the base of the leat stood at a higher level than the tail races of both the earlier and the later mills, suggesting that the water was flowing through with little change in level, in contrast to the marked changes in level between the head and tail races of the watermills.

It is therefore suggested that this leat may have been a simple watercourse carrying the outflow from the pond during a period in which there was no functioning watermill. The change in mill technology from the original vertical-wheeled mill to the later horizontal-wheeled mills may therefore be seen to have occurred at a re-establishment of the mill system after a period of abandonment, rather than as a direct rebuilding and replacement of the original mill. The length of the period of disuse cannot be calculated, but may have been years rather than decades, given the limited period of use for the entire system.

The second watermill (M26)

The 53 sherds of pottery recovered from this mill largely comprised undiagnostic St Neots ware sherds, although there is a single sherd of Stamford ware and a single early St Neots ware bowl rim. It is therefore only broadly dated to the eleventh century (ph LS3/2, 1000–1100) but, given the more precise dating available for both the earlier and later mills, a date spanning the first half of the eleventh century can be suggested.

The head race

The end of the pond had apparently retreated westward by at least 5m, with the earlier silts left *in situ* beneath, and with a further accumulation of silts against the southern side, so that the pond edge lay 3.0m further north (Fig 6.7). At the eastern end the pond was 1.40m deep, at 32.40m OD, 0.40m deeper than the shallowest point of the head race. The junction of pond and head race was not defined, but probably lay immediately west of ditch system 8 (Fig 6.7). No evidence was recovered for any sudden change in level or the provision of a timber sluice.

The head race was a broad flat-bottomed leat, 30m long (Figs 6.8c). To the east, where it had suffered less from later disturbance, it was up to 3.00m wide, with a basal width of 1.50–1.80m (Fig 6.19). From the pond the head race initially became shallower, from 1.30–1.00m deep, 32.50–32.79m OD, but then deepened to 1.20m, 32.60m OD, at the sluice. The only evidence for a revetment lay along the final 3.6m of the northern side, where a few stakeholes survived, driven 100–350mm into the base of the leat. The southern side of the head race had been lost, but some isolated stakeholes may have been part of a southern revetment and would indicate a basal width of 1.80m. Two of these stakeholes contained decayed, square-sectioned stakes.

In the base of the leat there was a sub-square pit (Fig

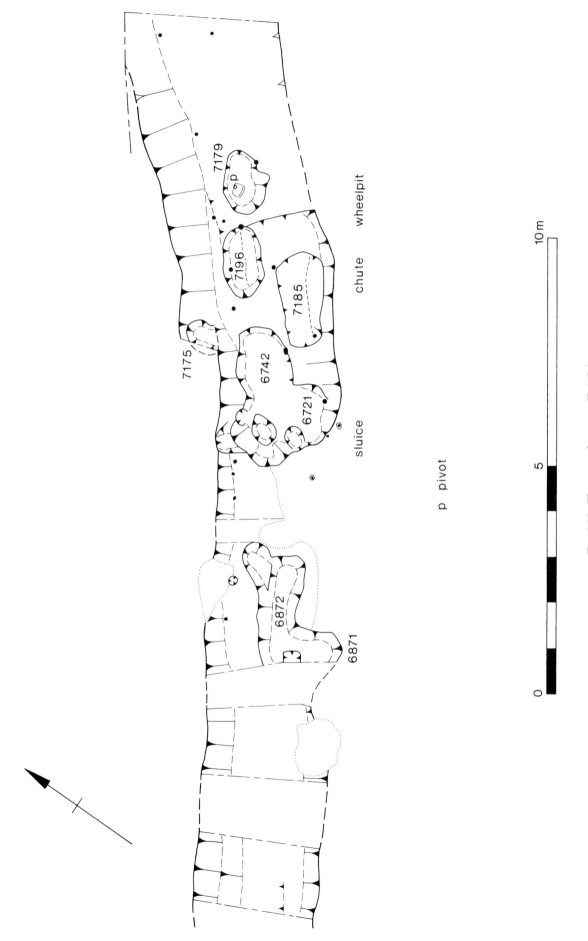

Fig 6.19: The second watermill, M26

6.19, 6871), 1.70m wide and 0.40m deep, and a linear slot (6872), 1.80m long, running along the length of the leat. Both had been filled with mixed sands and gravels prior to the accumulation of any silts within the head-race. It is uncertain whether they were directly associated with the functioning of the mill itself or were truncated earlier features.

The mill

The watermill was very poorly preserved, as it had been extensively disturbed by the construction of the final mill (M25). As a result the features recovered cannot be easily interpreted, but as the general form of the sluice, chute and wheel-pit areas are broadly comparable to the final mill, it too is assumed to have been a horizontal mill (Fig 6.19).

The dam/sluice

At the end of the head race there was a near vertical drop of 0.18m. Two oval hollows at the base, 0.60–0.70m in diameter and 0.10–0.17m deep, were probably the eroded remnants of post-pits supporting a sluice gate. They were both filled with grey clay and gravel and contained some fragments of limestone. A displaced oak stake, 685mm long with a rectangular cross-section of 90 by 35mm (6709, not illustrated), lay with its pointed base partly within the southern post-pit. A sub-rectangular recess to the north, cutting into the side of the leat, may have held the end of a horizontal beam also forming part of the sluice gate.

From the post-pits an elongated hollow (6742), 1.25m wide, ran eastwards for 3.00m, and a shorter hollow to the south (6721) was separated from it by a low ridge. In the northern edge of the leat there was a substantial post-pit (7175), 0.60m in diameter, with near vertical sides and a flat base, filled with clayey loam. A number of limestone fragments may have been displaced packing stones.

The whole of the sluice area was filled with tumbled limestone in a matrix of grey-brown sand and gravel, but this fill probably derived from the demolition of the mill structure.

The chute and wheel-pit

The only surviving evidence in this area comprised two shallow sub-rectangular hollows (7196 and 7185) and a further hollow to the east (7179). Hollow (7196) was 1.60m long, 0.85m wide and 0.20m deep. The northern, outer, half was filled with light grey sandy clay, and there was a near vertical edge between this material and the gravel and sandy clay, containing scattered fragments of limestone, filling the southern half, which may have come in after removal of the horizontal timber beam. The southern hollow (7185), 3.00m long, 1.00m wide and 0.12m deep, had a similar form and fill, with the southern, outer, half filled with grey clayey loam, and a near vertical edge against a fill of limestone in sand and gravel. These two hollows are tentatively identified as having contained

timber beams, set along the length of the leat, which may have supported a timber chute to carry water from the dam/sluice to a wheel-pit.

Along the northern side intermittent stakeholes, from 100–250mm deep and from 50–90mm in diameter, suggest the provision of a revetment.

The only evidence for the wheel-pit location was an oval hollow (7179), 1.40m long, 1.00m wide and 0.20m deep. This contained a square limestone block with a 50mm deep pivot hole on its upper surface (see Fig 11.15, 28). Immediately beyond the pivot stone there was a flat-lying slab of limestone and the remainder of the fill comprised steeply-pitched fragments of limestone tightly packed around the two flat-laid pieces. It is possible that the pivot stone was *in situ* and, if so, it may be postulated that it had held the base of the vertical axle supporting the horizontal mill-wheel. However, it did not appear to be substantial enough for this task, especially as the socket lay at the very edge of the stone block, and it may have been a displaced pivot stone from some subsidiary element of the system. At a more recently excavated and well preserved horizontal-wheeled watermill in stone, at Nendrum, Northern Ireland, the sluice gate had swung on a similar pivot stone (McErlean and Crothers 2007, 94–95)

The tail race

The tail race had been extensively disturbed by later activity. It had a basal width of 2.50m and two *in situ* driven stakes on the northern side, 650mm and 600mm long with square sections of 60mm, may indicate the provision of a revetment.

The abandonment of the mill

The head race had primary silting, 0.10–0.20m deep, of mixed sands, gravel and silty clay. The remainder of the fills all derived from deliberate backfilling with clean sand and gravel, which contained some inclusions of brown sandy silt and pieces of limestone.

The mill area had a more complex sequence of backfilling. It would appear that all the structural elements were removed before the entire area was backfilled with limestone rubble, sand and gravel and some clay to restore the ground level. A lump of charred horse dung, containing straw, oats and wheat came from this rubble dump. To the south of this backfill, a substantial revetment of limestone and clay formed the northern side of the wheel-pit and tail race of the final mill (M25), see below.

The third watermill (M25)

The third mill had a broad wheel-pit containing one of a pair of oak sill beams that would have supported a broad rectangular wheel house (Figs 6.20 and 6.21). This provided a marked contrast to the plan of the original mill, and this new structure is interpreted as a horizontal-wheeled watermill on the basis of the close comparison in general form to the well known excavated mill at Tamworth, Staffordshire (Rahtz and Meeson 1992) and also to the documented horizontal mills from the Shetlands (Goudie 1886).

Pottery from the clay and limestone around the *in situ* sill beam consisted mainly of T1(2) St Neots ware, along with sherds of Stamford ware and Cotswold Oolitic ware. This indicates a construction date in the eleventh century (ph 3/2, 1000–1100). The clay and stone revetments along the southern side of the wheel-pit and tail race produced a small pottery group indicating that at least a final refurbishment took place into the twelfth century (ph 0, 1100–1150). The fills of the leats and the wheel-pit, the later drainage ditches and the clay flood bank overlying the entire area are also dated to the earlier twelfth century and indicate that these successive changes all occurred within the space of no more than 50 years.

In addition, three radiocarbon dates were obtained from timbers from this mill. An unworked oak trunk within the wheel-pit revetment is dated to the tenth century, and may be regarded as an old timber (cal AD 880–1020; 95% confidence; 1086±29 BP; UB3326). More informative are the dates for an *in situ* post (6691) in the sluice (cal AD 890–1160; 95% confidence, 1014±51 BP; UB3327) and for the *in situ* oak sill beam (cal AD 990–1220; 95% confidence; 941±53; UB3325), which are both centred on the eleventh century.

The combined evidence of the pottery and the radiocarbon dating indicate a construction date for the third watermill at around the middle of eleventh century, with abandonment before the middle of the twelfth century. This would imply that it was this final, horizontal-wheeled mill that was in use at both the time of the Conquest and the Domesday survey. It was, perhaps, the cheaper of the two Raunds mills, worth 12d, as recorded in the Domesday Book.

The head race

The eastern end of the pond had retreated further westward and was not located, suggesting that the pond was then some 20–25m long, only just over half of its original length (Figs 6.7 and 6.20d).

The gently curving head race was 38.0m long (Fig 6.9). Along the western half, which lay west of a high point along the base of the leat, at 33.00m OD, the primary fills of silts and clays were pond-like deposits. To the east of this high point the primary fills were sandy silts with gravel, derived from flowing water deposition. There may have been a sluice set at this high point, but this area lay beneath an unexcavated baulk, and no evidence of a structure here was obtained. Along the entire length of the head race the bottom was ironstained and generally ironpanned, indicating that water flowed over the gravel bottom. At 6.5m from the eastern end the basal width was 2.50m and thereafter it tapered to a width of 1.60m at an abrupt, near vertical step, 100mm high (Figs 6.9 and 6.21). There were a number of features in the base of the head race. Substantial stakes had been driven in at each side (Fig 6.21, 6874 and 6875). The tapering stakeholes were 280mm deep and 150–200mm in diameter. Part of a decayed post survived in the southern stakehole while the northern hole had apparently held a rectangular-sectioned stake. It is suggested that they may have retained a fish trap.

Two pairs of shallow hollows, from 0.06–0.15m deep, flanked either side of head race at its eastern end (G6696). They lay within a rectangular area, 1.4m long by 1.15m wide, which was slightly sunken and uneven, perhaps as a result of erosion by turbulent water. The pits were all filled with mixed sand, gravel and grey clay and contained some small fragments of limestone. They had probably held posts supporting a revetment protecting the stepped end of the head race.

The mill

THE DAM/SLUICE

The pits (G6696) at the end of the head race may also have supported the western end of a timber dam structure spanning the 1.30m long ridge between the head race and the sluice. Ironstaining of the gravel base of this ridge does suggest the presence of water here, but perhaps as leakage from around and under a timber superstructure rather than from continuous water flow over the gravel, as a timber dam would have been a necessity to contain the water flow prior to it entering a feeder chute.

At the eastern end of the ridge there was a near vertical drop of 0.20–0.30m, with major post-pits at either end that would have held posts retaining the horizontal timbers of a controlling sluice gate. The southern post-pit (Fig 6.21, 6702), 1.10m long by 0.70m wide and 0.40m deep, may have been double, holding a larger post to the south and a smaller post to the north, perhaps 300mm and 100mm diameter respectively. A single fragment of limestone steeply-pitched against the cut side suggests that the other disordered stones within the fill had come from packing disturbed at the removal of the posts. The northern post-pit (6703) was 1.30m long by 1.0m wide and 0.40m deep. Compact gravel and sand against the northern edge may have been *in situ* packing, indicating that it had contained a post at least 300mm in diameter. The shallower eastern lobe of the pit may have held a further post or posts.

In addition, an *in situ*, rectangular-sectioned, oak stake, 510mm long and driven 50mm into the underlying gravel, stood in the north-eastern corner of the northern post-pit (Fig 6.21, 6691). A tapering stakehole, 80mm deep with a rectangular section of 60mm by 45mm, in the corner of the deeper western end of the pit, suggests the former presence of a second similar stake. They may indicate the provision of a timber revetment along the northern side of the wheel-pit. To the east, a shallow hollow and a short length of transverse, steep-sided, flat-bottomed slot (6713), at least 0.70m long by 0.30m wide and 0.12m deep, may also have been associated with the provision of a revetment.

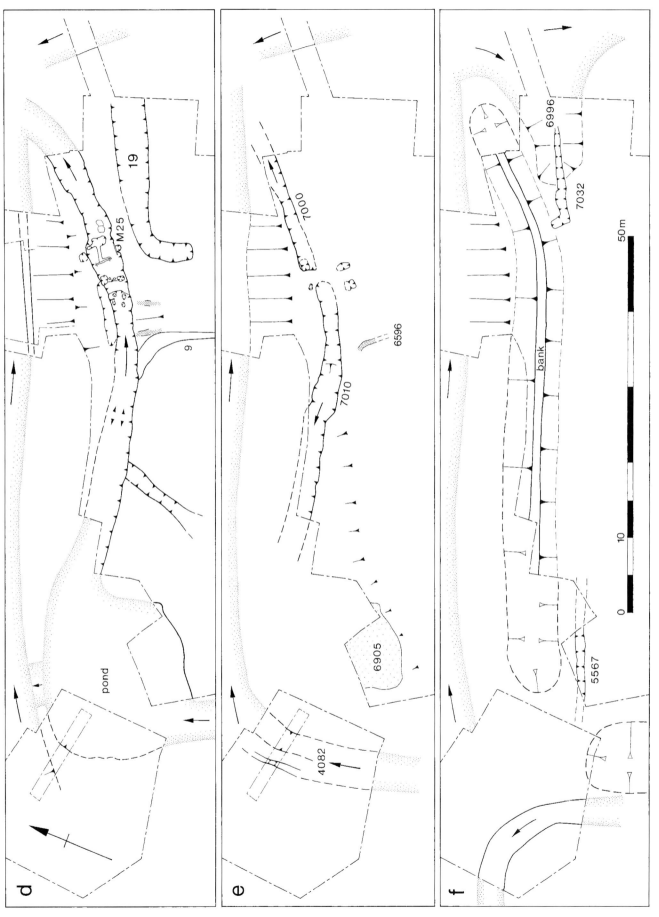

Fig 6.20: The watermill system; later development: d) the third mill, M25, e) drainage ditches on the former mill leats, f) the flood protection bank

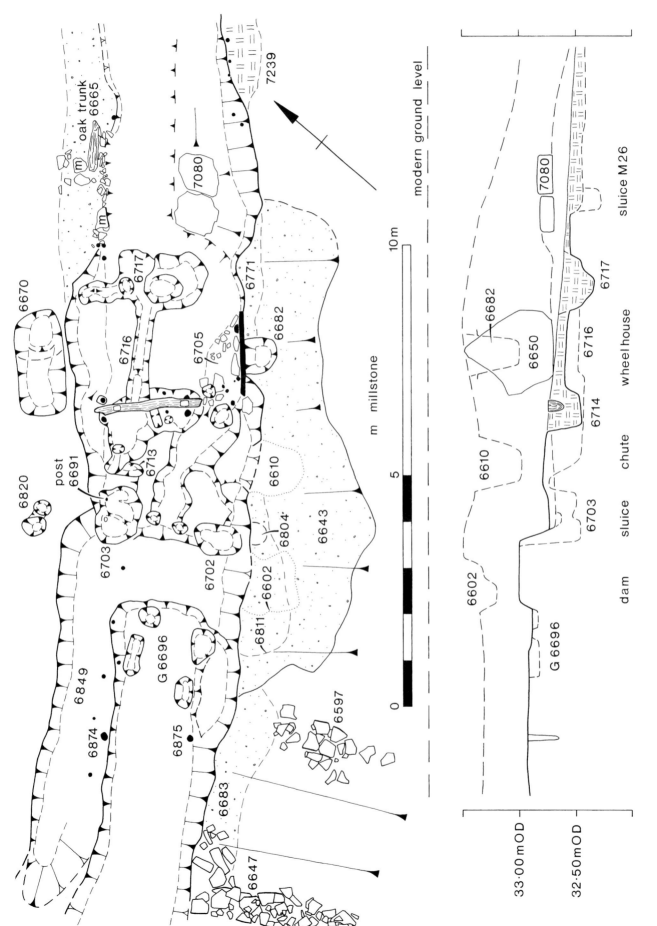

Fig 6.21: The third watermill, M25, with reconstructed longitudinal profile (exaggerated vertical scale)

The chute

Between the sluice post-pits (6702 and 6703) there were two small postholes, 0.25–0.30m in diameter by 0.15m deep, set 0.6m apart. These may have held smaller uprights supporting a central timber chute feeding the wheel house. The smaller post setting at the northern edge of the southern post-pit (6702) may also have been related, perhaps to support a second chute to feed water to a bypass channel south of the wheel house. (This interpretation is depicted in the reconstruction of the lost timber sub-structure (see Fig 6.25), which draws heavily on the intact timber structure of the mill at Tamworth.)

From the central postholes a shallow channel, up to 1.20m wide and 50–100mm deep, with irregular sides and an uneven base, followed a sinuous course running obliquely towards the southern side of the wheel-pit, and was filled with dirty sand and gravel. It may have been formed by water erosion associated with the flow to the bypass channel, perhaps suggesting that there was a regular, if not constant water flow bypassing the wheel house.

The wheel house and bypass channel

Two transverse slots define the probable location of a rectangular wheel house (Figs 6.22 and 6.23). The western slot (6714) was 2.40m long. It was 0.25m deep with respect to the chute area and up to 0.10m deep with respect to the surface beneath the wheel house. It was filled with grey clay mixed with some gravel, and an oak sill beam survived *in situ*, resting on this clay fill so that its upper surface was near level with the floor of the chute area to the west. The 2.39m long by 270mm diameter sill beam comprised a cleft trunk, which retained its bark, laid with the split face upwards (Figs 6.23, 6.24 and 11.35, 1). It was perforated by rectangular mortice holes, 170mm long by 130mm wide, set 1.33m apart. There were also two drilled perforations of 30–35mm diameter. In the base of the underlying slot there were pairs of stakeholes, set 0.35–0.40m apart and lying towards either end of the sill-beam. Three were circular-sectioned, 100–150mm in diameter, and penetrated 250mm into the gravel, while the fourth had a rectangular section of 90mm by 50mm. A pair of smaller intermediate stakeholes, 60mm in diameter, had been driven 100mm into the gravel. These stakes may have held or clamped the oak sill beam in position.

The eastern slot (6717) was of a similar general form, and was also clay filled. It is presumed to have held a second sill beam, most probably the other half of the same split oak trunk. At the time of excavation the bottom of this feature lay below the water table and further details, such as the stakeholes recovered in the western pit, may have been missed. A displaced and partially decayed length of oak plank (6690, see Fig 6.23 and Fig 11.36, 4) lay within the clay fills.

Running at a slightly oblique angle between the two transverse slots, there was a well defined, flat-bottomed linear slot (6716), at least 2.20m long by 0.40–0.50m

Fig 6.22: The third watermill, M25; showing the leat (top), the dam and sluice (centre) and the wheel-pit (foreground), looking west (upstream)

Fig 6.23: The third watermill, M25, showing the sluice and wheel-pit with in situ oak sill beam (centre), looking west

wide and 0.08–0.15m deep. This slot was only observed following the removal of the clay fill, 0.10m thick, that covered this area, but it may have held a removed timber associated with the wheel house structure that had been abutted by these clay fills.

The 1.0m wide gap between the wheel house and the southern side of the wheel-pit probably served as a bypass channel. There were two postholes, 0.55m and 0.30m in diameter and 0.15m and 0.20m deep, to the immediate south of the *in situ* sill beam. These may have supported the eastern end of a bypass chute. The side of the pit here was protected by a large vertical limestone slab (6650), described below. A hollow in front of the slab was filled with pebbles, cobbles and small fragments of limestone with frequent small voids between the stones. Above this there was a rough surface of flat-laid limestone (6705), which was water worn and ironstained. Patchy remnants of disturbed limestone surfacing continued eastward towards the two large slabs of limestone (7080) that lay beyond the eastern end of the wheel house, and at a slightly higher level.

The wheel-pit revetments

Along the southern side of the sluice area there was a broad shelf (Fig 6.21, 6811) filled with mixed sand and silty clay containing several large fragments of water-worn limestone and with a concentration of smaller fragments and cobbles along the northern edge. This appeared to form a consolidation and revetment of the edge. A circular pit (6804) 0.60m in diameter and 0.10m deeper than the base of the shelf, had a similar fill, and may have held a post related to the sluice gate structure.

Along the southern side of the wheel-pit the revetment had been partially lost, but it had probably run for a length of 9.8m from the sluice to the eastern end of the wheel house. To the east there was a 2.00m-wide gap and then a similar revetment (7239) flanked the tail race. It is uncertain whether this was an actual break in the revetment or merely a short collapsed length. The revetment comprised tenacious grey clay containing frequent fragments of limestone, pebbles, small cobbles and a single piece of Millstone Grit, all set on a distinct cut shelf (6771), with its base 0.10m higher than the base of the wheel-pit. There was no surviving evidence that the clay and stone was retained by timberwork, but within the similar tail race revetments there were some stakeholes, perhaps suggesting that evidence for similar supporting stakes within the wheel-pit may have been lost.

To the south of the wheel house the revetment included a large slab of limestone set vertically against the side of the construction pit (Figs 6.21, 6650 and 6.24). It was 1.90m long and up to 0.84m high, but tapered to 0.30–0.40m high at either end, and was 0.10m thick. The sides, right to the apex, were worn smooth. At least one function of this slab would have been to protect the post-pit immediately behind it (6682), while it would also have provided a general protection against erosion at a point where a bypass chute

may have deposited water into the bypass channel. The flat base of the slab stood on up to 120mm of clay and limestone fragments lying within a roughly semi-circular hollow within the base of the bypass channel (6705). A cluster of five stakeholes, up to 100mm deep and 100mm in diameter with either circular or rectangular sections, lay around the western end of the slab. At the eastern end there was a single stakehole, 200mm in diameter and 80mm deep, in front of the slab and a further stakehole was observed within the clay behind the slab as a rectangular-sectioned void, 80mm by 60mm, with a total height of 450mm and penetrating 70mm into the base of the pit. These stakes appear to have held the slab in place.

Along the northern side of the wheel house the former presence of a similar clay and stone revetment was indicated by a layer of clay and limestone fragments slumped against the pit side and overlying the northern end of the *in situ* sill beam. It was probably contiguous with the surviving revetment to its east, and it may have collapsed when the wheel house was dismantled.

The wheel supports

For a length of at least 11m the ground surface to the south of the dam, sluice, chute and wheel-pit, had been raised by the dumping of up to 0.30m of orange-brown sandy silt and fine gravel (Fig 6.21, 6643). The mill house structure would have been founded on this surface but later truncation of the upper levels had removed any indications of its presence.

A sub-square post-pit (6682), with steep to near vertical sides, was cut into this raised surface and abutted the rear face of the large revetment slab. It was up to 0.80m wide and 0.30m deep, but allowing for later truncation of the ground level an original depth of at least 0.45m is indicated. A flat-lying slab of limestone, 0.47m long, just above the base of the pit may have been either a pad-stone or a displaced packing stone.

A further post-pit (6670) lay beyond the northern side of the wheel-pit. It was 2.30m long by 1.10m wide, but had two phases of use. The original feature was a sub-square post-pit, 1.00m diameter by 0.45m deep, later replaced by an elongated post-pit, 2.00m long by 0.35m deep. It is suggested that the post-pits on either side of the wheel house would have held the uprights supporting a 5.00m long cross beam that held the vertical axle holding the wheel and millstone assemblies.

The tail race

A 10m length of the tail race was excavated. It had a basal width of 2.80m immediately beyond the wheel house, and probably maintained much the same width further to the east. Variations in the width as excavated are a result of the partial collapse of the clay and stone revetments before the area was backfilled.

Two flat-laid limestone slabs (Fig 6.21, 7080), each

Fig 6.24: The third watermill, M25, showing the limestone slab revetment and the in situ oak sill beam, looking south

around 0.90m square and heavily ironstained, lay to the south. They stood above the level of both the bypass channel to the west and of the outflow from the wheel house to the north, suggesting that the bypass water flow did not run straight through but was directed to the north and back into a common channel with the wheel house outflow. The outflow from the wheel house was initially contained within a narrow channel, 1.50m wide, but to the east this gradually widened until it occupied the full width of the leat.

A 4.00m length of the clay and stone revetment on the northern side of the tail race survived *in situ*. It overlay the wheel-pit of the second mill (M26) which had been backfilled with loose limestone rubble, with frequent voids between the stones. The revetment survived up to 0.35m high with a 0.30–0.40m deep vertical facing of fragments and blocks of limestone, and some millstone fragments, set irregularly within a matrix of sticky grey clay. Behind this the remainder of the earlier wheel-pit was backfilled with grey clayey loam containing a lower density and generally smaller fragments of limestone and some pieces of millstone. A single stake void was observed within the revetment face and penetrating the floor of the construction pit, while remnants of thin lengths of wood, up to 15mm thick, lay horizontally at the base of the face; indicating

that the revetment had been at least partially retained by stakes and wattles. Several fragments of Millstone Grit lay in the uppermost part of the revetment, including the single largest piece recovered from the mills, which was set into the top of the clay and stone facing. In addition, a length of unworked oak trunk or branch (6665), 1.20m long and 0.23m in diameter, was also set into the top of this revetment.

Along the southern side, the revetment (7239) comprised grey silty clay with gravel and some cobbles and small limestone inclusions. It also contained lumps of either sticky clay or ironpanned sand and gravel and there were some irregular voids within the fill. As with the revetment of the wheel-pit, it was set on a ledge bottoming up to 0.50m above the base of the tail race. At the western end six stakeholes were located as partial voids, typically 50–70mm in diameter and 80–150mm deep, spaced 0.3–0.4m apart, perhaps forming a localised reinforcement of the revetment.

The bridging point

Above the watermill, at the eastern end of the head race, there was a ramp flanked by walls on the southern bank and a ledge on the northern bank. These features had no obvious connection with the functioning of the mill and it is suggested that they relate to the provision of a timber bridge spanning the mill leat and providing access to the river channel beyond (Figs 6.21 and 6.25)

The ramp was 3.10m wide and 4.50m long, with a fall of 0.40m. The northern end lay 0.40m above the base of the head race. A shallow hollow along the edge of the head race (6683), 1.00m wide by 0.10m deep, was filled with sand, gravel and small fragments of limestone. Only a short length and a single course of the eastern wall (6597) survived *in situ*. The western wall (6647) was 3.80m long by 0.65m wide, with up to two courses of flat-laid limestone surviving. It had subsequently collapsed onto the ramp, and the quantity of rubble indicates that it had stood to a greater height.

The ledge (6849) along the northern side of the head race was 8.75m long by 1.00m wide. Its base lay 0.15m above the bottom of the head-race. Along much of the ledge there were stakeholes, typically 60–80mm in diameter and 170mm deep, set 1.0–1.2m apart. Sill beams forming the foundation for a timber bridge may have rested on this ledge and on the southern bank between the two side walls (Fig 6.25).

The horizontal-wheeled watermill

The later two mills at West Cotton have been identified as of the horizontal-wheeled form on the basis of their broad wheel-pits. The earlier example (M26) was very poorly preserved and no detailed interpretation of its structural form can be provided. In the final mill (M25), while only a few timbers survived *in situ,* the palimpsest of post-pits and other cut features define the former positions of further timbers so that it has been possible to provide a general reconstruction of the ground plan that has drawn heavily upon the excavated and reconstructed form of the mill at Tamworth, Staffordshire (Rahtz and Meeson 1992, figs 95–7), with which it appears to be closely comparable in general form and overall size (Fig 6.25).

Given the survival of the single oak sill beam with mortice holes at either end, which was set within one of a pair of parallel construction slots, it is clear that the West Cotton mill had contained a rectangular timber wheel house. While no direct evidence survived to indicate the provision of a timbered floor, the level and apparently undisturbed gravel bottom between the sill beam slots, which contrasts with the convoluted surfaces within the chute area to the west and in the bypass channel to the south, does indicate that the wheel house had been floored. The function of the slot running across this area is unclear, unless it held a timber providing additional support for a floor, perhaps directly beneath the water wheel. On the reconstruction, the wheel has therefore been placed above this longitudinal slot and between the post-pits set beyond either edge of the wheel-pit, which are believed to have held the uprights supporting the cross-beam carrying the vertical axle that held the wheel and millstone assemblies.

While such uprights could have carried the load, the lack of any lateral support seems surprising given the forces created by the functioning system. It is therefore likely that both the uprights and the cross beam were also tied into the structure of the mill house, which could then have provided the necessary lateral support. As no evidence for further earth-fast timbers was recovered, we must assume that the rest of the mill house was founded on ground laid sleeper beams spanning the wheel-pit, which have left no trace of their presence.

The millstones

The full report on the assemblage of millstones is within the finds report, and here only a brief summary is provided. The quantity of material recovered leaves no doubt that the primary functions of the successive mills was the grinding of grain into flour. There is a total of some 277 fragments, weighing 337kg, from sandstone millstones, the majority of which came from the structure and fills of the first and third watermills. In addition, there are some 55 recorded finds of lava, weighing 31.6kg, which has come from millstones in use only with the first watermill.

Stones in Millstone Grit from the Northern Midlands, most probably Derbyshire, form the largest group, although there are pieces from a millstone in finer-grained sandstone that was in use in the first watermill. By determining joining pieces and matching geologies it is suggested that for the Millstone Grit a minimum of seven separate upper stones and five lower stones had been in use through the lifetime of the first and third mills (Figs 6.26–6.28). The fragments of lava stone, which had been imported from the Eifel region of Germany, comes from a minimum of a further two sets of stones. The lava stones may have been of comparable diameters to the sandstone millstones, but as the circumferences of the lava stones often comprise flattened facets, the overall diameters may have been over estimated.

From the better preserved fragments it is seen that the millstones were typically 950–1000mm in diameter, and had been around 120mm thick when new, when a full set would have weighed 300–350kg (Fig 6.26). The used stones had typically been worn down to around half of their original thickness, and in one exceptional case an upper stone had two worn surfaces, indicating that it had been inverted and reshaped for reuse, and was used until it was only 32mm thick (Fig 6.26). In one case the distinctive shape of the surviving part of an upper stone suggested that it may have been recut to provide stone for a much smaller diameter rotary quern (Fig 6.27). The upper stones appear to have worn more rapidly than the lower stones, with this perhaps accounting for the greater number of upper stones identified.

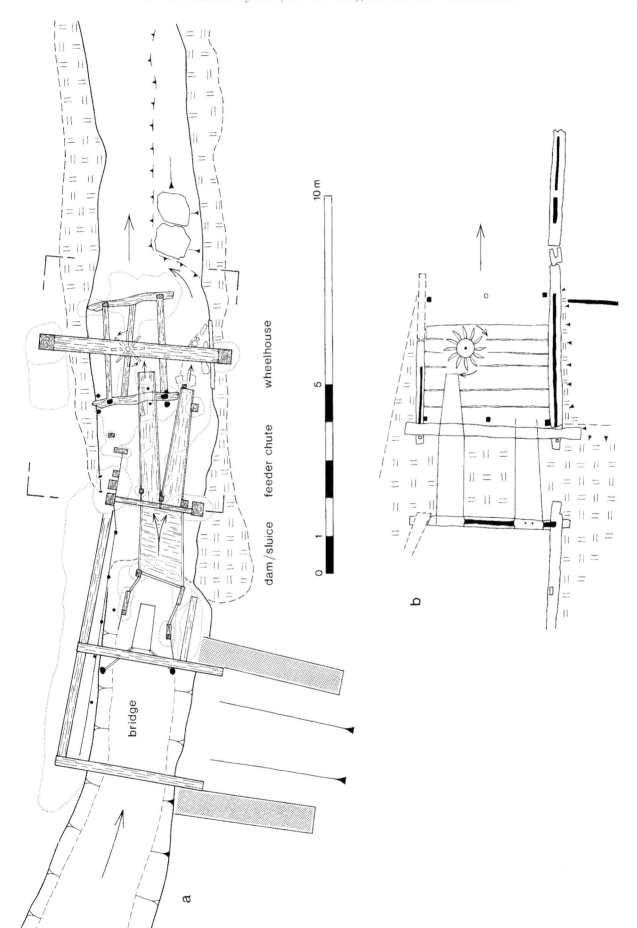

dam/sluice   feeder chute   wheelhouse

bridge

a

b

Fig 6.25: The horizontal-wheeled watermill; a) West Cotton, reconstructed, b) the ninth-century mill at Tamworth, Staffordshire

The abandonment of the mill system (AD 1150)

The abandonment of the mill system at West Cotton was a direct consequence of the disruption to the water supply caused by a catastrophic and abrupt episode of flooding and the subsequent deposition of alluvium, which remodelled the topography of the local landscape. Around the mill system itself, it is possible to describe a sequence of events that chronicle the onset of this episode.

The watermill area

Following the disuse of the final watermill (M25) the nature of the fills along the head race, wheel-pit and tail race provide evidence for a complex sequence of events occurring within a short period of time, some of this was evidenced in plan (Fig 6.20 e–f) but the overall sequence was largely derived from the section evidence (Fig 6.5b). The pottery from the entire sequence up to formation of the overlying flood bank falls within the first half of the twelfth century (ph 0, 1100–1150).

To the east of the final watermill, and above the area that had been occupied by the first mill (M27) and leat 6790 (Fig 6.9), there were very mixed layers of water deposited silts, denser pebble concentrations concreted by ironpanning, as well as dumped deposits of limestone, charcoal, burnt sands and fragments of fired clay derived from oven/hearth debris, and considerable quantities of fragmented animal bone and pottery, which included much Stamford ware, dated to the earlier twelfth century (ph 0, 1100–1150). This is all marks a period, shortly following abandonment of the final mill, in which either the leat systems were overflowing across the surrounding areas, or flood water was coming

Fig 6.26: Upper millstone, with fragment of rectangular socket (left)

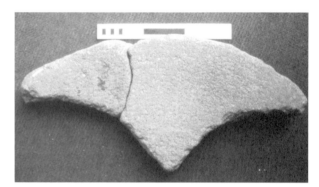

Fig 6.27: Upper millstone after recutting, possibly to provide stones for a small rotary quern

Fig 6.28: Lower stone in Millstone Grit

in from outside, with this particular area also being used as a convenient dump for occupation debris.

The primary fills of the wheel-pit of the final mill (Fig 6.5; section b–b', 6660) were of mixed sandy silts and clays, gravel, water worn fragments of limestone and frequent pieces of broken millstones. Some of this may have accumulated during the use of the mill, but much of limestone and millstone fragments must have been dumped following the demolition of the mill, perhaps to raise the wheel-pit and tail races to the same level as the head race. This allowed a smooth flow of water through the area, and this resulted in the deposition of sands and gravels (6603) heavily ironstained and partially ironpanned. A slowing of the rate of water flow is suggested by the later deposition of clayey-loam with some gravel.

Subsequently, the sluice and wheel-pit area was infilled with tumbled dumps of limestone rubble, including slabs of building stone up to 600mm long. This created a raised area some 10m long that would have stopped the flow of water through the system. However, water was still present to either side of the raised area. To the east there was an accumulation of generally coarser silts, including mixed sandy clays, sand with fine gravel and coarse yellow-brown sand (Fig 6.4, section b–b', 6569). To the west, sandy clays accumulated within the head race to a depth of up to 0.35m, and also over the ramp of the possible bridge approach and within the northern end of the adjacent ditch system (Fig 6.20d, 9). Following the filling of the boundary ditch, it was redefined by the introduction of a boundary wall (Fig 6.20e, 6596), 0.55m wide and surviving up to 0.30m high in three courses of flat-laid limestone bonded with yellow sandy mortar. A length of 3.00m of wall survived, which curved abruptly to the west as it approached the head race.

Once the head race had fully silted a new channel was cut along its northern side (Fig 6.20e, 7010). This was up to 3.50m wide and deepened towards the west, carrying water away from the raised area over the former mill. For part of its length the bottom was roughly surfaced with limestone and cobbles, heavily water worn and ironstained. To the east the evidence was less clear, but there may have been a similar channel along the northern side of the wheel-pit and tail race (7000). This also deepened away from the raised area and may have carried water eastward.

Two post-pits on the southern side of the former mill area (Figs 6.20e and 5.19, 6602 and 6610), were probably contemporary with this phase and may indicate the provision of supports for a new bridge. The pits were 1.50–2.00m long by 1.00–1.20m wide and 0.30–0.45m deep, with shallower shelves at the southern ends. To the north, a pair of smaller postholes (6820) and the elongated recut at the western end of post-pit (6670) may have formed an opposing pair of post settings. These four features would suggest the provision of a bridge some 3.00m wide by 5.00m long set slightly obliquely to the underlying, but by then largely backfilled, sluice and wheel-pit.

The pond and the western leats

The tenacious clays forming the primary deposits at the western end of the pond had probably accumulated after the abandonment of the final mill (M25). Above this there was a further 0.40m of light grey-brown sandy clays, and a final fill of light brown sandy clays with moderate pebble inclusions filled the pond almost to a level with the contemporary ground surface. The high level to which these silts had accumulated indicates they must have largely post-dated the demise of the entire western leat system, being contemporary with the higher level streams, described below, that had replaced them. They are therefore most likely to derive from flood inundation at a period when there was no longer any controlled outflow from the pond into the river (Fig 6.20e).

A final fill of dark grey clayey loam (Figs 6.7 and 6.20, 6905), was up to 0.40m thick and contained much occupation debris; pottery, animal bone, charcoal scatters, mottles of reddened (burnt) sand and burnt pieces of limestone, and was contemporary with the similar deposits to the east over the former watermills.

The identification of watermill systems

The previously excavated early watermills in England were recognised when substantial portions of the timber structures had survived. In this they differ markedly from the mills at West Cotton, where the timber structures had been almost totally removed.

It would seem likely that the situation encountered at West Cotton cannot be unique and may well be representative of many abandoned mill sites of pre- or immediate post-Conquest date. It is therefore of interest to consider what understanding of mill form and usage would have been achieved at two classic English mill excavations, Tamworth (Rahtz and Meeson 1992) and Bordesley Abbey (Astill 1993), if the timber structures had been largely lost. If the West Cotton mills had been encountered in, say, a watching brief or limited trial trenching, their very presence may not have been recognisable. In this context, it may be of use to future researchers to summarize the processes of thinking, investigation and chance that led to the discovery and excavation of the watermills at West Cotton.

The possible presence of a watermill at West Cotton had not been considered prior to the excavation. Retrospectively, this seems a curious oversight given the location of the settlement in the river valley beside a tributary stream. However, the expected peasant status excluded the possibility of a medieval manorial mill being sited here. In addition, the extensive leat and pond system and the watermills themselves had been totally concealed by a twelfth-century flood protection bank, so that the earthworks gave no indication of the presence of a mill system beneath. While the process of concealment may be unique to this site, there is clearly the potential for broadly comparable processes, such as stream migration and the deposition of alluvium, to have resulted in the concealment of mill systems at other similar settlements.

The first problem at West Cotton was, therefore, the recognition of the potential presence of a watermill system. The post-medieval stream channel with its sharply angled turns at the southern and northern ends (Fig 6.1), could have been seen as potentially indicative of an artificial origin, but this possibility was not recognised in advance of excavation. Indeed, the pre-excavation earthwork survey covered only the evident core of the settlement as defined by the building platforms, and ended at the inner edge of the flood protection bank. The stream course beyond was partially surveyed following the commencement of excavations, but was only fully surveyed once its significance to the understanding of settlement development had been recognised. Given broadly comparable circumstances at other deserted settlements, it might be possible to postulate the probable former presence of a mill system from anomalies in the courses of later stream channels, but to postulate the probable location of the mill itself presents a further difficulty which might not be resolvable purely from earthwork evidence.

At West Cotton the western stream course and the leats pre-dating it were partially uncovered at the southernmost end of the site in the first season of excavation, 1985, but this area had a low priority and no systematic attempt was made to understand the nature and development of the watercourses partly revealed in plan and section. The potential significance of the western stream system was finally recognised during the third season of excavation, 1987. However, this area was only examined in order to establish the extent of a prehistoric monument, the Long Mound (Fig 3.1), and without this additional impetus the western streams may not have been examined in such detail. Once the presence of the long sequence of watercourses was revealed, its potential use for generating water-power was appreciated, with Dr Mark Robinson instrumental in reaching this conclusion. As a result, a detached trench to the north-west of the main excavation area was opened to investigate the possibility that a medieval mill had lain at the northern end of the western stream channel system. The absence of a mill here was a disappointment, but retrospectively it can be seen that whilst the general reasoning was correct the detailed hypothesis was flawed, as the visible western stream post-dated both the abandonment of the mill system and the creation of the flood banks.

The location of the watermill system on the northern side of the settlement in the fourth season of excavation, 1988, was a result of chance. A broad trench was opened to link a previous detached trench across the river palaeochannel to the main excavation area, in order to provide a continuous stratigraphic link and to examine two large timbers within the palaeochannel which were then thought to represent either a watermill or a river edge revetment or landing stage. The northern leat system and watermill was located within this new area, however, it was totally unrelated to the timbers which had originally raised this possibility, as these were later shown to be of prehistoric date.

It was also a matter of chance that this trench encountered the wheel-pit area of the final mill (M25), the most readily explicable part of the entire system and producing such a quantity of millstone fragments that the presence of a watermill could not be doubted. If this trench had lain further to the west and encountered the mill leats near their junctions with the millpond, the resulting complex palimpsest of channels would have defied comprehension. The exposure of an area further east would have provided a slightly less complex but still largely incomprehensible sequence, and both of these areas produced no more than a sparse scatter of millstone fragments.

It must also be noted that initially only the presence of the final mill was recognised. The two earlier mills were largely filled with clean sands and gravels, often consolidated by iron panning, and barely distinguishable from the natural gravel. It was only following the full excavation of the final leat and mill that the presence of odd bands of silt within the consolidated gravel in the sides of the latest leat and wheel-pit suggested that these deposits were not natural. Given a greater time pressure, perhaps in combination with a strict excavation brief and limited funding, it would have been easy to dismiss these hints and deem the excavation complete, thereby missing two earlier phases of mill structure.

From this account of the process of discovery at West Cotton there can be no doubt that there may be no easy answers when facing the questions; did this settlement contain a watermill and if so, where? The excavation of the mills at West Cotton was achieved by a mixture of logical deduction, intuition and good fortune, but all generated by a positive and ambitious attitude in seeking to explicate aspects of the archaeology physically peripheral to the evident core of the settlement. The problems would only be compounded for mill systems detached from a settlement, as at Castle Donington, where it was noted that, "One of the major challenges now facing archaeologists is in the detection and recording of archaeological remains buried beneath deep alluvial deposits" (Clay and Salisbury 1990, 276).

Mill systems are extensive and given any significant duration of use, with multiple recutting of leats and the relocation of the mills themselves, they will not be easily understood. In particular, limited trial trenching might not be sufficient to determine the difference between a leat system and natural stream channels and, unless extremely fortunate, would be unlikely to determine the actual location of the mill. It may therefore be concluded that a similar broadly-based approach to the consideration of the morphology of the local tributary streams and their relationship to the main river channel, and to any adjacent settlement, would be a necessary prelude to selective trial trenching to explore the earlier history of the system. Beyond analysis and good judgement, it is still likely that a generous slice of luck would also be required.

New watercourses and the creation of the flood banks (AD 1150)

The southern flood bank and stream channel

The earthwork and contour surveys show that there were flood banks along the northern side of Cotton Brook from the eastern edge of the floodplain to the Cotton Lane. The bank continued along the southern side of the settlement to the junction with the western mill leats (see Figs 1.3 and 1.6). This southern bank was not excavated, so its date of origin is unknown, but there can be little doubt that it originated in the mid-twelfth century at the same time as the western and northern flood banks. The Cotton Brook meandered along the top of this flood bank, presumably raised above earlier streams channels. The stream course is preserved in earthwork, having lost its water flow at the end of the eighteenth century, when the Hogg Dyke was constructed.

A related feature may be a deep, clay-filled ditch beyond the south-western corner of the hamlet and running along the western margin of the field system to the south of the settlement (Fig 6.1 ditch, and see Figs 1.3 and 1.6). This may have been an attempt to reduce flooding across the fields. It was evidently no more than a partial or temporary success, as the ditch was filled with clay and alluvial clays had also accumulated over the ridge and furrow within the western half of the field system to a depth of up to 1.0m. The alluvium became gradual thinner to the east and the earthworks of the former ridge and furrow field system became more prominent to the east. This area is subsequently recorded as the "Short leys" indicating its later use as pasture.

The western flood bank and stream channels

Following the demise of the mill system a flood bank was raised over the western mill leats (Fig 6.2). The water flow was then carried by a sequence of raised stream channels running along the western side of the bank. The bank was recorded in a single section (Fig 6.5, section a–a', 5560). It was 6.5m wide and up to 0.75m high with gently sloping sides, and comprised orange-brown sandy clay with some gravel pebbles. It certainly contained water-deposited silts, which presumably had been dug from nearby alluvial deposits. There were occasional pieces and slabs of limestone, mainly towards the outer edges and perhaps deriving from later refurbishment. On the eastern side, above the former mill leats, there was a tail of more mixed silts some 3m long, While no dating evidence was obtained for the bank itself, the presence of only earlier twelfth-century pottery (ph 0, 1100–1150) in the deposits beneath it suggests that it was constructed at around the middle of the twelfth century.

A series of watercourses lay beyond the flood bank and these must originate, like the leat system that they replaced, in an artificial channel (Fig 6.4, e). However, it is likely that subsequent development, with a westward migration into the more sinuous channel owed much to natural evolution (Fig 6.4, f). The steady rise in the successive bottom levels probably reflects the steadily rising ground surface created by the progressively accumulating alluvium to the west (Fig 6.5, 4145, 5414 and 5399).

It has been suggested that the new stream course may have been constrained between the recognised clay bank and an outer bank. If so, it was not possible in section to distinguish an outer bank comprising dumped alluvial silts from the general accumulation of alluvial silts beyond this. These silts were up to 0.70m thick and were seen in section for a length of 35m, although only part of this length is depicted (Fig 6.5, section a–a', 5396/7). If there was originally an outer bank, the later stream migration and its sinuous course indicate that it was soon effectively absorbed into the general accumulation of alluvium. Further alluvium also accumulated across the inner slopes of the main flood bank and onto the margins of the settlement area, partly filling some of the boundary ditches. So, whilst the flood bank was an evident success in enabling the settlement to survive, despite the ground levels eventually lying up to 1.0m below the level of the adjacent floodplain, there were inevitably repeated incidents of over-bank flooding.

The earliest of the new watercourses (Fig 6.5, section a–a', 4145) was up to 3.25m wide and 0.60m deep, bottom level 33.67mOD deepening to 33.55mOD to the north. Above a 200mm thick primary silt of mixed gritty silts, sand and silty clay there was a general fill of yellow sandy silts and clay sealed by a possible dumped layer of gravel containing some limestone. The bottom level of the next watercourse (5414) lay 0.30m higher, at 33.85mOD. The primary silty clay fill, with inclusions of fine grit, was overlain by yellow-brown sandy clay virtually indistinguishable from the adjacent flood bank.

In the detached trench at the western end of the former millpond successive linear channels that cut into a layer of alluvial clays sealing the pond deposits (Fig 6.20e, 4082), may have been the continuation of the new western channels. If so, they indicate that the water flow was then directly into the river channel to the north, running over the silted millpond. By this time it is likely that the river course itself was on its way to redundancy, but it was still capable of carrying at least the flow of the Cotton Brook, although whether there was still any flow along the river system is uncertain.

The third western stream course (Fig 6.4f) is the one that survived both as an earthwork feature and on the enclosure map of 1798 (Figs 1.6 and 1.4). A double edge on the western side, as seen in section, suggests that it was scoured out at least once (Fig 6.5, section a–a', 5399). It was 3.0m wide and up to 0.80m deep. A primary fill of yellow-brown silty clay with fine gravel was overlain by a fairly homogeneous fill of yellow-brown sandy clay with fine gravel inclusions, indicating a prolonged period of silt accumulation whilst there was continuous or near continuous water flow.

Unlike its predecessors, at the north-west corner of the site the stream turned abruptly onto a south-westerly course to flow the wrong way along the silted course of the former river channel (Fig 6.20f). It was, therefore, this third western stream course that evidently post-dated the cessation of all water flow along the former river channel. Its sinuous course further to the west, carrying it to the river channel on the west edge of the floodplain is shown on the enclosure map of 1798 (Fig 1.4). While there is no direct dating evidence, it is suggested that the sequence of events was so rapid, that it is likely that the river channel had probably become redundant by around the end of the twelfth century.

The northern flood bank

Flooding along the northern side of the settlement, over the former mill system, was prevented by a combination of drainage ditches and a flood bank.

To the west there was a linear ditch, up to 1.40m wide by 0.50m deep, which was filled with clay. It was cut through both the pond silts and the overlying layer of occupation debris (Fig 6.20f, 5567). It probably terminated to the east within the former limits of the pond, while to the west it may have run beyond a northern terminal of the western flood bank to join the stream channel. To the east, south of the former mill system and over ditch system 19, there was a similar linear ditch that ran eastward into a sunken area (6996) containing pond-like deposits of grey to blue-grey tenacious clays (Fig 6.20f, 7032). It too was filled with yellow tenacious clay. The relationship of these drainage ditches to the flood banks was not established, they may have appeared either shortly before it or as accompanying features to provide drainage through breaks in the flood banks.

The northern flood bank lay over the former watermill system (Figs 6.20f and 6.5, section b–b', 6552). The bottom levels were of greyish-brown sandy clay mixed with orange brown sand, and contained much pottery, animal bone and some millstone fragments, probably as redeposited alluvial silts mixed with occupation debris. The similar clayey silts above this formed a bank up to 5.0m wide by 0.70m high. It is likely that it terminated shortly to the north-east of the excavated area, adjacent to the former northern stream channel.

The northern flood ditches

There does not appear to have been a bank along the north-eastern side of the settlement, but along the course of the old northern stream channel a new drainage ditch was established, also lying partly over the silted boundary ditch system 17 (see Fig 4.31, later ditch). This too was evidently successful, as alluvial clays accumulated only across the area to the north-east of this. By the middle of the thirteenth century (ph 2/0–2/2) the southern terminal had retreated to the north (Fig 7.1), and was filled with tenacious clays containing quantities of limestone rubble

and associated pottery dated to the later thirteenth century (ph 2/2, 1250–1300). This ditch was maintained through to the desertion of the settlement, and survived as one of the most prominent earthwork features (Fig 1.6).

The late Saxon to medieval river channels

The modern course of the River Nene adjacent to West Cotton lies along the western margin of the river valley, at its closest 400m west of the settlement (see Figs 1.2 and 1.3). This had become the only river channel sometime prior to the late eighteenth century; as a map of 1779 and the enclosure map of 1798 (Fig 1.4) both show the river much as it is today. It can be suggest that is was perhaps the only channel by the end of the twelfth century. However, as a result of survey, observation and some limited excavation it has been possible to establish the general location of the two major palaeochannel systems of former river courses that were contemporary with the late Saxon settlement of West Cotton (Figs 1.2 and 6.1). One channel ran along the eastern side of the valley and directly past West Cotton, the eastern palaeochannel. The other lay to the north, the northern palaeochannel. This ran west to east, linking the western channel with the eastern palaeochannel.

These palaeochannels were exposed during successive stages of the machine removal of the overburden within the quarry. To the immediate west and north of West Cotton much of the information was obtained during 1987 by the West Cotton team, while to the south the palaeochannels were recorded during survey work conducted by Steve Parry, and by the Central Excavation Unit teams during the excavation of the Stanwick Roman settlement and the investigation of the prehistoric landscape. In addition, a contour survey of the depth of the overburden across the valley floor, produced by the Central Excavation Unit utilising the borehole information obtained by ARC, also defined the locations of the main palaeochannels. Sampling of the palaeochannel deposits for both macro- and micro-biological remains was conducted by Mark Robinson and Tony Brown, who also recorded partial sections of the palaeochannel systems at several locations (Parry 2006, 23–29).

The eastern palaeochannel

This palaeochannel ran along the eastern side of the valley for 1.5km. To the south it branched from the modern eastern channel of the Nene to the west of the Stanwick Roman settlement, and ran around the northern side of West Cotton before turning back towards the north to a confluence with the Scalley Brook, to the south of Mallows Cotton. Its continuation northward is marked by the modern course of Scalley Brook and the post-medieval Hogg Dyke, which rejoin the river between Mallows Cotton and Mill Cotton (Fig 1.2).

In 1986 the location of this palaeochannel at West Cotton was determined in a series of boreholes. In 1987 a 32m long trial trench was cut by machine across the southern part of the channel system for the specific purpose of providing a section for environmental sampling within a recorded stratigraphic sequence (Fig 6.5, section c–c'; located on Fig 6.9). In 1988 the northern limit of the main excavation area was extended northward to provide a stratigraphic link between the dry-land excavation and this palaeochannel, and the area was further enlarged in 1989 to permit the investigation of the late Neolithic levels within the palaeochannel, which demonstrated the longevity of this channel system (Harding and Healy 2007, 113–115). The middle Saxon and the late Saxon to medieval river edges almost directly overlay the prehistoric river edge, illustrating the stability of the channel. While the general sequence of silting was obtained in a single major section, the complex sequence at the river edge was only fully resolved with the additional evidence obtained from several partial sections, and these have been combined with the major section to form a single composite section across both the river and watermill sequences (Fig 6.5, sections b–b' and c–c').

The river edge revetments and bank

The middle Saxon utilisation of the river has previously been described, and the deposits above this are all presumed to broadly date to the tenth to twelfth centuries, when the channel was 17m wide.

The river edge was artificially raised by the deposition of up to 0.50m of tenacious clays (Fig 6.5, section c–c', 7181) sealed by mixed gravels (7147). To the north the clays terminated at a near vertical edge and this and other evidence has suggested the possible presence of successive timber revetments along the river edge (Fig 6.9). A lower revetment was defined by a single *in situ* stake (7111), 60mm diameter by 350mm long and sharpened to a point, and driven into the underlying gravels (Fig 6.5, section c–c', b projected onto section). Two sections also show a rectangular cut, 0.40m wide by 0.20m deep, filled with grey-brown clay (c), and a narrow, vertically-edged cut, 0.30m deep by 0.14m wide, with a loose fill of mixed grey and brown clay (not illustrated). There was also a slight step, up to 0.10m high, in the exposed surface of the gravel layer (7111), and a single block of limestone lay on the gravel in line with this step. Taken together, these features suggest that there was a linear revetment formed of stakes and horizontal planks set on the riverbank against a slight step cut into the gravel layer.

An upper revetment was defined by a single *in situ* stake, up to 80mm in diameter by 200mm long, while two sections show a near vertical northern edge to the clay layer (7181), and in one instance this was flanked by a narrow, vertically-sided cut (Fig 6.5, section c–c', d), 200m high by 90mm wide, filled with dark grey clay. This upper revetment was abutted on the river side by clayey river silts (6661) which largely sealed the lower revetment, suggesting that

the upper revetment had replaced the lower revetment as water levels rose within the adjacent channel.

The final layers at the river edge were dumped deposits broadly contemporary with the use of the watermills. Above and partly within a shallow linear hollow, up to 0.15m deep, there was a deposit of grey loam containing much charcoal and charred seeds, including sprouted barley from a malt oven, as well as some pieces of fired clay and some small pieces of heat reddened limestone (7153). Above this there was up to 0.30m of gravel in a mixed matrix of yellow-brown to grey-brown sands and silts with some mottles of grey clay and some charcoal flecking (7147). This layer merged with the upper fill of the northernmost mill leat (M26), indicating that it was contemporary with the construction of the latest mill leat (M25). The dumping of gravel here may have been to raise the ground level adjacent to the mills to prevent over-bank flooding into the leats.

The silting of the river channel

The river silts broadly contemporary with the possible lower river edge revetment (Fig 6.5, section c–c', b and c), and also the watermills, comprised a layer of grey to near black peaty silts, up to 0.75m thick (6762). Immediately in front of the lower revetment the upper surface of this layer was convoluted and there was a deposit of coarse light grey-brown sand containing numerous shells of water molluscs. This deposit was up to 0.20m thick and had presumably been deposited at the river edge. The layer above this (6661) was of grey to blue-grey tenacious clay mottled with brown clay and containing some silt and peaty clay. It was up to 0.70m thick and abutted the upper revetment, d. The accumulation of peaty clays would suggest that at this stage the water flow in the channel was fairly slow, and perhaps that it was at least seasonally cut-off from the main channel or channels so that there was no longer a continuously flowing river, although it must still have been permanently under water or at least waterlogged.

Above the peaty layer blue-grey tenacious clay had accumulated (7361), sealing the upper revetment. These clays also interleaved with lenses of gravel probably derived from erosion of the adjacent gravel bank. The high level to which these silts had accumulated would suggest that they must have been deposited following the abandonment of the final mill. By this stage a near horizontal surface was established and the former river channel had become no more than a slightly sunken area, likely to have contained only seasonal flood water. A layer of sticky mottled brown clay with some sand and frequent small pebbles accumulated (7360).

The upper part of the sequence relates to alluvial deposition following the demise of the river channel. A layer of mottled orange-brown to light grey-brown sandy clay with inclusions of fine grit, up to 5mm, showed some banding, particularly towards the river edge where there were multiple near horizontal trails of fine gravel with numerous mollusc shells (7359). The upper surface of this layer was near level with the highest point of the gravel bank beside the watermills, suggesting that it accumulated following the construction of the flood bank over the former mills.

The final deposits (7355–8) comprised up to 1.0m of fairly homogeneous light brown tenacious clays with few inclusions. These were part of the widespread cover of alluvial clays seen to extend across the entire area to the south-west of the settlement. In a single section (not illustrated), it was possible to identify stratification within the alluvium. Successive, homogeneous clay layers 0.30–0.35m thick, were each overlain by thinner, 0.10–0.14m thick, and sandier layers containing water mollusc shells. This may indicate the presence of two successive accumulations of alluvial clays each followed by a period of relative stability. While the lower level can be assumed to have accumulated against the flood bank during the later twelfth century, no date can be provided for the accumulation of the upper level. The lower part of the accumulation would have built up against the flood bank (6552), while the upper part ran across the bank and into the interior, presumably as a result of regular seasonal over-bank flooding.

The latest feature recorded in section was a substantial ditch (6810), up to 3.00m wide by 0.90m deep, cut into the alluvial clays. This lay partly beneath the modern hedge line, and both respected a field boundary shown on the enclosure map of 1798 (Fig 1.3). This ditch may therefore have provided the original definition of the field boundary, while also serving as a flood protection to the West Cotton closes.

The fish weirs

To the immediate west of West Cotton the eastern palaeo-channel was not exposed as this area was excluded from stripping and extraction because of the known presence of the palaeochannel. The areas to either side were quarried, leaving the palaeochannel standing as an unexcavated ridge. Along the northern margin of the palaeochannel four or five separate minor channels, each no more than 13m wide, were observed to run either closely parallel or at oblique angles to the main channel (Fig 6.1). The relationship and dates of these channels is unknown, but as the main channel was redundant by the end of the twelfth century they must have been functioning no later than this date.

On three of these channels there were man-made structures of limestone and timber stakes, seen following the machine removal of the overburden. They were recorded by measured sketches at the arbitrary levels revealed, but it was not possible to conduct any further examination of either their form or of the channels on which they lay. It would seem most likely that these structures were fish weirs, although it was not possible to identify the characteristic V-shaped arrangement of stakes supporting wattle screens to corral the fish into a central basket or trap (Steane and Foreman 1988, 170–172). It would appear

that the channels on which they lay could not have been of any great depth, perhaps 0.5–1.0m deep, and they were clearly separate from the main palaeochannel system. One possibility is that they represent minor meander channels within a complex braided river system.

The best preserved structure (Fig 6.1, 6429) lay across channel E, which was 13.0m wide and largely filled with grey-black clayey silts. It comprised a C-shaped structure of stakes, horizontal planking and withes, and was backed by limestone, which in part comprised at least two courses of flat-laid and some pitched stones, to a depth of at least 0.30m. At either end there were arms of limestone rubble returning to the west. The structure was 5.5m long by 0.75m wide, with the return arms 2.5m long. The main vertical stakes were up to 1.00m long by 100mm in diameter and had been driven up to 400mm into underlying tenacious clay silts, and smaller stakes were interspersed between them. Running northwards from the structure there was a line of at least four stakes, which probably supported a timber revetment extending to the northern edge of the channel. A short line of four closely-spaced stakes running south from the southern arm suggests that a similar revetment ran to the southern edge of the channel. Within the grey-black clayey silts abutting the western, upstream side of the structure there were further stakes as well as a dense scatter of fresh-water mussel shells.

A second and probably similar structure (6431) lay to the east, across what may have been part of the same channel G. This had been badly disturbed and it was only possible to record that a limestone platform lay within a silted river channel.

A third and better preserved structure (6430) lay across a separate channel to the north, channel D, which was 11m wide and filled with grey-black clayey silts and orange sandy silts. The structure was set at a sharply angled turn in the channel and comprised a roughly rectangular platform, 7.0m long by 6.0m wide and at least 0.30m thick, of closely packed limestone rubble, including blocks of limestone up to 400mm long. Two *in situ* vertical stakes, 50mm in diameter by at least 0.30m long, lay within the platform and the presence of much displaced wood within the disturbed limestone rubble suggests that there were originally other timbers associated with it, probably including further stakes. From the eastern end of the platform to the southern bank there was a 4.0m long line of numerous closely-spaced stakes, some only 100mm apart. To the north-east of the limestone platform, and presumably on the northern-eastern stream bank, there was a linear spread of disturbed limestone rubble, 13m long by 1.0m wide. Beyond its north-western end there was a less disturbed area of limestone which appeared to be faced with at least three courses of limestone blocks, suggesting that there may have been an adjacent wall or revetment running along the northern bank of the channel for at least 19m.

Short lengths of two further channels were observed to the north, H, and south, F, of those containing the possible fish weirs.

The northern palaeochannel

A second palaeochannel lay to the north of West Cotton. It ran near west to east for a distance of 400m (see Figs 1.2 and 1.3), linking the present western channel with the eastern palaeochannel to the north of West Cotton. To the west the overburden above the channel was not removed but the quarrying of the adjacent areas defined its location. To the east, where it was exposed, three separate parallel channels were observed. The southernmost channel (Fig 6.1, A) was 25m wide and the central channel (B) was 9m wide. At the level exposed both were filled with grey-black clayey silts containing unworked wood ranging from small twigs up to small trunks or branches 250mm in diameter. The northernmost channel (C) was 20m wide; and was also filled with grey-black clayey silts, but these were seen to lie beneath a layer of tenacious blue-grey clay itself sealed by light brown tenacious clay.

There is no direct dating evidence for this northern palaeochannel. However, aerial photographs show that at least part of its course was more prone to flooding than the adjacent areas of the valley floor, including the palaeochannel directly adjacent to West Cotton. This would suggest that the northern palaeochannel had been active at a later date than the channel adjacent to West Cotton. It is possible that while the eastern palaeochannel up to West Cotton had silted up by the end of the twelfth century, its continuation further to the north, and running past Mallows Cotton, may have been sustained by this west-east channel, as well as by the Scalley Brook to the immediate south of Mallows Cotton. The date of the demise of this northern channel has not been established, but it must have occurred well before the late eighteenth century, as maps of this date do not show it.

7 The Medieval Manor and Hamlet (AD 1250–1450)

In the thirteenth century the buildings within the excavated part of the settlement were converted from a small manor house, to the north, and part of a possible second manor, to the south, to an arrangement that eventually comprised four substantial peasant tenements (Fig 7.1, A, B, C and E) and a single cottage, D. These building groups were set around a central yard, with further similar tenements to the east flanking both sides of Cotton Lane, although these have not been excavated, tenements F–I.

The simplistic interpretation would have been to view this as comprising the desertion and abandonment of the manor house and the division of the plots into a series of smaller properties, or crofts, with each containing its domestic and agricultural buildings, the toft. While this was the ultimate conclusion of the process, marking the abandonment of direct farming of the manorial demesne in favour of the collection of rents and dues from tenant farmers, some of the new buildings, particularly the barn, detached kitchen range and malt house on tenement C/D, appear to have been of manorial status.

This indicates that there was an intermediate phase that involved both the relocation of the manor house onto the eastern plots adjacent to the Cotton Lane, and thus the maintenance of direct farming of the manorial demesne into the later thirteenth century, and the contemporary provision of new tenements on the former site of the manor. The abandonment of direct farming of the manorial demesne was therefore a staged transition that took over 50 years to complete.

The context for the relocation of the manor house most probably lay in the twelfth-century abandonment of the watermill and the silting of the adjacent river channel, together with the agricultural reorientation that had been initiated with the introduction of the barn and processing room on the original manorial plot. With the loss of the mill there was no incentive to retain the manor house adjacent to the river, which was also silting, and the relocation provided the opportunity for both a further expansion of the processing activities and their physical separation from the domestic buildings of the manor, which could not have been achieved within the confines of the old manorial enclosure. The opportunity to introduce a more modern arrangement was taken, and the relocation would also have provided more convenient access to Cotton Lane and to the fields that now formed the principal economic base for the settlement.

The relocation of the manor (AD 1250–1300)

A new tenement on the manorial plot: tenement E

Slightly before AD 1250, most of the former manorial buildings on the northern holding were levelled and new buildings were constructed (Fig 7.2, tenement E). The hall of the manor was levelled and new domestic ranges were built around a new open courtyard at the northern end of the central yard. These included an attached kitchen range and adjacent processing room, and a detached building to the east with a broad doorway may have been a stable or byre. Some of the former manorial ranges were initially retained. The range containing the malt oven was levelled but a new oven was built over the remains. This was now either free-standing or under a new cover building that left few traces, and was set in one corner of a new walled yard, which occupied the area of the former courtyard. The dovecote may also have been retained and, to the south, the barn and processing room was probably also still in use. One possibility is that while new domestic ranges were provided for an incoming tenant, the agricultural ranges may have still been used directly by the manor, perhaps through an interim period whilst comparable and improved facilities to the east were still under construction, tenement C/D.

The new manor: tenement C/D and tenement F

By the mid-thirteenth century a substantial new complex of service and agricultural buildings, including a barn, detached kitchen/bakehouse and a malt house, had been constructed at the northern end of the eastern enclosures (Figs 7.2, tenement C/D and 7.3). The substantial barn, which fronted onto the eastern side of the central yard, was not fully excavated, but if the broad, opposed doorways were central it would have been 20–22m long. Geophysical survey also indicated that there was perhaps a further building beyond the south-eastern end of the barn (Fig 7.2). Abutting the northern end of the barn there was a large kitchen/bakehouse containing a circular oven, open hearths and a possible small processing trough. To the rear of the barn there was a walled yard, initially surfaced with gravel and later with limestone metalling, and beyond this stood a malt house, the most complex of the four excavated.

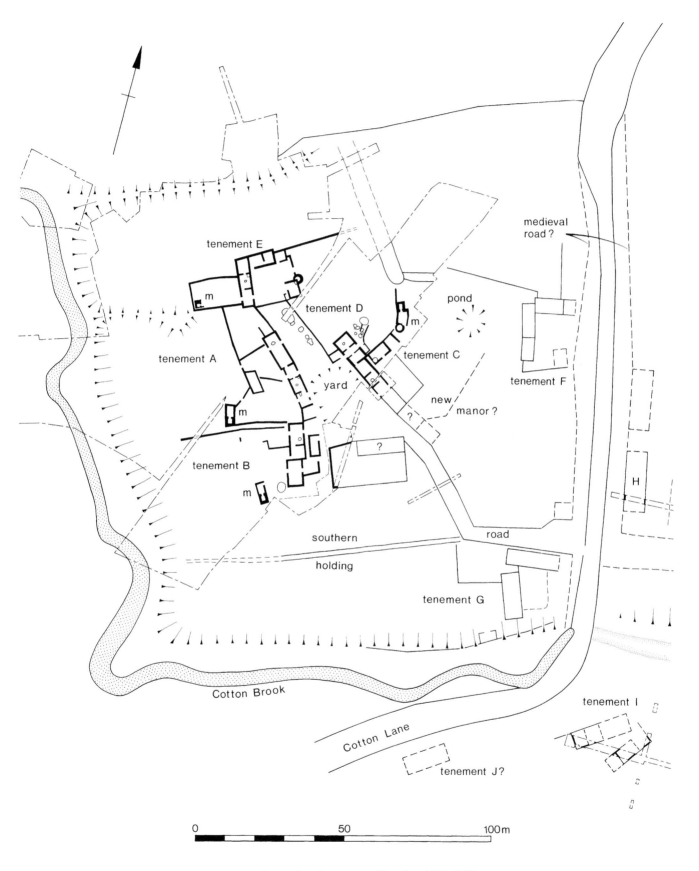

Fig 7.1: The medieval manor and hamlet, 1250–1450

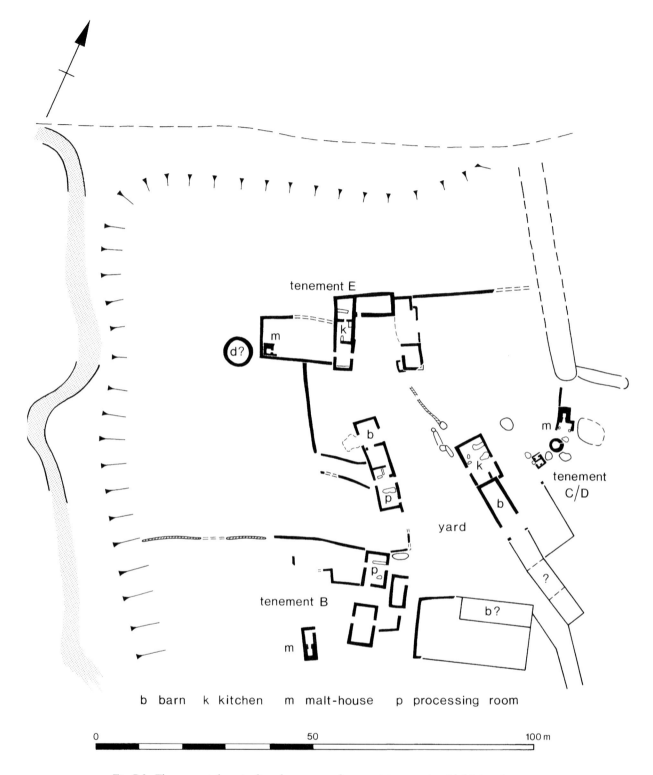

Fig 7.2: The manorial agricultural ranges and peasant tenement, mid thirteenth century

Originally it comprised a free-standing oven and a circular structure, perhaps holding a vat for steeping the barley prior to malting. An adjacent H-shaped stone-lined pit was also associated, and burnt debris from the firing of the oven was dumped into nearby pits.

Subsequently, the malt house was partially rebuilt to provide a fully enclosed room (Fig 7.4). The kitchen range was also partially rebuilt, and when a narrow partition wall was inserted the oven went out of use. It may have been replaced by a nearby new and separate bakehouse (Figs 7.4 and 7.5). In addition, a new room with an external door may have been added to the frontage at this time,

Fig 7.3: The medieval tenements in 1985, looking west, showing tenement C/D (foreground), tenement A (top right), tenement B, unexcavated (top left), the silt-filled yard (centre) and the ditches of the Bronze Age round barrow (right)

along with the provision of a boundary wall that ran to tenement E to the north.

It is suggested that the contemporary domestic buildings, the new manor house, lay further to the east adjacent to Cotton Lane (Fig 7.1, tenement F). These buildings survive as well-preserved earthworks, with many walls evident as parch marks in dry summers, and they have also been subject to geophysical survey. A central courtyard may originally have opened directly onto Cotton Lane, and it was flanked to the west by a range with two or more rooms and to north by a second range of similar length. Along the southern side there was a boundary wall and possibly a further, detached building to the east.

Geophysical survey indicates that there was a boundary wall along the northern side of the new manorial enclosure, and to its south a rectangular area of metalling flanked the northern side of a pond or large well pit, which survives as an earthwork and still retains water in the winter months. There may have been a north-south boundary wall, but this sub-division might only have been introduced when the manor was subsequently converted to peasant tenements. There is an absence of stone scatters in the south-eastern part of the area, south of tenement F, although at some date a small building may have stood near the junction of the internal road with the Cotton Lane (Fig 7.1).

Together, the two building complexes, C/D and F, would have formed a substantial farm that is interpreted as the new manor house, relocated from the northern holding onto the eastern enclosures, and with the domestic and agricultural ranges now physically divorced by being set on opposite sides of the new manorial enclosure.

Further new buildings: tenement A

Slightly after AD 1250, the old manorial barn and processing room was extensively rebuilt to form the main domestic range of a new tenement occupying the southern part of the old manorial enclosure (Fig 7.4, tenement A). While this tenement formed a linear frontage, the accommodation provided was closely similar in terms of room space to that of tenement E, to its immediate north, and included an attached kitchen with similar internal fittings.

This new tenement was provided with a malt house, set in the yard to the rear, but rather than supplementing the production of tenement E, it may have replaced it, as by this time both the dovecote and the malt house had been demolished. A new boundary bank separating the two tenements ran over the levelled dovecote. Once both were established, the northern tenement possessed a processing room containing a trough, perhaps used for fulling cloth,

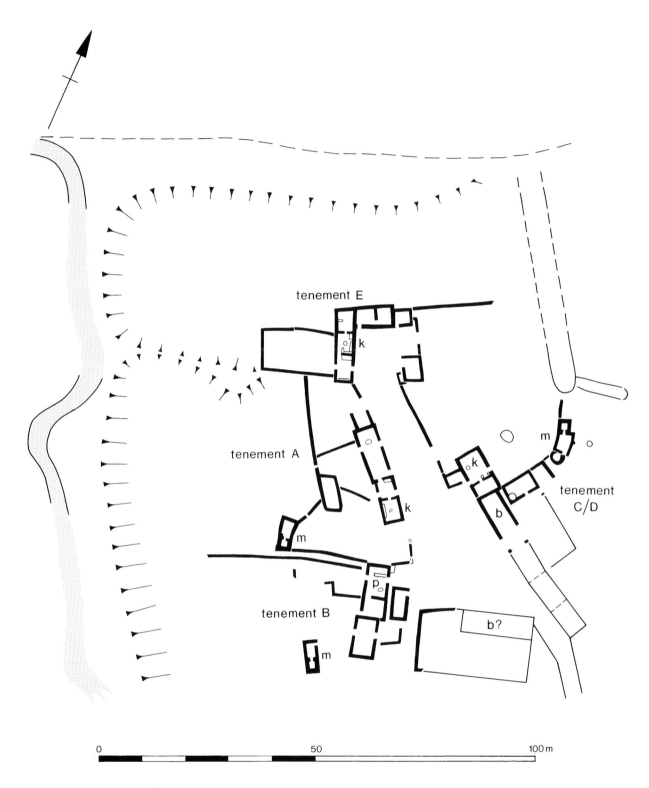

Fig 7.4: The manorial agricultural ranges and peasant tenements, late thirteenth century

while the southern tenement had a malt house. So each carried out one supplementary processing activity, perhaps directly contributing to the productive capacity of the new manor house, where perhaps both processes were carried out.

The southern holding: tenements B and G

Despite the replacement of the manor house with two tenements, the boundary between the former northern holding and the southern holding was both retained and re-emphasised. Initially, a single wall may have supplemented a remnant bank and perhaps a partial timber fence (Fig 7.2), but with the full development there was a double-walled boundary, perhaps with each wall provided and maintained by the separate property holders (Fig 7.4).

Further buildings appeared on the northern part of the southern holding to supplement the existing processing room (Figs 7.2, tenement B). An open room was attached to the processing room and a malt house was built in the yard behind. The small bakehouse at the frontage may have been either retained from the earlier development or was constructed at this time, although it was subsequently rebuilt, removing the oven (Fig 7.4). To the north of the bakehouse and in front of the processing room there was a small yard with successive metalled surfaces of neatly pitched limestone and a similar walled yard probably lay to the rear.

These facilities partly paralleled the development of the agricultural ranges on the opposite side of the central yard, and at the eastern limit of excavation there was a boundary wall indicating the presence of further related structures to the east. Without excavation, the nature of these buildings cannot be established but, taking the geophysical survey evidence into account, it appears to have comprised a building set within a walled yard and directly facing the barn and walled yard on the manorial enclosure to the north-east. It is therefore suggested that this building was perhaps also barn, with the two barns facing each other.

As with the new manor house, the related domestic ranges may have lain to the east forming a frontage onto Cotton Lane. This building complex is known from both poorly defined earthworks and geophysical survey (Fig 7.1, tenement G). Western and northern ranges flanked a metalled courtyard to the east, while a walled yard lay to the west.

To the south, a wall along the top of the bank flanking the Cotton Brook was abutted by a small building, but these features could be later medieval or even post-desertion in date.

As in previous periods, it is therefore suggested that there were still two manors at West Cotton, with closely comparable arrangements and facilities. The farm buildings were set on either side of the central yard, while the domestic ranges occupied the prime locations, fronting onto the Cotton Lane.

Other tenements: H and I

It may have been with the establishment of two major domestic ranges fronting onto the Cotton Lane that a further tenement or tenements appeared on the eastern side of the lane (Fig 7.1, tenement H). These buildings were located by geophysical survey and were investigated with a single trial trench.

A further two ranges of buildings lay to the south-east, and to the south of the Cotton Brook (Fig 7.1, tenement I). These buildings were in use in the fourteenth century, but only the demolition levels were investigated in limited trial trenching, so an earlier origin is possible.

The environmental evidence suggests that the agricultural activities still included the preparation of grain for milling, and the only possible location for a new mill would have been to the east, beyond the area where alluvial silts had been accumulating, and therefore in the vicinity of tenement I. It is suggested, therefore, that tenement I may have been a later medieval watermill complex, and there is documentary evidence for a watermill attached to the Chamberlain holding of West Cotton in the early fifteenth century. The only physical evidence to support this suggestion is part of a well-worn millstone from tenement H, to the north. It is, of course, also possible that grain was being prepared for milling elsewhere, perhaps at Mallows Cotton, where both documentary and archaeological evidence indicate the presence of a medieval watermill.

The medieval organisation and status of West Cotton

By the mid to late thirteenth century the whole focus of the settlement had shifted dramatically from a clustering of holdings around the central yard, to domestic ranges set alongside Cotton Lane while their agricultural complexes and two subordinate tenements occupied the central area (Fig 7.5 and Plate 7).

The presence of two major holdings and the tenements might be reflected in the documentary evidence as, by the later thirteenth century, it is recorded that men of both Ralf Normanville and Henry de Albotesk were in West Cotton. The earliest documented date of AD 1274–5 for this dual holding, might suggest that the relocation of the manor and the comparable development of the southern holding, had coincided with the acquisition of West Cotton by Henry de Albotesk and Ralf Normanville around the middle of the thirteenth century. The identity of the respective holdings cannot be established with certainty, however, the earlier decline of the southern holding might suggest that this was held by the Normanville family, as by the early fourteenth century this is recorded as the lesser of the two, 1/40 of a knight's fee in comparison to 1/16 of a knight's fee for the other, then held by the Chamberlain family. In the later fourteenth century the Chamberlain family were in possession of both.

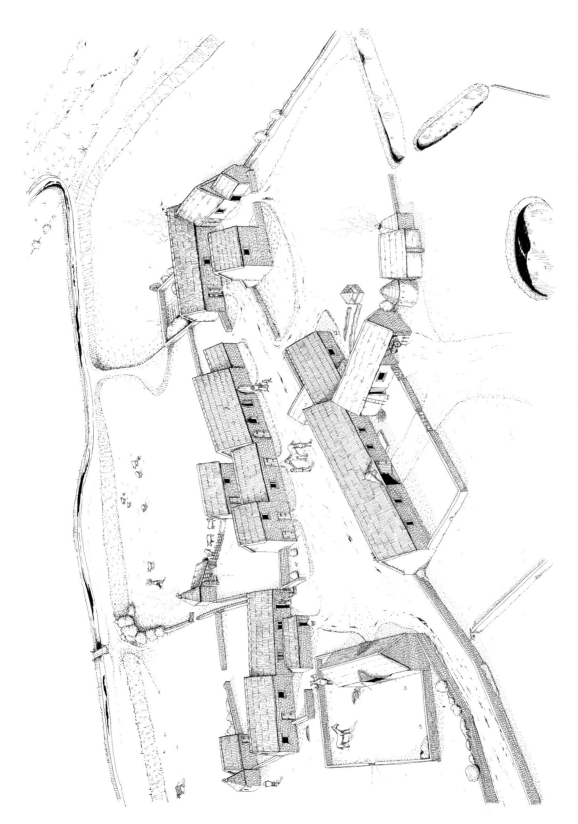

Fig 7.5: The manorial ranges and peasant tenements as they may have looked in the late thirteenth century (Alex Thompson)

From manor to hamlet (AD 1300–1350)

The relocated manorial buildings of the northern holding, with their emphasis on the storage and processing of arable agricultural products, and the probable comparable development of the southern holding, had represented a considerable investment in establishing substantial, well-organised and well-equipped farms. However, this was to be a short-lived phase of activity.

By the beginning of the fourteenth century most of the buildings, on both the manorial enclosure and the southern holding, which had been related to specific agricultural activities, had been either abandoned or reused for other purposes. In particular, both the barn and the kitchen of the manorial complex were converted to domestic buildings (Fig 7.6), to form a tenement, C, comparable to those already existing to the north and west, and an adjacent cottage, D. This in itself implies that direct farming of the manorial demesne had ceased, and it may be that there was a full abandonment of the manor at this time, with the domestic range adjacent to Cotton Lane perhaps also converted to a tenement.

Whether it was the desertion of the manor that caused the redundancy of the agricultural buildings or an agricultural decline that led to the desertion of the manor, cannot be established from the archaeological evidence. It is perhaps most likely that the two went together, reflecting the national decline in arable agriculture and the shift towards pastoral farming.

The southern holding underwent a similar decline, indicated by the disuse of the processing room at the beginning of the fourteenth century. The further short-term use of these buildings into the early fourteenth century may have been as ancillary buildings to a tenement, perhaps with its domestic buildings formed by conversion of the possible barn within the walled yard.

It is of interest that on both holdings the agricultural decline did not lead to total desertion of the buildings but to their conversion to tenements, tenanted crofts. It is therefore possible that through the first half of the fourteenth century, with the settlement now forming a hamlet of several crofts, its population may have reached its highest ever level. For a time there may have been seven tenements within the main settlement area. Tenements A and E were certainly still in use, the manorial complex may have been broken into two tenements, C and F, and a smaller cottage, D, and the southern holding probably contained two tenements, B and G. A further one or two tenements, H, lay to the east of the Cotton Lane. To the south a further building group, I, possibly a watermill, was also functioning at this time and may only have been introduced in the mid-fourteenth century. The fully excavated tenements exhibit a diversity of forms. To the north, tenement E had a croft of around one acre. To the south of this, tenement A had a very similar building arrangement but a smaller croft, at under 3/4 of an acre. To the east, the smallest tenement, D, possessed only a cottage on a croft of less than 1/2 an acre.

It has already been suggested that the lesser value of the fourteenth-century Normanville holding may identify it as the southern holding, which was at least partially deserted before 1350. Before the end of the century the Chamberlain family was in possession of both holdings, and this may reflect the continuous occupation of the tenements on the Chamberlain holding while the partial, and perhaps by then total, desertion of the Normanville holding had perhaps rendered it of so little value to the Normanville family in generating an income that it was not worth retaining.

While the Clare/Gloucester fee dominated West Cotton, with little doubt that the holdings occupied the main settlement area, we are left with the question of the location of the Duchy holdings, which comprised a meadow, recorded in the fourteenth century, and a cottage, recorded in the fifteenth century. Orders in the Duchy court rolls for the scouring of ditches at Cotton Bridge and references to the cottage with an acre of willows by the Cotton (Tipping) Brook, may provide sufficient clues when combined with the enclosure map of 1798 (see Fig 1.3). From this it can be seen that the ancient enclosure comprised two separate blocks; the Gloucester fee enclosure west of Cotton Lane and north of the Cotton Brook, and a further enclosure east of the lane and south of the brook. It is therefore possible that it is the enclosure to the south-east that formed the Duchy holding, and the Duchy cottage might have been a building to the south of the brook, where stone walls were observed in a pipe trench dug in 1967 (Fig 7.1, tenement J).

It may also be noted that of the various names applied to the settlement within the later medieval documents, the Duchy records generally refer to West or Little Cotes while the Gloucester fee documents use Wilwencotes. If the holdings of the respective fees were located as described above, and the differing names were specifically applied to the two distinct entities, than this would imply that what was actually excavated was the Gloucester fee holding of Wilwencotes and not the Duchy fee of West or Little Cotton.

The conversion of the manorial buildings

The tenement C/D malt house was abandoned and probably demolished around the end of the thirteenth century, while the barn and the kitchen were converted into separate domestic ranges (Fig 7.6, tenements C and D).

Tenement C

The broad barn doors were partially blocked to form narrow doorways, and two partition walls were inserted to form a series of smaller rooms. The internal arrangement was closely comparable to that of tenements E and A, with a clay-floored hall to the north, a kitchen, k, with a central hearth and no external doors, while the central room, with its opposed doorways, was at least partially floored with limestone slabs. The separate bakehouse was also retained, although the oven was removed. As noted earlier, a possible boundary wall running from the eastern end of the frontage to the pond to the north may have been introduced at this stage to separate the croft of tenement C from a further separate tenement occupying the former domestic buildings to the east, tenement F.

Tenement D

The former kitchen was divided into three small rooms by the addition of a second partition wall. The northern chamber served as a kitchen, k, there was a central cross-passage and the southern chamber probably had a flagged floor. A small, sunken chamber with a flagged floor and an external door, probably used for storage, was added to the rear. A walled passage provided access to a well, which may have been retained from the previous phase. The room abutting the front of the building was probably retained, along with the boundary running to tenement E to the north.

This building could be appropriately described as a cottage, as there is a striking contrast with the extensive ranges of tenements E, A and C. The small croft extended to the buildings of tenement E and it was probably with the appearance of the cottage that access from tenement E onto this area was blocked.

The northern tenements

Tenement E

This was retained with only minor alterations. The kitchen was frequently refurbished, and there was a succession of central hearths. In the chamber south of the kitchen at least the western external door was blocked, and the room was furnished with a full limestone floor, suggesting that it was used as a storeroom. The processing trough in the northern room was rebuilt twice, each time becoming shorter, with this indicating a progressive decline in the quantity of material being processed. This may mark a decline from commercial and domestic use to purely domestic usage. The hall was subdivided into two small rooms and the abutting, open-sided chamber was turned into a closed room. The detached building, formerly a stable or byre, was also partially rebuilt. The doorway was partially blocked and a massive circular foundation was set around one corner. An external area of burning suggests that it functioned as an oven with an internal step providing access to a raised oven chamber, similar to post-medieval bread/baking ovens.

Tenement A

There were similar modifications to this tenement. The kitchen was reorganised when a southern door was inserted to provide access to a new chamber abutting the southern wall. The provision of a stair-base within this extension indicates that it was of two storeys. The later blocking of its external doors suggest that it later functioned as a flag-floored storeroom with access only from the kitchen.

It may be noted how the later development of the kitchens in tenements A and E ran closely parallel. Both had access to an adjacent chamber in which the external doors had been blocked when they were provided with floors flagged with limestone slabs. This indicates a need for increased storage space, presumably for domestic foodstuffs, within the individual tenements, perhaps a need that followed the loss of the barn or barns of the two manorial holdings.

The conversion of the southern holding

The excavated buildings of the agricultural complex, tenement B, had fallen out of use as specialised buildings by the end of the thirteenth century. The bakehouse had been replaced by a new building, while the malt house was demolished and the trough in the processing room was filled in. The final use of these buildings was therefore merely as ancillary buildings, and they appear to have fallen out of use before 1350. A curving boundary wall then blocked access from the central yard and the levelled rubble over the former buildings may have been utilised as an external yard.

The medieval hamlet: decline and desertion (AD 1350–1450)

Tenement B had a short lifetime, as it was deserted before 1350 (Fig 7.6). In contrast, the desertion of the tenements of the northern holding probably began no earlier than the mid-fourteenth century. Tenement E was the first to go, possibly as early as 1350, but the dating evidence is far too imprecise to confirm any direct association with the Black Death, which reached this area by the end of April 1349. There was some reuse of the buildings in the later fourteenth century. A central doorway was opened in the main range, giving access into the former kitchen, and the partition wall separating the kitchen from the northern room may have been demolished. The building was perhaps then utilised as an outbuilding by the adjacent tenement, A. The provision of a continuous boundary wall, physically separating the tenement courtyard from the central yard, may either have coincided with this late reuse or even post-dated the desertion and demolition of all the tenement buildings.

By the early fifteenth century water-deposited clayey silts had begun to accumulate within the central yard, the access road and also within the Cotton Lane itself. The cause of this flooding is uncertain, but it may have resulted from the abandonment of control of the tributary stream, perhaps following desertion of the postulated medieval watermill. It is likely that domestic occupation of tenements A, C and D ceased at about this time, but at least some rooms in all three tenements were provided with thick clay and rubble or pitched-stone floors and raised doorway thresholds. In the cottage of tenement D,

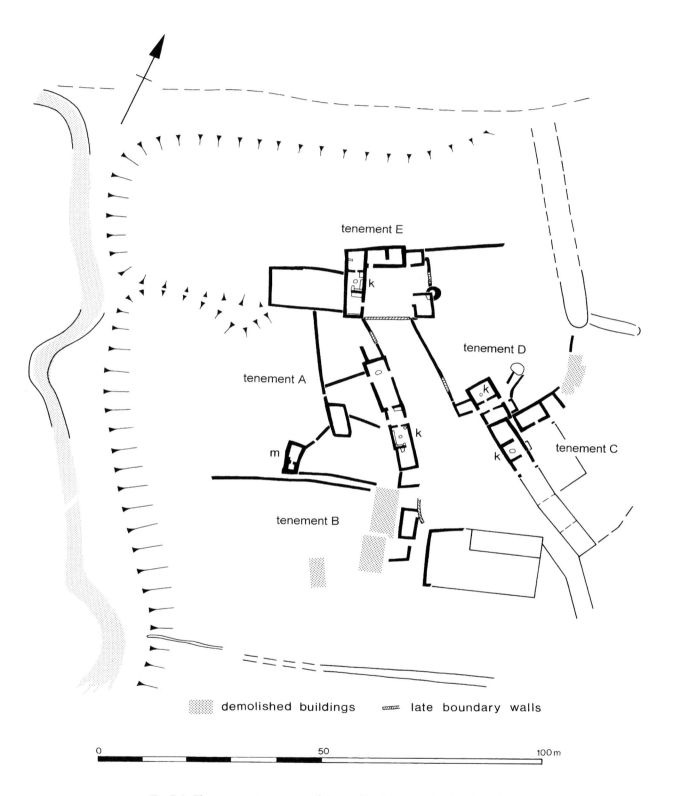

Fig 7.6: The peasant tenements of the medieval hamlet, fourteenth century

the southern wall to the central and eastern rooms may have been totally removed and the pitched-stone floor in the eastern chamber had been carefully laid, suggesting a specific use, perhaps as a byre or cart shed. These new floors were probably inserted to raise them above any threat of flooding, and the absence of any associated features, such as hearths, suggests that they were then only being used as outbuildings, perhaps by the tenements adjacent to the lane, which may have been the last to go.

The cutting of a ditch around much of the central yard indicates that an attempt was made to drain and maintain it (Fig 7.7, PM2). This ditch ran along the frontage of tenement A (Plate 9), suggesting that these buildings had totally fallen out of use, while its absence in front of tenement C and the very eastern end of tenement D, suggests that these buildings, perhaps specifically those with raised floors, were still in use when this drainage ditch was excavated

Tenements A, C and D all had been deserted by around 1450. The desertion date of the tenements adjacent to Cotton Lane is unknown, and these may have been in use later, but the general absence of later fifteenth-century pottery on the site would still suggest a general date of desertion at around the middle of the fifteenth century.

The levelling of the deserted buildings appears to have occurred fairly soon after desertion, probably through the later fourteenth to early fifteenth centuries. In some instances walls were totally robbed, but those fronting onto the central yard were generally retained to a sufficient height to complement the drainage ditch in preventing flooding from inundating the former crofts, although some intermittent flooding is indicated by accumulations of silty clays in hollows over the demolition rubble.

It is possible that stone from the first tenements to be deserted may have been partly utilised within the settlement, perhaps for further building or rebuilding alongside the Cotton Lane. This may explain why tenement E had been more extensively robbed than tenement A. Conversely, the well-preserved earthworks of tenement F and G, adjacent to the lane and perhaps the last to be occupied, suggests that these were not extensively robbed. Perhaps the effort of carting the stone up the hill to Raunds for reuse was not considered worthwhile as more immediate sources were available.

By the later fifteenth century the documentary evidence indicates that only a single cottage survived, held by the Duchy and tentatively equated with tenement J, lying well to the south of the main settlement. It was deserted by or before the late sixteenth century, bringing to an end 600 hundred years of continuous occupation.

The material and environmental evidence

At the beginning of this period the coarseware pottery was dominated by the range of jars and bowls produced by the local pottery industries based on the villages of Lyveden and Stanion, in the north of the county, and also from Potterspury, towards the south of the county. The first half of the thirteenth century also saw the first appearance of quantities of glazed jugs, as the production of glazed vessels for widespread use started to become common in the local industries. Many of these were from Lyveden and Stanion, which produced coil-built, wheel-finished, thick-walled jugs, not of the best quality, boldly decorated with vertical or diagonal white slip stripes, or applied strips of white firing clay commonly accompanied by stamped pads, which contrasted with the green body. Glazed jugs of better quality from the Potterspury industry were also common although sometimes it is uncertain whether these are genuine Potterspury vessels or similar finer, wheel-thrown jugs being produced in imitation at Lyveden and Stanion. Brill/Boarstall ware jugs, from the villages near the Buckinghamshire border east of Oxford, were also relatively common.

A handful of vessels also came in from slightly further away; including a couple of Oxford ware jugs and a tripod pitcher, two London ware drinking jugs, and a couple of Nuneaton ware jugs. The superior status of tenement C/D, as the suggested agricultural and kitchen ranges of the relocated manor house, may be reflected in the presence of these rarer vessels; with a Nuneaton ware jug coming from a primary deposit in a pit behind the kitchen/bakehouse, D12, while the Oxford ware tripod pitcher was from the adjacent tenement C.

It may be noted that the relatively lowly status of the site is reflected in the pottery assemblage, as it is dominated by local and then regional products, and clearly there were few wares being imported from further away and no exotic imports from the continent. However, the range of medieval glazed wares is basically the same as those from the site of Furnells manor in Raunds, which again emphasises how little difference there was between the outlying hamlet and the manorial centre in Raunds.

The range of other finds also illustrates aspects of the domestic life of the medieval tenements. There were many small items, particularly copper alloy buckles, buckle plates, strap ends and other small decorative fittings, all of basic simple forms. There was a large range of whittle tang knives, with the tang set in a socketed handle, while the presence of only twelve scale tang knives, where side scales of bone or antler are riveted to a flat tang, reflects the late introduction of these knives. It is notable that none came from tenement B, which was deserted soon after AD 1300.

Specific tool groups were rare, although the presence of spindle whorls and bone pins denoted that spinning was still a daily activity, although the absence of pinbeaters indicates that the two-beam loom was no longer in use. There is a notable scarcity of agricultural or woodworking tools in iron; which is restricted to parts of two pairs of shears, two sickles, a weed hook, a spoon bit, some wedges and a small draw knife only suitable for use on

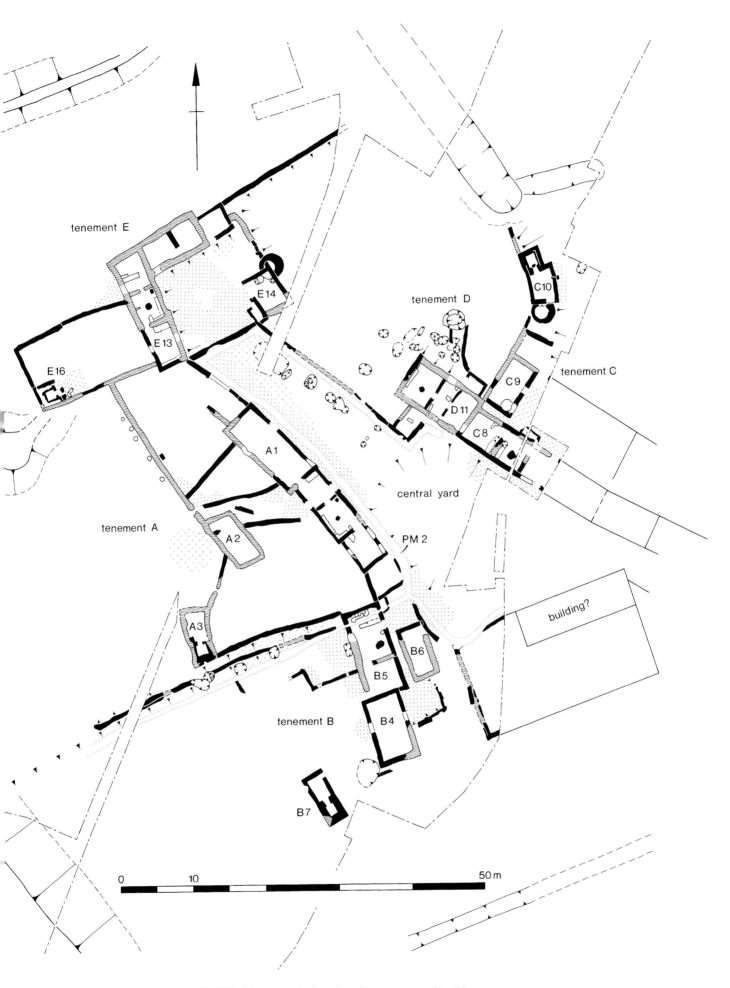

tenement E

E14

tenement D

C10

E13

tenement C

E16

C9

D 11

C8

A 1

tenement A

central yard

A 2

PM 2

building?

A 3

B 6

B 5

tenement B

B 4

B 7

0   10   50 m

Fig 7.7: The excavated medieval tenements and buildings

small domestic items. Ironwork relating to the buildings is also surprisingly sparse, but there is a range of sizes of staples, and eight L-shaped hinge pivots to hold window shutters or doors and gates.

In fact, it can be argued that, despite the recovery of around 1000 nails, iron in general is under-represented in the finds assemblage, suggesting that much of it, including the humble nail, had been recycled as scrap to the local blacksmith. This under-representation is well illustrated by the desertion of the domestic range of tenement C. This building appears to have been left derelict but with some fittings, either a door or chest or perhaps a number of such items, left stacked in one of the rooms. They were left long enough for the wood to decay, leaving behind a collection of nails, iron sheet and staples and parts of three lock mechanisms including a barrel padlock and sliding bolts from two mounted locks. Similarly, when the manorial kitchen/bakehouse, D12/D11, underwent a major rebuild a dense scatter of nails, presumably debris from demolition/construction, was sealed beneath the new floor.

The most common single item in iron, after nails, was the horseshoe, with 78 recovered. Only 10 came from twelfth-century contexts, and the remainder are of thirteenth to fifteenth century date. A considerable proportion might have been deposited during use of the closes following desertion of the tenements. However, the riding of horses during the lifetime of the hamlet is indicated by a small collection of spurs and bridle bits. Some of these were associated with the twelfth-century manor, while a number of others come from tenement E, and could either be residual from the underlying manor or add corroboration to the interpretation of the free-standing building with a broad doorway as a possible byre or stable.

Other items of interest relate to more leisurely activities. There are two simple musical pipes worked on lengths of sheep tibia, and perforated pig metapodials were spun on cord as buzz-bones. Other items include three nine-men's morris boards, all crudely scratched on irregular fragments of limestone. All of these were recovered from either the manorial kitchen/bakehouse range or its later use as a peasant cottage, D11/D12. This building also produced the only figurative carving from the site (Plate 13), set at one end of a small stone-lined pit with the floor of the pit including a scratched nine-men's morris board (see Fig 7.27).

Soil samples taken from the medieval tenements generally produced few charred plant remains, with the exception of samples from some of the malt-house ovens. Tenement A produced more material than the others and, like the twelfth-century manor house, the charred remains were dominated by weeds, and wheat was generally still the dominant cereal. It is also of interest that tenement A was apparently receiving some of its crops from the floodplain, as had the manor house in the twelfth century, perhaps suggesting that a specific piece of land originally under the control of the manor had come under the control of tenement A, with the area of remnant ridge and furrow to the immediate south of

West Cotton a possible candidate, although it might have lain further away.

Chaff remains were relatively scarce, but both types of free-threshing wheat, and hulled wheat chaff were present. Rye chaff was in the richer samples, though rye grain was only present in the tenement B, C and E malt houses. Sprouted grain and sprouts came from three of the four malt houses; with sprouted oat and barley grain from tenement B, and sprouted barley from tenements A and E. No sprouted grain came from the tenement C malt house, although wheat was present, perhaps suggesting that this malt house was also, if not primarily, used for grain drying.

Another striking feature of the samples from the malt houses is the number of cabbage and mustard seeds (*Brassica* spp.) recovered. Large legumes were also present, with peas from the tenement A malt house, and single peas from tenement C and B, which may have been deliberately used in brewing. There were lentils from the tenement B malt house and a single possible lentil from the tenement E malt house, although these may have grown as contaminants of the cereal crops.

The weed assemblages from the samples are somewhat different to the previous period. Species typical of winter and spring sown cereals are again present but leguminous weed seeds form a much larger proportion of the assemblages.

In the animal bone assemblage, as previously, sheep was the most common animal, followed by cattle, pigs and horses. In this later period, as also noted with regard to the medieval manor, while the range of ages in the kill-off pattern for sheep indicates a mixed economy exploiting the meat, milk and wool, there was an increase in slightly older animals, of 3–4 years, indicating a greater interest in wool production. This suggests that the animals were now providing two or more fleeces before being slaughtered, although at this age they would also have provided the best mutton, so there does not appear to have been a shift to specialised wool production.

The cattle show a slightly younger kill-off pattern than previously, which may suggest a small increase in beef production, but otherwise most animals were still kept to maturity for traction power and milk production. Many of the cattle bones bore butchery marks, and cut marks on the phalanges and metapoidals indicate that animals were skinned for their hides, and a single chopped horn core may relate to horn working. All slaughter and butchery probably took place on site for both sheep and cattle.

The exploitation of young pigs, with few older animals, for a quick return of meat and lard was unchanged.

The horse bones are of interest, as they show an unusually high incidence of cut marks indicative of skinning. In addition, there are also chop marks that come from the butchering of the carcases for meat in the same fashion as for the cattle and sheep. It may be that this horse meat was being fed to the many dogs around the site, but at least one horse bone had been smashed apparently to extract the marrow and, in the context of the wet seasons, poor harvests and animal diseases that were such a common feature of the early fourteenth century, the use of surplus horses for human consumption cannot be ignored.

As just mentioned, dogs were common throughout the life of the settlement both directly in the bone record and indirectly from the widespread evidence for dog gnawing of other bones. Cut marks show that dogs were skinned, and the pelts may have been used for producing gloves. Cats were also quite common, although many of the bones were from young cats, perhaps suggesting that they were largely exploited for their pelts, although a secondary use of keeping vermin under control was no doubt also useful.

As previously, fish were scarce but there was eel and carp from freshwater, and herring and ling from the sea.

The buildings of the later medieval manor and tenements: C, D and F

Tenement C/D contained the agricultural ranges of the later manor (Fig 7.7 and Plate 10). These buildings were constructed within the former eastern enclosures in the decades prior to the mid-thirteenth century (ph 2/0, 1225–1250). Initially, there was a barn, a multi-purpose kitchen range and a malt house with various ancillary features (Fig 7.8: C8, D12 and C10). At around the middle of the thirteenth century the kitchen range was rebuilt (Fig 7.9, D11) and the circular baking oven was probably relocated to a new building, C9. The malt house was also redeveloped and the barn was retained. At this stage, if not earlier, a walled yard was attached to the rear of the barn.

At the end of the thirteenth century (ph 2/2, 1250–1300) the buildings were converted into two peasant tenements, C and D. Both the barn, C8, and the kitchen range, D11, were partitioned into smaller rooms to form two separate domestic dwellings, tenements C and D (Fig 7.9). The malt house complex fell out of use and was probably demolished.

The new tenements were in use through the fourteenth century (ph 3/2, 1300–1400) but may have been abandoned at the around the end of the century. The insertion of raised floors in a few rooms of both tenements in the early fifteenth century (ph 4, 1400–1450), probably relates to the reuse of these rooms as agricultural outbuildings, with the raised floors a response to the onset of flooding within the central yard.

The barn and later domestic range, C8

This building was only partly excavated but the opposed broad doorways identify it as a barn. If the doors were central, they would indicate a total length of 20–22m (Figs 7.10–7.12). The building was 5.00m wide, and the internal width of 3.80m suggests that the internal area would have been of the order of 80sq m, probably making it the largest single building in the history of the settlement.

The southern wall was well-preserved, surviving five to

seven courses high, 0.40m. It was 0.60m wide with broader foundations, 0.65–0.70m wide, and an internal offset at the western end. The central doorway was 3.00m wide. At the western end of the wall the neatly faced northward return formed the southern side of a doorway opening, giving access into the adjacent kitchen range. The central door jamb recess had projecting pad stones at its base.

The northern wall had been extensively robbed, but the partly surviving surrounds indicated that the doorway was 4.10m wide. The western door surround had an external thickening suggesting the provision of a strengthening buttress.

A remnant of an early floor comprising large, flat-laid limestone slabs, cracked, fragmented and with worn surfaces, survived between the opposed doorways and suggests the provision of a threshing floor. A neonatal infant (3065) had been buried within a shallow pit beside to the northern wall, to the west of the doorway.

The barn was converted to a domestic range by the partial blocking of the barn doors and the provision of partition walls to form a series of smaller rooms. The blocking wall of the southern door was 0.55m wide and was founded on a course of large flat-laid limestone slabs. At the eastern end there was a new doorway, with a door jamb recess in the eastern surround. The blocking wall of the northern door had been robbed, but a new threshold comprising a double layer of flat-laid limestone, was 1.20m wide. A kerb of pitched limestone ran northward and flanked a better laid surface of pitched limestone that formed a path leading to the new door.

The westernmost partition wall was 0.55m wide, and within the internal doorway at the northern end a shallow slot and a pair of postholes, each up to 0.30m in diameter by 0.18m deep, would have held the door-jamb post and a sill beam. The other partition wall between was 0.60m wide.

The western room, 1, was 4.50m long by 3.90m wide; an area of 17.5sq m. A floor of clean yellow clay was up to 70mm thick against the walls, but had been eroded within the centre of the room and through the doorway leading to room 2. A shallow, linear robber trench adjacent to the partition wall, and a similar feature in room 2, probably held the foundations for stone-built benches.

In the angle of an L-shaped stone setting against the northern wall, there was an irregular clay and loam-filled hollow sealed by a flat-laid slab of limestone. This was similar to the corner bins seen in other buildings (eg D11/1 and A1/2). A later pit to the east was steep-sided, 0.53m in diameter by 0.30m deep, with a loose fill of limestone pieces and brown sandy loam.

In the surface of the clay floor and within the overlying layer of brown sandy clay, there was an exceptional quantity of domestic artefacts and a primary pottery assemblage, from which some nine vessels could be partially reconstructed. A particular concentration around the doorway between rooms 1 and 2 included parts of three lock mechanisms, iron sheet and numerous nails

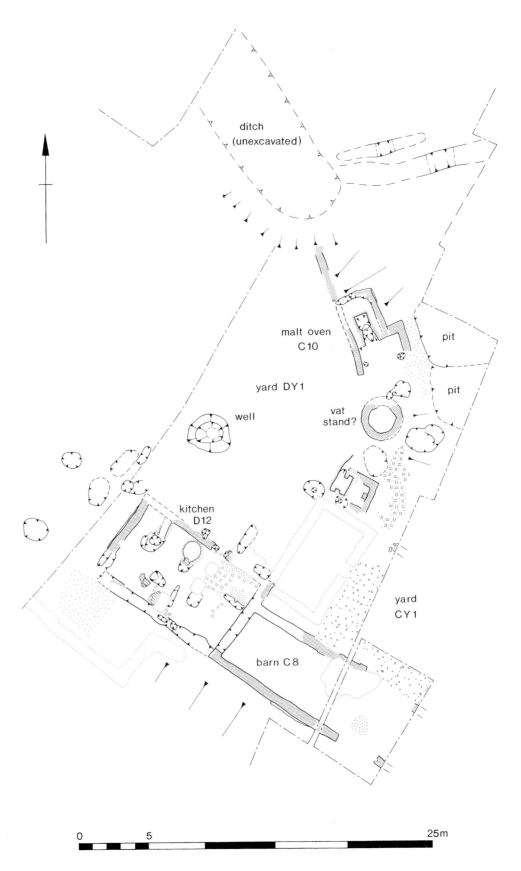

Fig 7.8: The agricultural ranges, tenement C/D

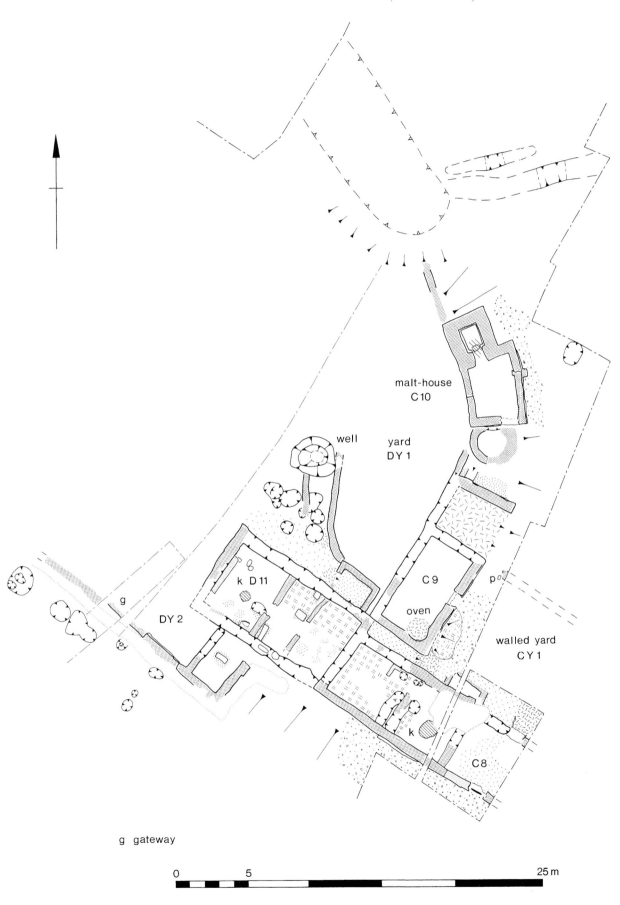

malt-house
C 10

well

yard
DY 1

k D 11

C 9

oven

p

DY 2

g

walled yard
CY 1

k

C 8

g gateway

0   5   25 m

Fig 7.9: The agricultural ranges and their conversion to peasant tenements, C and D

and staples. These fittings probably came from a door or chest, or perhaps more than one such item, apparently left to decay *in situ*. These deposits suggest that there was a period of temporary abandonment in which quantities of domestic items were left in rooms 1 and 2. This material was then sealed beneath the raised floors inserted when the building was brought back into use.

Room 2 was a kitchen, 3.60m long by 3.90m wide, with an internal area of 14.0sq m. To the south there were intermittent patches of a yellow clay floor beneath an earth floor. There may have been a stone bench against the partition wall to the west but, if so, it had been totally robbed. The open hearth, lying just south of centre, was 1.00m in diameter and comprised a heavily burnt hearth stone flanked on its eastern side by an arc of pitched limestone and pot sherds. Further fragments of burnt limestone above this were probably from an overlying hearth base that had been disturbed.

Room 3 provided a cross-passage, at least 3.9m long. The floor comprised light brown sandy clay with frequent pieces of limestone.

An external, stone-lined pit against the northern wall, was 2.20m long by 0.85m wide and 0.20m deep, with a partial floor of large limestone slabs (Fig 7.10, s).

In the final use of the building there were raised floors and thresholds. In the cross-passage, room 3, the earlier floor was covered by a 0.15m thick layer of disordered limestone rubble in a matrix of yellow-brown clay, with an area between the doorways comprising closely-set, pitched limestone slabs. In the northern doorway a massive slab of limestone, 0.90m long and 0.15m thick, with a worn surface, formed a new threshold. At the southern threshold a large slab of ironstone, 0.82m long, was set vertically across the width of the doorway, suggesting that there would have been a step down to the external surface, and an abutting internal threshold of flat-laid limestone sat on the new floor level. The partition wall between rooms 2 and 3 was retained but the western partition wall was levelled to create a single room spanning former rooms 1 and 2. There was a similar raised floor of disordered limestone rubble in a matrix of yellow-brown clay, with areas of tightly packed, pitched limestone.

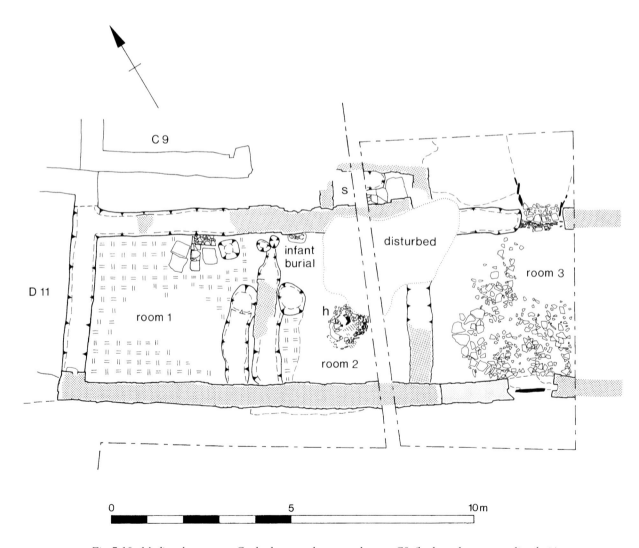

Fig 7.10: Medieval tenement C; the barn and peasant house, C8 (h=hearth, s=stone-lined pit)

Fig 7.11: Building C8, showing blocked barn doors, looking south

Fig 7.12: Building C8, looking north, showing rooms 1 (left) and 2

At some later date a large irregular pit, up to 3.80m long by 2.70m wide, had cut through the floors of rooms 2 and 3.

The walled yard, CY1

The walled yard to the rear, north, of the barn was 8.0m wide by around 16m long (Fig 7.9). Only the very end of the northern boundary wall lay within the excavated area, although further east it was partially visible as a low earthwork and was also located by resistivity survey. Two ironstone pivot stones, probably *in situ*, lay beside the wall terminal, and indicate the provision of a timber gate set within this opening, which was 1.5m wide. The pivot stones have larger sockets, up to 120mm diameter, than those recovered from building doorways.

To the west, in front of building C9, the yard surfaces had been heavily disturbed by later activity, but in front of the blocked barn door there was a well-preserved early surface of gravel pebbles, typically 20–40mm in diameter, with moderate small pieces of limestone.

At the conversion to a domestic range the yard was neatly resurfaced with flat-laid small pieces of limestone incorporating some small areas of pitched limestone, possibly later repairs. In front of the new narrow doorway there was an even more carefully laid area of pitched

limestone edged by kerbs of vertically-pitched limestone. In front of building C9 the metalling had been largely lost, but its former presence was indicated by the patchy survival of flat-laid limestone in a matrix of yellow sandy clay. This was best preserved beneath a dump of clayey mortar, 0.30m high, which had been heaped against the wall of the bakehouse, C9.

The bakehouse, C9

This single-roomed building was 7.60m long by 4.60m wide, and the internal dimensions of 6.40m by 3.20m gave a floor area of 20.5sq m (Fig 7.13). The southern wall was 0.60m wide and stood up to eight courses high, 0.60m. The internal face was of well-squared stones, while externally they were less well-squared. There were remnants of yellow-brown sandy loam bonding within the core. Only the bottom one or two courses of the eastern wall survived, at 0.65m wide and set on a 0.70–0.75m wide foundation course of large limestone blocks with an external offset of 0.05–0.10m.

The doorway at the southern end of the eastern wall was 1.20m wide with door jamb recesses, 0.15m square, overlying postholes up to 0.30m deep. It was blocked when a corner oven was inserted (Figs 7.14 and 7.15). The doorway just north of centre was 1.00m wide, and may

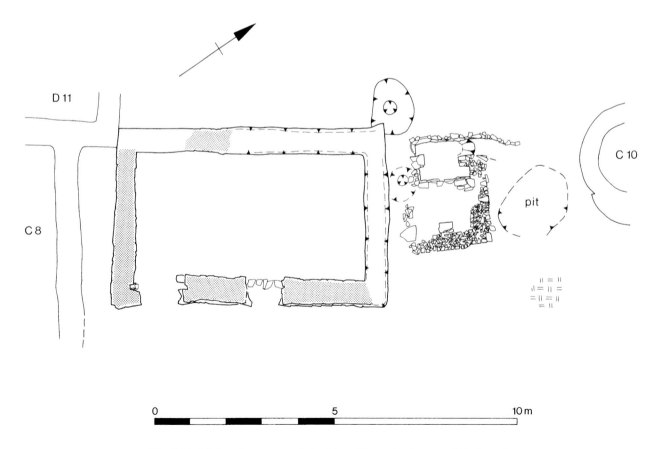

Fig 7.13: Medieval tenement C; building C9, early phase and H-shaped pit

have been inserted when the other doorway was blocked. Flat-laid limestone slabs set in a shallow hollow at the inner side of the doorway formed either a threshold or a step.

The corner oven was recessed into the standing walls, which had been refaced to follow the curve of the oven when the doorway was blocked (Fig 7.14). The oven base was 1.40m in diameter and comprised closely-set, flat-laid and pitched limestone sealed by a 20–30mm thick layer of yellow sandy clay, which was partially heat reddened (see Fig 7.79). A mixed layer of yellow-brown sand, bright yellow clay and some pieces of limestone that had accumulated over this foundation to a depth of 0.15m was probably debris from the levelling of a clay and limestone superstructure.

In the north-east corner of the room there was a steep-sided, flat-bottomed pit, 1.10m long by 0.40m wide and 0.15m deep, filled with grey sandy silt which contained some charcoal flecking and pieces of limestone. Around its southern end a tight cluster of small limestone pieces were set into the earthen floor, which comprised brown loam with some small pieces of limestone and some pebbles. An area immediately inside the central doorway was eroded into a broad shallow hollow, up to 1.80m in diameter, filled with a greyer loam and a higher density of limestone pieces.

The bakehouse was retained as part of the peasant tenement although the oven was levelled and covered by a new earth floor. An open-sided cart or shelter shed, 3.50m long by 4.00m wide, was added at this time (Fig 7.14, room 2). The new wall survived up to six courses high, 0.32m, and was 0.65m wide.

In the cart or shelter shed, there was a disturbed remnant of a probable original earth floor. This lay beneath a raised floor, 0.35m thick, which comprised a mixture of a single and a double layer of large, closely-set, vertically-pitched slabs of limestone, generally aligned across the width of the room and partly set in yellow sand (Fig 7.16). The raised floor inclined downward to the east to meet a mixed deposit of loam with much scattered limestone and gravel, which was probably derived from the trampling and churning of earlier laid surfaces.

A short length of blocking wall, 0.50m wide with two rough courses surviving, was inserted between the end of the cart or shelter shed, room 2, and the malt house, C10. A shallow, 0.15m deep, stone-lined pit lay beside the blocking wall (Fig 7.14, s). This area was later sealed by a layer of yellow-brown sandy loam that abutted the new walls and spread patchily over the levelled circular structure of the malt house.

To the south, the narrow space, 0.80–1.05m wide, between the bakehouse, C9, and the barn, C8, contained a succession of limestone surfaces, perhaps suggesting that it was utilised for storage. The surfaces stood above the yard level and there was a sloping surface of pitched

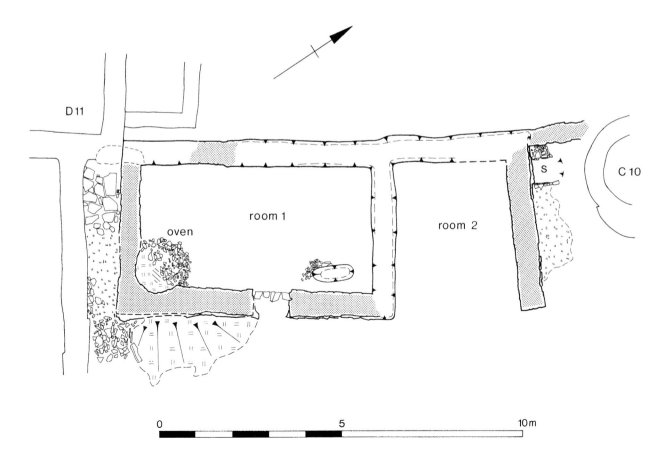

Fig 7.14: Medieval tenement C; building C9, with inserted oven (s=stone-lined bin)

Fig 7.15: Building C9, looking north-west, showing corner oven (left) and part of structure beneath room 2 (right)

Fig 7.16 : Building C9, room 2, showing late pitched-stone floor in section

limestone at the opening onto the yard (Fig 7.14). It would have been protected from the elements by the overhanging roofs of both adjacent buildings.

The malt house, C10

This was the best preserved and most elaborate of the excavated malt houses, with the walls standing 0.50m high. Specific constructional details are described below, and this is one of the specialised building types also covered in the general discussion of medieval buildings.

In its original form this was a free-standing oven, with the outer wall of the chamber continued southward for 1.50m to form an open-ended protective shed, although postholes adjacent to the walls may indicate that there was a timber end wall (Fig 7.17). To the south, a free-standing circular structure probably contained a vat for steeping the barley prior to malting.

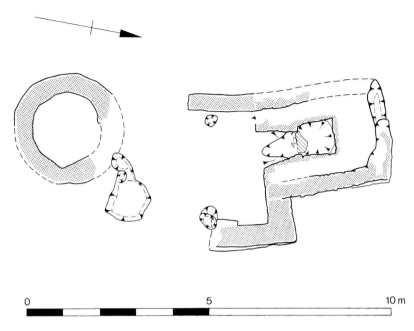

Fig 7.17: Medieval tenement C; the malt house C10, original form

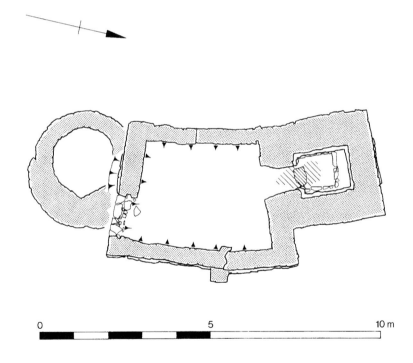

Fig 7.18: Medieval tenement C; the malt house C10, later form

Subsequently, the oven was rebuilt and enlarged, and the flanking walls were extended southward to form a fully enclosed room (Fig 7.18, and see Figs 7.74 and 7.75 and Plate 11). The circular vat stand was retained and would then have abutted the south wall of the malt house.

The oven chamber

The bottom course survived of the original near-square sunken chamber, 0.95m long by 0.80–0.90m wide and set in 0.20m deep construction pit (Figs 7.17 and 7.19). The chamber floor was yellow-brown sandy clay covered by a thin spread of blackened silt. A blackened slab of limestone was set in the opening of the flue, and the bottom one or two courses of the adjacent walls were reddened. The tapering flue was 1.10m long and from 0.60–1.00m wide.

The outer wall of the oven was built from ground level. To the west and north it was 0.50m wide, and an extra course of foundations were provided to the north where it overlay ditch fills. To the east an L-shaped length of wall abutted the oven build, and was slightly broader, at 0.55m wide with a 0.65m wide foundation course of large limestone slabs and blocks.

The enlarged oven chamber was 1.45m long by 1.10m wide (Fig 7.18). A lining of flat-laid limestone stood 0.50m high, and was battered so that at the upper level the chamber measured 1.65m by 1.30m. The flue was retained from the original oven and there was a ragged joint between this and the new lining. The oven walls were 0.85–0.95m thick in total, with the space between the chamber lining and the outer walls filled with limestone rubble in a soil matrix.

The original chamber was filled with closely-set, pitched limestone covered with yellow clay. An area of intense burning, 0.52m wide by 0.35m long, and some *in situ* burnt limestone showed the former presence of a stone fire base in the flue opening. This was covered by a new surface of yellow sandy clay and a new fire base comprising a single slab of limestone set immediately inside the chamber, rather than at the flue opening. This was overlain by a spread of grey-brown to dark grey charcoal flecked loam derived from the final firings.

The enclosed room

The new lengths of wall abutted the ends of the existing stubb walls (Fig 7.18). The western wall was 0.45m wide and it was founded 0.10m higher than the original wall, indicating that the external ground level had risen since the construction of the original building. To the south the wall was thicker, at 0.60m wide, and at the eastern end there was a corner doorway, 1.10m wide, with shallow door jamb recesses. A raised threshold setting of limestone slabs formed a stepped entrance.

The new eastern wall was 0.55m wide. The original wall terminal had been partially demolished, presumably to enable the new wall to be keyed into it. There was an internal wall thickening, and additional support was provided by a well-built, free-standing buttress.

The room was 3.20–4.10m long and 2.80–3.00m wide, an area of 10.4sq m. The earth floor was sunken, lying 0.10–0.20m below the base of the walls. Intermittent deposits of yellow-brown sandy clay against the walls may have been either a remnant of a clay floor or decayed wall rendering that had accumulated against the walls during a period of abandonment prior to demolition.

The circular chamber

The detached circular structure was 2.90m in diameter and the enclosing wall was typically 0.50m wide, leaving an internal space 1.90m in diameter (Fig 7.17 and see Fig 7.74). It is assumed that a doorway lay to the north within the demolished length. A floor of closely-set, pitched limestone was covered with yellow clay, and an upper floor of pitched stone, partially survived (Fig 7.20). At

some stage the eastern side had been rebuilt, with the wall thickened at foundation level.

An adjacent sub-square pit, 1.15m long by 1.05m wide and 0.25m deep, was largely filled with heavily charcoal-flecked, blackened loam (Fig 7.17).

With the creation of the fully enclosed room, the northern side of the circular chamber was removed, with the ragged wall ends abutted by the new wall (Fig 7.18). If the vat stand was still in use, it must have been accessed from an opening on the eastern side, as otherwise the thickened wall here would have blocked the adjacent doorway.

To the east of the malt house there were remnants of several contemporary surfaces, some pre-dating the full enclosing of the room. The uppermost comprised mixed yellow sandy clay, grey-brown clayey loam and small pieces of limestone, along with many small, abraded pottery sherds. This was overlain by a single width, linear setting of near vertically pitched limestone, which directly abutted the wall of the malt house.

At demolition, the walls were levelled to a consistent height as a single operation, and there was no subsequent wall robbing.

The H-shaped stone-lined pit

This lay to the south of the vat stand and is assumed to be related to the use of the malt house (Figs 7.8, 7.21 and 7.22). The stone-lined pit was 1.40m long by 1.05m wide and 0.50m deep, with 0.30m square buttresses forming the H-shape of two linked chambers each 0.40m wide. It was constructed in a combination of flat-laid and vertically-pitched slabs of limestone. The base was not surfaced and the lining showed no signs of burning or other discolouration. The northern end of the western chamber was unlined but steeply sloped, and a shallow channel, partly lined with limestone, extended 1.50m to the north. A pair of post-pits, up to 0.50m deep, lay to the south, and may have held posts 300mm in diameter. A shallow, U-shaped footing to the east, largely in small pieces of limestone, enclosed an area 1.50m long by 1.30m wide.

The specific function of this feature is unknown, although the primary fill of loose and soft grey-brown sandy silt suggests that the stone-lined pit served as a sump. The two buttresses may have held a mechanical device or container positioned above the sump. The post-pits and the U-shaped footing presumably held associated parts.

Pits east of the malt house

There was an extensive sunken area to the east of the malt house. This lay over former boundary ditches, and the upper fills may have been partially dug-out at this time (Fig 7.8). The fills of these hollows contained quantities of charcoal and small pieces of burnt clay and stone, suggesting that debris from the malt oven was dumped here. A partly stone-lined oval pit, 1.60m by 1.20m and 0.50m deep, was cut into these fills (Fig 7.9). It was filled with loosely

Fig 7.19: Malt house C10, the oven chamber partially dismantled to show method of construction

Fig 7.20: Malt house C10, showing pitched stone floor within circular chamber

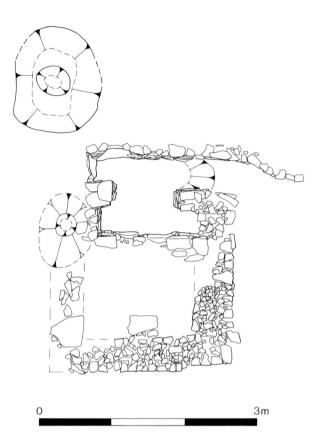

Fig 7.21: Medieval tenement C; the H-shaped, stone-lined pit and associated footings

Fig 7.22: The H-shaped, stone-lined pit, looking north-east

packed limestone rubble that was stained yellow-brown, indicating that it was used as a soak-away.

The kitchen, D12

This building was 11.00m long by 6.20m wide, with internal dimensions of 9.65m by 5.50m providing a room space of 53.1sq m (Figs 7.23 and 7.24). It was constructed on a slightly raised area over a partially surviving Bronze Age round barrow mound, and abutted the western end of the barn, C8.

The foundations of the western wall were well preserved as a result of being partly founded within a narrow construction cut into the sloping surface of the barrow mound. The wall above this was 0.65m wide. Part of the northern wall survived to either side of a doorway, which was 1.00m wide. The door jamb recesses in the wall surrounds were 0.15m square, and to the east a square posthole at the base of the recess contained a limestone pad stone, indicating that it was probably this jamb that carried the door. There was a slot beneath the other recess, but no pad stone. The presence of an opposed doorway in the robbed southern wall was defined by a similar but less well-preserved door jamb posthole and slot. An

adjacent pivot stone appears to have had no functional purpose in this location, but it may have been displaced in a refurbishment of the doorway. In addition there was a doorway in the south-east corner providing access to the barn, C8.

To the west of the southern doorway a shallow slot that ran part way across the room may have held a timber partition wall. A similar feature to the north had been largely removed when the circular oven was constructed. There would have been a central access between the partition and the oven, linking the chambers to either side.

In the eastern chamber the floors had been largely lost, but in the south-eastern corner a floor of flat-laid limestone slabs was contiguous with the stone-lining of an elongated pit or trough, 1.60m long by 0.35m wide and 0.30m deep (Fig 7.23, t). The lining comprised two rough courses of limestone blocks with a partial central division. There was no distinctive discolouration of the pit lining, but the form was similar to the processing troughs seen in other tenements. The trough was later taken out of use and was sealed by a new limestone floor over which a yellow clay floor only partly survived. There were also isolated patches of similar clay across the southern half of the room. Immediately beneath the clay floor in the

Fig 7.23: Medieval tenement D; kitchen range, D12 (h=hearth, s=stone-lined bin, t=trough, p=pivot stone)

Fig 7.24: The kitchen range D12, looking north

south-east corner there was a dense scatter of iron nails, and further nails were recovered from the disturbed floor to the south, suggesting that they were deposited during this refurbishment. The only other feature in the eastern chamber was a sub-square pit, 0.90m diameter by 0.15m deep, partly floored with limestone slabs (Fig 7.23, s).

The western chamber had an earth floor. A hearth against the southern wall, h1, comprised a clay base, 1.30m long by at least 0.60m wide, set in a shallow hollow, and a single piece of burnt limestone was a remnant of a larger hearth stone. A small open hearth lay nearby, h2.

In the north-western corner of the room there was a rectangular stone-lined pit, 1.30m long by 0.45m wide and 0.15m deep. A small area of one floor slab was lightly scorched, but otherwise there was no burning or other discolouration, but iron-staining of the underlying natural gravel suggests that water had been percolating through the base of the pit. To the south it may have opened directly into a complex bowl-shaped pit, 0.30m deep.

The circular oven was the best preserved from the site, and there is further discussion of these features in the section on detached kitchens (see Fig 7.77). The construction pit was 0.25m deep. A floor of neatly pitched limestone was covered by a layer of yellow sand, and the oven lining were built on this foundation in courses of small flat-laid limestone. The oven chamber was 1.26m in diameter and a large slab of heavily burnt limestone lay within the flue, which was 0.46m wide and opened into a small stokehole. Much of the stone lining was reddened and blackened, as was the sandy floor.

The rebuilding of the kitchen, D11

The kitchen was at least largely rebuilt (Fig 7.25 and 7.26). The northern wall was new and lay inside the levelled wall of the earlier building, while the western wall was probably rebuilt over the foundations of its predecessor, but with a slight shift to the east of 0.15m. The southern wall was either retained or rebuilt on the same line. The kitchen was then 10.8m long by 6.20m wide. A new room, 4, was added to the front of the building. The circular oven was removed at this time, and was perhaps replaced by the oven in a new separate bakehouse to the north-east, C9.

On the southern wall an external threshold of worn limestone suggests that there was still a central doorway, and there may have been an opposed doorway to the north.

The narrow, eastern partition wall, which was only 300–400mm thick, was probably built at this time. This may have been a dwarf wall supporting a timber partition, to form two rooms of unequal lengths. There was a central doorway, 1.10m wide, with a narrow door jamb recess in the surround to the south.

The smaller room to the east, 3, was 2.70m long, with an internal area of 11.6sq m. The disturbed floor of brown sandy clay was scattered with flat-laid slabs of limestone, including a large square slab with a heavily cracked surface set against the partition wall. It had probably been more

extensively, if not fully, surfaced with limestone slabs, suggesting its use as a storage chamber; there were no internal fittings.

The western room, 1, which was 6.30m long by 4.80m wide with an internal area of 30.2sq m, still functioned as a kitchen. Against the western face of the partition wall there were two stone-lined pits. The larger pit, 0.85m long by 0.55m wide, which lay adjacent to the doorway, was partially floored with two flat-laid slabs of limestone overlain by the lining of three courses of flat-laid limestone, s1. No lining survived around the western and southern sides of the pit, but a lining may have been removed. The eastern floor slab had a nine-men's morris board crudely scratched on its upper surface, executed before the stone was inserted into the pit. The eastern end of the pit was more crudely lined with three vertically pitched pieces of limestone, and the central stone, which stood on a smaller stone, carried a high relief carving of a figure with a stylised, shield-shaped face, and wearing a long robe or surcoat with the hands held together in front as if in prayer (Fig 7.27 and Plate 13). As a result of the juxtaposition of the figure and the nine-men's morris board, the figure was immediately christened 'Norman Morris' by the digging team.

This is the only figurative piece of worked stone from the site and it is an unusual, if not a unique item of exceptional interest but uncertain interpretation. It may be viewed most simply as a foundation deposit associated with the rebuilding of the manorial kitchen, D11, but the presence of both the carved figure and the nine-men's morris board at its feet could imply religious or mystical associations. The fill of the pit contained a small pottery assemblage dated to the earlier thirteenth century (ph2/0) while the overlying floor is dated to the later thirteenth century (ph2/2), suggesting that the figure itself is no later in date than AD 1250.

The pit containing the figure was subsequently backfilled and overlain by a later floor, but even following this the very top of the carved stone may still have stood above floor level, with the face perhaps at least partially visible.

To the north there was a smaller stone-lined pit, s2, 0.40m square by 0.23m deep, floored with flat-laid limestone and lined on three sides with two courses of limestone. On the northern side a single pitched limestone may have leant against the adjacent wall.

To the west of the southern doorway a well built stone-lined pit, s3, abutting the southern wall was 1.05m long by 0.35m wide and 0.45m deep, with a lining of six or seven courses of limestone and a floor of flat-laid limestone (see Fig 7.86). To the west there was an open hearth comprising a burnt hearth-stone set on and surrounded by a layer of burnt clay, h1.

Between the stone-lined pit and the hearth there was a less regular pit that may have been either introduced at this time or was a reuse of a pit within the earlier building. The primary silts, from a previous use, were overlain by some limestone rubble in clayey loam and above this the pit was lined along its northern side with steeply pitched slabs of limestone while there was a flat-laid slab of ironstone at floor level to the south. The fill of loose limestone rubble, frequently steeply pitched and in a matrix of grey-brown sandy loam, suggest that it may have functioned as a soak-away.

The stone bench abutting the western wall was 0.38m wide and survived one or two courses high, 0.10m. A posthole at its northern end was 0.25m deep, and vertically pitched pieces of limestone suggest that it had held a squared post of at least 100mm diameter.

The single-room extension, room 4, was 3.25m wide by 4.40m long, with internal dimensions of 2.15m by 3.85m; a floor area of 8.3sq m. The walls were 0.55m thick, and thickened to 0.66m adjacent to the doorway.

The doorway opening was 0.85m wide, with a shallow door-jamb recess to the south and an *in situ* pivot stone to the north, p. A small scratched, nine-men's morris board had been incorporated into the build. The new room was earth-floored and contained a central stone-lined pit, 0.85m long by 0.35m wide, which had replaced an earlier similar feature (Fig 7.25, s).

At the south-western corner of the new room, the wall extended 0.60m to the west. Beyond this the boundary wall was more crudely built, and ran from the end of the room 4 to the detached building range of tenement E, E14, to the west. The wall was 0.55m wide and survived up to three courses high, 0.30m. A change in the build suggests that there was a gateway, 3.5m wide, to the west of the

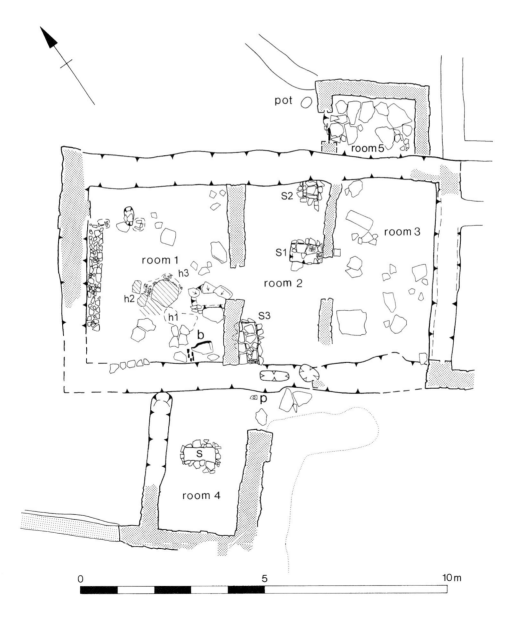

Fig 7.25: Medieval tenement D; the rebuilt kitchen and peasant cottage, D11 (h=hearth, s=stone-lined bin, b=raised bin, p=pivot stone)

Fig 7.26: The peasant cottage, D11, looking north

kitchen range (Fig 7.9, g). A single course of stone within this gateway was probably a later blocking wall. This was only faced on the southern side, indicating that the ground level within the plot to the north was higher than the surface of the central yard. At tenement E the boundary wall abutted, but also partially overlay the levelled wall of a small, stone-floored chamber attached to building E14.

The peasant cottage, D11

With the conversion of the manorial ranges, C/D, to two tenements the former kitchen was retained, but with further modifications (Figs 7.25 and 7.26). A second partition wall was introduced to provide three rooms, and a sunken, stone-floored storage chamber was added at the rear. The doorway giving access to the barn must have been blocked, as this was then a separate tenement, but this area had been totally robbed.

The new partition wall was 0.50m wide with a central doorway, 0.85m wide. The door surrounds contained narrow door-jamb recesses.

The shortened western chamber, 1, which was 3.75m long with an internal area of 16.1sq m, served as a kitchen. There were two successive open hearths. Of the earlier, fragments of a hearth stone and some adjacent pitched stone survived,

h2. The second hearth lay slightly to the east and comprised a single, large slab of limestone, 0.70m in diameter, with its surface reddened, blackened and heavily cracked, h3. It was flanked to the north by a narrow band of pitched pieces of limestone. Both hearths were partially surrounded by patchy areas of reddened and blackened loam, suggesting that there was an earth floor immediately around them.

In the southern corner of the room a large, upstanding slab of limestone suggests the presence of a corner bin, 0.90m long by 0.40m wide, b. A remnant of limestone surfacing survived against the southern wall adjacent to the bin. The stone bench abutting the western wall may have been either retained or levelled.

The new central chamber was only 2.15m long, an internal area of 9.2sq m, and probably formed a cross-passage between opposed doorways. The well-built stone-lined pit adjacent to the southern doorway was retained, while the two stone-lined pits against the eastern partition wall were both filled and sealed beneath a new floor of sandy clay and small pieces of limestone.

The eastern chamber, which was 2.70m long, an internal area of 11.6sq m, contained no internal fittings.

The small, sunken chamber, room 5, abutting the rear of the building had internal dimensions of 2.30m by 1.50m, an area of 3.45sq m (Fig 7.28). The wall was 0.40–0.45m

Fig 7.27: The carved stone figure, in situ in a stone-lined pit in building D11

thick with a slightly battered inner face, and the door surrounds contained narrow door jamb recesses. An external surface of pitched limestone sloped down towards a low step, 0.10m high, partly edged with vertically-pitched limestone. The sunken floor of the chamber comprised large limestone slabs.

The final use of the building probably post-dated its abandonment as a dwelling and marked its reuse as an outbuilding. The eastern end of the southern wall was totally demolished, along with the end of the eastern partition wall, to leave at least room 3 open-ended. Within room 3 a new raised floor comprised a double interlocking layer of vertically-pitched limestone, 0.35m thick, set in a matrix of sandy clay. This may suggest that it then served as an open-ended cart or shelter shed. To the south this surface sloped down to meet an external surface of scattered limestone that ran across the former wall line.

Within room 2, the final floor was a 0.15m thick layer of brown sandy clay with some scattered limestone. Within room 1, which was still fully enclosed, there was a similar floor but to the south it incorporated large limestone slabs, covering the final hearth and probably derived from disturbance of the earlier floors in this area. There was an eroded hollow within the centre of the room and through the doorway into room 2. Within room 4 a layer

of disordered and pitched limestone rubble in a sandy clay matrix may have been either a similar raised floor or merely demolition rubble.

Pit groups and a well

Three pit groups were contemporary with the kitchen range, D12/D11. Two pits lay to the immediate north-east (Fig 7.8), and both had been disturbed by the construction of the sunken chamber. The smaller eastern pit, 1.30m long by 0.75m wide and 0.45m deep, contained a compact mass of limestone rubble that included one of the few later medieval primary pottery groups, which comprised numerous large sherds from a small number of vessels, particularly glazed jugs, dated to the later thirteenth century (ph 2/2, 1250–1300).

A group of shallow pits, up to 0.30m deep, to the west of the kitchen were broadly contemporary with the rebuilding, D12 (ph 2/2, 1250–1300) (Fig 7.8). To the north of the building there was a tight cluster of eight small pits (Fig 7.9). The westernmost and largest, at 0.50m deep, contained only later thirteenth-century pottery (ph 2/2) indicating that is was contemporary with the rebuilt kitchen range, but some were open into the fourteenth century (ph 3/2). Once these pits had fallen out of use,

Fig 7.28: The sunken, stone-floored chamber at the rear of building D11

a pair of parallel walls, 1.5m apart, flanked the approach to a probable well (Fig 7.9). The eastern wall of this pair abutted the corner of the new sunken chamber and both walls contained a much higher proportion of ironstone, at up to 40%, than was encountered in the other tenements buildings or boundary walls.

The well shaft was up to 3.00m in diameter by 1.63m deep. The upper sides were moderately steep, at 45 degrees or more, and from a depth of 0.70–0.80m it was steep to near vertically-sided, with a basal diameter of 1.00m. It cut through the compact natural of mixed sands and gravel and bottomed in loose calcareous gravels at the modern water table. The bottom 0.60m of the pit was filled with sandy silts and much disordered limestone rubble. Large slabs of limestone, up to 0.40m long, and one ironstone block, 0.70m long, were pitched against the more shallowly-sloping north-western side. The stone content of the fill was not building stone, and it is possible that it was the debris from the robbing of an original stone lining. The shallower slope, with its cut step, may have provided an access ramp for the robbing.

The secondary fill of the shaft contained a small pottery assemblage dated to the earlier thirteenth century (ph 2/0), while the small, mixed assemblage from the final fill spanned the thirteenth century (ph 2/0 and 2/2) and contained three sherds dated to the fourteenth century (ph 3/2).

To the north of the parallel walls there was a general,

homogeneous soil horizon of brown sandy loam with scattered small pieces of limestone. The underlying subsoil and prehistoric barrow mound had been disturbed and truncated, suggesting that the area was in use as a garden/horticultural plot through the thirteenth and fourteenth centuries. The ground was similarly disturbed to the north-west adjacent to tenement E.

The manorial domestic range: tenement F

This tenement lay adjacent to Cotton Lane, and the evidence for its general form and its buildings is provided by earthwork and resistivity surveys (Fig 7.29).

The building along the western side of the courtyard probably formed the main domestic range (F39). It has a total length of at least 18.5m, and perhaps as much as 25.0m. Changes in the alignment of the long walls suggest that it may have comprised two abutting structures of separate build. The northern room is 10.5m long by 4.5m wide. A wall extending a further 2.4m to the north may be a boundary wall or part of a small northern chamber. The southern room was 7.5m long by 4.5m wide. At the southern end there may have been an additional square room, 3.5m long.

The building flanking the northern side of the courtyard was probably 11–12m long (F40). A poorly defined cross-wall indicates that there are at least two rooms.

The courtyard is up to 18m long by 14m wide, and is deeply sunken with respect to the building earthworks. A low linear ridge, 4m wide at the crest, probably with stone metalling, runs across the courtyard and was perhaps an access road. The southern side of the courtyard is bounded by a wall, although a raised platform and stone concentration at the eastern end could represent a further building, perhaps as much as 10m long and partly concealed by a later boundary bank. The boundary bank along the eastern side of the courtyard continues beyond the tenement in both directions and is most probably associated with post-desertion embanking along the Cotton Lane.

This was the only tenement for which clearly defined building outlines were visible in earthwork, and in the exceptionally dry summer of 1990 several walls appeared as sharply-edged, linear parch-marks, 0.30–0.70m wide. Probing established that the walls lay immediately below the modern turf, with some stones showing through at ground level, and the upper courses were only abutted by topsoil. In the excavated tenements the lengths of standing wall were always abutted by demolition rubble, and the lack of such rubble here accounts for the exceptional clarity of the earthworks and the sharply defined parch marks. It also suggests that most of the walls probably still stand to an appreciable height, indicating minimal robbing and even better preservation than in the excavated tenements.

There is no direct evidence for the date of origin of these buildings. However, the southern end overlies the probable former course of the northern stream, which had become redundant by the end of the twelfth century. This indicates

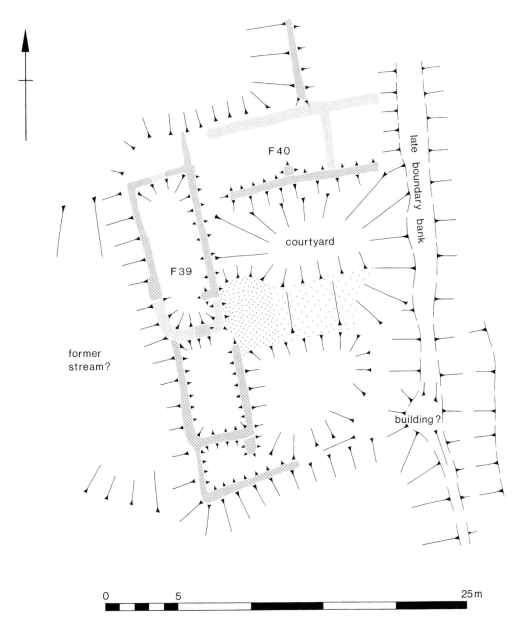

Fig 7.29: Medieval tenement F; the earthwork and parch-mark survey

that tenement F was a new development between the later twelfth and mid-thirteenth centuries, at least broadly contemporary with the appearance of tenement C/D.

The apparent lack of wall robbing is taken as an indication that this was one of the last tenements to be deserted, and that it was left as a derelict ruin. One possibility is that it was still occupied when the buildings of tenements C and D were in their final phase of partial use as outbuildings with raised floors, perhaps serving the occupants of tenement F. It is therefore suggested that this tenement probably remained in use well into the fifteenth century.

The buildings of the southern holding: tenements B and G

Two separate building groups occupied the area defined as the southern holding, with the northern buildings, tenement B, perhaps providing the agricultural and service facilities to a domestic complex, tenement G (Fig 7.1). This interpretation would imply that the southern holding had formed a second small manor, with a similar arrangement to that proposed for the manorial complex of tenements C/D and F; but again, the partial excavation of only one of the two building groups leaves the validity of the overall interpretation uncertain (Figs 7.30–7.31 and Plate 8).

The origin of tenement B apparently lay in the provision of a purpose-built processing room, B5/1, in the early thirteenth century (ph 1, 1200–1225), probably contemporary with the addition of a processing room and barn as the final phase of development of the original northern manor. The open, hall-like building, B4, was introduced slightly later as part of a second stage of development, with the tenement fully formed by the mid-thirteenth century (ph 2/0, 1225–1250), contemporary with the relocation of the northern manor onto the eastern plots. In its fully developed form tenement B was in use through much of the second half of thirteenth century (ph 2/2, 1250–1300), but by the end of the century the specialised functions had all been removed and buildings were either demolished or reused. Final abandonment of all buildings occurred early in the fourteenth century (ph 3/2, 1300–1400), perhaps well before 1350.

Building B4

This single-roomed building was 9.4m long by 5.5m wide, with internal dimensions of 7.95m by 4.35m, an internal area of 34.6sq.m (Fig 7.32 and 7.33).

The walls were more deeply founded than in any other contemporary building, perhaps as a response to constructional problems posed by the uneven existing ground surface. Two or three foundation courses were set within a construction trench 0.15–0.20m deep and, unlike all the other excavated buildings, the foundations were carried through under the doorways. There were considerable variations in the widths of the foundations

and the standing walls from 0.50m wide on 0.55–0.60m wide foundations on the northern end wall to the 0.80m wide southern end wall.

Opposed doorways were set immediately north of centre. They were 1.20m wide externally and slightly splayed, broadening to 1.32m wide. Shallow door jamb recesses, 70mm wide by 50mm deep, were set towards the outer wall faces and each had a pad stone at the base of the left hand jamb, as viewed from outside, probably indicating the side on which the doors were hung.

The room had either an earthen or a sandy clay floor, slightly hollowed within the centre of the room. There were no internal fixtures or fittings. It is suggested that it originally functioned as a store or workroom related to the agricultural and service functions of the adjacent buildings and as a domestic hall when the buildings may have been converted to a single tenement.

Directly abutting the walls around much of the interior there was a distinctive layer of clean, bright yellow, sandy clay. This may have been a remnant of a clay floor preserved only against the walls, or it might represent an accumulation of former wall rendering eroded during a period of dereliction prior to demolition. This interpretation may be supported by the presence of similar material abutting the external wall faces and similar deposits in the room to the north, B5, room 2.

The processing room, B5

Originally there was a single room, 1, and the second room was a later addition that linked this building to the southern range, B4 (Fig 7.32). The two-roomed building was 12.4m long. This is one of the specialised processing facilities that are subject to a general discussion at the end of this chapter (see Figs 7.87–7.89).

Room 1 was 6.55m long by 4.25m wide internally, a floor area of 27.8sq.m. The eastern long wall was 0.60m wide, with the lower two courses broadening to 0.70m. At its northern end, adjacent to the stone-lined trough, the inner face was built down into the end of the construction pit for the trough, indicating that the trough had been installed as part of the building construction and not merely as an internal fitting. Similarly, the foundations for a stone footing against the southern wall extended beneath the robber trench as another pre-determined internal fitting.

The ends of the northern end wall were contiguous with the long walls but oblique ragged joints indicate that the central section of this wall had been rebuilt, and was slightly narrower, at 0.50m wide (Fig 7.34). The rebuilding may have been necessitated by subsidence into an underlying ditch.

There were opposed doorways immediately south of the stone-lined trough, and a doorway at the western end of the largely robbed southern wall. The eastern doorway was 1.15m wide, with door jamb recesses set towards the inner wall face and including a pad stone at the base of the northern recess and a probable slot for a sill beam.

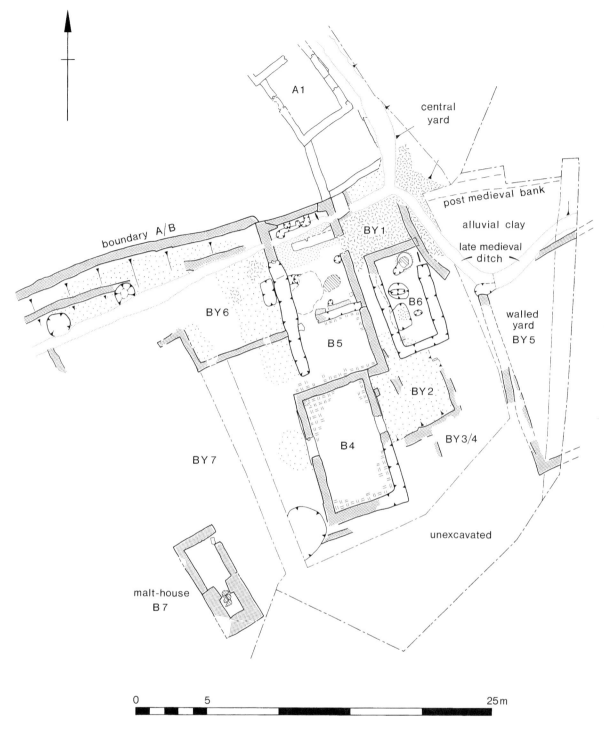

Fig 7.30: Medieval tenement B

The western doorway was similar. The southern doorway was 1.10m wide, with a door jamb recess to the east and a pivot stone to the west, probably slightly displaced. To the north the doorway opening was flanked by a rectangular respond.

The internal arrangements comprised the stone-lined processing trough, a stone-foundation against the southern wall, an open hearth and a large pit probably serving as an internal soak-away. The stone-lined processing trough was 3.0m long by 0.30m deep, with a basal width of 0.60m (see Fig 7.87 and 7.89). It was floored with limestone slabs, and included the lower stone of a rotary quern. A partial transverse division was formed by a block of ironstone projecting a third of the way across the trough. The southern

Fig 7.31: Medieval tenement B, looking north

side and the western end of the northern side were vertically faced with flat-laid limestone while the remainder had a stepped facing, which had partially collapsed. The floor and the facings of the pit were all discoloured by a thin grey encrustation.

To the south and west there was a surface of worn limestone slabs. Between the trough and the northern wall there was a complex setting of postholes and slots, which probably derived from at least two successive arrangements that comprised end posts, successively 2.0 and 1.5m apart, with shallow linear slots running between them. These arrangements indicate the provision of some form of timber framing set against the wall, presumably to support whatever was being processed within the adjacent trough.

The stone foundation against the southern wall was at least 1.7m long and comprised three mortar-bonded courses within in a construction pit, 0.20m deep and 0.60m wide, with half of its width beneath the adjacent robber trench (see Fig 7.87). At the western end there was a small posthole and a patch of clay and pitched stones, unexcavated, suggest that a further posthole lay against the eastern wall. The deeply set foundations suggest that this base had to carry a substantial load, while the small postholes may have supported an associated timber frame.

There was a large open hearth east of centre. A flat-laid, but unburnt, slab of limestone and an adjacent setting of cobbles, were probably a remnant of an early hearth. The later hearth measured 1.30m by 0.95m, and comprised a mortar bed for a flat-laid hearth stone, with pitched pottery sherds to the west flanked by a rough kerb of small, flat-laid limestone (see Fig 7.87). The heavily burnt and fragmented remnants of two successive hearth stones survived, surrounded by a spread of burnt debris, grey ash and blackened and reddened loams with much comminuted charcoal.

West of the hearth there was a large pit, 2.6m long by 2.4m wide and up to 0.50m deep, partially filled with loose limestone rubble (Fig 7.32 and see Fig 7.87). At the northern end this rubble was exposed at floor level and contained some near vertically pitched stones. Over the rest of the pit the rubble was covered by an upper fill of mixed sands sealed beneath a floor of mixed clayey to sandy loam. The pit would appear to have functioned as an internal soak-away.

A posthole inside the eastern doorway and a broad but short slot inside the western doorway may have held short wooden screens.

When the trough was taken out of use it was backfilled

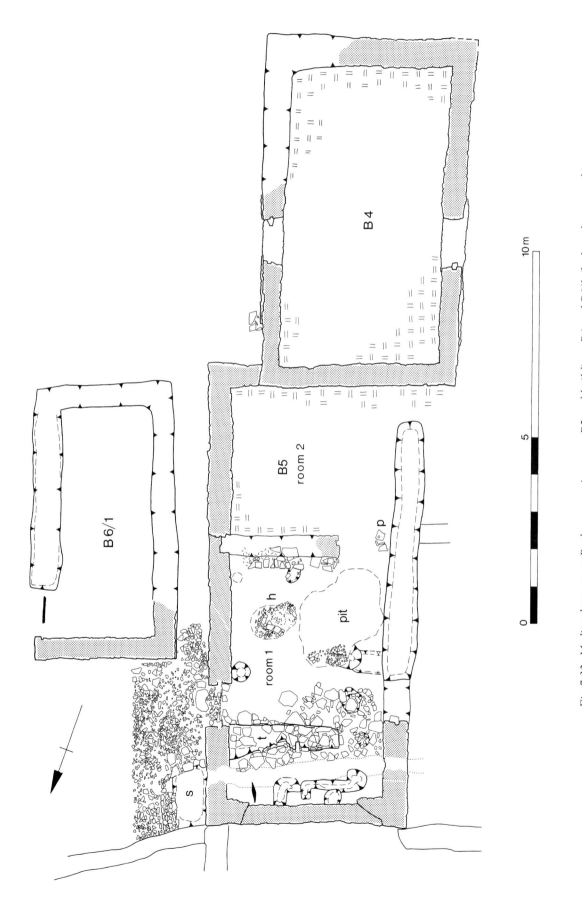

Fig 7.32: Medieval tenement B; the processing room B5 and buildings B4 and B6/1 (h=hearth, t=trough)

Fig 7.33: Building B4, looking east

Fig 7.34: Building B5, the processing room, showing the angled joint between the rebuilt (bottom) and original lengths of the northern wall

with limestone rubble, containing much charcoal, and the area was floored over with disordered limestone containing some patches of smaller, pitched limestone. The stone foundation against the southern wall was also levelled and partially removed. The final hearth stood above the latest floor surface and was probably still in use. In the north-east corner an upstanding slab of limestone may have formed one side of a corner bin, perhaps 0.70m square and at least 0.20m deep. The retained hearth and the corner bin suggest that the room was then functioning as a domestic kitchen.

Room 2 was 4.0m long by 4.6m wide, an internal area of 18.4sq.m, and was formed by infilling between the two existing buildings. The eastern wall was 0.65m wide, broader than the eastern wall of room 1, and was founded at a slightly higher level. There was access into room 1 and an external doorway at the southern end of the western wall, which had been totally robbed. Directly abutting three of the walls there was a patchy layer of yellow sandy clay. As in building B4, this may have been either a remnant floor or decayed wall rendering that accumulated during a period of dereliction.

The bakehouse, B6/2, and its rebuilding, B6/1

The original building, B6/2, was around 5.7m long by 3.0m wide internally, but as it had been totally levelled it was only defined by the extent of the internal features and floor surfaces (Fig 7.35). A slight scarp to the west indicates that the floor level was partly sunken below the base of the walls.

In the south-west corner there was a broad, shallow hollow, up to 0.15m deep, floored with two large flagstones. In the centre of the room there was a steep-sided pit, 0.5m deep, with a rectangular slot, 1.0m long by 0.15m deep, in its base. This may have held a timber base-plate supporting a timber superstructure that needed to be well founded. To the north, shallow postholes and some intervening stones are of uncertain function and may either have been remnants of an internal fitting abutting the northern wall or a door jamb and sill beam setting within the wall, although doors were not often set in end walls. In the north-east corner there was a circular oven with a slightly sunken chamber, 1.10m in diameter, but only the bottom course of the facing and a large, burnt floor slab survived (see Fig 7.78).

A layer of pitched limestone ran the entire length of the room alongside the western wall. It contained a high proportion of edge-reddened stone probably derived from the demolition of the oven superstructure, and may have been a levelling layer prior to the rebuilding, which took place in the later thirteenth century (ph 2/2, 1250–1300).

The new building, B6/1, was 7.30m long by 3.90m wide, with internal dimensions of 6.15m by 2.60m, an internal area of 16.0sq.m (Fig 7.32). The surviving northern wall, which stood up to eight courses, 0.46m, high, was 0.62m wide, and there was a broad doorway, 1.4m wide, in the north-east corner. A straight joint in the facing 0.45m from the eastern end of the wall indicates that the wall end was rebuilt at some stage; it contained a door jamb recess 80mm

wide by 70mm deep. There were no internal features and the floor was a light brown sandy loam with some small pieces of limestone.

In its final use, dated to the fourteenth century (ph 3/2, 1300–1400), the building was given a raised floor of compact limestone rubble, which abutted a vertical limestone slab standing 0.10m high within the doorway. Externally the threshold slab was abutted by rubble metalling.

Five knives or knife fragments came from the late floors of this building, with a further five from the surrounding yards; the only concentration of knives from the settlement. There was also a possible concentration of schist hones in the same contexts. This suggests that the final use of the building may have been in a food processing or some manufacturing process involving the use of sharp knives. One possibility is that it was used as a slaughter house or for the butchering of carcasses, but perhaps only following the abandonment of the adjacent buildings.

The malt house, B7

This building was 7.30m long by up to 3.15m wide (Figs 7.36 and 7.37), with nearly half of this length taken up by the oven itself, which was 3.50m long by 2.90m wide. The rectangular oven chamber, 1.40m long by 1.10m wide, had slightly battered internal facings, built down into a 0.20m deep construction pit. The oven walls were 0.90–1.00m thick, with a core of mixed loam and limestone rubble. The

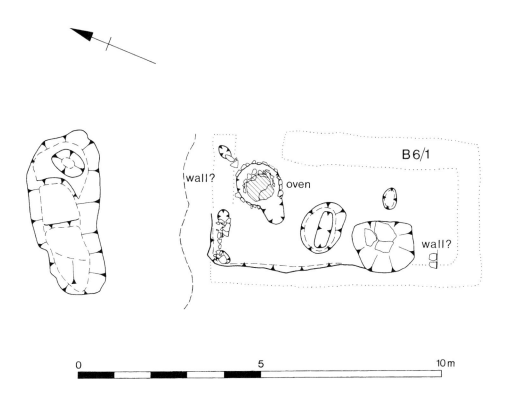

Fig 7.35: Medieval tenement B; the bakehouse, B6/2, and the sand-filled pit

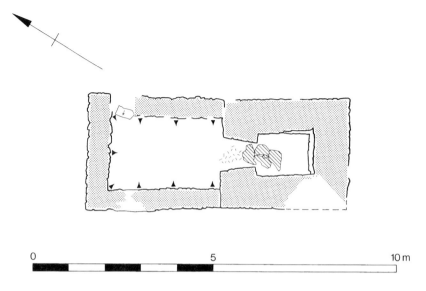

Fig 7.36 : Medieval tenement B; the malt house, B7

Fig 7.37: The malt house, B7, looking north

flue was 0.96m long and narrowed towards the chamber from 0.90m to 0.63m wide, and the wall faces leant slightly inwards, indicating the former presence of a flue arch. Two successive fire bases survived within the flue opening. The earliest comprised a layer of mortar extending along

the flue and into the chamber, with an area of intense scorching immediately inside the chamber indicating the former position of a hearth stone. Above a thin layer of mixed burnt debris, a second fire base comprised three large limestone slabs, with the central slab the most heavily burnt and cracked. The entire chamber and flue area contained a spread of burnt debris.

The oven chamber could have been a free-standing structure prior to the addition of the room, but no evidence was recovered for any post-pits suggesting the presence of an abutting timber shed. The abutting room was 3.10m long by 1.90m wide, a floor area of 5.9sq.m, with walls from 0.50–0.66m wide. The earth floor was sunken and lay below the base of the walls by up to 0.05m. Within the narrow, 0.60m wide, doorway at the north-east corner, there was a partially displaced threshold slab.

At its demolition the entire building was consistently levelled so that one or two courses of the walls of the attached room survived standing level with the compact limestone rubble, and both wall tops and rubble had a weathered surface indicating that it had been left exposed to the elements for sometime.

The boundaries and yards
The northern tenement boundary, A/B

The northern wall of the paired boundary walls was the earlier construction. It abutted a tenement B building, B5, to the east and the tenement A malt house, A3, to the west (Figs 7.7 and 7.26). The southern wall overlay early metalling within yard BY6, and was a later addition, forming a double-walled boundary. It also continued further to the west.

Both walls were constructed on a sloping surface and directly overlay an earlier boundary ditch The southern wall was 0.55–0.60m wide, and to the west of the tenement A malt house it sat on a low bank, up to 0.35m high. A length of at least 4.0m towards the west had been thickened by the addition of a 0.40m wide facing along the southern side, to give a total width of 0.95m.

There was no evidence to indicate that the narrow gap, 1.0–1.4m wide, between the two walls was utilised as a passageway. The space was largely filled with disordered limestone rubble that may have accumulated over an external period from progressive collapse of the walls as maintenance was neglected. Pottery of fourteenth to fifteenth century date (ph 3/2 and 4) suggests that much of this rubble accumulated after the desertion of the tenement B buildings. At this time four large pits were cut through both the rubble and the southern wall, and were filled with soil and stone rubble (Figs 7.7 and 7.26).

The yards

Isolated remnants of an early north-south boundary wall probably abutted the south-east corner of the original processing room, B5, and ran south across what was later yard BY2 (Fig 7.26). This wall certainly pre-dated the southern room of range B5 and perhaps also pre-dated building B4. A further remnant of early wall lay to the south of building B4. These early walls may have formed a walled yard to the south of the original processing room and with the malt house at the south-western corner.

With the full development of the buildings three small walled yards were introduced. To the north of the bakehouse, B6 there was a semi-enclosed yard, BY1, with multiple successive surfaces of neatly pitched limestone at the frontage of the processing room, B5 (see Fig 7.72).

To the north there was a 0.50–0.60m wide boundary wall with tenement A that abutted the corner of the processing room, B5. In the earlier use of the yard there was a large pit closely adjacent to the boundary wall (Fig 7.35). The pit was 4.20m long by 2.00m wide and up to 0.50m deep, with steep-sides, a rounded base and a shallower shelf at the eastern end. The bulk of the fill comprised a single, clean and homogeneous deposit of yellow to orange-yellow sand, with sparse small pieces of limestone, and contained pottery dating to the first half of the thirteenth century (ph 2/0). Over this there were successive layers of disordered limestone. It is suggested that the pit was utilised as a soak-away for surplus water from the adjacent processing room. To the south of the pit there was patchy metalling of gravel with some mortar, and above this there was a pitched limestone surface contemporary with the original ancillary building to the south B6/2.

To the east, the surfacing extended several metres beyond the frontage and sloped steadily downward to the lower level of the central yard. A second surface of pitched limestone covered much the same area, but was contemporary with the second building, B6/1. Immediately in front of the doorway of the processing room, B5/1, this surface included an area of larger, flat-laid limestone with worn surfaces (see Fig 7.72).

A third surface was of flat-laid limestone, and there was again an area of larger limestone with worn surfaces at the processing room doorway. To the north-west, in the corner between building B5 and the boundary wall with tenement A, there was a stone-lined pit, 1.50m long by 0.80m wide and 0.30m deep. This was later rebuilt, when it was floored with two large limestone slabs (see Fig 7.73). These surfaces and the pit overlay the large, sand-filled pit, which had evidently become redundant.

Subsequently, a layer of light brown clayey loam with scattered small pieces of limestone accumulated across the entire area. A final metalling of limestone rubble was laid on top of this layer, and was probably contemporary with the final use of building B6/1, when it was provided with a raised floor and an upstanding threshold slab.

Subsequent activity post-dated the abandonment of the buildings. A curving wall ran across the final rubble surface, in front of the doorway of building B6, and terminated to the south (Fig 7.30). This wall and the retained northern wall of building B6 formed the northern limits to a late rubble hard-standing, see below.

There was a small walled yard, BY2, in front of building B4. The boundary walls, which stood slightly above the sunken yard, had been largely levelled, but there was a 0.80m wide entrance adjacent to building B6/1.

The earliest surface, of limestone rubble in clean yellow sand, lay below the threshold of building B4, suggesting that there was either a stepped entrance or that the surface pre-dated the building. Above this there was a levelling layer, contemporary with the demolition of the bakehouse, B6/2, and rough metalling of small pieces of limestone in a clayey loam.

Following the demolition of building B6/1 in the early fourteenth century (ph 3/2), the entire area was surfaced with compact limestone rubble. To the west it abutted the frontage of buildings B4 and B5; to the north it abutted the retained northern wall of building B6/1 and the new curving wall to the east. To the south it may have abutted another new wall overlying the levelled walled yard, BY5, but only a short remnant survived running at a slight angle to the levelled yard wall.

A walled yard to the west of the processing room, BY6, had originally been surfaced with flat-laid and pitched limestone (Fig 7.30). Immediately outside the doorway to the processing room small patches of pitched stone indicate that a more extensive surface, probably similar to the metalling in the yard to the east, had been largely lost. Following the introduction of the southern tenement boundary wall, A/B, which overlay this early surface, there were no new surfaces and the earlier metalling was heavily disturbed by later activity. Immediately south of the processing room doorway there was a shallow rectangular pit, 1.70m long by 1.00m wide and at least 0.15m deep.

The dark loams across the eastern part of the open yard, BY3/4, to the south of the buildings, contained considerable quantities of occupation debris, including pottery of thirteenth century date (ph 2/0–2/2), animal bone and a wide range of other domestic finds, suggesting the presence of a midden heap immediately south of the walled yard BY2. In addition, a neonatal infant (1648) had been buried in this area, probably in a pit cut through the accumulated soils.

To the west of room B5/2 there was an area of flat-laid limestone, some of which had worn surfaces, and immediately outside the western doorway to building B4 there was a semi-circular area, 3.0m long by 2.0m wide, where successive layers of limestone rubble filled a shallow, eroded hollow. A steep-sided, flat-bottomed pit, 3.50m in diameter by 0.35m deep, beyond the south-west corner of building B4, was filled with yellow-brown sand and much limestone rubble.

Across the remainder of the croft, BY7, the contemporary soil horizons were largely removed by machine excavation. There was a general layer of mixed clayey loams overlying the alluvial silts and clays which had accumulated over much of the area in the earlier twelfth century. Above this, and sealed by the modern topsoil, there was a further accumulation of clean, alluvial clays that post-dated the abandonment of the tenement, probably accumulating in the later fourteenth or fifteenth centuries at the same time as similar deposits were accumulating within the central yards.

The walled yard, BY5

To the east of the excavated buildings there was a large walled yard, BY5, measuring 25m east-west by 12.0m north-south. Only the western end lay within the excavated area (Fig 7.30), but geophysical survey has defined the extent of the yard and the probable presence of a building range, perhaps 10–15m long by 5–6m wide, on the frontage (Fig 7.7).

The limited dating evidence suggests that the construction of the northern yard wall, which was 0.5m wide, occurred no earlier than the late twelfth or early thirteenth century, as it overlay layers dated to ph 1 (1150–1225). Demolition rubble adjacent to the walls is dated to the late thirteenth century (ph 2/2, 1250–1300) and this suggests that the yard boundary wall was levelled at the same time as the abandonment of the tenement B buildings to its west.

The domestic range: tenement G

The general location of these buildings, which were not excavated, was evident in earthwork, where the sunken central yard was clearly defined (Fig 1.4). Further details come from a resistivity survey, which indicates that building ranges flanked the western and northern sides of a yard in an arrangement closely comparable to tenements E and F (Fig 7.1), with the northern range fronting onto the eastern end of the access road. The lack of more detailed definition in the geophysical survey was at least partially a result of the dumping of brick and other building debris within and around the central sunken courtyard. Below

ground the state of preservation may well be broadly similar to tenement F, with only minimal robbing of the walls.

The western range was 15–17m long and 5–6m wide, with at least one major transverse wall. The northern range was at least 17m long by 5m wide, but the eastern end lay beyond the limit of the resistivity survey. The northern wall may have been concealed by a bank belonging to the late medieval to post-medieval ditches and banks enclosing the road and the central yard. There are indications of two internal divisions, suggesting that the building contained at least three rooms. To the west of the buildings there was a rectangular walled yard, 15m long by 11m wide.

The central courtyard was 20m long by 10m wide, and at least the southern half was probably metalled. There would probably have been direct access to the Cotton Lane but, as with tenement F, there was a late medieval to post-medieval bank along the frontage.

The peasant tenements: E and A

Following the demolition of the medieval manor in the earlier thirteenth century (within ph 2/0, c1225–1250) its enclosures were occupied by two tenements, E and A (Figs 7.1 and 7.7). Tenement E may have appeared towards the middle of the thirteenth century, with the manorial barn and processing range, S17, and perhaps the dovecote, S22, retained, while the malt oven, E16, was rebuilt as a free-standing oven within a walled yard. The malt oven and dovecote were probably demolished into the second half of the century (ph 2/2, 1250–1300) when the barn and processing range was remodelled and partially rebuilt to form the main range of a second tenement, A, which had a very similar arrangement of rooms. Both were occupied through the fourteenth century (ph 3/2, 1300–1400). Before the end of the century tenement E had been abandoned, while Tenement A was occupied into the fifteenth century, with a final reuse of some rooms prior to its abandonment and demolition.

Tenement E

Tenement E comprised an L-shaped range set around two sides of a central yard, with a further walled yard to the west (Fig 7.38). Its excavation provided a vivid illustration of the state of the buildings following demolition, with upstanding walls and fairly stone-free robber trenches set within a sea of scattered rubble from the levelled walls (Fig 7.39). The building plans only fully emerged once the rubble, which had concealed and protected the original floor levels, had been removed (Fig 7.40 and Plate 12).

The domestic range, E13

The total length of the L-shaped range was 29m, and the floor area of the five rooms, 86.3sq.m, was closely similar to the main range of tenement A (see Fig 7.67).

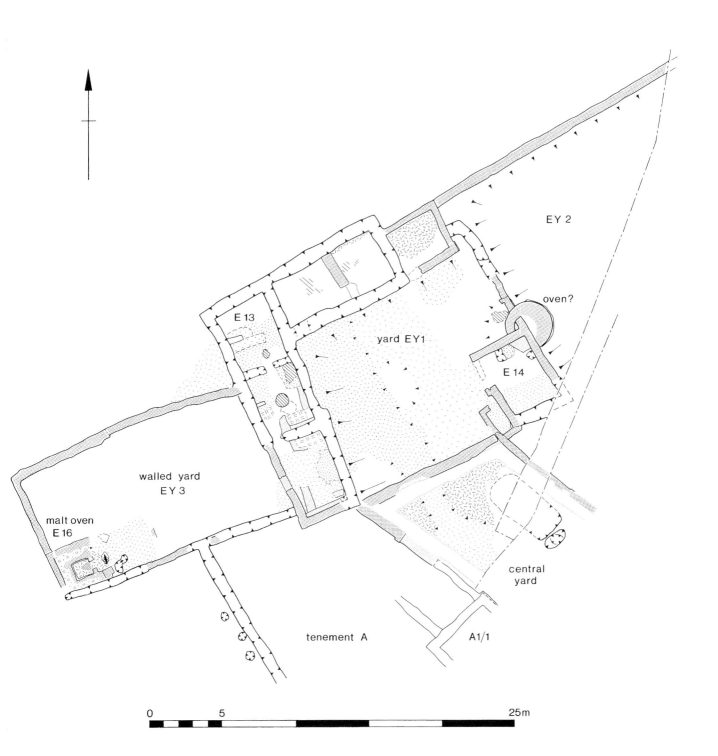

Fig 7.38: Medieval tenement E

Fig 7.39: Medieval tenement E; the demolition rubble, looking south-east

Fig 7.40: Medieval tenement E; the buildings, looking south-east

The western wing

This wing was 16.60m long by 4.90m wide (Figs 7.41 and 7.42). The long walls of rooms 2 and 3 directly overlay the levelled walls of the medieval hall, S18, although the end walls were slightly offset from their predecessors. Rooms 2 and 3 were of a single build, and the southern wall of room 2 was founded at the same depth as the long walls, suggesting that room 1, which was slightly narrower at 4.50m wide, was a separate abutting build.

The southern and western walls of room 1, which stood from to six to eleven courses high, 0.40–0.70m, was 0.65m wide at its base and was slightly battered, tapering to 0.55m wide at the highest surviving level. The surviving doorway was well preserved as a result of the later insertion of a blocking wall. The opening was 0.98m wide at the door jamb recesses, which were set slightly towards the inner face, and the wall ends were slightly angled so that the opening widened both internal and externally to around 1.05m (see Fig 7.69).

Room 1 was 5.35m long by 3.25m wide, an area of 17.4sq.m. A levelling layer of sandy loam and small pieces of limestone largely sealed the pre-building surfaces,

although in the south-west corner a length of the levelled wall of an earlier building, S19/20, still stood above both this layer and the earliest floor. Against the southern wall there was a narrow, 0.30m wide, stone bench standing up to 0.45m high, six or seven courses, coincident with the levelled top of the adjacent end wall. There was a single-course setting of flat-laid limestone in the south-east corner of the room.

The earliest floor was of light brown sandy loam, which to the east abutted a setting of large, squared limestone slabs patchily worn smooth, probably through the use of an adjacent doorway (Fig 7.43). A broad bench against the northern wall could have been introduced at this time or later.

The second floor was of yellow sandy clay, with the frequent presence of finely crushed limestone suggesting that it contained some mortar. It abutted the blocking of the western doorway. The bench against the northern wall, 2.25m long by 0.80m wide, comprised a platform of sandy loam and small pieces of limestone overlain by clean, yellow clayey loam, with the western end retained by a low stone revetment.

The third floor surface comprised limestone slabs,

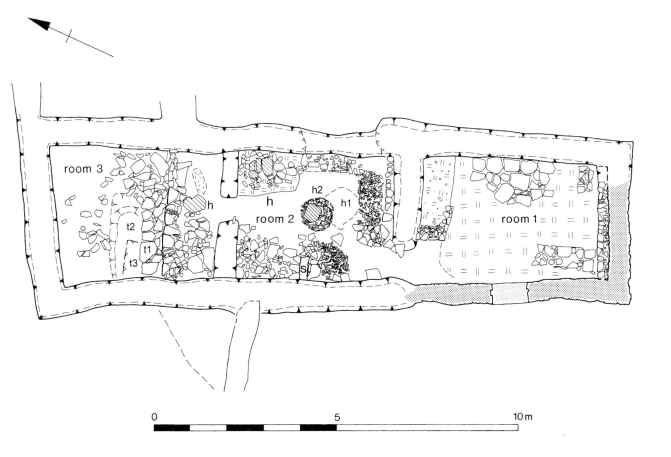

Fig 7.41: Medieval tenement E; the domestic range, E13, west wing (h=hearth, s=stone-lined bin, t=trough)

Fig 7.42: Medieval tenement E; domestic range, E13, west wing, looking south

from 0.1–0.6m in diameter. These were largely unworn and had therefore probably been covered by a lost upper surface of clay or earth. The two benches were retained, and within the northern doorway an eroded hollow had been patched with mixed deposits of loam, yellow clay and some limestone.

Room 2 was 4.20m long by 3.40m wide, an area of 14.28sq.m. It contained an extremely complex arrangement of features related to its use as a kitchen and, like all the later medieval kitchens, there was no external door to this room. Most of the internal fittings had been replaced at least once, and there was a sequence of four central hearths. This kitchen is discussed and illustrated further in the general account of the medieval kitchens (see Figs 7.83 and 7.84).

There was a narrow, 0.30m wide, stone bench against the southern wall. A similar bench was later built against the eastern wall, and broader foundations of pitched stone overlain with yellow clay against the southern bench may have been the base of a much broader bench, similar to the one in the room to the south.

In the north-east corner a rectangular hearth or oven base was replaced by an almost identical structure, comprising a rectangular clay base, 1.50m long by 1.10m wide, with flat-laid pieces of limestone surrounding a single, but fragmented hearth stone. Only this and the immediately adjacent stones, an oval area up to 1.30m long by 0.95m wide, had been burnt.

The original, circular open hearth lay towards the southern end of the room, h1, but with the introduction of the broader bench it was relocated further to the north,

Fig 7.43: The domestic range, E13, showing the partial stone floor in room 1

h2. The new hearth was 0.75m in diameter, comprising an arc of pitched limestone with a scorched area to the north where the hearth stone had lain. This was almost directly replaced by an almost identical hearth and, finally, by a further hearth which survived intact and was the best preserved example on the site (see Fig 7.86). It was sub-circular in plan, 0.90m in diameter, and comprised a near square, burnt and blackened limestone slab, measuring 0.46 by 0.40m, surrounded by a crescent of pitched limestone, incorporating pitched pottery sherds, carefully laid in a series of concentric rings. The hearth was surrounded by an homogeneous layer of brown to grey-brown sandy loam containing much comminuted charcoal.

Against the western wall there were two layers of flat-laid limestone slabs, with the upper surface worn. Bordering the southern margin of this surface was a stone-lined pit, s, similar to the example in building D11 (see Fig 7.86). It measured 0.65m long by 0.15m wide and 0.35m deep, but was built within a much larger construction pit. It was floored with a single large slab of limestone, covering much of the base of the construction pit, and was lined with three to four courses of flat-laid limestone. The apparently unnecessarily large size of the construction pit may suggest that either a solid, stone base was required as part of its functioning or that it may have replaced an earlier stone-lined pit of square plan. To the south of the stone-lined pit there was a well-laid quadrant of pitched limestone.

Room 3 was 4.50m long by 3.40m wide, an area of 15.30sq.m (Fig 7.41). The floors in the northern end of the room had been disturbed, but the remainder was well preserved. Three successive stone-lined troughs indicate that it was devoted to the same processing activity as seen in other tenements, and this room is discussed and illustrated further in the general discussion of these rooms.

The original trough, t1, was 2.30m long by 0.60m wide and 0.23m deep, and abutted the western wall. It was floored with large limestone slabs which were smoothed, rounded and discoloured and encrusted to a light blue-grey colour (see Fig 7.90). The lining on the southern side had an untidy bottom course of flat-laid and pitched limestone and an upper course of flat-laid limestone that was discoloured in a similar fashion to the floor. The lining on the northern side and the eastern end had been removed in the construction of a later trough. To the south the trough was flanked by a surface of flat-laid limestone slabs, which included an *in situ* heavily burnt hearth stone.

The original trough was infilled with clay and limestone and a new trough was built immediately to the north. This too had been partially robbed, but it was 0.65m wide by 0.30m deep and probably around 1.80m long, t2. The floor comprised scattered pieces of flat laid limestone with their surfaces discoloured grey, but these may only have been remnants of a once more extensive surface. The southern side of the trough had a vertical lining of up to three courses of flat-laid limestone, and the facing was also stained grey. The northern and eastern sides, which had been largely robbed, may have been stepped or inclined, rather than vertically faced.

The eastern end of the second trough was filled in with limestone and clay, including much discoloured limestone, and a shorter stone-lined pit, t3, 1.0m long, 0.40m wide and 0.25m deep, was built at the western end. The southern wall of the preceding trough was retained and new, vertically-faced walls, three courses high, were built to the north and east and it was floored with flat-laid limestone slabs. The facings of the new walls were not discoloured, except for the occasional stone that was probably reused, and the floor stones were discoloured red to purple, rather than the typical blue-grey of the earlier troughs. It would seem, therefore, that this final structure may have had a different function from the earlier troughs.

The later reuse of the western wing

A 2.0m length of the robber trench of the eastern wall of the kitchen, room 2, had a distinctive fill of brown loam and limestone that was partially overlaid by a late external yard surface. This suggests that a broad doorway had been opened in the eastern wall, and the room was given a new floor of brown loam and limestone. The partition wall between rooms 2 and 3 was probably removed and the robber trench was filled in and concealed by a final floor of small limestone pieces in clay.

The northern wing

The northern wing comprised two rooms of separate builds. The main room, 4, was 7.80m long with an average width of 3.70m, an area of 28.86sq.m (Fig 7.44).

Beneath room 4, earlier road and yard surfaces were sealed by a levelling layer of brown loam and small limestone pieces. The robbing of the walls had removed any direct evidence for doorways, but there was a slightly shallower section of robber trench at the western end of the southern wall. Against the southern wall there was a small stone-lined pit, 0.80m long, 0.30m wide and up to 0.30m deep. The fill of the pit was sealed by a well defined rectangle of pale yellow sandy clay, measuring 1.90 by 1.15m. A small central area was scorched red, as was a larger area to the south-west, above the stone-lined pit, suggesting that it may have formed the base for a brazier stand.

The room was subsequently split into two separate chambers by the insertion of a partition wall (Fig 7.46). At 0.70m wide, it was broader than most structural walls, and it is presumed that the standing partition was narrower than this. The internal doorway was 1.05m wide, with a single course of flat-laid limestone forming an offset threshold. The western chamber was 4.0m long by 3.5m wide, an area of 14.0sq.m, and had a floor of light yellow-brown sandy clay with a sparse scatter of small pieces of limestone. Just east of centre an irregular area reddened by light scorching may indicate a brazier location.

The floor within this chamber was around 0.10m higher than the floor within the eastern chamber, which was 3.00m long by 3.80m wide, an area of 11.40sq.m. Against the northern wall there was a linear setting of pitched limestone, 0.25–0.30m wide, possibly the foundation for a narrow bench. Against the partition wall there was a sub-square area of yellow sandy clay and the floor immediately to the east of this was patchily reddened by scorching.

Room 5, which abutted room 4, was 3.50m long by 3.00m wide, an area of 10.50sq.m. Originally it formed an open-sided cart or shelter shed with a sunken but well-laid floor of closely-set, pitched limestone (Fig 7.44 and 7.45). The northern and eastern walls were of a single build and 0.40–0.45m wide. To convert it to a closed room, a broader southern wall, 0.60m wide, was added. There was a straight joint in the external wall face, but internally the wall had been partly refaced to conceal the join (Fig 7.46). At the western end there was a doorway, 1.0m wide, with a central door jamb recess in the wall end. There were two phases of threshold stones, each edged with vertically pitched limestone standing above the floor level by up to 100mm, indicating that there was a step down into the room, where the later floor was of clayey loam with some pieces of limestone.

Building E14

This building was 5.80m long by 4.50m wide, with the room measuring 4.60m by 3.40m, an area of 15.64sq.m (Fig 7.47 and 7.48). The northern wall and western walls were 0.60–0.65m wide and stood up to six or seven courses high, 0.40–0.50m. The northern wall has been used as the exemplar for wall construction in the medieval period (see Fig 7.68).

The broad doorway, 2.10m wide, suggests provision of access for animals or goods, and the building probably served as a byre or stable, perhaps with storage for fodder and bedding in the roof space above.

A rectangular pit abutting the northern wall was 1.30m long by 0.85m wide and 0.40m deep with a shallower shelf to the west. The deeper part was filled with loose disordered limestone suggesting that it was a rubble-filled soak-away providing drainage. A small sub-square pit against the eastern wall was clay-lined. South of the doorway there was a well-laid floor of closely-set, small pieces of flat laid limestone. A single larger slab of limestone immediately inside the door was probably the sole survivor of an original kerb of larger stones, largely removed when the later floor was inserted. The stones were not worn and were probably a sub-floor for the overlying surface of brown clayey loam.

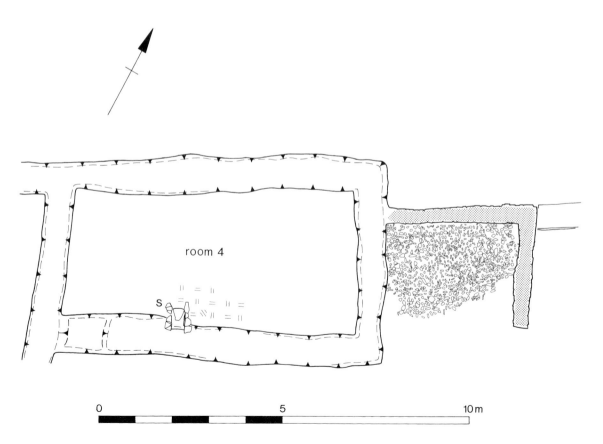

room 4

0   5   10 m

Fig 7.44: Medieval tenement E; the domestic range, E13, north wing original form

Fig 7.45: The domestic range, E13, showing the early pitched-stone floor in the room 5

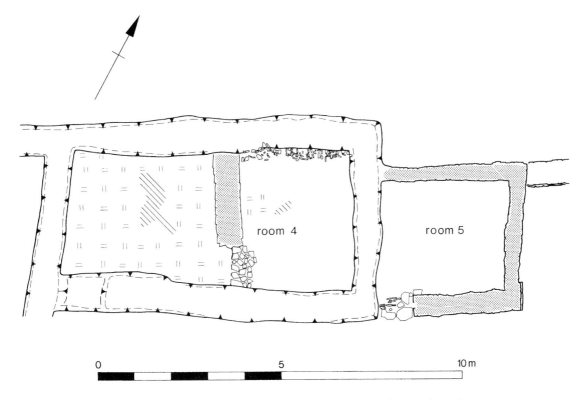

Fig 7.46: Medieval tenement E; the domestic range, E13, north wing, later form

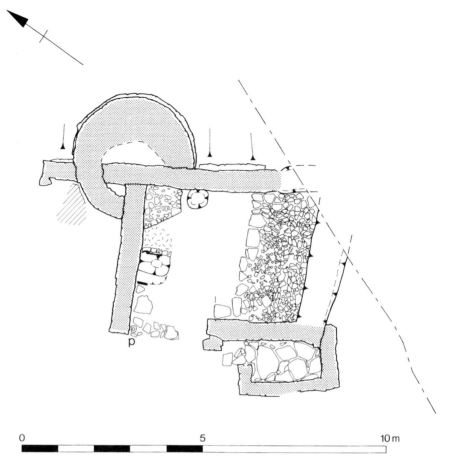

Fig 7.47: Medieval tenement E; building E14

Fig 7.48: Building E14, looking north, showing the broad doorway and the partial stone floor

The second floor was identical, but did not extend quite as far to the north; and had a kerb of larger, roughly squared, slabs. This surface was partly worn and the central area had been lost.

A small, stone-flagged chamber abutted the western wall (Fig 7.49). It had a floor of several very large slabs of limestone carefully fitted to form a near continuous surface. This was laid prior to the construction of the standing wall, which was 0.40m thick and stood on the laid stone surface. The doorway was 0.60m wide with a central recess in the door surround.

The eastern wall was subsequently completely rebuilt, when it then continued to the north to form a yard boundary wall. It was flanked and partly overlain by a massive circular foundation wrapped around the north-eastern corner of the building (Fig 7.50). To the east the wall stood up to eight courses high, 0.50m, and was up to 1.25m thick, with a battered face and a core of limestone rubble that merged into a central fill of loam and rubble. To the west it was as little as 0.65m wide.

The wall probably enclosed a chamber 2.0m in diameter. Any internal surfaces, which would have stood well above the floor in the adjacent room, had been lost, but the structure was most probably a raised baking oven. An adjacent layer of yellow clay which had been partly hardened by burning to a blue-grey colour may indicate that it was fired externally. Directly above this burning there was dump of mixed burnt debris, comprising small pieces of limestone, typically heavily reddened on both faces, as well as small pieces of burnt and fired clay, all

Fig 7.49: Building E14, showing stone-floored external chamber

Fig 7.50: Building E14, base of probable circular raised oven, looking west

probably from the demolished superstructure. Access to a raised oven chamber was perhaps via a stepped stone platform within the corner of the room.

Probably at the same time as the addition of the oven, the doorway was restructured. A pivot stone was set at the northern side of the opening (see Fig 7.71), while to the south the external quoins were removed and a door jamb recess was formed on the inner side of a newly constructed buttress, founded on a single large block of ironstone. Within the doorway a stone threshold formed a step down to a lower floor level.

The malt oven, E16

A malt oven had previously stood here within the southern range of the manor, S19/2, and the new oven was constructed over its levelled remains, probably as a free-standing structure (Figs 7.51 and 7.52). The small quantities of associated pottery suggest that it was in use for a short period at around AD 1250 (ph 2/0, 1225–1250), with its demolition occurring at about the same time as the formation of tenement A.

The earlier oven was sealed by a layer of neatly pitched limestone that formed both the floor of the new oven and a base upon which the new walls were constructed. The elongated chamber was 1.05m wide by 2.0m long, as defined by the location of the burnt limestone slab of the original hearth base. This slab remained *in situ* when the original flue was demolished and new responds were inserted to form a shortened oven chamber, 1.15m long, with an area of burning just inside the flue opening.

To the south and west the outer walls of the oven were provided by retained lengths of the earlier building walls, while to the north there was a new facing retaining a core of loam with some mortar and limestone. Beyond the end of the southern side of flue there were two shallow pits containing mixed burnt debris.

To the east of the oven there was a roughly 4.0m-square area of clay, mortar, limestone and burnt debris that defines a working surface or floor and suggests the possible presence of some form of cover structure (Fig 7.38).

The yards of Tenement E

There were two fully or semi-enclosed yards attached to the tenement; a metalled yard, EY1, at the northernmost end of the central yard and surrounded by the main buildings, and a walled yard, EY3, to the west of the buildings (Fig 7.38). At least in the earlier use of the tenement there was also access onto an enclosed plot to the east, EY2.

The central yard (EY1)

Within the area enclosed by the buildings a sequence of metalled yard surfaces was well preserved (Fig 7.38). The earliest comprised irregular pieces of flat-laid limestone, including slabs 0.30–0.40m in diameter, with gravel pebble infilling, was probably a levelling layer over the earlier

roads. To the east, the ground level stood at a higher level where it lay beyond the earlier eastern ditched boundary alongside the roads. To accommodate this disparity the shallow ditch was filled with limestone rubble and there was a thicker layer of stone to smooth out the gradient.

Above the levelling layer a metalled yard of smaller flat-laid limestone, frequently with worn surfaces, was particularly well preserved adjacent to the domestic range, E13, and was more patchy to the east. The final extensive resurfacing was of even smaller pieces of limestone, generally no larger than 100mm, but subsequent repairs were indicated by distinctive patched areas, up to 1.0m diameter, which in one instance contained a high proportion of ironstone. Another was largely of pebbles, and a number of small areas comprised pitched limestone. This upper surface was contemporary with the final, non-domestic use of building E13, when a broad doorway was opened into the former kitchen.

In the south-western corner of the yard a dump of loam and limestone against the wall of building E13 contained mainly large pottery sherds and other finds, suggesting that it may have been a remnant of a midden heap. Either there was never any surfacing directly beneath it or the periodic removal of the heap had also removed former metalling from beneath it.

Across the eastern end of the yard there were no surviving metalled surfaces of any great extent, although immediately outside the open-ended cart or shelter shed, E13 room 5, a layer of clayey loam contained frequent small pieces of limestone some of which were worn and had come from disturbed metalling.

There was a boundary wall at the eastern end of the yard, between E13 room 5 and the byre/stable, E14. The southern end was a continuation of the rebuilt eastern wall of building E14, and the northern end was represented by a robber trench. A broad gateway, 3.0m wide, had been subsequently blocked with a wall that was well faced only on the eastern side, indicating that the open yard to the east, EY2, was at a lower level than the central yard, EY1.

The midden deposit in the south-west corner of the yard pre-dated the construction of the boundary wall that ran between the southern ends of buildings E13 and E14, to form a closed courtyard, now separated from the central yard. The wall was 0.80m wide and survived up to six courses, 0.30m high. Following the construction of this boundary wall the courtyard was never remetalled with limestone, and the latest layers across the southern half of the yard comprised deposits of sandy to clayey loams interspersed with patchy areas of worn limestone that were possibly redeposited from the earlier surfacing. A hollowed area in the centre of the yard was similarly filled with clayey loam containing numerous pieces of worn limestone.

The construction of the boundary wall apparently removed all direct access to the courtyard and the buildings of tenement E, while the absence of any late metalled surfaces in yard EY1 also indicates a contemporary change in usage. This suggests that the boundary wall probably

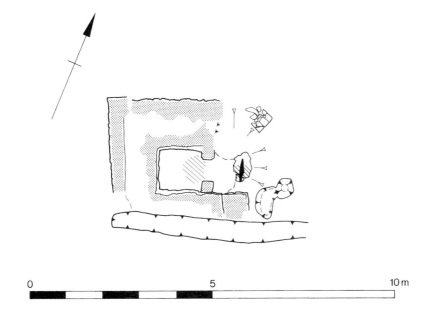

0   5   10 m

Fig 7.51: Medieval tenement E; the malt oven, E16

Fig 7.52: The malt oven, E16, looking east

appeared at the desertion of the tenement to cut off the abandoned buildings from the rest of the settlement, parts of which were still occupied.

The walled yard (EY3)

The walled courtyard occupied both the courtyard of the preceding building phase, SY1, and also extended over the levelled southern building range, S19 (Fig 7.38). Initially, a malt house, E16, stood in the south-western corner but this was levelled early in the use of the tenement.

The southern courtyard wall was the retained southern wall of the earlier building range, S19, while the western wall and the western end of the northern wall was a new construction, up to 0.70m wide. The narrower eastern half of the northern wall was of a separate build, more roughly built and on a slightly different alignment, perhaps suggesting that it formed a later closing of access from the north.

In the south-eastern corner of the yard a small area of closely-set, flat-laid limestone with worn surfaces was probably originally more extensive, and may have formed an area of metalling outside the western doorway of the domestic range, E13. Across much of the yard there was a build-up of sandy or clayey loam with few stone inclusions but containing much pottery and other finds, a proportion of which was residual from the earlier periods of occupation, the manor house.

An area of surfacing comprising a compact layer of small pieces of flat-laid limestone with worn surfaces lay in the external angle of the northern boundary wall and the domestic range E13. A substantial pottery scatter on this surface was of fourteenth century date (ph 3/2).

The eastern yard (EY2)

The area to the east of the buildings was slightly sunken with respect to the central yard. It was bounded to the north by a well-built linear wall, 0.65m wide and surviving five courses, 0.30m high, which abutted the end room of the domestic range, E13 room 5 (Fig 7.38). To the south the yard was open to the buildings of tenement D/C, leaving some uncertainty as to which tenement it belonged with, although in its latest use access from tenement E was apparently blocked.

Away from the boundary walls the area was covered by an homogeneous layer of brown, slightly clayey loam with a sparse scatter of small pieces of limestone, showing little differentiation down to the truncated and disturbed subsoil, which suggests that the area may have been used as an horticultural or garden plot.

Tenement A

Tenement A comprised a long frontage onto the central yard, with walled yards and two ancillary buildings to the rear (Figs 7.53). To the east it shared a double-walled boundary with tenement B.

The domestic range, A1

This range was developed by extensive rebuilding of the manorial barn and processing room, S17 (Fig 7.54 and 7.57). Some standing walls may have been retained while others were rebuilt on or adjacent to their predecessors. The domestic hall, A1/1, the narrower cross-passage, A1/2, and the kitchen, A1/3, were of a single build, while the storeroom to the south, A1/4, was an abutting addition that contained a stair-base, indicating that it had an upper storey. There was also an open-ended shelter or cart-shed to the north, A1/5. Together, they gave the range a total length of 31.0m and a total ground floor room area of 103sq m, closely similar to the main range of tenement E.

The cart or shelter shed

The open-ended cart or shelter shed attached to the northern end of the range was 3.70m long by 3.00m wide (Fig 7.54, room 5). Its construction was probably contemporary with the provision of a gateway opening onto the northern end of the central yard (Figs 7.53 and 7.38). The eastern wall was built in two abutting lengths, which may suggest that originally there was a 2.0m wide doorway at the southern end of the wall that was subsequently blocked. The interior was surfaced with clay and flat-laid limestone, and a remnant of a later floor of clay and pitched stones survived against the western wall.

The hall

The open hall, room 1, was by far the largest room, measuring 11.25m by 4.10m, an area of 46.1sq m. This space reflected the size of the barn that had preceded it (Figs 7.54 and 7.55). There were opposed doorways a third of the way along the walls, forming a three-bay room. The eastern doorway was 1.15m wide, with a large and heavily worn threshold slab of limestone edged across the doorway opening with vertically pitched limestone. The robbing of the quoins of the doorway opening, in an otherwise well-preserved length of wall, may indicate that an elaborate surround had been removed, perhaps for reuse elsewhere. Two limestone fleur-de-lys found within rubble in front of room 2 to the south might have come from a decorative finial surmounting such an elaborate door surround (See Fig 11.16).

There was a doorway, also 1.15m wide, at the southern end of the eastern wall, which had been subsequently blocked. In addition, there was a doorway at the western end of the southern wall to provide access to the cross-passage to the south. Both surrounds were partially removed, but there was an *in situ* pivot stone and a threshold of flat-laid limestone. The subsequent blocking of this doorway was indicated by the presence of an upstanding internal fitting in the room to the south.

The hall floor was of yellow clay mixed with some mortar, and it had probably been relaid in a similar fashion at least once. There were no internal fittings and no

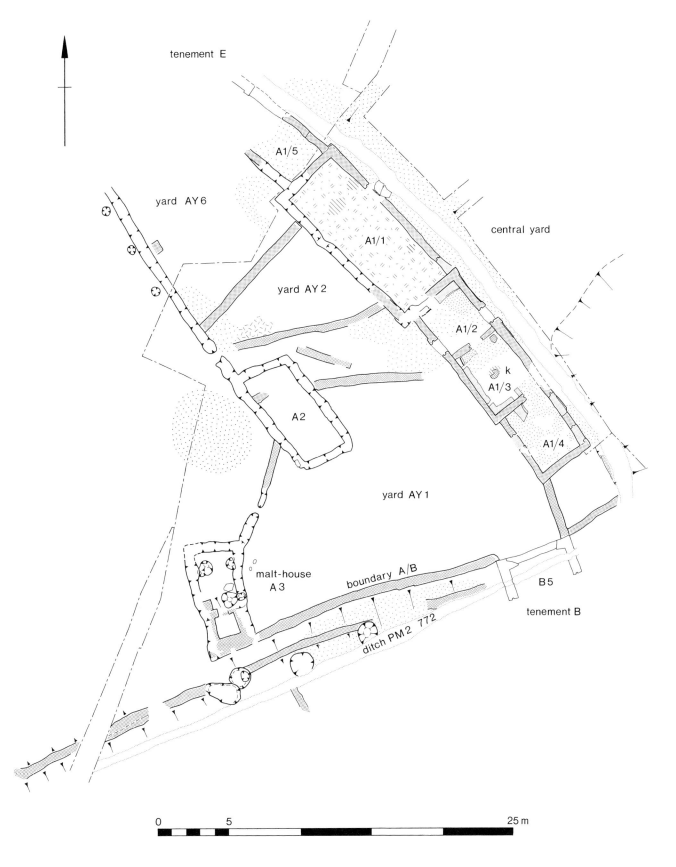

Fig 7.53: Medieval tenement A

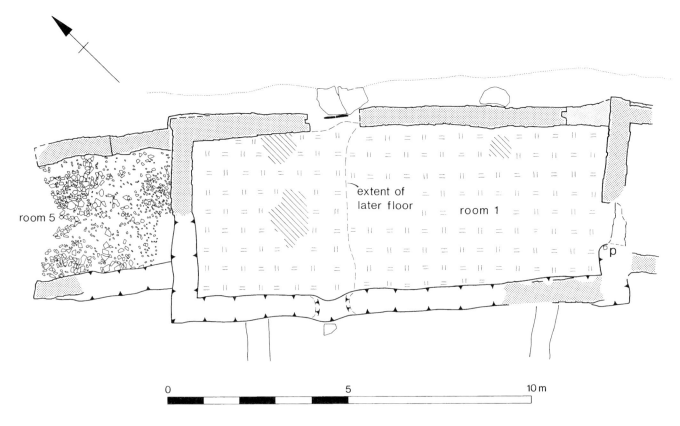

Fig 7.54: Medieval tenement A; the domestic range, A1 rooms 1 and 5

Fig 7.55: The domestic range, A1 room 1, looking south-east

evidence for the former presence of a stone-built hearth, but an area of scorched and blackened floor to the north of the opposed doorways might denote the location of a brazier. Two smaller areas of similarly scorched floor adjacent to the eastern wall may denote further brazier locations. Later, a floor of clay and limestone pieces, including areas of pitched stone, was laid across the northern end of the room, extending to the southern side of the opposed doorways (Fig 7.54, dashed line and Fig 7.56). This suggests that there was a functional division of the room even though there was no evidence for any physical partitioning. This later partial floor might have been contemporary with the late provision of raised floors in the rooms to the south.

The eastern end of the wall between the hall and the cross-passage, room 2, projected beyond the line of the frontage by up to 0.2m to form a shallow pilaster buttress. The wall was contiguous with the eastern wall of the rooms to the south, which suggests that, despite the greater width of the hall, this and the cross-passage and the kitchen were probably of a single build.

The cross-passage

The cross-passage, room 2, was 4.00m long by 3.45m wide, an area of 13.8sq m (Figs 7.57 and 7.58). The opposed doorways at the southern end of the room, which were 1.10m wide, were flanked externally by narrow, pilaster

Fig 7.56: Building A1, room 1, showing late floor of clay over pitched stones

buttresses, which makes them more elaborate than the typical tenement doorway. In both doorway openings there were square door jamb recesses, and each had a threshold of laid stones.

The earliest floor was of small slabs and pieces of limestone, and there were probably no internal fittings at this time. It was resurfaced at least once in a similar fashion, when a stone-built bench, 0.46m wide by 1.75m long, with an offset bottom course that was heavily worn, was set against the northern wall to the east of the doorway to the hall. In front of this bench the floor was of large, worn flagstones. In the north-west corner, a slab of limestone standing up to 400mm high, and the probable stumps of further such slabs, suggest the provision of a box or bin structure (b), inserted following the blocking of the adjacent doorway.

Rooms 2 and 3 were separated by an internal partition wall, 0.4m wide, which abutted the main walls. The length west of the central doorway was later refaced on the northern side, broadening it to 0.6m wide. The doorway was 0.9m wide, and the door jamb recesses had underlying postholes. There was a single course threshold of flat-laid pieces of limestone.

The kitchen

The kitchen, room 3, was 4.50m long by 3.60m wide, an area of 16.2sq m (Figs 7.57 and 7.58). This is discussed below as one of two exemplars of medieval kitchens (see Figs 7.80–7.82). There were no external doorways and initially the only access was via the central doorway to room 2. The room to the south was a later addition, and a corner doorway was opened in the southern wall of the kitchen to provide access between them, which had necessitated a rearrangement of the internal fittings.

Throughout there was a central open hearth, but in the earlier arrangement there was also was a hearth or oven in the south-east corner (Fig 7.59). This was disturbed, but remnants of burnt clay, a limestone hearth base and part of a kerb of pitched limestone survived. In the north-east corner there was a stone-lined pit, s, although the stone lining along the southern side had been totally removed. It was 1.0m long and may have been 0.3m wide when both sides of the lining were intact, making it comparable to the small stone-lined pits recovered in other buildings. The northern end of the room had a floor of limestone slabs while the remainder was earth floored. Along most of the western wall a single course of stonework, 0.36m wide, was probably the levelled base of a stone bench.

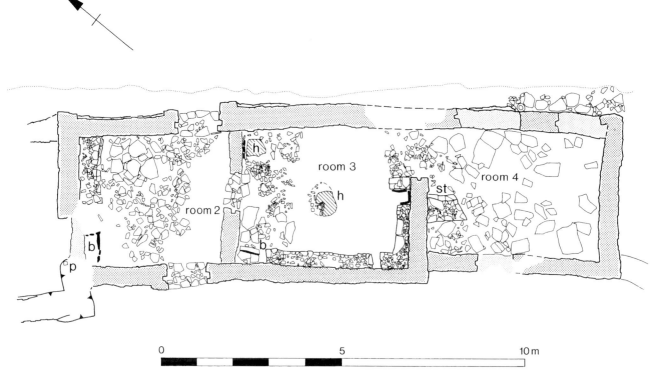

Fig 7.57: Medieval tenement A; the domestic range, A1 rooms 2–4 (h=hearth, b=bin, p=pivot stone)

Fig 7.58: The domestic range A1, showing the cross passage, room 2 (right) and the kitchen, room 3

Following the insertion of the southern doorway, many of the same fittings were present but they had been relocated (Figs 7.57 and 7.80). The corner hearth or oven was now in the north-east corner, replacing the stone-lined pit. The main hearth stone, 0.50m square and heavily burnt and cracked, was set on a layer of clay adjacent to the partition wall with vertically pitched stones set against the wall. To the west and south there was a surrounding surface of mixed flat-laid and pitched pieces of limestone, set into the clay base, and the surfaces of the stones to the immediate west of the hearth stone were lightly burnt.

The lost stone-lined pit may have been replaced by an upstanding stone-lined box or bin in the north-west corner, b, formed by an upright slab, 0.60m long and standing up to 0.40m above floor level. It was set between the end of the stone bench and the partition wall. Adjacent to the box or bin there was a well-laid surface of three large flagstones within a general surface of smaller limestone across the northern end of the room.

A new L-shaped bench, 0.37m wide with a rubble core faced with up to seven courses of flat-laid limestone, was built against the southern wall (see Fig 7.82). The surviving surface was at a height of 0.4m above floor level, and was probably the originally surface, which included two large slabs of limestone, each 0.40–0.44m long. Adjacent to the doorway there was a stone-built respond and vertical slabs within the space between the respond and the bench supported a remnant of an overlying slab that had carried the bench surface over this small alcove (Fig 7.82). As before, the remainder of the room was earth-floored with a concentration of burnt debris around the central hearth.

The original central hearth, not depicted, comprised a base of yellow clay beneath a single large slab of limestone, 0.90m long, which was burnt, blackened and fragmented. The later central hearth comprised a sub-rectangular hearthstone, 0.66 by 0.48m, heavily burnt and cracked, flanked to the north and east by a 0.2m wide setting of small pieces of pitched limestone interspersed with pitched pottery sherds (Fig 7.81). Part of the slab appeared to have been lost while the hearth was in use, and this area was patched with further pitched limestone.

The southern chamber

The abutting southern chamber, room 4, was 4.75m long by 3.30m wide, an area of 15.7sq m (Figs 7.57 and 7.60). There were two doorways in the eastern wall, and the northern doorway had a wider than average opening of 1.65m. There was a further doorway in the western wall.

The original use of this room is uncertain. The wide doorway could suggest that it served as a stable, perhaps in a similar fashion to building E14 in tenement E, but if so, this use might be expected to pre-date the opening of the doorway into the adjacent kitchen. Subsequently, all three doorways were blocked, although not necessarily simultaneously, and it is likely to have been the blocking of at least the broader doorway that coincided with the opening

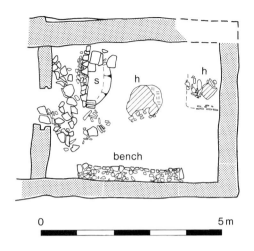

Fig 7.59: Medieval tenement A; the kitchen, A1 room 3, early arrangement (h=hearth, s=stone bench)

of the internal doorway to the kitchen. The original wall was levelled down to floor level, leaving the lower wall courses *in situ* beneath the new earth floors. The ragged wall end was refaced to form the door surround, which included a square door jamb recess. The fully enclosed room was probably used for storage, and at this time it was floored with large flagstones, although many had later been lifted and disordered.

Against the northern wall there was a stone-built stair-base of trapezoidal plan, 1.1m long and standing 0.45m high (Fig 7.57, st and Fig 61). The lower step on the eastern side had worn edges and surfaces, and there was a rise of 0.20m, although the surface of the second tread was unworn. The outer end of the western side was not faced, leaving the core of loam and rubble exposed, suggesting that it had been built against a timber support, possibly a newel post supporting a timber stairway set in a slightly hollowed area between the stair-base and the western wall. The presence of the stairway indicates that there was either a full upper storey or at least frequent usage of the loft space.

There was a late reuse of at least some of the rooms, which was most clearly seen in the kitchen. The southern bench was left standing but the remainder of the internal features were sealed beneath a layer of clay and limestone that included areas of pitched stones. A 2.0m length of the eastern wall may have been removed at this time to provide a broad opening into both this room and the adjacent store to the south. It was probably during this late use as an agricultural range that the flagged floor was so badly disturbed. The cross-passage to the north of the kitchen was also given a raised floor of clay and disordered limestone. The presence of small amounts of fifteenth-century pottery (ph 4, 1400–1450) within the final floor surface of the hall and within the demolition rubble suggests that the building was only demolished in the early fifteenth century.

Fig 7.60: The domestic range, A1, showing the kitchen, room 3 (right) and the storeroom, room 4

Fig 7.61: Building A1, showing the stone stair-base in room 4, looking south-west

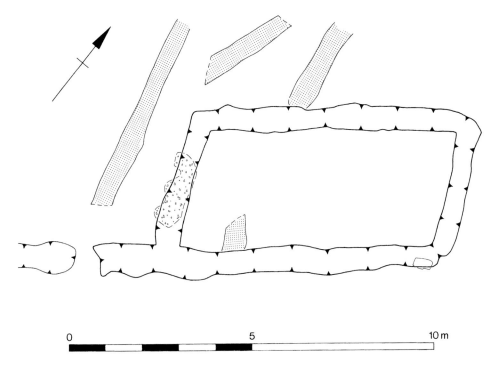

Fig 7.62: Medieval tenement A; building A2

Building A2

This building had been more thoroughly robbed than any other excavated medieval building. It was defined by the robber trenches and a spread of demolition rubble, and was 8.0m long by 4.2m wide although the plan formed a parallelogram, with the end walls at an obviously oblique angle to the long walls (Fig 7.62). The internal dimensions of 6.9m by 3.10m provided an area of 21.4sq m. Along the western wall a single course of stonework may have been a remnant of either a deeper foundation course or an earlier surface preserved beneath the later wall. The room had an earthen floor and there was no evidence for any major internal fittings.

The malt house, A3

Only the inner lining of the oven chamber, within a 0.35m deep construction pit, survived (Figs 7.63 and 7.64). The chamber was near square, 1.4m long by 1.5m wide, with slightly battered walls. A surface of irregular limestone, set within a shallow hollow, formed a hearth base at the inner end of the flue.

Originally, the oven was probably free-standing and abutted by a timber-built room or lean-to shed, some 3.0m long, founded on a pair of corner posts to the north and perhaps with further posts adjacent to the flue opening.

The walls of the later stone-built room had been totally robbed apart from a short length abutting the western side of the oven chamber. The shallow robber trenches indicate that the internal dimensions were 3.8m by 2.4m, an area of

9.1sq m, giving the building an overall length of 7.8m.

Two complete pottery vessels had been buried upright just beyond the western wall, one of Lyveden A coarseware and the other of Lyveden D glazed ware, indicating activity around the building in the later fourteenth century.

Tenement A boundaries and yards

The boundaries

The boundary walls between tenements A and B (Fig 7.53, boundary A/B) followed a former boundary ditch and a bank, which was partly retained within the new boundary. In its original form it had been defined by only the northern wall, which was 0.70m wide. For most of its length this wall was built across a sloping ground surface largely resulting from the presence of an underlying prehistoric mound. To the east it abutted the end of the processing room of tenement B, B5/1. To the west it probably abutted the malt house, A3, but this area had been robbed. The southern wall has been described as part of tenement B.

The boundary between tenements A and E was provided by the walled yard of tenement E to the north (Figs 7.6 and 7.7). To the west this line was continued by a low clay bank that would have abutted the main flood bank along the western side of the settlement. At its narrowest, the bank was 3.50m wide by 0.30m high, but to the west, as it approached the flood bank, it was broader and higher, 5.50m wide by 0.50m high,. It was also broader and higher to the east, up to 11.50m wide by 0.50m high, and formed a sub-circular platform beyond

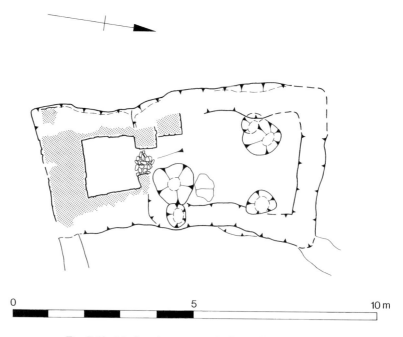

Fig 7.63: Medieval tenement A; the malt house, A3

Fig 7.64: The malt oven, A3, looking south

the corner of the walled courtyard, partly overlying the levelled malt house, E16.

The yards

Three walled yards lay to the rear of the frontage, probably at least partially respecting yards that had been introduced with the earlier barn and processing range.

The southernmost yard, AY1, was covered with homogeneous brown sandy to clayey loams, containing only a sparse stone scatter. It was bounded to the west by the ancillary building, A2, and the malt house, A3. A length of boundary wall, largely robbed, ran between these buildings and included an opening giving access into the croft to the west. The chamber at the southern end of the domestic range, A1/4, had been a later addition, so initially this yard opened directly onto the central yard. Subsequently, the opening was blocked both by room 4 and by a boundary wall running between room 4 and the northern end of tenement B.

The central yard, AY2, had originally comprised a narrow, limestone-surfaced access way, which was flanked by parallel boundary walls standing only 3.0m apart. In this form it was probably contemporary with the barn and processing room, S17, and it certainly pre-dated the introduction of the ancillary building, A2, which lay above the original western end of the yard southern wall. With the appearance of this building, perhaps at the formation of tenement A or shortly after, the northern wall was levelled and replaced by a new boundary wall further to the north and set at a right angle to the hall, to form a larger yard. This wall was 0.60m wide and was well built, and had not been disturbed in the same fashion as the two walls to its south. It was probably retained until the very end of the use of the tenement.

Although only small areas of well-laid limestone surfacing survived, the general dense scatter of limestone across the entire yard indicates that it was originally extensively metalled in this fashion.

The northern yard, AY6, ran up to the buildings and walled yard of tenement E. To the west there was a linear boundary wall, totally robbed, which had probably been introduced at the appearance of the barn and processing room, S17. Along the western side of this wall there were five small pits or post-pits, 0.50–0.60m in diameter by 0.20–0.30m deep, four of which lay at regular intervals of 3.1–3.2m, perhaps suggesting the provision of substantial fence at some stage.

To the north-east access to the central yard was provided by a gateway in a boundary wall running between tenements E and A (see Fig 7.38). The wall was at least 0.45m wide, but the outer face had largely collapsed into a later ditch. The southern end of the northern length ended at a broader buttress, with a central recess overlying a substantial post-pit, 0.40m deep and largely filled with vertically-pitched packing stones. A similar post-pit lay beneath the terminal of the southern part. These indicate the provision of substantial timber gate posts flanking an entrance, 2.80m wide. Subsequently, this gateway was blocked with a crudely constructed blocking wall in very rough courses of mixed limestone and ironstone.

The croft

The open croft beyond the walled yards contained no pits or other cut features. An earlier large shallow pit, which

lay immediately west of the ancillary building, A2, was finally fully filled with limestone rubble during this period, probably to consolidate the surface over earlier softer fills. The entire area was covered by amorphous mixed loams suggesting that it was perhaps utilised as either paddocks or for horticultural activities.

Access in and around the settlement

The central yard

Trial sections across the central yard had shown that it was filled with up to 0.5m of water-deposited clays, which had been laid down at around the time of desertion in the later fourteenth and fifteenth centuries. As a result, the limits for full excavation of the medieval levels were set around the margins of the central yard, so that only narrow strips immediately adjacent to the tenements were fully investigated. In 1986, following excavation of the stone buildings of tenements A, B and C/D, the central yard was fully stripped by machine down to the natural gravel as part of the investigation of the underlying prehistoric monuments (Fig 7.7).

The medieval yard overlay the open yards that had been established at the formation of the settlement in the late Saxon period. However, by the time the medieval tenements were established, encroachment of the boundary system and the final phase of building associated with the twelfth-century manor, had reduced the extent of the central yard and its original form was lost.

There were two distinct areas to the yard: a broad southern end between tenements B and C, with the access road entering at the eastern end, and a narrower continuation between tenements A and D running up to tenement E (Fig 7.7). The southern area was up to 25m long by 17–22m wide, and was slightly sunken in comparison both to the adjacent tenements and to the northern end of the yard. Metalled surfaces survived along the margins of the southern area and generally comprised rough spreads of flat-laid limestone rubble, although the well-laid, pitched stone yard of tenement B to the west extended onto the central yard and sloped gently down from the tenement frontage, which was some 0.20m higher. The absence of any metalled surfacing across the sunken central part of the southern area may have resulted from intensive usage creating a hollowed area, a hollow-way effect. However, the clays directly sealed the natural gravel, when it might be expected that there would at least have been an intervening deposit containing disturbed limestone from former metalling. It is therefore suggested that this southern end of the yard had been partly dug-out at a later date, perhaps with this material contributing to the late embankments around the margins of the yard.

The northern end of the yard was 9.5–12.0m wide. Although originally it ran right up to tenement E, there was always a clear distinction between the tenement E courtyard, with its flat-laid limestone metalling, and the northern end of the central yard, where there was well-laid, pitched-limestone metalling. Further south there was flat-laid limestone along the frontage of tenement A. The survival of a pitched stone surface at the northern end of the yard was probably partly due to the later introduction of the wall cutting off access to the deserted tenement E, so that later usage of the central yard did not then extend far enough north to result in its removal.

Several pits alongside the boundary wall between tenements E and D were in use in the fourteenth century. They were typically 1.00–1.80m in diameter and from 0.10–0.40m deep, and were filled with clay and frequent pieces of limestone. At the northern end of the group there was a larger, sub-rectangular, flat-bottomed pit, 5.20m long by 2.30m wide and 0.20m deep. An elongated pit at the southern end of the large pit contained a central post-pit packed with disordered limestone, but the specific use of the pit and adjacent standing post is unknown. There was no metalling across the area occupied by the pits, but scattered disordered stone suggests that metalling may have been disturbed and removed whilst the pits were in use.

It is suggested that at the establishment of the medieval tenements, and probably continuing from the twelfth-century manor, much of the central yard was metalled with laid limestone, which in some areas comprised neatly pitched surfaces. Most of this was then lost at around the end of the life of the settlement. Much of the damage was perhaps a result of the final phase of occupation, when some of the buildings fronting onto the yard were given raised floors and were apparently used as sheds and byres. Animal trampling across the central yards would have disturbed and churned these surfaces, especially if the raised floors do indicate that at least periodic flooded of the yard was already occurring. This model also accounts for the survival of metalling at the frontage of tenement B, which had been the first to be abandoned, and in association with tenement E, probably the second to be abandoned, and thus avoiding animal trampling in the final phase of activity.

The Cotton Lane

Adjacent to West Cotton and running south for 1.25km, the former medieval road between Higham Ferrers and Thrapston survives as an unsurfaced track to the immediate east of the new road (see Fig 1.3). It is typically 10m wide between the flanking field hedges, although immediately south of West Cotton it is now much overgrown and the effective width is often less than 5m. The track adjacent to West Cotton had still been some 5m at the time of excavation, but by 2008 a new wooden fence along the field to the east of the lane had reduced the former track to little more than a wide footpath.

Adjacent to West Cotton the modern track is approximately level with the general ground surface. However, the former presence of a hollow way was demonstrated by a trial trench across tenement H (Fig 7.1). The eastern side of the lane was located 4.0m beyond the present track, with limestone

rubble abutting the building frontage and sloping down to the west. This indicated the presence of a hollow way at least 1.10m below modern ground level and 0.40m below the floor level of the adjacent building, H. On the western side of the lane a low bank is visible in earthwork inside the modern hedge line (see Fig 1.6) and while perhaps late medieval in origin, it may define the former western limit of the road. This would suggest that adjacent to West Cotton the road had widened to around twice its normal width, from 10m to 20m.

The accumulation of at least 0.75m of water deposited, tenacious clays within the hollow way repeats the pattern seen within the central yard to the west, with this process perhaps beginning in the late fourteenth century but probably largely occurring through the fifteenth century (ph 4–5, 1400–1500).

The filling of both the central yard and the Cotton Lane with water-deposited clays was clearly a result of extensive flooding of the lower lying road system and this must have been caused by frequent over-bank flooding of the Cotton Brook. This may merely have been a result of a lack of general stream management through the period of progressive desertion, but if tenement I was a medieval watermill, then a lack of maintenance of the mill leats following desertion may have provided a specific context for this flooding.

To the north of West Cotton, where the Cotton Lane begins to climb uphill and runs past the Mallows Cotton settlement, the lane largely survives as an evident hollow way. It is remembered by local residents as having been in use as a footpath until the 1940s or 50s, but had since fallen out of use and was badly overgrown. A section cut across the hollow way between West Cotton and Mallows Cotton (Parry 2006, 183–184, fig 6.18) exposed limestone surfacing at the base of the hollow way, which was 1.0m deep. The surface was sealed by clays overlain by a later gravel and limestone surfacing, but no dating evidence was obtained.

The course of the Cotton Lane between Mallows Cotton and Mill Cotton has not survived, but it is depicted on the first edition of the one-inch Ordnance Survey (Sheet 53, Bedford and Northampton, first published in 1835).

Tenements east of Cotton Lane: H, I and J

Evidence for the former presence of stone-built tenements to the east of the Cotton Lane is derived from a variety of sources, but particularly from the survey and trial trenching conducted by the Raunds Area Survey team under the direction of Steve Parry (Parry 2006, 172–177, fig 6.13).

Tenement H

In 1990 a series of trial trenches were cut in the field to the east of West Cotton as part of the second stage of the

Rauns Area Survey. These were mainly located to test for the presence of subsoil features related to early Saxon pottery scatters, but a single trial trench immediately east of the lane, 27m long by 1.30m wide, located part of a medieval building in a area that had previously produced a surface scatter of limestone and medieval pottery (Fig 7.1, H).

The western wall of the building was 0.60m wide, and was abutted by a 0.40m wide internal stone facing, perhaps a bench. The former eastern wall was denoted by a ridge of limestone rubble, indicating an internal width of 6.50m. The floor levels were largely concealed by rubble, which was not removed, but an area of burnt clay and limestone, and including pitched stones, 1.0m in diameter, indicated the presence of a hearth or oven to the east. To the rear of the building and at a slightly lower level, a compact layer of small, worn pieces of limestone formed a metalled yard, 8.0m wide.

A fragment of an upper millstone, 800mm in diameter by up to 95mm thick, in a type of sandstone not present within the assemblage of millstones from the main excavations, was built into the bench abutting the western wall. It provides some support for the suggestion that tenement I, to the south, may have been a medieval watermill, see below.

Pottery recovered from the hearth indicates that the building was in use in the later thirteenth century (ph 2/2, 1250–1300), while sherds of late medieval reduced ware and oxidised ware suggest that the building may have been in use into the early fifteenth century (ph 4, 1400–1450) and was perhaps only demolished in the second half of the century (ph 5, 1450–1500), although the later date may relate to the deposition of clays over the levelled building remains.

The full extent of the medieval frontage along the eastern side of the lane remains uncertain. Resistivity and magnetometer surveys along a 180m length of the frontage did not reveal clearly defined wall lines, possibly because of the effect of the overlying alluvial clays, but did suggest the possible presence of a total length of 50m of building, perhaps as two separate tenements each around 20m long.

Tenement I

In 1988 an area east of Cotton Lane and south of the Cotton Brook had also been trial trenched by the survey team under the direction of Steve Parry. Previously unknown medieval buildings were located beneath a layer of water-deposited clays (Fig 7.1 tenement I). Only the uppermost levels were exposed, revealing the tops of walls, demolition rubble and some probable areas of internal floors and external metalling (Fig 7.65). Trenches beyond the buildings indicate that they sat on alluvial clays, presumably filling earlier channels of the Cotton Brook and probably associated with the twelfth-century alluviation seen to the west.

While no direct evidence was obtained to define the function of this building complex, its location over earlier

alluvial silts and directly beside the Cotton Brook opens the possibility that it could have been a later medieval watermill, and the fragment of millstone from tenement H adds some support to this suggestion. The buildings lay at the western end of a close, measuring about three acres, Cotton Close, as recorded on the enclosure map of 1798 (Fig 1.4).

Building 144

The trial trench ran obliquely across the western end of a major medieval building (Fig 7.65). The walls were 0.70–0.75m wide and constructed in flat-laid limestone with some ironstone. They were significantly broader than the typical building walls located within the central area of the settlement. The building was perhaps 6.0m wide, with an internal width of 4.50m.

A partition wall, 0.45–0.50m wide, abutted the southern wall to form a room 3.30m long. There was a stone bench, b, 0.45m wide, against the western end wall, and a trapezoidal stone foundation, s, against the southern wall may have been a stair-base. There was a corner doorway to the next room, which may have been at least partially floored with pitched limestone, and which had a external doorway in the southern wall.

The full extent of the building was not established. The two rooms give a minimum length of 9.0m and it may have been up to 20m long, containing four or five rooms. The stair-base and the unusually thick walls suggest that it was of two storeys.

The yard

Between the two buildings there was a yard which had been at least partially metalled with flat-laid slabs of limestone, some of which had worn surfaces (Fig 7.65).

Building 145

The walls to the east, which were 0.60m wide, probably belonged to a second building, with an internal width of 4.0m (Fig 7.65). The northern end wall was located, and a robber trench of a possible internal partition wall indicates that there was a further room to the south. The building may have been around 17.5m long with three or four rooms.

The outer face of the eastern wall was abutted by limestone rubble, including pitches stones, and it was suggested by the excavator that this may have been deliberately banked against the wall.

Immediately following the levelling of these buildings a layer of yellow-brown clay was deposited across the entire area, directly overlying the demolition rubble. It was as little as 0.05m thick over the standing walls and up to 0.50m thick within the yard.

Pottery from the alluvial clay, the demolition rubble and from the yard surfaces is dated to the fourteenth century (ph 3/2, 1300–1400) and there were no residual ceramics of earlier date. It would appear therefore that the construction,

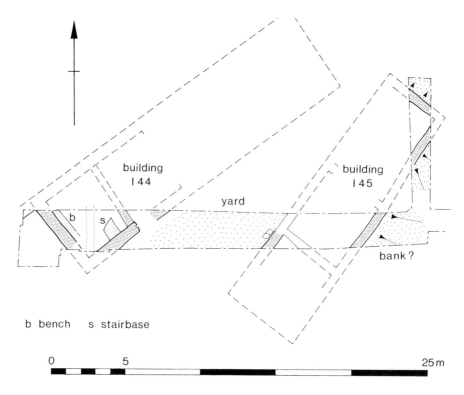

Fig 7.65: Medieval tenement I; trial trenches

use and demolition of these buildings all occurred in the fourteenth century.

Tenement J

The only evidence for the existence of a further tenement to the east of Cotton Lane comes from the observation of a pipe trench in 1967 by A E Rowlings, when a limestone wall footing and pottery sherds of the twelfth to early fourteenth-century date were recovered (Brown 1967, 28). This provided the first identification of the location of West Cotton, and a later reference to this same observation records that the pipe trench had cut through "a building with foundations 3ft deep" (Hall and Hutchings 1972, 15). The recorded grid reference is consistent with the known location of the pipe trench and it places this building both to the east of Cotton Lane and south of the Cotton Brook (see Figs 1.3 and 7.1). No surface scatters of limestone or medieval pottery have been recorded in this area, but this may result from the concealment of the building beneath a layer of alluvial clay, in a similar fashion to that demonstrated with tenement I.

The southern field system

The only extant area of the contemporary ridge and furrow field system in the vicinity of West Cotton lay to the west of Cotton Lane and south of the main settlement area and the former course of the Cotton Brook (see Figs 1.3–1.6). It was surveyed by David Hall in 1973 and appears on several aerial photographs (see Fig 1.5). In earthwork, a length of 50–60m survived, gradually fading out to the west as it was obscured by an increasing depth of alluvium.

In the investigation of the southernmost prehistoric monument, ridge and furrow preserved beneath the later alluvium was exposed and sectioned near the western edge of the field (Fig 1.6). The furrows were generally quite regularly spaced at 9–11m, although to the north the spacing was narrower at only 7m. They were formed within a 0.60m thick soil horizon of homogenous sandy loam almost free of stone inclusions, and where they crossed the prehistoric monument the furrows bottomed on or slightly into the underlying mound (see Heading and Healy 2007, 70, fig 3.20). The western side of the field was bounded by a ditch, 3–4m wide and up to 1.0m deep, seen in section in a machine cut trial trench, cutting through the western edge of the prehistoric mound and slightly into the underlying natural gravels (see Harding and Healy 2007, 68, fig 68). The inner edge of the ditch stood 0.40m higher than the outer edge and the greater depth of soil at this point probably indicates the presence of a head or butt at the end of the strips. The ditch was filled with light brown tenacious clays indistinguishable from the overlying alluvial clays covering the entire area. Over the ridge and furrow system the alluvium was as little as 0.35m thick over the tops of the ridges, but it was up to 1.0m deep over the furrows.

Despite the partial investigation of this field system it is not possible to provide any date for its origin. Similarly, the date of the alluvial cover has not been directly established. However, by analogy with the evidence from elsewhere on the site it can be suggested that the earliest possible date for the alluvium is AD1150, so the ridge and furrow system had been fully formed by the mid twelfth century at the latest. The western ditch may have been introduced as an original field boundary, as given the low-lying location seasonal flooding may always have been a problem, but it could have been introduced in the twelfth century specifically to protect the field system from flooding after the commencement of the period of catastrophic alluviation.

The earthworks indicate the presence of a later linear ditch at this same location and running south-westwards from the angle of the southern stream channel. No ditch was recorded in section within the upper alluvial clays, but if largely filled with these clays it would have been barely discernible. The coincidence of location does indicate that a ditch was either maintained during the period of alluvial deposition or was re-established once it had ceased.

The prominent linear and curvilinear ditches appearing in earthwork show a respect for the alignment of the ridge and furrow, but these clearly post-date the alluvium and are probably post-medieval drainage ditches carrying the outflow from a spring on the eastern side of the Cotton Lane and lying directly opposite the end of the northernmost ditch (Fig 1.4). At least part of this drainage system has remained in use for this purpose until the present day, although now carried by a field drain lying towards the southern end of the field. From the 1739 records of the field names the identification of this field as Short leys (Hall *et al* 1988, fig 6 and table 1) suggests that it had reverted to pasture, with this perhaps occurring as a direct result of the twelfth-century flood inundation.

The medieval stone buildings

The exceptional state of preservation of the buildings constructed between the mid-thirteenth and earlier fourteenth centuries, and the excavation of an extensive sample of the available tenements, has provided a vivid illustration of the argument that the size, quality and complexity of late medieval peasant buildings has frequently been underestimated (Dyer 1986). The general characteristics of these buildings are considered below, along with the less well-preserved stone buildings of the twelfth-century manor, and this is followed by an overview of the specialised buildings that contained a range of distinctive internal fittings.

Building dimensions

Despite the wide variety of local construction traditions, it has been recognised that among the common characteristics of later medieval peasant buildings is the frequent presence of two or three-bay houses or barns at around 30ft and 45ft (9.2m and 13.8m) long and 15ft (4.6m) wide (Dyer 1986).

These general conclusions are supported by the evidence from West Cotton. The two-bay arrangement is particularly well seen in the buildings of the twelfth-century manor (Fig 7.66). The hall, S18, the southern range, S20 (not illustrated) and the kitchen range, S21, at 9.5–9.6m long and 4.8m, 5.5m and 5.75m wide respectively, all possessed central or slightly off-centre doors indicating the presence of two bays. The later two-roomed southern range, S19, at 18.2m long by 5.0m wide, comprised a pair of two-bay structures, and the hall with opposed doorways in tenement B, B4, probably dated to the earlier thirteenth century, was a two-bay structure 9.5m long by 5.5m wide.

The barn and processing room, S17, added to the manor in the later twelfth century was comparable in width, at 5.2m, but had an overall length of 21m. The processing room conformed to a two-bay length, at 9.5m long, while the barn, at 11.5m long was appreciably longer. The only other building of probable later twelfth-century date, the processing room of tenement B, B5, was 7.8m long by 5.5m wide.

The majority of the twelfth-century buildings therefore showed regularity in length but a slightly broader range of widths, indicating that they were typically set out to a standard two-bay plan and to a standard length of around 9.5m (31ft). The exceptions, the barn, S17, and the processing room in tenement B, B5, were both specialised buildings, and the latter was certainly purpose built for its specific function. In addition, the thirteenth-century kitchen/bakehouse range of the later manor, tenement C/D, D11, at 11.0m long by 7.0m wide, was longer than a standard two-bay structure and, like the earlier bakehouse, S21, was unusually wide. It would therefore appear that it was the buildings with specialised functions which departed from the standard dimensions of the basic medieval two-bay structure.

In the thirteenth to fourteenth-century tenements there was consistency of room organisation, as was very clearly evidenced by the two purpose-built tenements, A and E, which comprised almost identical sets of rooms (Fig 7.67). A square kitchen with no external access was flanked on one side by a cross-passage chamber, while an open hall stood at the end of the range, abutted by an open-ended cart or shelter shed. The room on the other side of the kitchen, which in the case of tenement A was a later addition, had their external doors blocked and were then furnished with limestone-flagged floors, indicating use for food and crop storage. The same pattern of room arrangement was also seen in tenement C at the conversion of the barn to a peasant tenement, with the excavated rooms again comprising a cross-passage, a kitchen, a store room and a domestic hall, together with an open-ended cart or shelter shed.

Behind the consistency of form in these tenements there was a wider range of building and bay lengths within which it is difficult to isolate examples of Dyers' standard lengths.

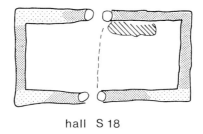

hall S 18

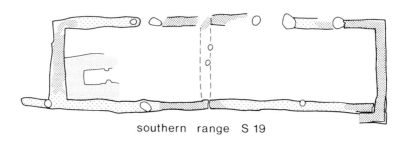

southern range S 19

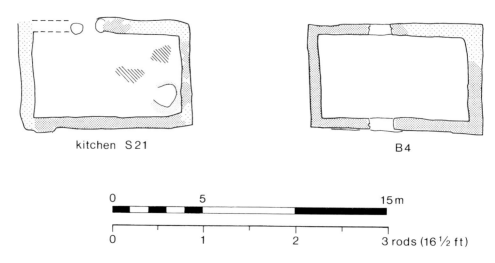

kitchen S 21   B 4

```
0              5                           15 m
■■■□□□■■■□□□■■■□□□■■■□□□■■■
0              1              2           3 rods (16 ½ ft)
```

Fig 7.66: The twelfth-century manorial buildings, comparative plans

This may suggest that the building dimensions were determined on a more *ad hoc* basis, but the complex way in which these tenements had replaced earlier buildings, often largely but not precisely overlying earlier wall footings, may itself have provided a complicating factor that tended to result in departures from standard lengths.

The 12.5m long hall of tenement A had opposed doorways well to the north of centre, indicating a basic three-bay structure of a fairly regular form, but this was largely formed over, and may have retained some of the walls of the earlier barn, S17, which may explain its exceptional length in comparison to the other contemporary tenements. The central rooms of this range formed a regular two-bay structure 9.6m long, but this was an almost direct rebuilding over the earlier standard two-bay processing room, S17.

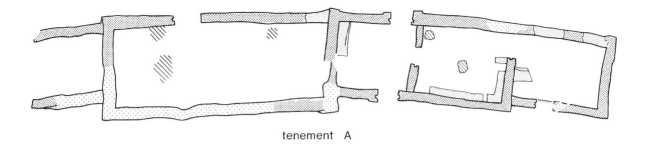

tenement A

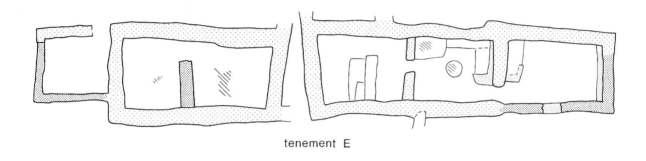

tenement E

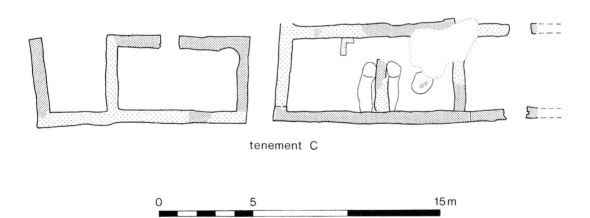

tenement C

Fig 7.67: The peasant tenements, comparative plans

The main range of tenement E was a new build, and possessed three rooms, although two of these did overlie the levelled hall of the manor, S18. At 16.6m long it exceeded the typical length of a three-bay structure. In contrast, the adjacent domestic hall was 8.5m long and so somewhat short for a two-bay room. The cottage, D11, of tenement D had three rooms but two were particularly short, so the building may be considered as a simple variation on the standard two-bay theme, although at 10.2m long by 6.2m wide it was both longer and wider than average.

However, these dimensions were largely determined by the underlying kitchen/bakehouse, D12, one of the specialised buildings that appear to depart from the norm.

While we cannot provide a simple analysis for the later buildings in terms of regular bay lengths, tenements A and F do vividly illustrate the size, quality and complexity of the peasant tenement in the later thirteenth and fourteenth centuries. In its final form, the four main rooms of the tenement A range, together with the open-ended shed to the north, presented a continuous facade 31m (101ft) long. This may, however, be placed in perspective by contrasting it with the agricultural buildings of the contemporary manor, tenement C/D, which had a continuous facade perhaps 44m (144ft) long, over half of which comprised an impressive barn.

It may be noted that each of the four tenements also contained a small detached range both narrower and shorter than Dyer's typical two-bay structure. These buildings were from 6.0m to 8.0m (19ft 8in–26ft 3in) long and 3.9m to 4.5m (12ft 9in–14ft 9in) wide, and in at least three instances they originally had corner doorways indicating that they were single rooms (Fig 7.7; A2, B6, C9 and E14). They were all evidently ancillary structures, detached from the main ranges, and perhaps serving a range of specific or general functions. Two were used as small bakehouses for part of their usage and another was a small stable or byre. The rooms attached to the malt ovens were also of similar dimensions (Fig 7.7; A3, B7 and C10).

The evidence therefore shows a diversity of approaches. There was evidently a considerable regularity in size and form in the typical two-bay structures of the twelfth-century manor, but greater diversity in size within certain specialised buildings such as barns, detached kitchen/bakehouses and processing rooms. In the tenements of the thirteenth and fourteenth centuries there was considerable consistency of form and arrangement, indicative of buildings of some quality and complexity, but with a diversity of building lengths, although this was partly derived from the way in which earlier buildings had been remodelled or rebuilt.

Building stone

The main building stone was limestone, the Blisworth Limestone of the Great Oolite Series which outcrops locally in the vicinity of both Raunds and Stanwick. Medieval stone pits and quarries have been excavated immediately to the north of the parish church in Raunds (Audouy and Chapman 2008; 127 and fig 5.74; 136 and fig 5.84) and the one-inch Ordnance Survey map of 1835 shows lime kilns 1.5km to the east of West Cotton, at the junction of Meadow Lane and London Road in Raunds, and also in Stanwick, a similar distance to the south. While the limestone used at West Cotton may have been obtained from such local quarries, an alternative source would have been the Roman settlements to the south and north, at Stanwick and Mallows Cotton (see Fig 1.2), which both lay within 700m of West Cotton with direct access along Cotton Lane. Many of the residual finds of Roman date recovered at West Cotton may have been brought to the site on carts loaded with building stone robbed from these settlements. In particular, it is notable that more Roman than medieval coins were recovered, along with small quantities of Roman pottery and tile. The robbing of stone from the nearby Roman ruins, in which there may still have been many partially standing walls easily accessible, would have removed the need for quarrying and would have provided conveniently-sized stone for either direct use or reworking, with the transport distance to a minimum.

A small quantity of ironstone was used in the buildings, particularly the later building phases of the thirteenth and fourteenth centuries, where it typically appeared as large squared blocks in the quoins at the wall corners and within door surrounds. This Northampton Sand Ironstone, a ferruginous sandstone from the Inferior Oolite Series, is also available locally, outcropping on the valley slope immediately above West Cotton and within less than 1km. Ironstone quarries of Roman date were located within the nearby Mallows Cotton settlement, and the Roman buildings at both Mallows Cotton and Stanwick may again have provided a further or alternative source of ironstone.

Construction techniques

Superficially, there was little difference between the buildings of the twelfth-century manor and those of the peasant tenements dating to thirteenth and fourteenth centuries. All the standing walls comprised courses of flat-laid, rough hewn limestone set on shallow foundations of the same build but usually slightly broader than the standing wall. There was, however, one major distinction between them; the twelfth-century buildings all possessed mortared walls which were, on average, slightly narrower than those of the later buildings, which were merely bonded or packed with sandy clay.

Foundation courses

The foundations of the stone-built manorial hall, S18, which was probably of two storeys, were unique in comprising single or double courses of pitched stone set within a well-defined construction trench, 150mm deep. The pitched stone was sealed by a layer of mortar, which provided a level base for the standing wall.

The foundations of the other buildings comprised one and sometimes two courses, 100–150mm thick, of flat-laid limestone, and were 50–100mm wider than the standing walls, at 600–750mm wide, with external offsets. They tended to contain limestone slabs longer, wider and often thicker than the facing stones of the standing walls. These frequently met at the centre so that there was no more than a minimal core of smaller stones.

The lack of well-defined construction trenches made it difficult to determine the relationship of the foundations to the contemporary ground surface. In many of the twelfth-century buildings there were distinct but shallow construction trenches, 100mm deep, but construction trenches could not be identified in the later buildings. These may have been lost in the removal and relaying of both internal and external surfaces, as well as through subsidence of the wall foundations into underlying softer soils. However, it is possible that the technique used was to level the entire area of a building so that following wall construction the floor levels, and perhaps the adjacent external surfaces, were built up from the same level as the base of the wall foundations, so that the walls were ground laid.

In the earlier buildings it was recognised that additional support needed to be provided for walls running over softer ground, generally the fills of underlying ditches. The western wall of the southern range of the manor, S19, ran across a major boundary ditch and was provided with an exceptionally wide foundation course of particularly large limestone slabs, while the lowest wall courses were partially of pitched stone. The dovecote wall, S22, ran across a pit with exceptionally soft fills and these had been partially dug out and an additional depth of rubble foundations was inserted. The southern wall of the later thirteenth-century barn and processing complex, S17, did not possess a foundation course distinct from the standing wall, but the central length of the wall had been carried down into the upper ditch fills beneath. The earlier thirteenth-century kitchen/bakehouse, D12, of new manor, tenement C/D, was built over the remnant of a prehistoric barrow mound with its northern wall across sloping ground. Here, an additional depth of foundations for the external wall face was set within a narrow construction trench, presumably to prevent slippage down the slope.

The nature of the underlying ground appears to have been ignored in the later thirteenth to fourteenth-century tenement buildings, even though many walls ran along or across recently filled in ditches. There were no clear instances in the later buildings of the provision of broader or deeper foundations over such potential weak spots, while there were a number of examples of structural problems resulting from such situations. The central length of the northern wall of the processing room in tenement B, B5/1, which lay directly over an earlier ditch, was narrower than the remainder, with angled joints at the junctions with the original wall. It appears that subsidence had necessitated the complete levelling and rebuilding of this length of wall. Conversely, the southern end of the western wall of the domestic range in tenement E, E13/1, crossed the levelled remnant of an earlier wall and had subsided on either side, resulting in cracking at the corner, with the southern end wall leaning outward.

Standing walls

The standing walls were constructed in flat-laid courses of rough hewn limestone. The coursing was generally quite regular (Fig 7.68 a), indicating a fairly careful preparation and choice of stones of similar thickness for individual courses, although there were intermittent thicker blocks spanning two, or exceptionally three, courses, and sometimes two thinner slabs within a course. The typical facing stones were 150–300mm long by 50–100mm thick. In some instances the stones of the inner wall face were evidently either smaller or better squared than those of the outer wall face. The quoins at the external and, to a lesser extent, the internal corners and in the door surrounds were typically of larger stones, either of the same thickness, to maintain the courses, or spanning two courses (Fig 7.66 b). In the later buildings, the use of ironstone blocks for at least some of the quoins was common and these were typically two to three courses thick. The largest ironstone quoins occurred either in the foundation courses or at the base of the standing walls.

The facing stones generally took up some 2/3 of the total wall thickness (Fig 7.66c). The wall cores contained smaller limestone rubble but much of this was still flat-laid with interspersed smaller rubble, indicating that the wall cores had been carefully built-up along with the facings. Except for occasional instances within the foundations, there were no through stones.

The later medieval boundary walls were clearly more roughly built, without broader foundation courses and with smaller facing stones. The facings were also shallower, no more than half the wall width, and the cores comprised mainly disordered rubble, so that the wall faces were not tied together particularly well.

The mortared walls of the twelfth-century buildings were typically 450–600mm thick, although the walls of the possible two-storey hall were slightly wider, at 550–600mm. The walls of the later buildings were slightly broader, on average 550–650mm thick. The northern wall of the tenement A hall, A1/1, was exceptional wide at 700–750mm. On some of the best preserved walls battering was evident. The western wall of the west range of tenement E, E13/1, had a basal width of 650mm while at its maximum surviving height of 700mm (11 courses) it had narrowed to 550mm. To the east of Cotton Lane a building located in trial trenching, tenement I, was exceptional in having walls 700–750mm. Both the wall width and a probable stone stair-base within one of the rooms may indicate that this was a building with two storeys, and its interpretation as possibly a later medieval watermill may provide a explanation for the presence of both an upper storey and the exceptional wide walls.

The walls of the twelfth-century buildings were bonded with mortar; a pale yellow sandy lime mortar with small inclusions of friable limestone. The later buildings did not have mortared walls, but within the best preserved walls there was yellow-brown sandy clay both within the core and between the facing stones, indicating that they had been packed with clay, presumably used during construction as thick slurry.

The change from mortared to clay-packed walls may

partly reflect the difference in status between the twelfth-century manor and the later peasant tenements. However, the barn and processing room, S17, added to the manor at around the end of the twelfth century and the early to mid thirteenth-century buildings of tenement C/D, the new manor, had clay-packed walls similar to the peasant tenements.

The best preserved lengths of wall stood up to 900mm high. This, together with the substantial quantities of demolition rubble, clearly indicates that these were not merely dwarf walls. They would have stood to eaves height, perhaps typically some 1.8–2.1m (6–7 feet). Stone stair-bases in tenements A, A1/4, and I, I44, have been taken as indicators of the presence of some upper storeys, or at least a more formal use of the roof space. Both of these instances are quite late additions implying that this may only have occurred in the fourteenth century, with the exception of the two-storey hall in the twelfth-century manor.

Internal partition walls were typically 400mm wide and of the same general build as the external walls, although they only abutted the external walls. An exceptionally narrow partition wall in tenement D, D11, was only 300mm wide and, as found, was leaning considerably. It may have been a dwarf wall supporting a timber partition. A partition wall in the domestic hall of tenement E, E13/4, was 700mm wide, with shallow facings and a rubble core. It may have formed a foundation for a narrower partition wall, perhaps incorporating some piece of room furniture.

No direct evidence for external or internal wall rendering had survived, and none of the buildings had plastered walls. However, a strip of heat hardened yellow sandy mortar that appeared to have collapsed onto the hearth in the manor hall, S18, may have been uniquely preserved by being burnt on the fire. It is also possible that an external layer of yellow-brown sandy mortar abutting the lower wall courses along the front of the same building, may have been derived from the weathering of an external rendering. In a similar fashion, the walls of a number of the later buildings were directly abutted either internally or externally with clean yellow-brown sandy clay, similar to the packing used to bond the walls themselves. This too may have been derived from decayed wall rendering. Its survival in only a limited number of instances might suggest that only a few buildings had been rendered in this way, but alternatively it may only have accumulated around buildings left standing derelict for a period following their abandonment.

Doorways

In the twelfth-century manor buildings large, sub-square post-pits, typically 0.50m in diameter by 0.30m deep,

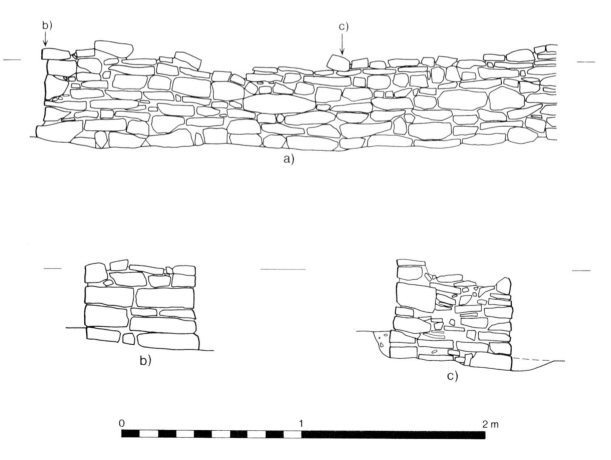

Fig 7.68: The medieval stone buildings; building E14 north wall, elevations; a) inner face, b) wall end, c) section

would have held square or rectangular door jamb posts, perhaps up to some 300–400mm thick, indicating the provision of substantial timber door surrounds.

In the thirteenth century, the use of such massive door posts ceased and thereafter doorways were provided with stone-built surrounds that typically possessed shallow, square recesses for slender door jamb posts, around 100mm square (Fig 7.69). This change was most clearly evident within the manorial hall, S18, where the original door-jamb posts were removed and the stone surrounds were extended over the backfilled post-pits. In some doorways there were either shallow postholes or pad stones at the base of the recesses, and in a few instances linear slots ran between the door jamb recesses, indicating the provision of timber sills. The sills were of comparable width to the door jamb posts, and were set within one or two courses of flat-laid threshold stones. Some of these slots had been carefully filled with small pieces pitched limestone, suggesting the later removal of the timber sills. Pad stones were only ever present beneath one of the recesses, indicating that they were provided to support the door jamb on which the door was hung. In nearly all instances the doors were hung on the left hand side, as viewed from outside, as in buildings through to the present day.

The intact door blocking in building E13 room 1, also illustrates shows the depth of accumulation of both the floor levels and the external surfaces during the lifetime of these buildings, with the base of the blocking wall raised some 200mm above the original floor level (Fig 7.70).

In addition, five pivot stones were found *in situ* within doorway openings, while a further nine displaced examples were recovered (Fig 7.71). None came from a doorway provided with door jamb recesses, indicating that they were not used in the main domestic accommodation. Two were on internal doorways where there was an abutting room of separate build, B5/1–2 and A1/1–2, two were on doorways of smaller ancillary buildings, D11/4 and E14, and the fifth was from the processing room of the late twelfth-century barn, S17, the earliest example. The conical pivot sockets indicate that the doors were equipped with metal studs (see Fig 11.15).

Floors and room function

There were three basic forms of floor surface: clay, stone and earthen, and some rooms had composite floors associated with different functional areas.

The twelfth-century hall, S18, possessed the most complex floor surface. A partial sub-floor of pitched limestone was probably provided to consolidate the fills of an underlying ditch. Above this there was a floor of yellow sandy mortar. Between the central doorways and within the northern chamber the floor was of flat-laid slabs of limestone in a matrix of yellow sandy mortar.

Fig 7.69: Door jamb recesses, building E13, room 2

Fig 7.70: Building E13, room 2, showing the blocked doorway and the change in level resulting from the accumulation of floor and external surfaces

Fig 7.71: Door pivot stone, in situ *within building E14*

At least one major domestic room in each of the ranges of the thirteenth and fourteenth centuries had a clay floor, and in tenement A, A1/1, the clay had been mixed with mortar. These rooms all contained few internal features indicating that they functioned as domestic halls. In tenements A, A1/1, and E, E13/4, areas of scorched clay suggest the possible locations of braziers providing heating.

In the main range of tenement E, a clay-floored room had an area of large limestone slabs adjacent to the doorway, E13/1. In the southern range of the twelfth-century manor, S20 and later S19 room 1, the eastern end of the room was surfaced with flat laid limestone and may have served as a storage room. In tenements A and E, rooms adjacent to the kitchens were re-floored with large flat-laid limestone slabs when the external doors were blocked in the fourteenth century, indicating that they were converted for use for food and crop storage, E13/1 and A1/4.

On a smaller scale, there were stone-floored external chambers in tenements E and D, which may have served as small storage rooms, with the tenement D example being slightly sunken, D11/5 (see Figs 7.28 and 7.49).

Some rooms fully or partially floored with smaller slabs of limestone in tenements A and D were cross-passage chambers, A1/2, which probably provided the main access to these ranges and certainly to the adjacent kitchens. The processing rooms in the twelfth-century manor and tenements B and E were also floored with large limestone, but usually only immediately adjacent to the processing trough, S17/2, B5/1 and E13/3. The kitchens were largely earth-floored but with some small areas of stone paving, including some pitched stone.

The only rooms provided with more robust floors of pitched stone were the open-ended cart or shelter sheds in tenements E, C and D, confirming their use for agricultural rather than domestic functions, E13/5, C9/2 and D11/3.

The detached ancillary buildings and the malt houses in tenements A, B and C were earth-floored.

A single piece of a ceramic floor tile was recovered from tenement C, and this may indicate that late in the life of the hamlet there was at least one room with a tiled floor, perhaps in the postulated fifteenth-century use of the unexcavated tenements adjacent to Cotton Lane.

Roofs

Only negative evidence is available for the nature of the roofing materials. The total absence of any stone or ceramic roof tile indicates that all the buildings were roofed with organic materials, most probably straw or reed thatch. The use of wooden shingles cannot be excluded, although in this instance it might be expected that more nails would have recovered.

External surfaces

The twelfth-century metalling of the central access road comprised a compact surface of small well-laid pieces of limestone, much worn through use and with some patched areas that included pitched stones.

In the thirteenth to fourteenth-century tenements many of the walled yards and much of the central yard comprised mixed deposits of disordered limestone in a clay or earth matrix. In some instances small areas of metalling survived beneath, indicating that more extensive areas had been largely lost, perhaps as a result of animal trampling during the late reuse of some former domestic buildings for agricultural purposes.

There were more extensive areas of intact metalling within tenements B, where a succession of flat and pitched-stone surfaces lay in front of the processing room (Fig 7.72). They may have been protected from later damage by soil accumulation following the early abandonment of this tenement. In one corner of this yard there was also a stone-lined external pit (Fig 7.73). There was a similar external stone-lined pit abutting the barn in tenement C.

An area of similar metalling survived at the northern end of the central yard, south of the boundary wall cutting of the courtyard of tenement E. In both instances there was little wear on the stones, indicating that they had formed a consolidated sub-base for overlying clay or earth surfaces.

Specialised buildings: malt houses, kitchens and processing rooms

Among the numerous buildings excavated at West Cotton there were three types that served such specific purposes that they required tailor-made internal fixtures and fittings, and in some instances these were evidently built into the fabric of the rooms in which they stood. This indicates that the rooms were pre-designed to serve these functions and they had not merely utilised an existing building shell. The buildings in question are the malt houses, the detached and internal kitchens and the processing rooms. In all instances a number of examples were excavated and from the particular details of each, as already described, a generalised account of their forms and functions can be provided.

The malt houses

The basic process of malting involves steeping barley grain in water, and then spreading the grain out on a surface or floor until it germinates and sprouts. It is then dried in a low temperature oven to kill the sprouting. The end produce of the drying is the malt, as used in brewing ale.

A linear earth-cut oven was operating at Furnells manor, Raunds as early as the sixth of early seventh centuries, although it is not certain whether this example was used for malting or just general crop drying (Audouy and Chapman 2009, 66, fig 5.6).

They were malting at West Cotton by the earlier twelfth century. In the northern holding there was an earth-cut

Fig 7.72: Tenement B, metalled yard, BY1, looking west

Fig 7.73: Yard BY1 with external stone-lined pit abutting the wall of the processing room, B5

oven with a sunken sub-rectangular chamber and a linear flue, and the debris indicated that its superstructure had been of fired clay over a wattle frame (see Fig 4.31). Carbonized, sprouted barley grain came from the oven and also from earlier twelfth-century deposits around the nearby watermills.

Stone-built malt ovens and detached malt houses are relatively common, and numerous medieval and post-medieval examples have been excavated on both rural and urban sites throughout Britain. Further examples within the Raunds area are known at Mill Cotton deserted medieval settlement (Parry 2006, 188–190, fig 6.21) and at Furnells manor and Burystead in Raunds (Audouy and Chapman 2009; 98–100, figs 5.38, 5.39; 105–106, figs 5.45 and 5.46 and 131–133, figs 5.79 and 5.80). A medieval manorial malt house and barn complex has also been excavated at nearby Irthlingborough (Chapman *et al* 2003, 81–86, plates 1–3 and figs 6 and 7).

A malt oven dated to the late eighth to early ninth centuries from the middle Saxon estate centre at nearby Higham Ferrers is a rare or even unique example of an early stone-built oven, as the middle to late Saxon examples from Raunds, Furnells and West Cotton were earth-cut ovens. The Higham Ferrers oven is also anomalous in that the lining of the entire chamber and the elongated stone-lined flue had been heavily burnt. This would suggest that it was either used for some other purpose, requiring much higher firing temperatures, or that it had been the victim of an accidental conflagration (Hardy *et al* 2007, 48–54 and 135–140).

The circular structure at the western end of the tenement C/D malt house is a rare instance of the survival of a structure related to other stages of the malting process (Figs 7.74–7.75). It is interpreted as having held a large wooden vat in which the barley grain would have been steeped in water to promote sprouting. A similar circular wall footing was attached to the end of the late medieval kitchen/bakehouse range at Furnells manor Raunds, and may have served the same purpose (Audouy and Chapman 2009, 105–106, figs 5.45 and 5.46). A malt oven related to the earlier, western manor house at Furnells lay close to a rectangular, stone-lined pit, which may also have been used for steeping the grain.

There is no specific evidence to indicate where the barley was laid out to sprout, but presumably it could have been spread across the floors of the rooms attached to the malt ovens, where a small fire may have helped to keep the room temperature up to promote more rapid sprouting. In examples of malt houses set at the end of barn-like buildings, there would have been plenty of space for spreading the grain to sprout, but the floor areas of the majority of the malt houses would appear to be too small, and presumably either other rooms were utilised or the grain was laid out within the walled yards.

It is the ovens themselves that provide most of the evidence. By the mid to later twelfth century the northern manor included a stone-built malting oven. In this instance the oven was constructed within a standing building, the southern range, S19, with the earth core behind the stone-faced chamber set against the existing standing walls (Fig 5.18). This is not the most common form of malt oven, which are more usually free-standing structures. A malt oven abutting the walls at one end of a barn-like building as part of a complex of manorial status has been excavated more recently at Irthlingborough, only a few kilometres to the south of Raunds (Chapman *et al* 2003, 82–86), while there is a further example at Brackley, although in this instance the status of the building in unknown (Atkins *et al* 1998–9).

It is the three malt houses that were constructed around the middle of the thirteenth century, attached to tenements A, B and C (Fig 7.7), that provide the model for the most commonly recorded form of malt house. In each example there was a free-standing oven that had a slightly sunken chamber with the stone-lining slightly inclined, battered, so that the dimensions increased up to the extent of the surviving walls. The rectangular chambers were typically 1.20–1.45m long by 1.10–1.40m wide. Behind the chamber lining there was an earth core and an outer stone facing, to make a well-insulated structure with walls around 1.0m thick (see Fig 7.20). While the ovens were free-standing, there was typically an attached stone-built room, as in tenement B (Fig 7.76). As the walls of the attached room and the outer facing of the oven chamber were ground laid, while the oven chamber was sunken, in excavated examples on truncated sites only the lining of the chamber itself might survive, giving little clue as to the full extent of the oven and the attached structure. In the tenement A malt house there were possible post-pits beyond the free-standing oven (Fig 7.63), suggesting that there was an abutting timber shed or shelter prior to the construction of the stone-built room.

The malt house attached to the agricultural ranges of the later medieval manor, tenement C/D, was the most elaborate of those excavated, and the only one where there were additional ancillary structures presumably related to other aspects of the malting process (Figs 7.74 and 7.75). It was also atypical as its structure was of an intermediate form. The oven chamber was built abutting a full-standing wall, in a similar fashion to the manorial ovens already mentioned, but these only projected a little way out from the oven as stub walls supporting a short open-ended shed, with postholes suggesting the provision of an end-wall in timber (Fig 7.17). Subsequently, the stone walls were extended to form a fully enclosed room, giving it a similar appearance to the other contemporary malt houses (Fig 7.18).

The exceptional thickness of the oven walls provided both heat insulation and support for the superstructure. Large slabs of limestone, surviving up to 500mm long, filled the chamber of the tenement C/D oven, and may have collapsed from a raised oven floor on which the sprouting barley was spread for drying.

The hearth stones were typically set at the inner end of the sloping flues, and partly within the rectangular chambers (Figs 7.74 and 7.76). While the hearth stones were burnt and blackened and the adjacent stones on the flue were

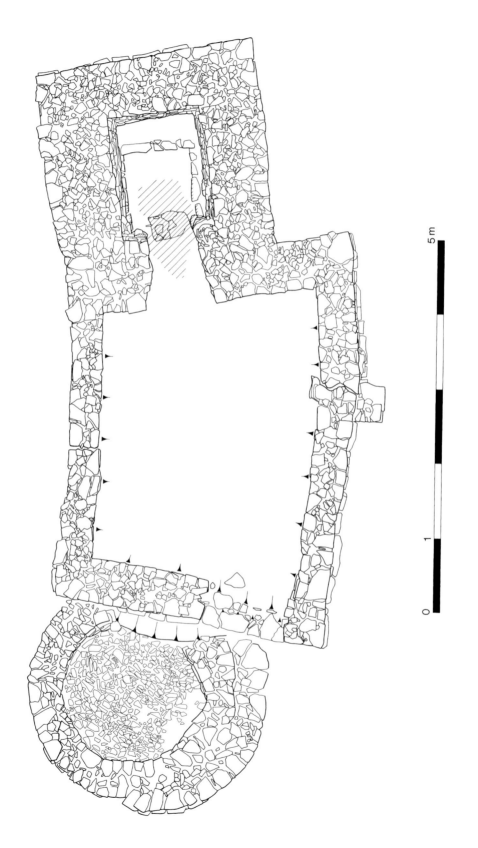

Fig 7.74: The malt house, tenement C/D

reddened, the low temperature maintained in these ovens was indicated by the absence of any general scorching of the floor of the chamber or on the chamber walls.

Deposits of burnt soils within a number of the ovens contained charred seeds, evidently from firings that had been overcooked (see Chapter 12, The charred plant remains by Gill Campbell, from which the following overview is abstracted). The charred seed evidence does confirm the use of these ovens for drying barley to kill the sprouted grain and thus to form the malt for brewing. However, a range of other carbonised seeds and material was also present. The abundance of chaff in the early earth-cut malt oven indicates that they had been using threshing waste as fuel, although this was less evident in the later ovens. In addition to cereal and pulse threshing waste, bracken, and possibly rough grassland vegetation lining hedges was also used as a fuel for drying grain.

The burning of chaff is thought to be associated with sites that can provide for their animals by other means, so the chaff is not needed as fodder, or sites associated with a particular product such as malt. The proximity of West Cotton to hay meadow would suggest that there would have been ample supply of winter fodder, and it is likely that there would have been some permanent pasture.

The choice of fuel for malting is particularly important as the malt takes on the flavour of the fuel used. Wheat straw was often regarded as the best fuel, followed by rye, oat, and lastly barley. Both types of wheat, and maslins of both together, along with rye, would be the most likely types of chaff to be used as fuel, which may explain the abundance of both types of wheat chaff, and rye with bread wheat chaff in assemblages from West Cotton.

In some instances barley was being malted on its own, with good evidence from the early earth-cut oven and from the tenement malt houses, E16 in particular. In the tenement B malt house there was both sprouted barley and oat grain, suggesting that these two cereals were grown together as a mixture, known as a dredge or drage, which was then used for malting. Two-row barley was particularly favoured for brewing, but in some instances hulled six-row barley was also used.

The malt houses attached to both the twelfth- and the thirteenth-century manors were also used for drying wheat prior to grinding, and in the tenement C/D malt house much wheat was recovered but no sprouting barley, perhaps suggesting that the broader use as a drying oven for grain was as important as its use as a malting oven.

The scale of the operation at West Cotton is taken as indicating that sufficient malt was being produced both for local consumption and to provide a surplus to go to market as a cash crop, as indicated by the documentary evidence for malt being traded from the market at nearby Higham Ferrers to as far away as London.

Detached kitchens and bakehouses

The twelfth-century buildings of the medieval manor included a detached kitchen/bakehouse range (Fig 5.19,

Fig 7.75: The malt house, tenement C/D, looking west

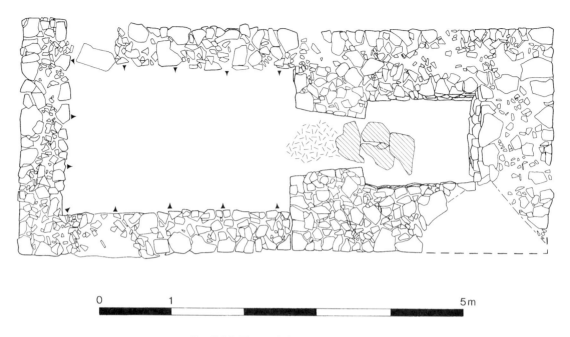

Fig 7.76: The malt house, tenement B

S21), which stood at the opposite end of the courtyard from the manor, surrounded by other activities that would also have produced strong smells, namely a malt house, a dovecote and a cess pit (Fig 5.7). With the relocation of the manor to the east in the early thirteenth century, a larger and more elaborate kitchen/bakehouse was provided in tenement C/D (Fig 7.23, D12) and, as earlier, this was kept well away from the domestic apartments, and abutted a barn with a malt house lying nearby. Later in the century this building was remodelled and became just a kitchen range, with a new and separate bakehouse provided nearby (Fig 7.14, C9). There was a similar detached bakehouse in tenement B (Fig 7.35, B6/2).

In three instances the circular baking ovens were located in the corners of rooms with the flue at 45 degrees to the walls, S21, B6/2 and C9, while in the fourth example it was set near centrally and at a right angle to the wall, D12. This was also the best preserved oven. It was built within a 0.25m deep construction pit, with a metalled surface of pitched stone covered by a layer of sand (Fig 7.77). The chamber lining, in flat-laid limestone, was built over this surface; and it had an internal diameter of 1.26m, with a 0.4m wide flue opening into a short stoke hole.

The others possessed chambers of 1.1 and 1.2m diameter (Fig 7.78), while in building C9 the chamber lining had later been fully removed but had been built up over a 1.40m diameter surface of flat-laid and pitched stones covered with sandy clay (Fig 7.79). This example had been a later addition to the room and was recessed into the wall, with the facing rebuilt. The other examples merely abutted the adjacent walls. No stone floor survived within the oven in building S21, and in building B6/2 much of the chamber

was occupied by a single hearth stone. In all the ovens the facing stones around the entire circumference of the chamber had been reddened and blackened by heating.

The superstructures had all been fully removed above floor level, but in building D12 the chamber was largely filled with pieces of limestone each with a reddened edge, and scorched, but not fired, sandy clay, indicating that the superstructure largely comprised limestone bonded with clay. Given the sunken chambers, these ovens evidently had a lower fire box which would have heated the floor of a second raised chamber into which the bread was placed for baking.

In buildings S21 and D12 there were open hearths in addition to the ovens, indicating that they also served as general kitchens, even through few internal fittings had survived. The hearths comprised flat-laid hearth stones surrounded by scorched and blackened floor surfaces. In building C9 a number of other features may have been contemporary with the oven; a shallow pit floored with limestone slabs lay beside a deep pit with a rectangular slot in its base; this pit may have held a sill beam supporting a vertical timber for some item of equipment requiring a solid foundation, some form of press perhaps. The largest kitchen/bakehouse, D12, also contained a stone-lined pit apparently opening at one end into a pit with stepped sides.

All of the excavated small circular baking ovens had gone out of use by the early fourteenth century. It is possible, however, that the detached range in tenement E, E14, was converted to a bakehouse in the fourteenth century (Figs 7.47 and 7.49). This was of a different form with a larger more substantial circular stone structure,

Fig 7.77: A circular baking oven with pitched-stone floor, detached kitchen range D12

Fig 7.78: Small circular baking oven, detached bakehouse, B6

Fig 7.79: Stone base for circular corner oven, detached bakehouse, C9

wrapped around the corner of the building. It contained no internal burning at the level it survived to. This indicates that rather than the separate fire box and oven chamber of the manorial ovens, this would have had a single raised chamber. A fire would have been lit and once the oven was raised to temperature, the ashes would have been swept out and the bread inserted for baking. A plinth provided access from inside the building, while an external area of heavily burnt clay may suggest that it was fired and raked out from outside. In this form and function, the structure would have been closely similar to post-medieval baking ovens, which sometimes still survive in standing buildings.

The detached kitchens and bakehouses of probable manorial status, were out of use by the fourteenth century. The new style bakehouse in tenement E perhaps served for the whole hamlet, while the individual tenements now included a kitchen within the main domestic building range.

The tenement kitchens

In the later medieval tenements the kitchens were a single room within the main range. The kitchens in tenements A and E possessed the same set of features and had closely similar internal arrangements, and may provide a model for kitchens at this time (Figs 7.80–7.86).

In both instances there was no external doorway: a central doorway at one end and a corner doorway at the other provided access to the adjacent rooms. The kitchen in tenement C also appeared to be similar, although it had two corner doorways and was less well preserved, so some internal fittings may have been lost (See Fig 7.10, C8/2).

The tenement A and E kitchens were provided with stone benches, one set against a long wall and the other along the adjoining end wall containing the corner doorway. In tenement E only the basal levels survived, but in tenement A the bench against the end wall was 0.37m wide and stood to a height of 0.4m (Figs 7.81 and 7.82). The large top slabs indicate that this was probably the original surface, so it seems likely that the others had all once stood to a similar height. They could therefore have served as seating, but it is perhaps more likely that they acted as shelves for storage, perhaps with timber superstructures above them for further storage of food or utensils, in fact forming the base for a medieval "cup-board". In front of the end bench in tenement E there was a surface of pitched limestone covered with clay, which may have served as a foundation to a new item of timber furniture perhaps replacing the narrow bench with a broader structure serving the same function. Similar high and narrow, and broad and low benches were also found in some rooms that had not served as kitchens.

The tenement E kitchen contained a stone-lined pit with adjacent areas of flat-laid and pitched stone surfacing (Fig 7.83, s and Fig 7.84). It had been constructed at one end of a square construction pit and the filling of the remainder with limestone might suggest the provision of an adjacent solid foundation, perhaps to carry some item of machinery functioning in conjunction with the pit. Alternatively, it may simply have served as a below ground cool box, perhaps covered with a movable wooden or stone slab (and was commonly referred to as the wine cooler during excavation, for which it would have served perfectly). There was a closely similar feature in building D11 (Fig 7.85). The

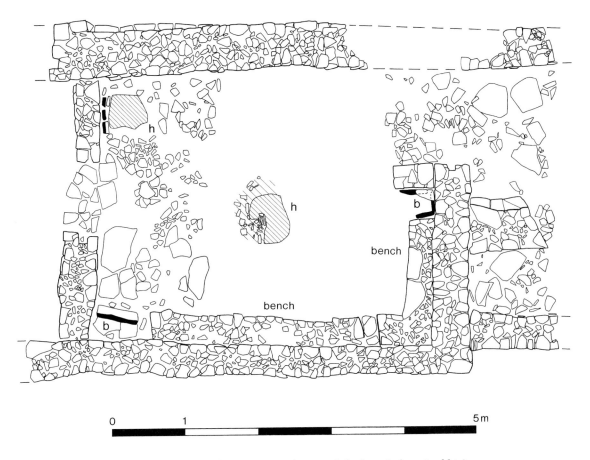

Fig 7.80: The kitchen, tenement A, room 3 (h=hearth, b=raised bin)

first phase of the tenement A kitchen probably included a similar stone-lined pit, much disturbed by later activity, while in its second phase a slab of limestone standing 0.4m high suggests the provision of an above ground bin in the corner of the room, with an adjacent area surfaced with large slabs of limestone (Fig 7.80, b). This bin may have served a similar storage function, although above-ground storage would not have had the same cool box effect. Both kitchens were partially surfaced with limestone, with this occupying the corner of the room adjacent to the stone-lined pits or bins.

The focal point of these kitchens was the central hearth, with the surrounding earth-floors rich in comminuted charcoal from the decades of use. The central hearths were 0.8–1.2m in diameter, comprising a large, flat-laid slab of limestone flanked by a crescent of small pitched stones, usually set within a clay base and often incorporating quantities of pitched pottery sherds (Chapman and Hurman 1991). The flat-laid slabs had clearly been the hearth stones as they were blackened, cracked and often quite friable, while the reddening and no more than slight blackening of the projecting edges of the pitched stones indicated that these had been subjected to less intense heating (Fig 7.86). This arrangement suggests the provision of both

direct and indirect heating; with metal vessels suspended over the fire itself and metal or ceramic vessels set beside the fire on the pitched stone area with hot ashes heaped around them to provide a slow cooker effect. In all of the kitchens, the hearths had been relaid a number of times, with their predecessor still at least partially intact beneath, so that the hearth area became slightly raised with respect to the rest of the floor surface.

The tenement A and E kitchens also possessed either corner hearths or, perhaps, small semi-enclosed corner ovens. They were of rectangular plan, measuring 1.5 by 1.0m, and comprised a single flat hearth stone, intensely burnt, set adjacent to the wall and surrounded by an area of smaller flat-laid stones, less heavily burnt. In tenement A, small slabs of limestone had been pitched against the adjacent wall, presumably to protect it from burning, but no other evidence for any enclosing superstructure was recovered (Fig 7.80, h, and Fig 7.83, h, both top left). How the use of these corner hearths/ovens supplemented or complemented the central hearths is uncertain, but their use in a different fashion, perhaps for roasting, as in a dutch oven, seems likely. This would imply that when in use they were partially enclosed perhaps by a portable metal screen.

Fig 7.81: The kitchen, tenement A, looking west, showing central hearth, corner hearth/oven (bottom right), raised bin (top right), and stone bench (left)

Fig 7.82: The stone bench, tenement A kitchen, room 3

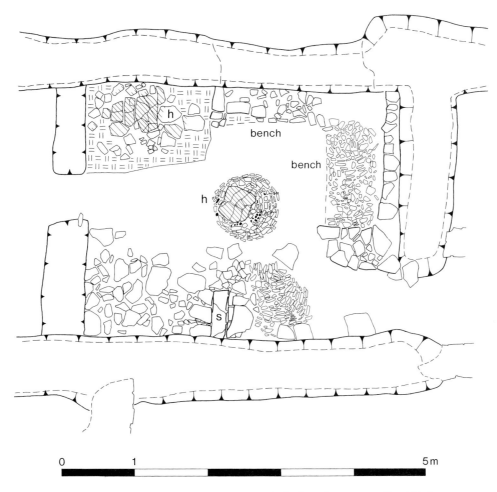

Fig 7.83: The kitchen, tenement E, room 2 (h=hearth, s= stone-lined bin)

0 1 5 m

Fig 7.84: The kitchen tenement E, looking east

Fig 7.85: A stone-lined bin, building D11

Fig 7.86: A typical central hearth, tenement E, kitchen

The processing rooms

These rooms were defined by the presence of elongated stone-lined pits, which were stained and encrusted grey or blue-grey by the action of powerful organic chemicals. The earliest examples are dated to the end of the twelfth century. One was attached to the manorial barn (see Figs 5.23–5.25, S17/2) and there was another in tenement B (Figs 7.87 and 7.88, B5/1). In the thirteenth century a room in tenement E was also devoted to the use of a processing trough, which went through three phases of rebuilding, getting shorter each time (see Fig 7.41). A shorter processing trough was in use in the kitchen/bakehouse range of the relocated manor house, building D12 (see Fig 7.23. t).

The processing rooms in buildings S17 and B5 also included a hearth and a stone-filled soak-away pit set beneath the floor of the room, with these features presumably related to other stages of the same processing activity (Fig 7.87).

The troughs were typically 1.8–3.0m long by 0.50–0.60m wide and 0.30m deep. They were fully stone-lined, and two possessed partial transverse divisions. They were all flanked by areas of limestone flooring, often with well worn-surfaces which were similarly stained and encrusted (Figs 7.89 and 7.90). In tenement B an irregular group of postholes and slots between the trough and the adjacent wall suggest that there was an adjacent timber structure, perhaps racking of some form (Fig 7.87).

The processing room in tenement B also contained a mortared stone footing. This was more deeply-founded than the adjacent wall, and extended partly under the wall, showing that the footings had been put in place before the walls were built. A pair of postholes at either end of this footing may have supported some timber structure related to it. At the end of the processing trough the inner face of the building wall was carried down into the construction pit to form the end of the trough. So, like the footing at

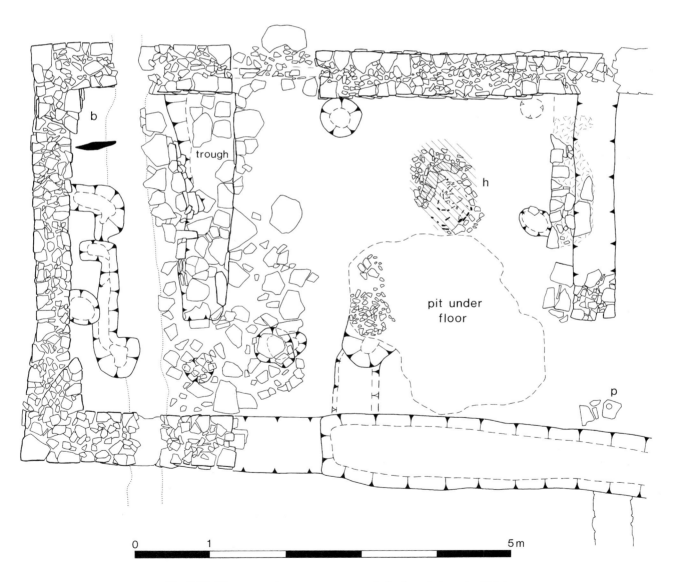

Fig 7.87: The processing room tenement B (h=hearth, b=raised bin)

Fig 7.88: The processing room tenement B, looking north

the other end of the room, the arrangement of the trough was also set out before the walls were built, showing that this was a purpose-built structure.

There seem to be few excavated parallels for these stone-lined troughs, although there was a similar feature with the same grey discolouration of the limestone lining, within the early use of the service wing of the later medieval manor at Furnells, Raunds (Audouy and Chapman 2009, 102 and Fig 5.41). With the lack of parallels, the specific function of these processing rooms remains uncertain. However, if it is accepted that the discolouration and encrustation derives from organic chemical staining, there are two main possibilities both relating to the processing of cloth.

The most likely option is that the troughs were used for the fulling of newly woven woollen cloth. The fulling process fulfilled the two requirements necessary to finish the cloth: *scouring*, the cleansing of the cloth to remove the natural oils and greases by soaking and pounding in a strong liquor of water and a cleaning agent such as fuller's earth, stale urine or soapwort; while the pounding of the cloth matted the fibres together to close and tighten the weave.

Fulling mills had been introduced on monastic sites by the later twelfth century to mechanise the process, but the use of human power to "walk" the cloth by trampling it underfoot would still have been the standard process beyond the monastic establishments, and in the late fourteenth century William Langland in his *Vision concerning Piers the Plowman* states (translated to modern English) that

Fig 7.89: The stone-lined processing trough, tenement B

"cloth that comes from the weaving is not comely to wear until it is fulled under foot or in fulling stokes".

The use of stale urine, forming an ammonia-based liquor, might well account for the staining and encrustation of the pit lining, and fulling is therefore the preferred option for the use of these troughs. The postholes and slots adjacent to the trough in tenement B may have supported a wooden rack on which the cloth, or part of a length of cloth, could be hung during the processing, while the stone-filled soak-away pits would have collected the surplus liquids.

The second option is the bleaching of linen yarn or cloth. This involves three basic processes (Baines 1985, 29–30): *bucking*, boiling the cloth in lye (alkalised water: wood ash, fern and seaweed ash and lime have all been extensively used); *grassing or crofting* on the *bleach green*, laying the cloth out on the fields to expose it to the oxidising effect of air and sun (the cloth had to be kept damp so that the lye could take effect without damaging the cloth, this could take from two to fourteen days); *souring*, soaking the cloth in a weak solution of acid as a neutraliser (buttermilk, sour milk and water fermented with bran or rye meal have been used), followed by complete rinsing.

It has been established that the water-retting of flax (submerging under water to decompose the woody matter and cellular tissue so that the fibres could be easily separated) was being carried out within the adjacent river channel in the eighth century. In addition, the spindle whorls and heckle teeth recovered in the excavations could be indicative of either flax or wool spinning, while a single glass linen smoother from tenement E indicates that the final finishing of linen cloth (pounding or *beetling* to close the surface by making it smooth and glossy) was carried out on the site.

As with the malt houses, the processing rooms would have been central to the evolving cash economy in producing a surplus of goods that could have gone for sale to the traders in the market at nearby Higham Ferrers.

Additional note

Following the preparation of this summary a probable parallel for these troughs has been recognised in a medieval house at the deserted medieval village of Upton, Gloucestershire, excavated in the 1960s, and dated to the mid to late thirteenth century. Building AD–AF comprised: an upper room; a kitchen, with central hearth and corner oven; and a lower room, with a cross passage to the north and two, probably successive, troughs with floor slabs and uprights to the south (Rahtz 1969, 86–98 and fig 6). As at West Cotton, much of the area between the cross-passage and the troughs was paved. No interpretation was offered in the published account, but in an article in Current Archaeology (Hilton and Rahtz 1967), this room was interpreted as "a 'working area', with troughs where some domestic industrial activity such as fulling or tanning was carried on".

Fig 7.90: The early stone-lined processing trough, tenement E, looking south, partially removed by later troughs

8   West Cotton, Raunds: a study of medieval settlement dynamics

For many people today the English village is seen as "a tangible symbol of an ideal rural life: simple, safe, stable and cohesive" (Lewis *et al* 2001, 5). The excavation of around a half of the outlying deserted medieval hamlet of West Cotton, along with the complementary evidence from the similarly extensive excavations of parts of the manorial centre in Raunds (Audouy and Chapman 2009), has provided a mass of high-quality information that reveals some of the reality behind the myths; and the results should be of use to researchers for many decades to come.

The term 'settlement dynamics' has been chosen to embody both the analysis of the processes of change through the lifetime of the settlement and also to emphasise that we are truly talking about a dynamic settlement: a place that was far from simple, safe or stable, although the survival of the settlement through five centuries of change does speak of an underlying social structure that was cohesive.

The overall story is, therefore, one of dynamic change in response to changing social and economic factors, but within a pattern of continuity that can be embodied in the survival of a field gateway that lay at the end of the access road off the Cotton Lane, as established 1000 years earlier, but which is now buried and almost lost within the hedge following disuse in the mid-twentieth century (as depicted in the frontispiece). It is such compelling evidence of continuity that leads many to believe that they are viewing a static rural landscape rather than a landscape of constant adaptation to changing circumstances.

The planned late Saxon settlement

There was no substantial domestic settlement at West Cotton in the ninth century, and the mid-tenth century date for its creation strongly suggests that it appeared in the decades following the reconquest of eastern England by the Saxon kings and the subsequent establishment of order within the Danelaw.

The work of the Raunds survey team has shown that the Anglo-Saxon settlement pattern was of dispersed farmsteads that were either abandoned at the creation of the new nucleated settlements (Parry 2006) or were absorbed into the new larger settlements. People were therefore brought in from their farmsteads and their fields in an episode of overt social engineering.

West Cotton was clearly a planned settlement comprising regular rectangular plots, nominally one-acre in extent and sub-divided into smaller functional areas of half- or a quarter-acre; although to the east regularity had to give way to the topographical limitations imposed by an old stream channel.

Work in Raunds has shown the appearance of similarly regular plots at about the same time (Audouy and Chapman 2009, 53–54, fig 4.1), so it can be argued that this was not a piecemeal process of change but probably a single episode of imposed and widespread reorganisation of settlement. West Cotton was a new foundation on a block of land beside the river that had seen some previous small-scale Anglo-Saxon settlement in the sixth century, and the use of the river for flax retting in the eighth century. It provides a contrast to Furnells manor in Raunds, where a similar plot system was imposed on an existing substantial farm of mid-ninth century origin, the so-called Anglo-Scandinavian farm, which contained several post-built halls standing next to a ditched enclosure, which contained a further hall (Audouy and Chapman 2009, 28–34, fig 3.5). At this point in the discussion it may be worth noting that the revised dating for Furnells presented in the final report (Audouy and Chapman 2009, 24–25, table 3.1), does indicate that it was only in the mid-ninth century that continuous occupation began, and not in the 6th century as was suggested in interim publications, which have been subsequently cited by others (eg Lewis *et al* 2001, 87.

An echo of the style seen at Furnells in the ninth century, with the provision of substantial ditches to provide both a practical and a psychological sense of defensibility, was evident in the original formation at West Cotton, where the principal buildings were partially enclosed by both a timber palisade and a substantial ditch. The success of the new political and social order may be reflected at West Cotton in the abandonment of this arrangement by the end of the tenth century in favour of a more open courtyard setting, a form that was to be retained in the twelfth-century manor house.

It has not been possible to provide an accurate date for the establishment of the open field system at Raunds, but it does seem most likely that it was formed, or at least formalised, as part of the same process of reorganisation, with the fields extending across the former farmsteads of those who had been brought into the new nucleated settlements.

There can be little doubt that such an all-encompassing reorganisation could only have been imposed from outside at the highest level as a response to the evident need to establish peace, or at least stability, within an area potentially liable to outbreaks of civil disobedience if not outright revolt. The political organisation behind the practical end results seen in Raunds at the lower levels of settlement hierarchy has been summarised by Lewis *et al* (2001, 47) in their overview of medieval settlement in Central England:

> "the kings of Wessex instituted in the east Midlands a hierarchy of administrative structures which provided them with an effective system of government, capable of imposing law and order, and of raising military service and taxation. In many respects it was this system that provided the framework for government for the rest of the middle ages".

The ultimate success of this reorganisation is demonstrated by the period of extended peace that followed, which was disrupted but not overturned by the Danish incursions at the end of the tenth century that led to the installation of Danish Kings in the earlier eleventh century (Swein 1013–14 and Cnut 1016–35). Its success must have derived from the fact that the system was sufficiently equitable to enable most individuals to maintain if not improve their standard of living, with the regularity of the planning of the settlements and the systematic organisation of the field system providing a ready measure of the fairness of the land allocation. There was, therefore, a common vested interest in its maintenance at all levels of local society.

One particular aspect of the early organisation of West Cotton that needs some further comment is the presence of so-called empty plots. It has been argued that "the presence of unoccupied tofts … suggests that the settlement was planned to allow for anticipated growth" (Lewis 2001, 82)". This statement originates in the assumption that the status of West Cotton was static, so that its final form as a peasant hamlet reflected an origin as a peasant settlement comprising a row of ditched plots each of which was a potential toft awaiting occupation.

The excavated late Saxon building group was of a higher status, and in fulfilling its role at the centre of a mixed regime of arable and pastoral farming it utilised the surrounding ditched plots as functional areas of the farm. The presence of a double-gated enclosure at the entrance to a plot south of the main residence, although of a slightly later date, demonstrates a use for stock control, with this shedding enclosure utilised for the separation of animals. The other plots opening onto the central yard, which can perhaps be most appropriately pictured as a farmyard, were probably also used as paddocks for stock, perhaps including the oxen for the plough team and maybe a horse or two, while other areas around the buildings may have had a horticultural use.

Seen in this light, these plots were far from unoccupied, but were never intended as potential tofts. The fact that each could have served as a peasant toft only underlines the difference in status, and therefore land holding, between the Anglo-Saxon peasant and the residents of the main building complex at West Cotton.

The status of the late Saxon occupants of West Cotton

The question of the likely status of the late Saxon occupants of West Cotton, and the nature of their tenure, has already been considered in relation to the documentary evidence. As concluded by Courtney, it is most likely that in the excavated late Saxon building complex we are looking at the residence of someone of relatively high status in local terms, probably either a minor thegn or a sokeman or freeman; and he has drawn attention to the likely overlap in economic status between these individuals. The suggested presence of two similar high-status holdings at West Cotton is considered as perhaps more appropriate to the presence of sokemen or freemen, although another possibility is that at least the excavated building complex, with its associated watermill, may have been the residence of a minor thegn, with the southern holding perhaps occupied by a sokeman or freeman, while the dependent peasants occupied the smaller plot to the east between the roads and an old stream channel.

The arrangement of the late Saxon buildings, with a hall at the end of an access road while the domestic range and other buildings were set around a central courtyard, closely paralleled the arrangement at Furnells, Raunds, a documented post-Conquest manor. A more substantial manor at Goltho, Lincolnshire had the same arrangement (Beresford 1987, fig 26), but on a slightly larger scale, and by the twelfth century it had been replaced by a motte and bailey castle. The well-documented manor at Faccombe Netherton, Hampshire (Fairbrother 1990) evidently possessed a similar hall with attached domestic range, showing that this form was not unique to midland counties. In all of these instances the factor that denoted the manorial status of Furnells, Goltho and Faccombe Netherton was the presence of an adjacent church, to reflect the parochial responsibilities attached to the manor, which were obviously absent from the social level immediately below even though economically there may have been no significant distinction.

The similarity in the general courtyard form of the building arrangement at West Cotton compared to those at Furnells, Goltho and Faccombe Netherton, and other examples, can be extended more specifically to the actual hall and domestic apartments. In all instances these comprised two adjoining ranges with an open hall and adjacent apartments, although the higher status sites were generally on a slightly larger scale, with broader and longer halls and perhaps a longer domestic range containing an additional chamber or two. A further discussion of these long ranges is contained in the report on the sites in north Raunds (Audouy and Chapman 2009, 53–55, fig 4.2), where it is suggested that the overall dimensions of the West Cotton and Furnells long ranges are so similar that they could have been off-the-peg designs, perhaps constructed by the same builder and maybe even utilising timbers prepared off-site to standard dimensions.

The difference in status only becomes physically evident a little later. At Furnells manor some of the ditches of the original plot system were realigned in the mid tenth century to make space for a new plot to hold a small church and churchyard. Later still, the hall at Furnells was rebuilt as a much wider aisled hall, presumably to add more physical substance to its seigneurial status, while the rebuilding of the hall at West Cotton added no appreciable additional ground floor space, and was perhaps related more towards the additional comfort of the residents.

The Norman Conquest and sub-infeudation

It has been argued by Courtney in this volume, that in the twelfth century all three of the Cottons were sub-infeudated, and he has identified West Cotton as the half-a-hide held of the Clare/Gloucester fee by Frumbold de Denford, in addition to his lands in Knuston. This was clearly not his main residence and we must envisage the West Cotton manor house as a manorial holding in which the demesne was directly farmed by a resident bailiff.

The suggested continued presence of a second major holding has support from documentary evidence, which tells us that men of both Ralf Normanville and Henry de Albotesk (later the Chamberlain family), both of the Clare/Gloucester fee, held land in West Cotton by the later thirteenth century, and perhaps this had a much earlier origin. It is possible that the southern holding was occupied by a freeman, as it may have been before the Norman Conquest, but the presence of a wealthy tenant of Frumbold is perhaps the more likely explanation.

As in the late Saxon period, the paucity of the documentary evidence leaves us unable to clearly define more than the broadest view of the status of the residents, while the archaeological evidence shows a complex pattern of multiple tenure in which the physical form of a prosperous holding may be little different from a documented manorial holding.

Although the post-conquest period may have seen a tenurial change at West Cotton, the twelfth-century rebuilding entailed the almost direct replacement of the timber buildings with new stone buildings offering much the same scale and range of accommodation as previously. There is therefore no reason to suppose that there was any immediate change in the economic functioning of the settlement. However, the provision of a dovecote clearly does reflect the manorial status of the holding at this time, together with a detached kitchen and bakehouse and a stone-lined cess pit, an uncommon luxury on a rural settlement. The manor house itself also showed some limited architectural pretensions, and was the only excavated building provided with distinct foundations of pitched stone, and the only building where timber scaffolding was systematically used in its construction. An external staircase provided access

to the upper chamber, and a hearth in the hall below was probably provided with a smoke hood.

Although the new buildings offered little additional space, there was a change in the organisation of the plot pertaining to the manor house, as this was enlarged by absorbing an adjacent plot to the south, so that the new buildings stood towards the centre of the enlarged plot. Part of this space was taken up by a new ancillary building, while areas to the west of the kitchen and dovecote and at the frontage onto the central yard were taken up with agricultural processing facilities, largely comprising ovens used for the general drying of grain and animal fodder for winter storage, although much of this activity occurred later in the twelfth century.

A new barn on the southern side of the courtyard would have provided storage, while at its western end there was an oven specifically for the production of malted grain, for brewing, the surplus from which may have provided a cash crop at market.

By the mid-twelfth century, shortly following the establishment of the new manor house, change arrived unasked for and unwanted when a catastrophic episode of flooding and consequent alluviation threatened the very survival of the settlement. Changes to the hydrology resulted in the abandonment of the manorial watermill, and to combat the flooding a series of drainage ditches were excavated around the margins of the settlement. When these proved to be ineffective, it became necessary to create several-hundred metres of flood bank to protect the settlement. With continuing flooding the deposited alluvial clays rose to the top of the flood embankment, and thereafter the ground level within the settlement was actually around one metre lower than the surrounding floodplain. Deposits of clays within the settlement show that over-bank flooding was not unknown.

Without the flooding, it would seem likely that the mill would have been retained, and perhaps even enlarged, to continue as a major part of the economic function of the manor. Its loss was perhaps compensated for by an expansion of other agriculturally-based industries. This was partly indicated by the external drying ovens within the manorial enclosure and by the provision of a specific malt house within a new and longer barn on the southern side of the courtyard.

However, the major expansion of these activities lay at the beginning of the thirteenth century with the addition of an entirely new range fronting onto the central yard, which contained a new barn and an adjacent chamber with a stone-lined trough and other features probably used for the fulling of woollen cloth. This involved soaking the newly woven cloth in an ammonia rich solution, probably made from stale urine, to remove the natural grease while also pounding it to close the weave, with both processes preparing the cloth for dyeing. This new activity may have run in parallel with a gradual increase in the age-of-death of the sheep from the site to three or four years, showing that an extra fleece or two was being taken from them before they were slaughtered for the mutton.

With both the expansion of the manorial enclosure and the introduction of the new barn and processing room at the frontage, the former open plots that had been used for stock control had largely been lost to new walled yard areas, utilised in relation to the activities taking place in the buildings. This is not to say that such routine pastoral activities as the infield penning and separation of stock were no longer taking place, just that they were no longer taking place so close to the principal residence of the manor house. In the next period of development we will see the continuation of this process as the domestic industries represented by the barn, processing room and malt house were themselves moved to a distance beyond the principal residence.

The surplus from the new activities of malting and the fulling of woollen cloth could have gone to market as part of an enlarged cash economy replacing the loss of the fees from the mill. Of course, even if the mill had continued in use, these other activities may well still have seen a similar level of expansion, as on the separate southern holding a purpose-built processing room, with a similar fulling trough, appeared as a new development on the frontage at about the same time, and therefore closely paralleled the expansion of the manor house to the north.

The decline of manorial demesne farming

The appearance of the new manorial barn and of new processing rooms on both the manor and the southern holding, marking an increased need for both crop storage and crop processing facilities, was the first stage in the expansion of arable-based industry. The second stage took place around the mid-thirteenth century within a major reorganisation of the northern holding and the eastern enclosures that marked the beginning of the end for direct farming of the manorial demesne.

There may have been both social and economic factors behind this change. With the demise of the mill and the silting of the adjacent river channel, the focal point of the manor had gone and, perhaps in order to reinstate itself in a position of primacy within the larger settlement, the manor house was relocated onto the eastern enclosures adjacent to the Cotton Lane, where it could dominate and control access to and from the settlement. A further factor may have been that within the physical constraints of the northern holding it would not have been possible to provide a better-appointed manor house. In the new manor the domestic ranges stood beside the Cotton Lane, well away from the functional ranges that fronted onto the central yard, and included a barn, a kitchen/bakehouse and a malt house.

It is possible that this move onto the Cotton Lane was associated with the establishment of a new watermill also lying adjacent to the lane and to the east of its crossing of the Cotton Brook, which later documentary records refer to as a bridged crossing, although the presence of a watermill at this date has not been proven.

The old domestic enclosure was then subdivided into two peasant tenements that would have been occupied by rent-paying tenants. Once fully developed, one of these tenements contained a processing room and the other a malt house, presumably directly complementing the production from the manor house itself. Although they have been described as peasant tenements, the new buildings were well-appointed and are well above a basic peasant cottage. The farmers who occupied them were clearly men of some substance, and one at least had a detached building that was either a byre or even a stable, while each tenement also had an open-ended shed that must also have served as either a cart or shelter shed.

At the same time, further development of the southern holding appeared to parallel the new manor house. There may have been the same separation of activities with a principal house fronting onto the lane, while a malt house and perhaps a barn were added to the processing room, and faced the manorial barn on the opposite sides of the access road. The new buildings on both plots overlay the former ditched boundaries between the plots and the central yard. This encroachment obviously narrowed the width of these yards to that of a street running between the tenements, although a broader area was left between the two barns, perhaps for ease of turning carts bringing goods into the barns for storage.

Given the presence of the new manorial barn and the malt house, there was evidently still direct manorial farming of at least some of the demesne land, but with tenants occupying new well-appointed tenements and evidently duplicating some of the functions it would seem that the process of transfer of the demesne to rent-paying tenants was well underway.

The desertion of the manor

At around 1300, no more than 50 years after the new manor house and tenements had been built, change was underway again. The new manor house was abandoned and both the kitchen and the barn were converted into peasant tenements. The broad barn doors were blocked to make normal-width doors and a series of partition walls were inserted. The end result was a range similar to the two northern tenements on the old manor site. The kitchen range was also subdivided with partition walls, but this formed a much smaller residence, that can perhaps truly be seen as a peasant cottage with few pretensions. The manorial malt house was abandoned and levelled.

The similar agricultural complex of the southern holding was also deserted at this same time, with the processing room, the malt house and perhaps another barn being abandoned, but in this instance without reuse of the buildings, perhaps indicating that the limit of land for rent by tenant farmers had been reached.

With the abandonment and conversion of these buildings it would appear that direct farming of the manorial demesne ceased, with the lands being farmed only by the tenants of what had finally become a peasant hamlet, most probably containing no higher-status residents. The possible watermill may have been the one manorial right that was retained, as clearly this function could not have been easily relocated elsewhere.

No specific reasons for the desertion of the manor are suggested by the archaeological evidence, and we must turn to the recognised general economic processes in action in later medieval England. Arable exploitation is believed to have reached its peak by the end of the thirteenth century, with virtually all possible land taken into cultivation, and by the later fourteenth century the land under plough was being reduced (Postan 1972, Chapter 2.4). Soil exhaustion, particularly on marginal land, would have led to decreasing yields, and this would only have been exacerbated by the climatic extremes occurring from the later thirteenth century onward, generally a colder and wetter period, but interspersed with occasional prolonged droughts (Beresford 1975, 50–2). These factors led to loss of crops and animals and in these more difficult times the abandonment of direct farming of the manorial demesne and the collection of rents from tenants was a sounder means for maintaining a reliable income from the land, while the tenants often found cash rents preferable to labour dues and tiths.

Concurrently, a rise in sheep farming for wool is well evidenced across the country. The bone evidence from West Cotton reflects this in showing an increasing proportion of sheep and with an increase in the age of death, indicative of both more sheep and the obtaining of more fleeces per animal before they were slaughtered for meat. The sudden decline in arable crop processing at West Cotton, as indicated by the abandonment of at least two malt houses, could be taken as an indication of a decline in arable exploitation, although it is possible that the processing of grain for malt was tied to the manorial holding and was relocated elsewhere. It may also be noted that while the manorial barn was converted to a residence, rooms within at least two of the tenements, both adjacent to kitchens, had their external doors blocked and were furnished with flagged floors, indicating a conversion to storage rooms for produce, perhaps to replace some of the storage capacity lost with the demise of the barn or barns.

The transition from manor to hamlet: some speculations

by Paul Courtney

By the mid-thirteenth century the manor house at West Cotton had been demolished and replaced by two peasant tenements. It may have been replaced by a new manor further to the east but, if so, this too had been replaced by peasant tenements by the end of the century. The abandonment of the manor house is unlikely to have reflected its closeness to the more important de Denford and Normanville estate in Knuston, 2km to the south. The continuing use of a residence would have been necessary for a steward or farmer (leasee), even though the post-

Conquest period may have seen the decline of West Cotton as a main residence of its lord.

The succession of the Normanville family, who may also have had a manor house in Raunds, could have played a role in its decline or abandonment, but the date of this event is uncertain. They had certainly replaced the de Denfords at Knuston by 1232. One explanation may be suggested by the archaeological evidence for the location of peasant tenements within the manorial enclosure. These may reflect the end of direct farming of the demesne and its subsequent splitting up between new peasant tenants.

The abandonment of the manor house certainly indicates a major and permanent tenurial change. Manorial buildings were normally maintained when demesnes were farmed to multiple peasant leasees later in the middle ages. The small extent of the West Cotton demesne may have made it awkward and not especially profitable to run. The purchase of the demesne by peasant tenants may therefore have been an attractive proposition for the lord. A similar phenomenon may have occurred on the newly acquired Waldeshef family fee in Ringstead and Stanwick in the early thirteenth century. The customary tenants had their work services commuted and tenures changed to free socage, either indicating a total reliance on hired labour or more likely the end of demesne farming (Kerr 1925, 83, fn.10).

The peasant hamlet and its desertion

The conversion of the manorial buildings to peasant tenements indicates that there was probably an increase in the population of West Cotton at this time, suggesting continued importance for arable farming. The possible retention of a watermill into the fourteenth century, together with documented mills at both Mallows Cotton and Mill Cotton, is indicative of the continued primary role of arable farming, but the increase in wool production does suggest that more land was now under pasture.

The peasant hamlet, as formed at around 1300 at the desertion of the manor, may have survived relatively unchanged for a period of some 50–75 years through the difficult decades up to an beyond the mid-fourteenth century, but subsequently there was a progressive process of desertion, tenement by tenement.

The northernmost tenement was probably abandoned between 1350 and 1375, when a wall was built across the end of the access road. Some of its buildings were left standing with new doorways broken through the walls to enable use as agricultural outbuildings, probably for the adjacent tenement. The other tenements around the access road were probably in use until slightly after 1400. Some of these buildings were also reused as outbuildings, with the provision of raised floors suggesting that maintenance of the Cotton Brook was being neglected, with water often filling the hollow way of the Cotton Lane and running into the centre of the settlement, with animals trampling the former metalled yards while these were also progressively buried by an accumulation of alluvial clays.

The reuse of some of these central building may suggest that one or more of the tenements fronting onto the lane were still in use, and these were most probably the last to be deserted, with this occurring at around 1450. The evidence therefore indicates a progressive desertion of the hamlet over the course of approximately a century from 1350 to 1450.

It is from this time, 1413, that we have a detailed account of the Chamberlain holding in West Cotton. In terms of buildings, land and rent (excluding the total of 3.5 virgates in the open field) it lists; a messuage, three acres of land and a watermill; two other messuages; and one cottage, two tofts, nine acres of land and 3s 5d of rent. Trying to equate these to the known tenements is fraught with uncertainty, but the attempt must be made.

We may identify the watermill as the buildings to the east of lane and adjacent to the brook, tenement I, while the messuage and three acres of land could all have belonged with the mill. The converted manorial kitchen, tenement D, might have been the cottage, but another possibility is that the two other messuages and the cottage were perhaps all tenements fronting onto the lane, F, G and H. The two tofts might take in the abandoned tenements, C/D and A/E, set around the central yard.

The sixteenth-century reference to the Duchy holding in West Cotton comprising a cottage with three acres of pasture and an acre of willows, cannot apply to any of the excavated buildings at the centre of the settlement and must relate to one of the tenements beside the Cotton Lane, and it has been tentatively suggested that this may have lain to the south of the main settlement area, tenement J.

The desertion of West Cotton must be seen within the national trend towards the desertion of minor settlements resulting from a complex combination of causal factors. One major factor was the social and economic reorganisation that followed in the wake of the Black Death. This is known to have arrived in the Raunds area in May 1349 (Groome 1983) but the desertion of only a single tenement occurred at around this time, indicating that it cannot be cited as the primary direct cause of desertion.

Given the marginal location and the small size of West Cotton, it could not be regarded as a prime settlement, especially when the depredations of the Black Death had left better land untenanted. The drastic reduction in the population had also led to a contraction of arable cultivation, although this ran in parallel with a contraction from land that had been rendered even more marginal as a result of the deterioration in the climate in the early decades of the fourteenth century. The evident local flooding is a further possible direct cause although, as already noted, it may have been a product of the abandonment of water management associated with the early stages of desertion, perhaps specifically the abandonment of a watermill beside the Cotton Lane.

The end result was probably a progressive relocation to more potentially profitable tenancies elsewhere, especially given the inducements offered by landlords to attract new tenants to such properties following the loss of tenants

caused directly by the Black Death. By at least the end of the fifteenth century the tenants of the Chamberlain's Gloucester fee holding had all departed and the buildings were levelled. The land was rented out as pasture closes and was eventually sold to a new generation of farmers acquiring land piecemeal as the old manorial system contracted.

The disappearance of the horizontal mill in England

The use of the excavated watermills at West Cotton spanned the mid-tenth to mid-twelfth centuries, with a vertical-wheeled mill replaced by successive horizontal-wheeled mills. Of the two Raunds mills mentioned in the Domesday Book, the horizontal mill at West Cotton may be the mill valued at 12d, among the lowest level of mill valuations nationally (Holt 1988, 11–16), and provides an extreme contrast with the other mill which was valued at 34s 8d and 100 eels, the second richest mill in the county.

In Huntingdonshire, all the low-valued mills were on the minor watercourses, while those of intermediate to higher value were on the rivers Ouse and Nene (*ibid*, 11–13). This model would appear to be applicable at Raunds, where the low-value mill at West Cotton was adjacent to the River Nene but fed by a tributary stream, while we may surmise that the high-value mill probably lay directly on the river, perhaps at Mill Cotton, where a mill on the river was still in use until the late nineteenth century (Parry 2006).

However, mill valuations were certainly not purely dependent on the nature of the water supply, and the possibility that a low-valuation may at least sometimes denote a horizontal-wheeled mill has been explored by Holt (1988, 117–122) in considering the chronology of the decline and eventual abandonment of the horizontal mill. From the demonstrated sequence at West Cotton and the possible valuation of this mill at 12d, we may now suggest that low-value mills are most likely to represent small mills situated on minor watercourses, either away from or closely adjacent to major rivers, and which could either be of horizontal form or small vertical mills of similar power-producing capacity.

The date of demise for the horizontal mill in England is poorly defined. West Cotton demonstrates that they were still in operation beyond the time of Domesday Book and into at least the mid-twelfth century, and Holt argues that they must largely have disappeared by the thirteenth century, which would suggest a rapid decline in the use of the horizontal mill through the twelfth century.

The technological implications of the sequence at West Cotton, where a vertical mill was replaced by a horizontal mill, are also worthy of comment. It is clearly generally true that the higher costs involved in the provision and maintenance of the more complex machinery required for a vertical mill was offset by the increased potential for the generation of power. However, at West Cotton there was no evident social or technological reason for the apparently regressive change from a vertical to a horizontal mill, and it may merely have been economic pragmatism, with the lower costs in maintaining a horizontal mill making it the more attractive proposition.

The horizontal mill was cheap to build, maintain and operate, and so could be equally as well worked as, for instance, a co-operative venture by groups of peasant families (as indicated in some Domesday Book references), as under direct manorial control. The decline in their use, as indicated by Holt (*Holt 1988*, 117–22), must therefore be viewed within the social context and not purely from a technological viewpoint. Holt's analysis indicates that their decline was linked with lords acquiring exclusive rights of milling in the post-Conquest period, with this perhaps having been largely achieved coincident with the disappearance of horizontal mill by the end of the twelfth century. Thereafter, the vertical mill in its many forms reigned supreme with the exception of areas where seigneurial control was never achieved; as denoted by the survival of horizontal mills in the Shetlands into the nineteenth century, where they were operated as family or co-operative enterprises (Goudie 1886).

The result of seigneurial control of milling was to remove another element of potential peasant independence, with the consequent and additional benefit for the lords that, apart from illegal hand milling, the peasants had no choice but to have their grain milled at the manorial mill whilst paying for the "privilege". In this context, we can see that the simple but effective technology of the horizontal mill was forced out of existence within most of England not as a result of its direct replacement by a superior technology but through the worst practices of the feudal system, the removal of self determination from the hands of the peasants and its replacement with dependence on, and subservience to, the lord.

We may take this argument even further. A decline in the horizontal mill was inevitable, given the tendency for milling to become more centralised at a smaller number of larger manorial mills, and clearly the horizontal mill could never complete with, say, a large vertical mill run directly on a major river. However, the total disappearance of the horizontal mill was not necessarily a logical and necessary outcome, either technologically or economically, of the change to manorial control. At West Cotton we have argued that the change from a vertical to a horizontal mill could have been merely a pragmatic change to a cheaper and simpler mill but with a near equal productive capacity. So, there seems no reason why the continued use of horizontal mills, which were cheap to build and maintain, could not have had a useful, if minor, role within manorial-controlled milling throughout the medieval period, at least within smaller manors. Indeed, by reducing the overheads it would surely have increased the profitability of small manorial mills.

We may therefore postulate an additional reason for the complete disappearance of this technology. The continued use of a mechanism clearly capable of being successfully managed at lower levels of society would have been a constant reminder of the iniquity of the new system of manorial control. The removal of the simpler technology would therefore have assisted in defining milling as something evidently beyond the control of the peasants. This is to suggest an Orwellian process; if the technology no longer existed how could there be a concept of any alternative to manorial control! It may be going too far to suggest that the technology of the horizontal mill was consciously forced out of existence as part of the process of establishing manorial control of milling; their natural decline through the progressive establishment of fewer and larger mills may have achieved this on its own. However, whether consciously achieved or not, the end result was still the same; the horizontal mill ceased to exist and its technology was lost in England, and there was thereafter no alternative to vertical mills which, by definition, were beyond the economic means of the peasants.

The disappearance of the horizontal mill therefore provides a vivid illustration of how technology can be controlled for the benefit of the few and to the clear disadvantage of the many; with the replacement of cheap and simple technologies by complex and expensive technologies providing a very effective means of market control. It can be concluded that without the post-Conquest establishment of manorial milling rights, it is more than likely that the horizontal mill would have remained a common sight within at least smaller villages and hamlets throughout England in the medieval period, as it did within marginal areas throughout Europe until recent times.

West Cotton: a future for its past

The title of this section is a paraphrase of the adopted motto of the Northamptonshire Archaeology Unit as it existed in the 1980s and early 1990s through the fieldwork phase of the Raunds Area Project – Northamptonshire Archaeology Unit: Making a Future for our Past.

In those days, the unit was under Alan Hannan as County Archaeologist and he headed both the field team and the team running the Sites and Monuments Record (SMR) and the associated activities related to the enhancement of that record, together with an education officer and assistant and an information officer. The funding for most of the fieldwork through the 1980s came from the Manpower Services Commission, with additional support from English Heritage, the County Council and often help-in-kind, such as the provision of heavy plant, from developers.

Since then, times have changed dramatically. The County Archaeologist gave way to a County Archaeological Officer in the 1990s, and into the 2000s the post was further reduced to the status of a section head under a broader umbrella of the Built and Natural Environment Team, and the education and information officer posts were removed one by one.

In 2006 further County Council cuts saw the disappearance of an archaeology section as a separate entity, with the SMR absorbed into the County Record Office. At the same time the curatorial role of providing advice to local authorities on archaeological issues relating to planning applications was downgraded and then removed altogether, undermining the basis of commercial contract archaeology in Northamptonshire.

Concurrently, in the early 1990s the field team had to adapt to survival in the world of developer-funded archaeology, with contract tendering and the resultant changes which have led most former County-based units into carrying out much of their work out of county, with developers often preferring an external organisation free of any taint of closed-shop practices with the partnering curatorial section.

This has seen a huge increase in the quantity of archaeological work being carried out, and has resulted in many important discoveries on sites that might have been let go in the days of more limited resources. It is certainly known to the author that while we were excavating West Cotton there were other sites of potential that passed with no more than token investigation, which should not happen today. However, developer funding has different demands and restrictions, and many present large-scale area excavations are carried out under severe time and financial schedules that can produce inadequate levels of sampling, while other sites of great potential will be preserved beneath modern developments that will render them inaccessible for many decades to come.

It may be worth pointing out that in the present situation West Cotton would most probably not have been excavated. Following geophysical survey and some trial trenching, it would have been argued that as the length of the new road from West Cotton northward required an embankment, the site could and should be preserved under that embankment. Of course, the initial evaluation would not have produced an understanding of the watermills and the adjacent river channel, and these areas may have lain beyond any scheduled or preserved area. As a consequence, they might have been lost to gravel extraction without adequate excavation, although a watching brief might have produced enough evidence to show that there had been a watermill there as, if nothing else, fragments of millstones should have been recognised as the silts were machined away.

However, West Cotton was excavated and we may finally consider the future for its past beyond the production of the present report.

For West Cotton and for all other aspects of the Raunds Area Project, an immediate problem is the lack of a permanent county archaeological store, let alone an archive suitable for researchers to access those archives. At the moment it is not possible to comment any further on how this may change in the future, and how a physical archive of the finds and the primary site record may be preserved and made accessible. All that is likely to be available for the foreseeable future is the report itself.

A further consideration that needs to be briefly mentioned is that half of the settlement of West Cotton still survives. A triangular area between the new road and Cotton Lane includes the remaining parts of two partially excavated medieval tenements and two complete medieval tenements, as well as late Saxon timber buildings and further prehistoric monuments. This area is a Scheduled Ancient Monuments and survives in good condition under pasture and represents a significant archaeological resource, not the least in that it has the potential to examine the extrapolated conclusions presented in this report concerning the nature and status of the unexcavated buildings. It may be worth mentioning that the planning grid was extended onto the unexcavated area and metal pegs have been driven into the ground so that any future fieldwork could be directly related to the original site grid.

The tenements east of the Cotton Lane lie beneath a field that has been subject to annual ploughing in its use for horticulture, but trial trenching has shown that the medieval buildings and cut features of prehistoric date further east, lay below the reach of the recent ploughing regime. By 2008 this area had been taken out of cultivation and is currently also under grass as paddocks for houses. The buildings adjacent to the old stream channel, the possible later medieval watermill, lie on land belonging to the Anglian Water, which has long been left as a neglected and overgrown wasteland.

With the publication of this volume, the results of the prehistoric and the Saxon and medieval aspects of the Raunds Area Project have now been made available, leaving only the Iron Age and Roman aspects, centred on the settlement and villas at Stanwick and Redlands Farm, still to come. Given the breadth of the study and the significance of the results for all periods, it would still be highly desirable to make these results available in a popular form to a wider audience, although whether this will be achieved is uncertain.

Conclusion
by Paul Courtney

The excavation at West Cotton, and indeed the Raunds Area Project as a whole, indicates the importance of understanding the process of settlement creation in explaining the varied character and success or failure of settlements over later centuries.

West Cotton has a lack of manorial records and the available documentation is highly biased to its feudal overlords, saying little about its medieval peasant inhabitants. In addition, there is a chronological bias to the period after its decline as a settlement. Such problems, though, are typical of minor subsidiary settlements and make nonsense of Sawyer's much quoted and infamous statement that archaeology is 'an expensive way of telling us what we know already' (cited by Rahtz 1983, 15).

Put another way, the archaeology of West Cotton has produced information of great interest to medieval historians, and for most of which the documentary evidence gives no inkling or adequate explanation.

9 Radiocarbon dates

Six wood samples and one charcoal sample of suspected Anglo-Saxon to medieval date were submitted for dating to The Queen's University of Belfast (UB), while organic material from environmental sampling was submitted to the Radiocarbon Accelerator Unit, Oxford University (OxA).

Radiocarbon dating was undertaken in order to obtain absolute dates for specific aspects of the site where stratigraphic sequences and pottery assemblages were either not available or were insufficient to provide the required definition.

In addition, a beaver bone recovered from river silts of mid to late Saxon date was submitted to Oxford, but this proved to be a residual bone of late Bronze Age date. The results of these determinations are summarised below.

The radiocarbon determinations have been calibrated using CALIB v2.1 (Stuiver and Reimer 1986) which uses datasets published by Pearson and Stuiver (1986); Stuiver and Pearson (1986) and Pearson *et al* (1986).

The date ranges have been calculated according to the maximum intercept method (Stuiver and Reimer 1986), with calibrated date ranges cited at two-sigma (95% confidence) and rounded to 10 years.

References

Pearson, G W, and Stuiver, M, 1986 High-precision calibration of the radiocarbon time scale, 500–2500 BC, *Radiocarbon*, **28**, 839–62

Pearson, G W, Pilcher, J R, Baille, M G L, Corbett, D M, and Qua, F, 1986 High-precision ^{14}C measurements of Irish oaks to show the natural ^{14}C variations from AD 1840–5210 BC, *Radiocarbon*, **28**, 911–34

Stuiver, M, and Pearson, G W, 1986 High-precision calibration of the radiocarbon time scale, *Radiocarbon*, **28**, 805–62

Stuiver, M, and Reimer, P J, 1986 A computer program for radiocarbon age calculation, *Radiocarbon*, **19**, 1022–30

Table 9.1: The radiocarbon determinations

Laboratory Reference Number	Context/ Structure	Sample	Radiocarbon age (BP)	Calibrated range (95% confidence)
OxA-4740	7109, river silts	Bone (beaver)	2900 ±60	1310–920 Cal BC
UB-3418	Early Saxon SFB, Str 36	Charcoal Hazel (*Corylus*)	1548 ±33	Cal AD 420–600
OxA-4079	River silts	Flax seeds & capsules	1295 ±70	Cal AD 620–890
UB-3328	Riverside *in situ* post 6778	Wood Oak (*Quercus*) Outer rings only	1297 ±49	Cal AD 630–860
UB-3323	Riverside *in situ* post 7120	Wood Oak (Quercus)	1264 ±52	Cal AD 660–890
UB-3322	M27, 1st mill Displaced stake	Wood Hazel (*Corylus*)	1258 ±36	Cal AD 660–880
UB-3326	M25, 3rd mill trunk 6665. in revetment	Wood Oak (Quercus) (outer 30 rings)	1086 ±29	Cal AD 880–1020
UB-3327	M25, 3rd mill *in situ* post 6691	Wood Oak (Quercus)	1014 ±51	Cal AD 890–1160
UB-3325	M25, 3rd mill Head sill 6444	Wood Oak (Quercus)	941 ±53	Cal AD 990–1220

Bibliography

Abels, R P, 1988 *Lordship and Military Obligation in Anglo-Saxon England*, Berkeley

Allison, K J, Beresford, M W, and Hurst, J G, 1966 *The Deserted Villages of Northamptonshire*, Leicester, Dept of English Local Hist, Occ Papers, **18**, 38

Archibald, M M, 1975 Coin Report, in Bryant and Steane 1975, 149–50

Astill, G G, 1993 *A medieval industrial complex and its landscape: the metalworking watermills and workshops of Bordesley Abbey*, Council for British Archaeol, Research Report, **92**

Atkin, M, Carter, A, and Evans, D H, 1985 *Excavations in Norwich, 1971–1978: Part II*, East Anglian Archaeol, **26**

Atkins, R, Chapman, A, and Holmes, M, 1999 The Excavation of a Medieval Bake/Brewhouse at the Elms, Brackley, *Northamptonshire Archaeol* **28**

Audouy, M, and Chapman, A, (ed) 2009 *Raunds: The origin and growth of a midland village, AD 450–1500: Excavations in north Raunds, Northamptonshire 1977–1987*, Oxbow Books

Ault, W O, 1972 *Open-Field Farming in Medieval England*

Baines, P, 1985 *Flax and linen*, Shire Publications

Beresford, G, 1975 *The medieval clay-land village: excavations at Goltho and Barton Blount*, Medieval Soc Archaeol Monog, **6**

Beresford, G, 1987 *Goltho: The development of an early medieval manor, c 850–1150*, English Heritage Archaeol Rep, **4**

Beresford, M, 1988 *New Towns of the Middle Ages*, 3rd edition

Blinkhorn, P, 1998–99 The trials of being a utensil: Pottery function at the medieval hamlet of West Cotton, Northamptonshire, *Medieval Ceramics*, **22–23**, 37–46

Bridges, J, 1791 *The History and Antiquities of Northamptonshire*, Whalley, P, (ed)

Brown, A E, (ed) 1967 Raunds (SP 9767 7243), *Bulletin of the Northamptonshire Federation of Archaeol Soc*, **2**, 28

Campbell, G, 1994 The preliminary archaeobotanical results from Anglo-Saxon West Cotton and Raunds, in Rackham, 65–82

Chapman, A, 2005 *Medieval Stylised Chess Pieces*, The Finds Research Group AD700–1700, Datasheet, **35**

Chapman, A, 2006 Prehistoric palaeochannels and a ring ditch at Stanwick Quarry, *Northamptonshire Archaeology*, **32**, 1–22

Chapman, A, 2006 West Cotton deserted hamlet, SP 976 725, in Parry 2006, 172–177

Chapman, A, and Hurman, B 1991 Late medieval potsherd hearths, *Medieval Ceramics*, **15**, 48–50

Chapman, A, Atkins, R, and Lloyd, R, 2003 A medieval manorial farm at Lime Street, Irthlingborough, Northamptonshire, *Northamptonshire Archaeol*, **31**, 71–104

Clay, P, and Salisbury, C R, 1990 A Norman Mill Dam and other sites at Hemington Fields, Castle Donnington, Leicestershire, *Archaeol J*, **147**, 276–307

Coles, B, 2006 *Beavers in Britain's Past*, WARP Occasional Papers, Oxbow Books

Courtney, P, 2006 Raunds and its region, and, Raunds Burystead: a manorial economy in decline, in S Parry 2006, 99–116

Courtney, P, 2009 Historical Background, in M Audouy and A Chapman 2009, 14–18

Crawford, H, (ed) 1979 *Subterranean Britain; Aspects of Underground Archaeology*, John Baker

Crosby, V, and Neal, D S, in preparation *Raunds Area Project: The Iron Age and Romano-British Landscapes at Stanwick, Northamptonshire*, English Heritage

Dallas, C, 1993 *Excavations in Thetford by B. K. Davidson between 1964 and 1970*, East Anglian Archaeol, **62**

Dix, B (ed), 1987 The Raunds Area Project: second interim report, *Northamptonshire Archaeol*, **21**, 3–30

Dyer, C, 1986 English Peasant Buildings in the Later Middle Ages (1200–1500), *Medieval Archaeol*, **30**, 19–45

Fairbrother, J R, 1990 *Faccombe Netherton: Excavations of a Saxon and Medieval Manorial Complex*, British Museum Occ Papers, **74**

Fernie, E C, 1991 Anglo-Saxon Lengths and the Evidence of the Buildings, *Medieval Archaeol*, **35**, 1–5

Foard, G, 1979 *Archaeological Priorities: proposals for Northamptonshire*, Northamptonshire Archaeology Unit, Occ Pap, **4**

Foard, G, 1983 *The Raunds priority area*, Northamptonshire Archaeology Unit

Foard, G, and Pearson, T, 1985 The Raunds Area Project: First Interim Report, *Northamptonshire Archaeol*, **20**, 3–22

Foard, G, and Parker Pearson, M, 1989 *The Raunds Area Project, Reassessment of the Research Design*, Northamptonshire Archaeology Unit

Gelling, M, 1976 *The Place-Names of Berkshire*, pt. III, English Place-Name Society, **LI**, Cambridge

Gibson, A, 1989 (ed) *Midlands Prehistory: some recent and current researches into the prehistory of central England*, British Archaeol Reports, British Series, **204**

Glover, J E B, Mawer, A, and Stenton, F M, 1938 *The Place-Names of Northamptonshire*, English Place Name Society, **10**, Cambridge

Goudie, G, 1886 On the horizontal mills of Shetland, *Proc Soc Antiq of Scotland*, **20**, 257–97

Grew, F O, 1987 Introduction, in Cowgill *et al* 1987, viii-x

Groome, N, 1983 The Black Death in the Hundred of Higham Ferrers, *Northamptonshire Past and Present*, **VI**, 309–312

Groves, C, 1989 *Tree-ring analysis of Timbers from West Cotton, Northamptonshire, 1988*, Ancient Monuments Laboratory Report, **95/89**

Hall, D N, and Hutchings J B, 1972 The Distribution of

Archaeological Sites between the Nene and Ouse Valleys, *Bedfordshire Archaeol J*, **7**, 2–16

Hall, D, Harding, R, and Putt, C, 1988 *Raunds: Picturing the Past*

Hall, R, 1972 Excavations at Full Street, Derby, 1972, *Derbyshire Archaeol J*, **92**, 29–77

Harding, J, and Healy, F, 2007 *The Raunds Area Project: A Neolithic and Bronze Age landscape in Northamptonshire*, English Heritage

Hardy, A, Mair Charles, B, and Williams, R J, 2007 *Death and Taxes: The archaeology of a Middle Saxon estate centre at Higham Ferrers, Northamptonshire*, Oxford Archaeol Monog, **4**

Hilton, R H and Rahtz, P A, 1967 Upton Medieval Village, *Current Archaeology*, **4**, 98–99

Hinton, D, (ed) 1983 *25 Years of Medieval Archaeology*, Sheffield

Holt, R, 1988 *The Mills of Medieval England*, Oxford

Howe, M D, 1984 Three Anglo-Saxon Burials from Alwalton, Cambridgeshire, *Northamptonshire Archaeol*, **19**, 53–61

Huggins, P J, 1991 Anglo Saxon Timber Building Measurements: Recent Results, *Medieval Archaeol*, **35**, 6–28

Kerr, W J B, 1925 *Higham Ferrers and its Ducal and Royal Castle and Park*, Northampton

Kosminsky, E A, 1956 *Studies in the Agrarian History of England in the Thirteenth Century*, Oxford

Lewis, C, Mitchell-Fox, P, and Dyer, C, 2001 *Village, Hamlet and Field: Changing medieval settlements in Central England*, Oxford, Windgather Press

Longworth, I, and Cherry, J, (eds) 1986 *Archaeology in Britain since 1945*, British Museum

Marshall, A, and Marshall, G, 1991 A Survey and Analysis of the buildings of Early and Middle Anglo-Saxon England, *Medieval Archaeol*, **35**, 29–43

Maull, A, and Chapman, A, 2005 *A medieval moated enclosure in Tempsford Park*, Bedfordshire Archaeol Soc Monog, **5**

McErlean, T, and Crothers, N, 2007 *Harnessing the Tides: the early medieval tide mills at Nendrum Monastery, Stranford Loch*, Northern Ireland Archaeol monog, **7**

Mays, S A, 1990 *The Human remains from West Cotton, Raunds, Northamptonshire*, Ancient Monument Laboratory Report, **56/90**

Mitchell, S K, 1951 *Taxation in Medieval England*, Yale

Parry S J, 2006 *Raunds Area Survey: An archaeological study of the landscape of Raunds, Northamptonshire 1985–94*, Oxbow Books

Platt, C, and Coleman-Smith, R, 1975 *Excavations in Medieval Southampton 1953–1969*, Leicester Univ Press

Postan, M M, 1972 *The Medieval Economy and Society*, Pelican

Rackham, J, (ed) 1994 *Environment and economy in Anglo-Saxon England: a review of recent work on the environmental archaeology of rural and urban Anglo-Saxon settlements in England*, Council for British Archaeology Research Report, **89**

Rahtz, P A, 1969 Upton, Gloucestershire, 1964–1968: Second Report, *Trans of the Bristol and Gloucestershire Archaeol Soc*, **88**, 74–126

Rahtz, P A, 1983 New Approaches to Medieval Archaeology, in Hinton 1983, 12–23

RCHME, 1975 *An Inventory of the Historical Monuments in the County of Northampton: Volume I, Archaeological Sites in North-East Northamptonshire*, Royal Commission on the Historical Monuments of England

Rynne, C, 1989 Early Irish watermills, *British Archaeol*, **14**, 13–15

Selkirk, A, 1987 West Cotton, *Current Archaeol*, **106**, 337–339

Smith, A H, 1956 *English Place-Name Elements*, 2 vols, Cambridge

Smith, R A, 1918 Anglo-Saxon Antiquities Discovered at Islip, Northants, *Proc. Soc. Antiq. London ser. 2*, **30**, 113–20

Todd, M, (ed) 1978 *Studies in the Romano-British Villa*, Leicester Univ Press

VCH Northants *The Victoria history of the Counties of England: Northamptonshire*

West, S, 1985, *West Stow: The Anglo-Saxon Village*, East Anglian Archaeol Rep, **24**

Williams, J H, 1979 *St. Peter's Street, Northampton. Excavations 1973–79*, Northampton Development Corporation Archaeol Monog, **2**

Williams, R J, and Zeepvat, R J, 1994 *Bancroft. A Late Bronze Age/Iron Age Settlement, Roman Villa and Temple-Mausoleum*, Buckinghamshire Archaeol Soc Monog, **7**

Wilson, D, M, and Hurst, J D, 1958 Medieval Britain in 1957. I Pre-Conquest, *Medieval Archaeol*, **2**, 183–5

Windell, D 1984 *West Cotton, Raunds: Trial-trenching*, Northamptonsire Archaeology Unit

Windell, D, 1987 West Cotton, in Dix 1987

Windell, D, 1989 A late Neolithic "Ritual Focus" at West Cotton, Northamptonshire, in Gibson 1989, 85–94

Windell, D, Chapman, A, and Woodiwiss, J, 1990 *From Barrows to Bypass: Excavations at West Cotton, Raunds, Northamptonshire 1985–1989*, Northamptonshire County Council

Wrander, N, 1983 *English Place-Names in the Dative Plural*, Malmo

Zeepvat, R J, Roberts, J S, and King, N A, 1994 *Caldecote, Milton Keynes, Excavation and fieldwork 1966–91*, Buckinghamshire Archaeol Soc Monog, **9**

Zupko, E R, 1968 *A Dictionary of English Weights and Measures: From Anglo-Saxon Times to the Nineteenth Century*, Wisconsin Univ Press

Index